What Others Are Saying About "Sell What You Sow!". . .

"The information Eric provides is as complete a book on agricultural marketing as has been written in the last century. I would recommend this book to anyone who is seeking new ways to obtain success in the farming business. If you buy only one book about farming then let it be *Sell What You Sow!* Too many farmers have learned the hard way that you can't raise it, then decide how you're going to sell it. Sell it first, then plant the seed. That's good marketing."

—*Robert "Matty" Matarazzo, Matarazzo Farms, Belvidere, New Jersey*

"You've produced an excellent and valuable book. I congratulate you. I'm sure small farmers everywhere are going to appreciate learning how to market better, and we as consumers are going to profit greatly from increased access to fresh, organic food. Survival of small farming is crucial to our health and environment. You are doing a great service."

—*Dave Smith, co-founder, Smith & Hawken*

"*Sell What You Sow!* has helped me tremendously in starting my greenhouse business. It not only gave me the much needed information required for a business plan for my new business, but also showed me various methods to achieve success. I highly recommend this book to anyone looking for the best way to succeed in today's new farming and greenhouse enterprises."

—*Bruce Catlin, Catlin Farms & Enterprises, Emigrant, Montana*

"You certainly have come up with a readable book on a subject that most farmers find difficult to deal with. Covers marketing alternatives thoroughly, down to specific details every farmer, whether direct marketing or wholesaling, must consider."

—*Richard VanVranken, county agricultural agent, Rutgers Cooperative Extension*

"This is the best book to date about the alternative marketing options available to farmers. To be successful today farmers have to be creative marketers as much as they are growers. In most cases they can not go head to head with large conventional growers. They need to find a niche both in what they produce and how they sell it.

This *how to* book deals with every aspect of marketing from selling to choosing crops and from regulations to advertising. Small family farmers in this country are ready for a book like this."

—*David Visher, Small Farm Center, U.C. Davis*

"*Sell What You Sow!* is a very readable book, full of great tips from experienced marketers across the country. I recommend it highly to any farmers looking for better ways to sell what they produce. It is not only a great source of information for growers new to the business, it is a real resource for those who have been in the business for many years. If you want to see what successful marketers are doing across the country, read this book."

—*Kevin Hosey, assistant manager, Knox County Regional Farmers Market, Knoxville, Tennessee*

"Diversification and direct marketing are a must for the survival of the small family farm. *Sell What You Sow!* addresses the area most needed by those wishing to tackle a diversified approach—marketing. For too many years, we farmers have let others do the real marketing of our products and as a result have let the profits slip away. *Sell What You Sow!* explains how to use direct marketing to recapture lost profits and boost the farm gate value of your work. This book takes the mystery out of how to make diversification work for you."

—*Curt Stutzman, Rural Innovation Center, Amana, Iowa*

The Fruit Of Our Labor

Love is the fruit of our labor;
Surely the toil of our days shall end
    Beyond the fruit of this earth;
Though the hand that sows the seed is born of the soil
    And must return to the soil;
Yet the eye that sees the light is born of the sun
    And shall return to the sun;
And as stars in the fields of the night
Our souls scattered in darkness
    Sprout forth into Light;
Out of the sands of Experience
    And the waters of Time
Love breathes Life into the Seed
    And the fruit of our labor is Love.

SELL
WHAT YOU SOW!

The Grower's Guide To Successful Produce Marketing

by Eric Gibson

Illustrations by Andrea Gibson

New World Publishing

*Sell What You Sow! The Grower's Guide
To Successful Produce Marketing*
by Eric Gibson

Printed in the United States of America on recycled paper.

Illustrations by Andrea Gibson.
Additional illustrations (logos) courtesy individual farmers,
agricultural-related companies, U.C. Davis Small Farm
Center, Dover Publications and Wheeler Arts.

Publisher's Cataloging in Publication
Gibson, Eric L.
    Sell What You Sow! The Grower's Guide To Successful
Produce Marketing/ Eric Gibson.
        p. cm.
        LCCN: 92-090951.
        ISBN 0-9632814-0-2
1. Produce trade--United States--Handbooks, manuals,
etc.
2. Farm management--United States--Handbooks, manuals, etc.
3. Gardening--United States. I. Title.
HD9000.65.G53 1994   630.068'8   QBI92-20126

New World Publishing
Auburn, California

Contents

Foreword   7
Author's Preface   8
Acknowledgments   10
Introduction   11

I. Getting Started
   1. Planning For Profits   19
   2. Choosing Your Enterprises   23
   3. Deciding What To Grow   32
   4. Market Research   39
   5. Making A Marketing Plan   45

II. Direct Marketing
   6. Is Direct Marketing For You?   49
   7. Farmers Markets   56
   8. Roadside Markets   66
   9. Pick-Your-Own   75
  10. The Rural Attraction   83
  11. Subscription Farming   90
  12. Mail Order   97

III. Marketing To Retail Outlets
  13. Introduction   100
  14. Selling To Restaurants   104
  15. Selling To Retail Outlets   110

IV. Specialty Food Products
  16. Specialty Food Products   117

V. Marketing Skills
  17. Merchandising   127
  18. Customer Service   136

VI. Wholesale Marketing
  19. The Wholesale Picture   143
  20. Getting Your Product To Market   153
  21. Making It Pay   159
  22. Cooperatives   167

VII. Business Matters

    23. Business Smarts   171

    24. Pricing For Profits   178

    25. Rules & Regulations   187

    26. Insurance   193

VIII. Promotion

    27. The Sales Call   197

    28. Promotion   203

    29. Advertising   219

    30. Group Promotion   233

IX. Harvestime

    31. Sharing The Bounty   243

    32. Enjoy! (Farm Festivals & Farm Humor)   250

X. Resources

    General Resources   255

    Chapter Resources   270

XI. Appendices

    Produce Handling & Storage   279

    Produce Display   282

Awards, Footnotes and Index

    The Thomas Jefferson Award   286

    The *Sell What You Sow!* Logo Awards   288

    Footnotes   290

    Index   293

Back Matter

    About New World Publishing. . .   298

    New World Bookshelf   299

    Order Form   304

Foreword

by Howard W. "Bud" Kerr, Jr.
Director, U.S.D.A. Office for Small-Scale Agriculture

FARMERS, AND PEOPLE who go to the ocean, fall into three categories: "sunners," "shiverers," and "surfers." A sunner goes to the ocean with no intention of getting wet, only to sun on the beach and never gets into the ocean. Some farmers fall into the sunner category. They have the right equipment, spend a lot of time preparing and caring for the crop and ultimately produce a good crop. They are farmers and good agricultural producers, but fail to target a market for the crop. They take the market for granted, just as the sunner always takes the ocean for granted.

The shiverer uses the beach and also goes into the ocean. However, such a person keeps both feet securely on the ocean floor. By always being in this position, two things can happen. If the water suddenly recedes, the shiverer is left high and dry. If the water rises, the shiverer drowns.

The surfer is a risk taker. Such a person quickly crosses the beach, gets into the water, and swims out to the action, breaking waves. Cautiously and patiently, he observes the situation and judiciously selects a wave. Astride the surfboard, he rides the surge and power of the wave, extracting every opportunity to reach new heights or goals. The surfer and the ocean are one, totally bound to each other.

In the future, if a farmer expects to be profitable, he or she will have to be similar to a surfer. Farmers must be committed, absorbed with details, have a target or goal established, and always keep a patient but cautious eye on changing situations. The farmer and the marketplace should be one, totally bound to each other.

In my positions both as director of the USDA Office for Small-Scale Agriculture and as a part-time farmer, I have always considered marketing as the keystone of any successful agricultural business. In the late 1960s, I bought a small tract of farmland and planted high-value crops—peaches, strawberries and thornless blackberries and opened Arrowhead Farm, a pick-your-own, part-time farm. Location, choice of crops, and innovative marketing methods were the key factors to success. Today, it is no different.

Several years ago, I wrote (in *The Future Of Agriculture Near Cities: Directions For Research*, June 1988): "Farms in metropolitan areas, which comprise only 16 percent of U.S. land area, account for more than two-thirds of fruit and vegetable sales. Yet faced with urban development pressures, future small-scale farmers must become involved with specialized intensive production systems. Further, their marketing skills must be honed to a sharp edge; maximum returns must be obtained from all production."

In the past, it was sufficient to be a good agricultural producer, but today—and in the near future—this is no longer enough. Farmers face tougher economic realities today and must be adept at selecting the most profitable crops and pinpointing the most opportune ways to sell.

The agricultural industry has continued to lose farms, and the number of people working on farms has declined continuously since 1960 when I began working for the USDA. Now, commercial farm producers of all sizes are learning a lesson that has long been known by small farmers: that they cannot afford to grow a crop that they cannot market profitably.

Sell What You Sow! The Grower's Guide To Successful Produce Marketing, is an outstanding example of the increasing volume of written information that is available to meet the marketing needs of farmers. The tools for profitable farming are in your hands. *Sell What You Sow!* can be your "surfboard," and the waters of farm marketing opportunities await you. Happy surfing!

A civilization begins to decline when it loses its connection to its agrarian origins.
    —Arnold Toynbee, historian

Author's Preface

Founder Sibella Kraus called it a "celebration of food." Renowned restaurateur Alice Waters called it "the most important food event in the country." The Oakland Museum seemed the perfect place for the seventh annual Tasting of the Summer Produce last August, as farmer-artists revealed their latest masterpieces.

From stalls spread out among the museum's terraced gardens, the picture-perfect produce of more than 100 growers sparkled like an artist's palette: blue potatoes, golden raspberries, green-grape tomatoes, yellow doll melons, royal burgundy beans, brown Turkey figs, baby red Romaine lettuce, pink pearl apples, red okra and pink flamingo mushrooms.

"There were more kinds of strawberries and squashes, ferns and figs, potatoes and peaches than even a savvy produce professional would have recognized a decade ago," crowed the San Francisco Chronicle.

—from "The Freshest and the Finest" by Eric Gibson, Rural Enterprise magazine

THE 1987 "Tasting of the Summer Produce" festival in Oakland was a magical event for me. As a journalist, it brought renewal, as I discovered a world of farmers who seemed to have a different, more vibrant and alive way of growing and marketing than the large-scale, conventional farmers I had previously encountered. These small-scale, niche-market growers were passionately in love with their products and their profession. They considered themselves artisans!

I grew up in a nonfarming family in California's Central Valley. Except for a few summers spent working on my grandmother's blackcap farm in Oregon, my impressions of agriculture were derived mainly from my classmates. Many of them came from 40-acre farms, and they milked the cows or did other farm chores before coming to school each day.

Fresno County, with its miles and miles of cotton, corn, alfalfa, almonds and grapes, is the nation's leading agricultural county, ranking ahead of all but 10 *states* in agricultural production. Yet even in the land of plenty of this great valley, farmers are struggling. I was dismayed to discover years later at a class reunion that nearly all of my classmates had drifted to the cities to take nonfarming jobs.

Only 2 percent of our nation's population today is involved in agriculture; yet Thomas Jefferson, one of our most illustrious presidents, was equally proud of being a farmer. He considered agriculture the highest of the arts. As a generation raised on concrete, we have been cut off from our roots—spiritually, socially and economically. Man cannot be severed from nature and survive; his feet and sustenance belong in the soil!

No small part of our society's slide away from a more balanced and harmonious way of life has been the decline of the family farm. Farming, as our direct link with the soil and nature, is our primary profession. Until our ideals of living in harmony with nature are interwoven with the way we obtain our food, we cannot, as a society, be healthy.

Yet while farming has fallen on hard times, there are farmers who are surviving and thriving, and one big reason is that they have taken control over their own marketing. Their story is told in these pages. As Karl Ohm III, editor/publisher of *Rural Enterprise* magazine, said: "You are part of a great and noble profession that deserves to be passed on to future generations." If this book makes any small contribution to helping farmers make the living they deserve, I am grateful.

Paul Muller and Dru Rivers of Full Belly Farm, Guinda, California, at the "Tasting of the Summer Produce" festival, Oakland, California, 1987

Dedication
To my parents

Acknowledgments

Truly speaking I am the editor more so than the author of this book. There have been many generous people involved in producing this book, both by sharing their verbal or written information, or in reviewing the manuscript. While the contributors to this book are too numerous to acknowledge in this space, primary consultants or peer reviewers for each chapter are listed at the end of each chapter under "Acknowledgments."

Special thanks to Sibella Kraus, *San Francisco Chronicle* food columnist and founder of the Tasting of the Summer Produce. She is a true friend of the farmer, and her work in agriculture helped pave the way for this book. My special gratitude also to Richard Smoley, former managing editor for *California Farmer* magazine and my agricultural writing mentor.

For their advice, support and enthusiasm, my appreciation to Claudia Myers and David Visher, of the California Small Farm Center; Karl Ohm III, editor of *Rural Enterprise* magazine; Vance Corum, an agricultural consultant in Oakland, California; Lynn Bagley, director of the Marin County, California, Certified Farmers Market; Matty Matarazzo, a farmer from Belvidere, New Jersey; Paul Vossen, Sonoma County, California, farm advisor; Kelso Wessel, agricultural economist at Ohio State University; Curt Stutzman, an agricultural consultant from Kalona, Iowa; Kurt Moulton, King County, Washington, extension agent; Howard "Bud" Kerr, director of the USDA Office for Small-Scale Agriculture; and Forrest Stegelin, agricultural economist with the University of Kentucky.

Above all, I extend my gratitude to the growers I've interviewed in my career as an agricultural journalist, many of whom are quoted in these pages. They are the real authors of this book.

Thanks again to my mother for her countless hours in helping with my career. As a church newsletter editor, she was my best example and inspiration as a writer. My eternal gratitude to the "prooofreading team." And to my wife, Andrea, for sharing the joys and burdens of this book.

It was the best of times, it was the worst of times.
   —Charles Dickens

Introduction

Nine generations of Cosmans, six generations of Clarkes and four generations of Crists have worked the land of the Hudson River Valley. Sometimes, their apple orchards have been bountiful; sometimes, they have not.

"The last two or three years, apples have not made money," said Steve Clarke from Prospect Hills Orchard Inc. in Milton. Consumers, and farmers, worry about chemicals. Farmers can get more money selling their land to developers than farming it. Competition from the Northwest and abroad is squeezing their apples off store shelves. And bad weather and pests, of course, never go away.

Coping with apple prices is tough. Though supermarkets were selling apples for up to 99 cents a pound, Mike Moriello said he was paid 19 cents a pound wholesale.

"We go from year to year and look at the future and hope we're going to be here," Larry Cosman said at his Mount Airy Farm in the hamlet of Middle Hope, where he grows 250 acres of apple trees. "I think the odds are kind of against us in the sense that progress will prevail sooner or later and push out some of the farms," he added later.

From the early 1800s, growers in the Hudson Valley shipped many fruits by sloop south to New York City and points beyond. Wholesale buyers from New York City would travel the valley, haggling with each farmer on their route. In the 1930s, there were 500 farms in Ulster County, on the Hudson's western bank. In 1990, there are fewer than 200 family farms all along the valley, from New York City to Albany, a 140-mile stretch.

"Sometimes you talk about it and get a little choked up," Cosman said. "Farming is not really a job, it's a lifestyle. And most farmers live, eat and breathe what they're doing."

Not that the farmers are railing against progress. "We brought you here to show you we don't have our heads in the sand," said grower Jeff Crist.

Farmers are adapting by getting closer to consumers, like the pick-your-own orchards at Clarke's farm, and with dwarf trees, which can be planted more densely and pruned and picked more easily. They also are starting sales organizations that market fruit from a group of farms, and are selling directly to restaurants, at farm markets and stands, and abroad.

"Ten years ago, it was enough to know what was going on in the confines of your orchard. It's not enough anymore," said Mike Moriello of New Paltz, trying to be heard over Joe Porpiglia's water dump, which washes apples and sends them down to the waxer.

   —"Frustration Growing Along With Their Apples," by Mary MacVean, Associated Press, *The Fresno Bee*, July 22, 1990

THE SUN SITS ON THE HORIZON of American farming, and it is either sunset or daybreak, depending on whom you talk to, and whether they are following the old or new ways of growing and

Middleman Marketing

by Al Courschesne

FARMERS, BE YOUR own middleman! Historically, when farms were in, around, or near the towns they served, the farmer would load his goods on a wagon and take them to the market—which usually meant he sold his products himself, directly to the townspeople.

Al Courchesne, president of the California Association of Family Farmers

As cities got larger and farms became further removed, other more complex methods of food distribution were developed. The farmer found himself further and further removed from the marketing process. He abdicated his role (and his profits) to the "middleman."

Today, largely because of distance, many farmers are out of touch with marketing. Indeed, in many cases, the minute a box of fruit is picked off the tree it is transferred to a packing house and the farmer is at the mercy of the packer/shipper to get him the best price for his crop. Often the farmer must wait for months to get paid—and must take the word of strangers as to the percentage of culls his fruit had, the sizes, etc.

You should be spending as much time on the telephone as you do on the tractor! Tractor work and field management are essential in growing the crop, but. . . when market time is

near, get into your office and *sell!* The larger, more successful farms have learned this. The big corporate farms are vertically integrated from production on up to the final sale to Safeway! They have established statewide, nationwide and even worldwide customers, with their own sales reps, distribution networks, storage centers, etc.

Small- and medium-sized family farmers can do the same thing on a smaller scale. It takes years to establish good customers. Start small and choose clients who fit the size of your operation. Start with your own neighborhood. Establish a fruit stand and sell direct. You would be amazed how much you will learn from talking directly to your customers—the people who actually eat your food. You will get a lot more personal satisfaction from that contact. And you will make more money!

---

marketing. "The days when small farmers could grow and profitably sell just about whatever they wanted are over," warned an article in a recent issue of *Rural Enterprise* magazine.[1] "Government subsidies are shrinking, consumer demand for variety is growing, and farmers can no longer rely on bulk production of one or two crops to provide them with income."

"Profitable crops are now determined by market signals, not by government subsidies," the article quoted John O'Sullivan, agricultural marketing specialist at North Carolina A & T State University's Cooperative Extension program. Urging farmers to utilize niche marketing to sell their products, O'Sullivan advised farmers to "plan be-

fore you plant. Establish your market before putting that first seed in the ground."

At a recent farming conference, Curt Stutzman, an agricultural consultant from Amana, Iowa, echoed the same thoughts: "The outlook for the decade of the '90s is not all that different from the '80s. Big farms will continue to dominate in commodity crops where high-volume, low-cost production is the only way to survive. Smaller farms, and family farms, will have to continue to adapt by diversifying into markets that meet special local and regional needs."

Similarly, Suzanne Vaupel, a marketing consultant from Sacramento, says: "In California, we're looking at a lot of specialized marketing segments, and that's what is coming to the rest of the nation. The markets for a lot of traditional crops just aren't there these days. Yet I see a lot of innovative farmers who are willing to try new products or new ways of marketing. These are the farmers who are going to make it."

Sell What You Sow! is the summation of lessons from farmers encountered in the fields, on the phone, through trade publications, or at farm conferences, who are practicing the "new" methods of marketing. At an Ohio Roadside Marketing Conference in the mid-'70s, Lee Jones, a third-generation grower from Huron, Indiana, recounted how his family had increased their net income by reducing their acreage from 1,500 acres to 200 acres and finally to 25 acres, while switching from marketing traditional commodity crops through traditional wholesale outlets to marketing gourmet vegetables through farmers markets, restaurants and an on-farm retail market. "My grandfather was production oriented; my father was production oriented; all of us as growers are production oriented," Jones said. "Production has gotten us into trouble. Last year's field corn prices were the same as in the '50s. We need to stop thinking like farmers and think like marketers."

TRADITIONAL AMERICAN FARMING is in trouble. While the number of Americans engaged in farming continues to decline (down by one million in the past 20 years), headlines have traced the twin trends toward the giant mega-farms and the "plight of the family farmer."

To be sure, American agriculture has been called the "wonder of the world," producing an abundance of cheap food. Americans spend less on their food than any other nation—only 16 percent of their total income. Yet overproduction has led to oversupply, and producers find themselves gripped in a cost-price squeeze. Wholesale prices for some crops, such as nectarines or apples, have remained relatively unchanged for over 30 years while production costs have skyrocketed. Profit margins on traditional crops have become so thin that only farmers with enormous acreage can survive.

In the terminal market system of distribution, set up for regular high-volume delivery of produce, the smaller growers are especially hard hit. The farmer's share of the consumer dollar has decreased significantly—from about 50 – 80 cents of every dollar spent on fresh fruits and vegetables fifty years ago, to less than 30 cents today. In 1988,

approximately 75 cents out of every dollar that consumers spent on food went for packing, shipping, handling, brokering, wholesaling, distributing and retailing.

In a recent hearing before the Agricultural Communicators Congress, Senator Bob Kerrey, D-Neb., called the farm crisis of the 1990s a "quiet crisis" being felt by families who are slowly losing their grip on their land and their livelihood. Kerrey said there is a "gnawing sense" among farm families, especially younger farmers and those with debt, that their operations and their way of life are no longer sustainable.

Much has been written about the deleterious effects of large-scale agribusiness. As a society, we have chosen sugar water over life-sustaining fruit juice, french fries over fresh-dug potatoes, convenience over value, and corporate farming over "real" farming. While small family farms go hand-in-hand with bustling local economies and a vibrant social milieu, large-scale agribusiness has been a cancer of greed and ignorance that has decimated our rural social fabric, and threatened to near extinction the irreplaceable quality of life inherent in family farming.

With only 2 percent of the U.S. population left on the farm, 98 percent of the population has to have what we have to sell. What an opportunity!

—Kelso Wessel, agricultural economist

YET OUT OF THE BELLY of the food-distribution beast, there has emerged—for the smaller, specialty grower—a plum. In a word, *taste*, and the marketing opportunities represented therein. For years, the produce industry, organized for the economics of mass production and distribution, has bred fruits and vegetables for durability, transport and storage. Products are picked unripened, harvested and sorted by machinery, shipped vast distances and stored for long periods of time. Taste and quality are in many cases the trade-off.

To meet the demand for taste, quality and variety in food, however, a "new" farmer has sprung up: the niche specialty grower, whose ways of marketing are often as unorthodox as the produce he or she grows. Anxious to gain a greater share of

Our American Food System: The Great Debate

Gross and excessive food transport from one region to another should be against the law. It's doing a hell of a lot more harm to us and the environment than many of the things that are currently considered criminal.

—Andy Lee, Backyard Market Gardening

Andy Lee: "Our American grocery stores and supermarkets offer a cornucopia of choices," writes Andy Lee, in his book, *Backyard Market Gardening*. "Anytime of the year it is possible to get almost any type of vegetables or fruit desired. The produce is almost always blemish-free, relatively inexpensive and is available in seemingly unlimited quantities. However, when we scratch below the surface of this apparent cornucopia, we don't like what we see."

The problem, according to Andy, is the vast distance our food travels before reaching our tables. Nearly 90 percent of the fresh fruits and vegetables consumed by people in most states comes from out-of-state, or from out of the country. Andy lists a whole train of evils resulting from the long-distance shipping of fruits and vegetables, including:

- long-distance shipping is expensive, energy consumptive and wasteful;
- the lack of agricultural jobs and ownership opportunities for residents in nonagricultural intensive regions, leading to a declining quality of life in the nonfood producing regions;
- the tendency toward large field monocropping in intensive food growing areas leads to heavy infestations of crop-devouring pests and diseases, which in turn leads to the heavy use of chemicals;
- the heavy use of chemicals leads in turn to soil erosion, farm-caused pollution, and barren, biologically dead soils;
- because food does not ship well, mega-farmers choose varieties that yield well and ship well. Flavor and nutritional value are secondary or even ignored.

"Most of us have no connection to the land at all," Andy continues. "We don't feel connected to the food that we are eating, or the farmers who grow it for us. Americans may be the best fed people in the world, but we are also the least nourished by the food we eat. Nationally, cancer and heart disease are the biggest killers, and they are often related to a nutritionally deficient diet. We are eating food that is laced with poison, placed there for the very purpose of making that food available to us in a convenient and inexpensive way.

"We are all in this mess together," Andy Lee concludes. "Missing most of all is the quality of life that we Americans once enjoyed, when the community was part of farming and the farmer was part of the community."

the food dollar, more and more farmers are looking to market direct to the consumer through selling at farmers markets, roadside markets and pick-your-own operations, as well as direct sales to restaurants, high-end retail outlets, specialty distributors—and even supermarkets.

And as consumers savor the lusciousness of tree-ripened peaches at farmers markets, or partake of squash blossoms at high-end restaurants, they demand the same from their local supermarkets. Tired of tasteless tomatoes and cardboard-like vegetables, they are willing to spend a few cents more for a tomato that tastes like a tomato.

Supermarket produce sections have begun to undergo dramatic changes, as sparkling displays of arugula, peak-season salad greens, herbs and alfalfa sprouts have sprung up alongside the potatoes and tomatoes. Twenty years ago most supermarkets carried about 75 different items in the fresh produce section throughout the year; today, many of the markets carry 200 to 250 separate produce items. "Five years ago there were very few high-quality specialty growers," noted Tasting

The Great Debate continued. . .

Kay Blonz: "If it weren't for the terminal market system of food distribution," says Kay Blonz, a specialty wholesale broker from Berkeley, California, "none of us would ever have eaten a banana. Of course, we should all eat and buy local food products seasonally when they are available. But the fact is, one-half of the country can't grow a lot of fruits and vegetables for one-half of the year. Neither can we blame chemicals and monocropping solely on large-scale agribusiness. Campbell's needs enormous amounts of tomatoes for their V-8 juice, just to pick one example. In our present society, we can't feed our enormous population on backyard gardening. Some of our food has to be shipped in from longer distances."

Ina Chun: "It's nice to be idealistic," says Ina Chun, a specialty grower and distributor from Graton, California. "But the reality is that people have to eat. As it is now, most people don't take the time to go to the farmers market or join a subscription farm. Until consumers choose to support community local agriculture, and buy locally and in season, the terminal markets will continue to fulfill a need. Change has to come from the consumer."

Gail Feenstra: "Let me start by describing a couple of scenarios. In the first, agricultural production has become more and more centralized, with land and capital concentrated in the hands of fewer, larger landholders. Many of these farms are highly specialized, growing mainly one crop. Small family farms are quietly disappearing, replaced by quickly expanding suburban developments, or in some regions, impoverished rural towns. All kinds of produce are now available year-round and food is relatively cheap at the supermarkets. Some people complain that the food doesn't have much flavor. Eventually, they begin to forget what produce used to taste like or how it was grown.

"In the second scenario, the food system is more decentralized. There are many more family farms on the landscape, particularly in certain farming regions of the country. These farms would be closely linked with nearby rural communities, supporting the economic, educational, and cultural vitality within those communities. Food distribution networks and food processing industries would be closely connected to nearby food production so that consumers in local communities and cities would benefit from the freshest, locally produced foods in season. Food producing resources—land, water, technologies, marketing, processing and distribution networks—are much more democratically controlled and equitably distributed among many individuals.

"Unfortunately, the trends in our present food system are much more similar to the first scenario than the second. Do we want to continue in this direction? I would like to suggest that we do not, and that we can go a lot further toward making our food system more localized, more democratic and more accountable."

—from "Should The Food System Be Decentralized?" by Gail Feenstra, *Sustainable Agriculture News*, Summer 1992

staffer Catherine Brandell. "But today, restaurants, brokers and retail outlets are eager to have this kind of produce."

In her book, *Cooking From The Garden,* Rosalind Creasey outlines her vision of cooking as "an unbroken arc from the garden to the table. We've lost our connection to the garden," Creasey claims. "The average American has had little exposure to the fantastic variety of fresh fruits and vegetables, and they don't know what they're missing. It's as if we've been raised on concrete and it's impossible to know what grass under your toes feels like."

"Even very few professional food people have their roots in the garden," Creasey points out. "The farmers don't cook the food, and chefs don't grow it." Times are changing, Creasey notes: women like Jan Blum and Renee Shepherd now own specialty seed companies, bringing along with them a cook's knowledge of the food business; and farmers are establishing dialogues with chefs of the restaurants they sell to, exchanging ideas about what to grow and how to cook the new produce.

At Farm Conference '90, Creasey advised farmers to learn about the specialty produce appearing

Lotus vs. SuperCalc: A Lesson In Marketing

HAVE YOU EVER HEARD of a computer program called SuperCalc? Probably not. It is a great product, very much like Lotus 1-2-3. If you own a computer, Lotus 1-2-3 is a household word. Both Lotus and SuperCalc were launched at the same time; one was a success, the other collects dust on the shelves. The people who developed SuperCalc spent a lot of time and money producing a great product. The people at Lotus developed a good product and spent a lot of money on great marketing. It doesn't seem fair, does it? A good product with great marketing beats a great product with poor marketing every time.

In this country we have some of the most efficient growers in the world. Their operations are highly automated and there is an efficient marketing system to move their products to the consumer. Many of you may even have been one of these growers; we used to call them farmers. Today many people refer to them as "poor farmers." They are "poor" because a funny thing happens on the way from the fields to the dinner table— the price of a 100-pound bag of potatoes increases from the $2 paid to the farmer to as much as $50 on the grocery shelf. Watermelons get 5¢ a pound at the farm auction and 30¢ a pound in the store. Every day a few more farmers go broke. It's pretty obvious that people are willing to pay a lot more than the farmer is getting for his product, but he lets someone else do his marketing.

—Gary H. Lucas in *Greenhouse Product News*, Sept./Oct. 1991

in the supermarkets. "It used to be enough for the farmer to produce sufficient food to feed people, but now the emphasis is on taste, flavor and health," she said.

FOR THE SMALLER GROWER, especially, the gaps in taste and quality and variety in the traditional American agricultural system have opened up profitable marketing niches, and, quite possibly, a way to make a living in farming. "Conventional farmers are wallowing in a desperate financial depression right now largely because agribusiness persists in thinking of food as plastic," Gene Logsdon wrote for *In Business* magazine (Nov./Dec. '86), "yet ironically there was never a better time to get into farming. This does not mean that mass-produced food is not going to continue to serve the mass market, but there is now room for what in small-scale food business circles is called 'niche marketing.' What you do is find a food product that large-scale production methods can't handle properly without exorbitant expense."

Smaller growers can concentrate on plants that the big wholesalers overlook because they require special care. Herbs and many specialty items; hand-picked, tree-ripened fruit; or organic fruits and vegetables, are examples of high-value, labor-intensive crops that do not lend themselves easily to large-scale commercial farming. For the niche-market grower, quality, taste and variety are the goal, rather than volume; net income, rather than yield.

Since the labor-intensive, hands-on requirements of high-quality and specialty products make them more adaptable to small farms than corporate farms, the mini-farms often resemble backyard market gardens rather than traditional row crop farms. The small farms are generally characterized by diversity of production and marketing, as well as high-yield, intensive gardening methods. Many of the small growers are deeply committed to soil conservation and ecologically sound soil practices, which they feel produce plants that are healthier and have less disease problems.

Many of the "new" farmers, in fact, see themselves as a throwback to the Jeffersonian ideal as respected pillars of the community. "The image of the farmer just driving around in his pickup with a stub pencil and notepad in his breast pocket is passe," says Howard ("Bud") Kerr, director of the

USDA Office for Small-Scale Agriculture. "The new entrepreneurial farmers are leaders in their communities, stewards of the land, and good farm managers and marketers."

Yet the most striking characteristic of the "new" growers is their passion for farming—it is a labor of love. Bud Kerr recalls how 20 years ago when he ran a pick-your-own farm eight miles out of Baltimore, and commuted 30 miles to his USDA office in Washington, DC, "I found myself putting lights on the tractor so I could mow or plow at night," he recalls.

I T IS YET ANOTHER ASPECT of the "new" farmers, however, that is the subject of this book: they are astute marketers. In the wholesale food distribution system, farmers overwhelmingly took whatever price the system offered them. One of the dozens of successful small, specialty growers I interviewed said: "Traditionally, farmers have not been concerned with what happens to their product once it leaves the farm gate. But in today's economy, you just can't have the attitude that you can spend all your time growing and not marketing."

Yet the "new" farmer/entrepreneurs bend an ear to the marketplace and produce foods consumers want. "Knowing what's happening in the marketplace," says Don Anderson, a specialty vegetable grower near Santa Cruz, California, "is the

difference between the farmer who makes it and the farmer who doesn't make it." By phone or personal contact, Anderson keeps in close touch with the Bay Area restaurant chefs to whom he delivers direct twice a week. He also subscribes to a variety of food industry magazines to keep abreast of market trends. "I know what I can sell before I plant it," he says.

The "new" grower is willing to spend the first hours of the day on the phone marketing, or traveling to the city to research markets. Warren Weber of Star Route Farms in Bolinas, California, developed a market for his specialty greens by demonstrating to a number of chefs how to use the greens in Mesclun salad mixes. Berkeley farmer Andrea Crawford worked alongside Alice Waters in the Chez Panisse restaurant to pioneer ways to use baby vegetables and edible flowers.

Marketing is not so simple, however, as finding the latest wonder crop to grow. According to Charlie Hoppin, a fruit and vegetable grower near Yuba City, California, "There was a panacea in the '80s that anything different was going to be profitable. That wasn't true. I know because I lost a hell of a lot of money on some of them. Things change very, very rapidly. The '80s were the decade of specialty crops; the '90s will be the decade of specialty marketing."

H OW MUCH CAN YOU MAKE as a smaller, niche-market grower? Kona Kai Farms, a one-half acre farm near downtown Berkeley, which raises specialty salad greens and edible flowers for high-end restaurants, has grossed up to $200,000 yearly, a figure that owner Michael Norton claims makes it the highest grossing farm per acre in the U.S. On their 20-acre farm near Capay, California, specialty growers Kathy and Martin Barnes consider their specialty melons, which gross $2,000 – $3,000 per acre, a marginal crop; their goal is $140,000 per year (*The New Farm*, February 1989).

These are, of course, high-end examples. "Realistically," says Carol Klesow, an agricultural marketing consultant from Santa Rosa, California, "it's hard to make substantial money on less than ten or five acres." Characterizing specialty produce as "not a fast buck area," Klesow says that lots of people are getting into it. "The ones making good money will be the ones willing to work hard and plan. You can't just read an article on the latest fad crop and discover what vegetable can make you a millionaire. The ones that survive will be the business-minded farmers willing to keep track of costs and prices, study seed sources, and study the market."

"It's not enough to grow a beautiful product," Klesow continues. "Farmers have to take responsibility for their own marketing. It's going to take money and time—up to one-third to one-half of your sales and time to market your product."

The rewards in farming are there. You can make a good living, but the real joy is the family farm and the lifestyle that it provides. Farming is a business, yet it is also a way of life that both farmers and an increasing number of consumers are not willing to let fade into history. Typical was one farm family I interviewed, who related how the evening before the opening day of their "subscription farm," many of their customer/clients had camped out at the farm in order to get an early start harvesting the crop the next morning. These were hardly supermarket shoppers, and it is obvious they were searching for something more than food!

At the Redondo Beach Certified Farmers Market, I met Brian McGraff, a fruit and vegetable grower from Camarillo, California, who farms five rented acres. In addition to growing for seed companies, Brian goes to four farmers markets a week. Five of Brian's ten children help with farming, which will provide the financing for their education. "The farmers markets are a breakthrough," says Brian. "They allow the small farmer a way to make a living."

In his fascinating book, *Barry Ballister's Fruit and Vegetable Stand,* Barry Ballister calls fresh produce the "greatest source of taste, health, beauty and value in the food world today. Imagine a fruit stand brimming with high pyramids of ripe, colorful fruit, wafting a honeylike aroma and a vibrancy that fairly shouts, 'Take me, peel me, eat me!' Imagine one in every small town, one in every neighborhood or, in the cities, one, two, or three on every block. That's the way it was when I was a boy."

Noting that the average carrot once travelled over 1,000 miles before being eaten by the consumer, Marin Certified Farmers Market manager Lynn Bagley says she believes the USA is returning to a day when farmers markets were the hub of communities. "We lost our local farmers and fresh food. We ended up getting food that tasted like cardboard," says Bagley. "The pendulum is swinging back now."[2]

NOAH'S ARK
ORGANICALLY GROWN PRODUCE

Planning For Profits

Why It Pays To Develop A Marketing Plan

CHAPTER

1

Paula Winchester, president of Herb Gathering, Inc., started her herb business eight years ago in her basement. She slowly built a wholesale business and then opened a retail operation in 1985. She cautioned cattle ranchers considering the herb business. "If you start with 100 acres of basil and don't know what you are doing," she said, "you will lose your shirt."

—Kansas City Times, December 4, 1987, reporting on the ADAPT 2 Conference

"UNFORTUNATELY FOR American agriculture, we've traditionally been poor planners," states Dan Block, a professor of agribusiness and marketing consultant from Ventura, California. "We have tended to live from season to season, and planning has often been viewed as a luxury for big companies that have executives with nothing else to do with their time. Nothing could be further from the truth. Developing a marketing plan can be a simple project that can yield tremendous, long-term benefits."

The major reason for developing a marketing plan is to maximize limited resources. "If you have unlimited money, unlimited time and unlimited customers, then you don't need to do much planning," Dan Block states. "But all of us in American agriculture know that our capital and time are limited, and we have to share our customers with an increasing number of competitors."[1]

Particularly in direct marketing, where so many farmers underestimate the time, effort and resources they will be spending in marketing, a marketing plan is vital. As one farmers market manager said: "Too many growers go into direct marketing without a plan. They decide to go into direct marketing, and immediately hit six farmers markets a week, or they drive all over the state making small-volume deliveries to grocery stores. Very soon, they're tired from being on the road all the time; and no one is taking care of the farm."

A marketing plan helps you think through in advance just what it is you want to accomplish, how you intend to accomplish it, and when. It helps you establish priorities to use as a guide in making decisions, decreases risks, and offers a way to monitor progress. How much product should you market through various outlets? Do you have the time, talent and experience to make your own advertisements, send announcements to the newspapers, find recipes, or develop a mailing list? If you are out selling at the certified farmers market, is there a trustworthy employee to make sure the irrigation gets done? A good market plan will reveal flaws in your thinking at the "paper stage," rather than in the real world, where mistakes can be costly. Generally, the survival rate for new enterprises is greater if some preproduction planning has been done!

Finally, having a marketing plan allows you to respond to changes more effectively when they occur. Too many small-business owners "react" to marketing problems rather than "acting" on situations. Having a marketing plan enables you to make your decisions based on your plan.

Put your plan in writing! Writing down your thoughts and ideas on paper helps you think them through more clearly. It's easier to refer to a plan and to revise it when it is outlined on paper. Putting your plan on paper also allows you to take your information to local or state experts who can help you decide what crops would work on your land, or how you should market them. Another reason to put your plan in writing is financial: bankers love to see things in writing!

The broader picture: making a business plan[2]

Hand in hand with investigating market potential for your prospective crops, you also need to look at what you'd like to raise, and your resources, desires and ability to carry out your prospective projects. Making a marketing plan, in other words, is only part of an overall business plan. A business plan—in addition to a marketing plan—includes:

- A *mission statement* is a brief, generalized statement of the purpose of your business. You should be able to capture the essence of your business vision in one or two sentences. The purpose of this book, for instance, is *to help farmers make a right livelihood by selling what they grow!*
- A *statement of goals, objectives and strategies.* (See Chapters 2 and 5.)

- A *production plan* describes in detail the production process, including input quantities and prices, labor, facilities and equipment requirements. Production plans should also identify potential production problems (insects, weeds and constraints caused by soil, water or crop variety) and management solutions.

- A *financial plan* is used to estimate capital needs, to project future financial circumstances, and to make decisions about financial actions needed to carry out a business development plan. Financial plans include projected balance sheets, projected income statements and projected cash flow statements. By developing projected versions of these three financial statements, a business manager can evaluate production and marketing plans to determine whether outside sources will be needed to finance a new enterprise. A cash flow statement should be projected for monthly intervals for the first year. Showing your projected income and expenses helps point out weaknesses in your working business plan and helps you keep from overspending during low-income months. Projected financial statements can be used as part of contingency plans to address possible problems, such as discontinued financing, cash flow concerns, effects of different depreciation methods, or rapidly increasing costs for a certain input. Having contingency financial plans makes it easier to evaluate possible solutions to problems.

- *Staffing and organization plans* describe the personnel and organizational structure needed to support a projected operation. Personnel duties and responsibilities, accountability, recruitment and training are considered. It is important, for example, for a producer to know when and where seasonal labor can be found; whom to deal with to arrange for such labor; expected labor costs; and what room, board, medical and other services must be provided for such laborers.

- *Management and contingency plans.* Management plans, which involve planning, organizing, directing, coordinating and controlling the operation, are necessary to assure that the organization's mission and objectives are accomplished effectively and efficiently. Contingency plans help make the operation flexible, since they deal with situations that may come up.

20

Examples are government intervention, supply and demand changes, price changes, changes in consumers' preferences, changes in produce grading and quality standards, or changes in marketing practices.

While the complete process of writing a business plan is beyond the scope of this book, many of these steps are gone through in Chapter 2, "Choosing Your Enterprises." In addition, Chapter 3, "Deciding What To Grow" and Chapter 4, "Market Research," provide a more in-depth look at analyzing your own situation and the marketplace. Once you've studied your situation, looked at potential markets and chosen your enterprises, you're ready to move on to Chapter 5—making a marketing plan to market your products. Your county extension agent can help you prepare financial statements and develop a business plan. Also, see the Chapter 5 listings in "Chapter Resources" for further information about writing a business plan.

What about finance?

Startup capital, to most people, means banks. Although financing your enterprises may come down to borrowing from a commercial bank, take a long, hard look at this option. Borrowing at high interest rates is often a road of no return. Can you finance the venture yourself, from savings or earnings from an off-farm job? Borrow money from family or friends at less than prime rates? Your county extension agent may be able to identify many other possible sources of startup capital, including federal and state-level assistance, or private sources of grants and assistance.

Here are some tips in seeking outside financial assistance: [3]

- *Research.* Thoroughly research your proposal and have accurate data and information. Document some sources.

- *Examples.* Have examples from someone who is already engaged in the enterprise that can help document your budgets and act as a mentor.

- *Market information.* Have reliable and documented information on markets, and how to access them.

- *Business plan.* Have a professional business plan.

- *Experts.* Suggest a third party who can provide an unbiased opinion about the business proposal, e.g., someone from a small business development center, Extension, etc. Take your banker to an operating farm if possible.

- *Self-finance.* Be creative in finding ways to finance up to 50 percent of the total costs yourself.

- *Risk management.* Find ways to spread or minimize the risk so that the lender does not carry the full financial weight of the proposal.

- *What if.* Do not present only a best case scenario to your lender. Also present a worst case scenario with an alternative pay-back plan.

- *Salary.* Document that you may not be withdrawing salary from six months to two years following startup.

- *Credit record.* Know that your past performance on loan repayments may affect your creditworthiness.

- *Resume.* The lender needs to know whether you have the skills to make your proposal work. Provide documented evidence of the successes you have had.

- *Small is beautiful.* Do not attempt to begin on a large scale. Earn your lender's confidence by beginning small.

What if the banker (or other lender) turns you down? Redouble your efforts to find innovative ways to carry out your vision. Start smaller and get an off-farm job to help support your farming passion. Look for ways to do the job better or more efficiently, with less money. Barter at every oppor-

© Dry Creek Herb Farm, 13935 Dry Creek Road, Auburn, CA 95603 (916) 878-2441

tunity: trade food for any outside services you need. Scale down your first year plan to fit your budget. Tom and Denesse Willey, of T & D Willey Farms near Fresno, California, are two of the most innovative farmers I've met. "We joke about it now," they say, "but the best thing that ever happened to us was that the bank refused to loan us any money!" Lack of capital forced them into being creative and innovative beyond what might have been the case if they had had a lot of money.

And if a lender gives you a loan? Conserve your capital. Spend it wisely. Andy Lee, author of *Backyard Market Gardening*, advises thinking of spending money as either vital, essential or nice. "In the first year, focus on the vital elements of your business plan. These can sustain your immediate future. Leave the essential items for the second or third year, and don't buy the nice items until your business is solidly established. For example, don't buy a new tractor or rotary tiller if you can rent or borrow one in the short term. Don't buy a new truck if a used truck will work just as well. You need to save money, so be as inventive and innovative as you can to keep your expenses at a manageable level."

Start small, think big: some startup tips

Match the scope of the project to the risk you can handle. Start small, and test your ability to grow and market new products before you scale up. In addition to protecting yourself so that you don't get knocked out if your experiment fails, starting small also helps assure you'll produce a quality product. Set aside a certain percentage of your acreage or gross income each year to experiment with new products. Plan to spend some time and money researching any new enterprises before you launch into them, and go visit some producers outside your area before you start anything.

Look at new enterprises as a part-time investment with the goal of providing supplemental income the first year. As each small-scale demonstration "seed" sprouts, expand acreage and varieties gradually on a phased schedule. Focus initially on producing a few selected specialties, and establish a reputation for quality specialty products. Establish brand identification as soon as possible. Marketing image, including promotion, sales and merchandising support (such as recipes) is important to consider even in the planning stages.[4]

Match your abilities to your market. In the beginning, don't worry about what you can't handle! Match your market prospects to your ability to supply that market not only with the correct amount of product but also with proper service and frequency. Until you build up your ability to deliver large volumes at frequent intervals, it's wiser to start out at a local farmers market rather than trying to supply a large retail market or a large wholesaler.

Diversify your markets and not just your enterprises. Adding mushrooms to the product mix you are already selling to local restaurants, for example, may not increase your economic stability so much as adding a farmers market to your marketing mix.

Sell before you grow! Too many growers tragically follow the process of growing the plant, then trying to sell it, and are left with an unwanted portion of their crops rotting in the field. Or, if they are lucky enough to sell it to a wholesaler or a processor, they will get a check for half the amount they should be getting for their product. By investigating market potential for a product before you grow it, you will choose enterprises with real markets, not just enterprises based on wishful thinking. That's what this section is about: planning ahead for profits.

Acknowledgments

Curt Stutzman, agricultural consultant, 4943 Cosgrove Rd., SW, Kalona, IA 52247; (319) 683-2495.

Choosing Your Enterprises

McFadden is an innovator. When he sees a new farm product that excites his imagination as a producer or marketer, he buys a sample. Then he analyzes every aspect of its production, distribution, pricing and even packaging. The shelves and floor of his office are cluttered with boxes, cans, bags and bottles from farms all over the country.

—The New Farm magazine

THE KEY TO CHOOSING an enterprise, according to Judy Green, coordinator of the Farming Alternatives Program at Cornell University, is to analyze your resources to find out if a new enterprise is going to be fun and profitable—or the last straw. And do it *before* you start investing money in a new enterprise.[1]

This chapter borrows extensively from *Farming Alternatives: A Guide to Evaluating the Feasibility of New Farm-Based Enterprises*, of which Judy Green is a co-author (see "Chapter Resources"). "It is surprising how often people jump into a new venture without taking a good, hard look at feasibility," Green continues. "Unfortunately, many end up wasting precious resources that could have been put to good use with proper planning."[2]

The steps involved in choosing an enterprise include taking a look at yourself, your family and your operation, as well as your physical, marketing, management, labor and financial resources. In addition, look at prospective customers, competition, length of time required to become established in a market, and market potential, trying to analyze your market for possible niches. The research you do will help you answer these questions: Does this enterprise satisfy my wants and needs? Do I have, or can I develop, the necessary skills to make it work? Is the current market outlook for the product favorable? Can I make the enterprise pay with realistic market prices?[3]

Set goals[4]

Ask yourself *why* you're considering a new enterprise. What are you trying to accomplish? Is your goal to make money? Be specific. How much? How soon? Is that a realistic goal? Perhaps an off-farm job may be a better solution than a new enterprise.

Is your prospective enterprise consistent with your family and farm business goals, as well as your skills and preferences? It's important to involve the whole family in the planning process, right from the start. Sit down together and discuss how everyone feels. The decision to diversify affects the whole family, so it's important to communicate and come to a consensus.

Assessing preferences is just as important as projecting profitability: "You have to love your new enterprise," says Judy Green. "It isn't going to make money for a while and you're going to take a few lumps. So you really have to believe in your product to have the perseverance to pull through. That spirit and strength is important, as long as it doesn't blind you to reality."

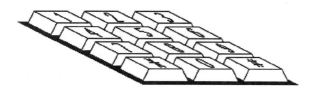

Inventory resources[5]

Match your market prospects to your ability to supply that market, not only with the correct amount of product, but also with service and frequency. Do not waste your time and endanger your reputability by trying to sell to Safeway, a major wholesaler, or a chain restaurant if you can't supply their needs! You need to take a detailed account of your resources.

Physical resources. Physical resources include land, soils, climate, water, buildings, machinery and equipment.

Management and labor resources. These include both the on-farm labor and potential labor pool in your area, and nontraditional as well as traditional agricultural skills. If your spouse has superior cooking skills, or teaching and lecturing skills, write it down; food processing or educational classes may be a possibility.

Match prospective enterprises so that labor requirements coincide with existing labor availability. A labor flow budget can help you do this. Set up a chart with a category for each month, estimating how much time in each month is already spent in working with your current enterprises. Look for months in your chart in which you have unused hours that could be utilized in new enterprises.

Marketing resources. If you are good at marketing you may be able to create your own market, but the more usual case is to take advantage of markets that are presently available. Look at the marketing alternatives in your area, including farmers markets, roadside stands (your own or others), restaurants, grocery stores, supermarkets and processing plants. Wholesalers, including terminal markets for produce, brokers, distributors, supermarket warehouses and marketing cooperatives are another possibility. Other prospective marketing channels include a pick-your-own operation or a recreational farming attraction, campgrounds, institutions, or other farmers to whom you may be able to sell products or services.

Financial resources. List the financial resources you have available, including cash, savings, credit and potential investors.

Miscellaneous resources. These include sources of information, suppliers, processors and distributors.

Time. Time is one of a farmer's most valuable resources. In most cases, it's also the resource that is in shortest supply. If your present enterprises are hard enough to handle, adding more may be overwhelming.[6]

Identify enterprises

After you've defined your goals and inventoried your resources, it's time to identify possible enterprises. Check with your current or potential buyers, such as specialty distributors, restaurateurs, or customers at your own PYO or farm market. Do they have any unfilled demands? Visit specialty wholesalers and distributors, as well as the produce section of a successful food store. Note what's being sold. Talk to the store manager about what types of produce are in demand. Visit local ethnic markets in your area. Is the food being imported? If so, you've found a potential for selling locally grown ethnic food.

There are lots of ideas for new farm enterprises. Extension publications list everything from artichokes to zucchini. Read Craig Wallin's *Backyard Cash Crops*, and browse through farm trade magazines and journals, as well as food magazines like *Cooks, Bon Appetit, Gourmet*, etc., to look for ideas. Read the food column in your newspaper, as well as cookbooks, such as Rosalind Creasey's *Cooking From The Garden*, a rich resource of ideas for growing specialty crops. Ask friends to lend you any copies of direct-mail food catalogs they receive.

Ask your seed company for suggestions on what to grow. Also send away for gardeners' seed catalogs, which offer a greater variety than standard commercial seed catalogs. Many food trends start with specialty seed companies. Seeds from garden catalogs may not always be of commercial quality and yield, however. The produce may be odd-shaped or inconsistent in size, so you'll need to grade it for selling through different outlets—some for restaurant buyers, some for farmers markets, others for juicing, etc.

Look for selections that boast of excellent flavor. Also, be aware of what they *don't* talk about.

If they talk about the variety's storage capacities, or yield, etc., but say nothing about flavor, you can bet it's not a great tasting product! Since larger companies often don't offer some varieties in their catalogs because the seeds are so scarce, you might investigate growing specialty seeds for seed companies.

Play around in the kitchen, experimenting with different ways in which your products can be used! Understanding how your products can be used can create excitement and enthusiasm which help with promotion and sales. If you don't like to cook, try to work with a chef who can develop new ways to use your product. Also, ask yourself: What would you *like* to grow? Chances are, that's what you'll grow best. A real enthusiasm for what is being grown can be felt by the customer.

While it is fun and useful to expose yourself to new ideas, don't get swept away by every new possibility that comes along. What's important is to take your list of new ideas and evaluate how each alternative matches your skills, preferences and resources identified in the previous section.[7] As a general rule, avoid enterprises which require resources which you are lacking, and take advantage of resources that are underutilized. For fur-

Al Weiser selling apples at the Santa Monica, California, Certified Farmers Market

ther discussion of possible enterprises, see also Chapter 3, "Deciding What To Grow."

Match prospective enterprises to your situation

Next, find out if the crops you are considering can be produced in your locale, and if they fit into your farm's capabilities. With the help of your extension agent, compare the conditions in areas now producing those crops with your conditions. Are they similar to your conditions? Check for things like soil, water and climactic requirements, rotation considerations, building and facility requirements, machinery and equipment requirements, pest management considerations, management and labor requirements, and harvesting considerations.

Consider production costs. Most specialty items will have a higher rate of return, but will also cost more to grow, and require a lot of hand-labor in seeding, transplanting and daily cutting and weeding. Some specialty crops have comparatively low yield—does your selection generate enough volume to make a profit? What are the alternatives for pest control? If no chemicals are registered for the crop, can you grow the crop organically at a profit?

Do you have the necessary management and labor resources to meet the demands of your prospective enterprise? Specialty crops often require intensive labor. Getting the crop out on time, and in good condition, is vital to profitability. Project management and labor requirements by season and job for your new enterprise, and figure what each will cost.

Also, do you have the facilities to pack and ship the product properly? Postharvest handling procedures are critical factors in creating a reputation for quality, which is crucial in developing return sales—do not neglect this vitally important aspect of farming.

If possible, conduct trials to see how well a crop does under your farm's growing conditions, and to test market acceptance on a small scale. Specialty crops are generally not easy to grow, and there may be less information available on how to produce some of these crops than for traditional crops. Experiment and find out how a crop does under your farm's conditions before making a major investment!

Are the marketing requirements of the prospective enterprise available to you? Let's say you'd like to sell to supermarkets, for example. Can you meet the minimum volume requirements, or are there other nearby producers with whom you can pool supplies? Can you provide the level of quality and service required for your product?

Check also such business aspects as regulatory, legal and liability restrictions, zoning and tax considerations, and leasing alternatives.

Finally, determine the value and productivity of the resources that will be allocated to the enterprise. You will need to have an idea of the financial resources required by the operation in order to determine profitablilty.

Research your market

Sell before you sow! Don't plant one seed until you know who your customers will be. Match your sales volume to the market—plan ahead and anticipate what you can sell to your outlets. There's nothing worse than producing a crop, only to find out that you can't sell it.

Market analysis not only helps determine if your prospective enterprise can be profitable, but also determines how you will promote and market your product. You must know who will buy your product or use your service, how many potential customers there are, where they are located, how they like to buy, how much they are likely to purchase, when they like to buy, what price they are likely to pay, what services they require, and who already supplies them.

By knowing your customers, you can zero in on the most productive market in which to promote your product, and not waste time trying to promote your product in the wrong market. Asian pears, for example, which are light, refreshing, and juicy, might be targeted to an upscale audience with an active lifestyle. Remember, each market segment that you identify will require a separate marketing plan. Marketing to ethnic restaurants, for example, will require a different strategy than marketing to a local grocery store chain.

If you are a retailer, develop a customer profile of your existing customers. How far away from your store do customers live? What products do they purchase? What will encourage them to make repeat purchases?

Similarly, develop a customer profile for your potential direct-to-retail or wholesale marketing methods. Which restaurants or grocery stores might purchase your product? What kinds of wholesale outlets might buy your product? What do they require in terms of delivery, price, volume, quality, etc.?

Estimate prices. Make a telephone survey of restaurants, grocery stores, specialty distributors, wholesalers and cooperatives, etc., to get a general picture of current market volume, prices, sources and quality. Extension agents, trade organizations and other producers are also good sources of information.

Another way to estimate prices you might expect to get for your prospective crop is to look at wholesale prices for your product or similar products. Study federal market news reports, as well as *The Packer's Produce Availability and Merchandising Guide,* both current and past issues. Look for these publications at a university library, state department of agriculture, or your extension office. Look at prices that have been paid for your product in the region you will be shipping to and at a similar time of the year. This should give you a reasonable estimate of the going market prices for your product. Look for "market windows," i.e., high prices that indicate a high-demand product at certain times of the year. Also look at prices of similar products that may be used as substitutes for your product. If the price of nectarines falls significantly below that for peaches, for example, the high price for peaches may be unstable, since buyers may easily switch to nectarines.

Find out all you can about past and projected future trends. Is consumption increasing, leveling off, or about to boom? Are prices likely to plummet as more people get into the business, or is this a fairly well-established, stable market?

Finding information on market trends for new or unusual products and services is difficult; study the market trends for similar or related products or services. If your product is a unique, non-mainstream product, or if you are selling through very unique marketing channels, you may be able to set your own prices according to demand. If your product or service is so new that there isn't already an established market, you will have to create a market by educating potential buyers. Are the

Choosing Your Enterprises: A Checklist

Personal and family considerations

- Have you identified goals and objectives for your business and personal life?
- Have you conducted a full inventory of your resources (human, physical and financial) which can contribute to accomplishing these goals and objectives?
- Are you willing to make sacrifices required to make this enterprise profitable (time, changes in lifestyle, privacy)?
- What do you wish your business to look like five years from now, and what are some intermediate steps or objectives required to get there?

Inventory resources

- Physical resources: land, soils, climate, water, buildings, machinery and equipment;
- Management and labor resources;
- Local marketing options available;
- Financial resources;
- Miscellaneous: sources of information, suppliers, processors and distributors;
- Time.

Identify enterprises

- Current and potential buyers, produce managers, books, magazines and publications, seed companies, chefs, etc.

Enterprise feasibility

- Is this enterprise technically feasible for your location given the following factors: climate, soils, water, insects, diseases, growing season?
- What are the building, machinery, equipment, management and labor requirements? If you don't have the necessary resources, what is the cost (in dollars and time) of acquiring them? Do you have the facilities to pack, package and ship the product?

Market factors

- Have you clearly defined what your product/service is (features such as size, quality, varieties, etc., and benefits to buyer or user)?
- Are there markets for the product, and if so, what is your target (niche) market(s)?
- Market outlet alternatives;
- Geographic location of market(s);
- Demographic characteristics (age, income, etc.);
- Behavioral characteristics (lifestyle, etc.);
- How large is the existing market demand?
- Number of potential buyers;
- Annual per capita consumption;
- Average purchase per buyer;

- Can the market be created or expanded to absorb an increased supply of the commodity. Are advertising and promotion efforts worthwhile?
- What are the favorable market windows for the product? (Compare historical prices against projected costs per unit);
- Does the market demand specific grade/quality/size standards?
- What is the cost of transportation to the targeted markets?
- Are there any middlemen services involved (brokers, wholesale distributors, etc.)? If so, do they have any specific requirements (delivery, volume, etc.)?
- How many competitors are located nearby? What do you have to offer to surpass your competitors?
- What prices does the market offer and how steady are those prices? What is the highest price and the lowest price you are likely to receive and what conditions create these price situations?
- What is your expected sales volume? What is the minimum and maximum volume of product you believe you could sell in one year?

(Continued on next page)

Choosing Your Enterprises: A Checklist continued. . .

If your market research shows that supply already exceeds demand for the product/service being evaluated, or that the trend is one of declining consumption and/or prices, do not pursue the enterprise any further. If your market research is favorable, continue with the following considerations.

Financial considerations

- Once you are in full production, what are the expected costs and returns (enterprise budgets)?
- What will be the impact of varying yield/production levels on profitability?
- What are the costs of production given varying climatological and pest problems?
- Are you able to acquire the necessary startup capital to establish the enterprise? What about the annual operating funds necessary to continue the enterprise?
- What is the impact of the new enterprise on the profitability of any existing enterprises?
- Is the proposed enterprise complementary or supplementary to existing enterprises, or

does it compete with them? If so, what is the impact on the profitability of the other enterprises?
- How will the additional costs and returns of the new enterprise affect the cash flow of the business?
- How will investment of additional resources and the diversion of existing resources from present uses affect the financial risk position of the farm?

Miscellaneous considerations

- Are there any legal restrictions, regulations or liability factors associated with the new enterprise?
- Does the enterprise require any special recordkeeping to provide information for both management decisions and/or government reports?
- Does the enterprise require an abundant or continuous supply of special production inputs?

- Will the proposed enterprise limit off-farm employment opportunities?

If you have satisfactorily answered all of the questions from this checklist, you probably have enough information to make a decision about the new venture. If you decide to go ahead with the enterprise, you should now develop an implementation plan, including a business development plan that specifies a timetable, production schedule, marketing plan, management structure and financial plan.

Adapted from *A Guide To Successful Direct Marketing* by Charles R. Hall and Jeff L. Johnson. (See "General Resources—Pamphlets & Booklets.")

time, effort and expenses involved in consumer education prohibitive to making a profit? If the market is already developed, on the other hand, you will need to differentiate your product or services from competing products already on the market.

Study the broader "environmental" aspects of your product. Is it politically correct, environmentally friendly and socially acceptable? In the '90s, these considerations are important!

To find out how to do market research, see Chapter 4, "Market Research."

Study the competition

Who is your competition? Where are they? How much do they sell? What kind of quality and service do they offer? At what prices? What kind of customers do they attract, and how well satisfied are these customers? What are their media and marketing strategies? What makes them successful? What can you do better than they do?

Studying your competition will help to determine the various segments of the markets that are being served, and help you identify an available niche in the marketplace.

Look for nondirect as well as direct competition. Competition for your farm recreation operation, for example, may come from books, movies or campgrounds, not just from other farm market operations.

There are a number of ways you can learn about your competition. Visit their businesses, use their products or services, survey their customers, or interview them directly if possible. Some competitors may refuse to share any information with you, but some may be quite helpful. Look for ways that can decrease direct competition, or that can even be of mutual benefit.

What must you do to claim market niches not being filled by the competition? Don't try to compete against the competition's strengths. It's impossible to compete against a larger grower in price, for example; find your niche, instead, in quality, uniqueness and service.

Choosing market outlets

Review your resources. Look at the time and financial resources you will have available in the next two or so years. Select a channel that is reasonable for you to address, in terms of volume of product required, prices, shipping costs, and other factors. If you will have only a small amount of product for the next year or so, you are probably not going to supply a wholesaler or chain warehouse unless they are willing to buy from a number of small growers.

Match your product's unique characteristics with the needs of the segment you are supplying. Soft-stemmed shiitake mushrooms might be appropriate if you are selling to very sophisticated chefs demanding the "totally edible shiitake," for example. The mushroom's unique qualities may not be seen as an advantage, on the other hand, if sold to a relatively uneducated consumer retail market.[8]

Identify subjective factors. Maybe you don't want to be bothered with plastic trays and prepackaging. Or you don't want to be bothered with customers driving up your driveway to ask if they can pick outside the posted hours of your pick-your-own operation. All of these preferences are legitimate. Just be sure that they are profitable!

Estimate your profit potential for each of the channels you are considering. Figure your costs of servicing each channel under consideration. Is further processing or prepackaging required? What are transportation costs? What are your expected volumes? What sort of sales effort will be required? What degree of promotional support is required or expected?[9]

Evaluate the profitability of your enterprise

Will this new enterprise be profitable and feasible? After you've gathered information about markets, competition, trends and prices, you need to project income and expenses to determine profitability.

Estimate the annual volume of sales, both minimum and maximum, you expect to generate when you enter the market. Similarly, draw up "best case" and "worst case" figures for costs. Identify any additional capital the enterprise will require, as well as operating expenses, and draw up sales and cost estimates for your enterprise. Include expected times of income and expense when drawing up a projected cash flow chart—this helps you determine the "low spots" of critical cash flow.

Don't worry if your estimates of sales and expenses are not pinpoint-accurate; they are utilized as a "most likely" estimate, and you can adjust them later. Sources of information to help you make projections include extension service, small business development centers, financial institutions (cost of money, land, etc.), local and state governments, personal operating records (if any exist), consumer surveys, trade publications and industry statistics, and information from existing marketers in similar areas.

Compare the source of your sales and cost estimates with your own unique situation, and revise your sales and cost estimates accordingly. For instance, if on the average there are three U-Picks for every 15,000 people in a regional market, and your U-Pick will be number four in a 15,000 person market, your sales estimate may be too high. Whatever the situation, adjust the initial estimate to reflect real life circumstances.[10]

Based on your sales and costs estimates, project the profitability of your operation. One method of evaluating feasibility is to divide expected profit (costs subtracted from sales) by the amount of capital allocated to the project. This ratio provides an expected rate of return on investment. It can be compared to the interest rate you receive at the bank. However, this return is nowhere near risk free.[11] For more sophisticated profitability analysis, seek help from your extension agent, a local SCORE volunteer (call a Small Business Administration office to locate a SCORE volunteer near you), or a local banker or accountant.

Also, remember that your money and time may be better invested elsewhere. You haven't really made a profit until you have made a return on your investment that is at least as good as you could get for the use of your resources in any other manner. If you can get a 5-percent return on your investment elsewhere, you should not be investing in a crop or enterprise that will yield only a 3-percent return on investment.

Do you have the capital, resources and experience to break into this market? A new enterprise may take several years to become profitable. Some

Are You Listening?

A few years ago, Bob Kirtlan, of Silver Bend Farm near Clarksburg, California took his young son to visit some railroad relics. On the way home his son said, "Daddy, buy me a train!" Bob did. Today a real train circles their farm and provides a major attraction for their operation. Are you listening when others are talking?

alternative crops take years to establish and require specialized machinery. The more capital you have, the better, because it's often difficult to get commercial credit for alternative enterprises.

If financing proves to be a problem, then you need to look at enterprises that require little up-front cash. Getting a new product onto supermarket shelves, for example, can be tremendously expensive, whereas setting up a booth at the local farmers market doesn't require much of an investment.

Select your enterprises

Select enterprises to utilize your farm's resources for their highest possible return. If, after having analyzed your business and the marketplace, your prospective enterprise matches available resources, shows promising opportunities *and* you have sufficient financial resources to undertake the project, you may want to start the new enterprise.

If, however, your research shows insurmountable barriers such as prohibitive competition, legal restrictions or declining marketing trends, or your financial resources are already stretched to the limit, you need to rethink your new enterprise. Your market research hasn't gone to waste, however; it may reveal new options that are better than your first ideas. For example, you may find that local restaurants already have all the carrots they need, but they need a supply of specialty greens.

If your research has shown that your resources are being used to full capacity, a better strategy than diversifying might be to focus on reducing costs and improving income from your present enterprises. Make maximum use of your on-farm resources with enterprises you already know before looking for something new and different.[12]

One way to exploit existing enterprises is to add value to your products by further processing: drying, freezing, canning, baking, juicing, etc. By getting involved in processing and distribution, you will receive as much of the total retail dollar as possible. Processing also provides a way to store crops for year-round sales. A pick-your-own blueberry farm, for example, might expand into making its own jams and jellies.[13]

Should you diversify?

Farmers have heard much of the advantages of diversification in recent years: if you lose money in one place, you can make it up somewhere else. With specialty crops, especially, market prices can be volatile, and it helps not to put all your eggs in one basket. Another advantage of diversity is that once you've established connections with buyers, increasing the variety you offer them is a good way to increase the overall volume they will accept from you.

But there's a tradeoff. If you are a potato farmer, for example, and decide to try to raise apples, you will have to learn new production technologies, buy new equipment and develop new markets.

Since diversifying production can be very knowledge- and equipment-intensive, diversifying markets can be simpler and more lucrative than diversifying production. Going organic, or developing "value-added" products such as soybean snacks are examples of diversifying your markets without changing what you produce.

Each situation is unique, and you have to apply common sense. If you have a roadside stand and are also selling to restaurants, it may make sense to diversify your production so as to offer a greater variety of products. If you are a potato grower selling to a processing plant, on the other hand, it may make sense to develop more markets for your product so as not to be dependent on one market.

Acknowledgments

Judy Green, coordinator, Farming Alternatives Program at Cornell University.

© Ronniger's Seed Potatoes, Star Route, Moyie Springs, ID 83845 (Catalog $1)

Deciding What To Grow

No longer satisfied with standard varieties which boast of uniformity and extended shelf life, consumers are seeking the unusual—from "Hopi Blue" corn to nasturtiums and lavender borage. Rosalind Creasey, author of Cooking From The Garden, compares this period of exploration to "the time in Europe when explorers were returning from the New World with ships full of potatoes, peppers, chocolate and tomatoes."

THE NAME OF THE GAME is niche marketing. Identify target markets, determine special needs, and position yourself to serve the markets you select. Find out what the large suppliers aren't supplying, e.g., what is too small for them to bother with; then develop products to fill those needs.

Look for ways to differentiate your product not only by what you grow, but how you grow it (i.e., organic); what you do with it (i.e., "added value," or processed products); or how you package or market the product. Ordinary spinach, for example, triple-rinsed, cut and placed in plastic bags as a ready-to-eat salad, becomes a specialty item!

Pettigrew Fruit Company, located near Sacramento, began marketing Berre-Hardy pears (French Butter Pears), an old standard which had fallen out of fashion. When the grandchildren took over the farm, the family had been selling them for juice. By picking them vine-ripe, and wrapping them individually in a fancy box, the grandchildren turned them into a specialty item. By the second year they were selling thousands of boxes,

as customers thought it was some kind of exotic French pear!

Most successful specialty growers find that their "specialty" comes naturally to them, out of their love of growing and marketing. Rather than looking for the wonder crop, they grow what they like to grow, do it well, and do a great job marketing.

Translating trends into profits

Changes in society have made U.S. food consumers more diverse. The ongoing decline in average household size, for example, will open a market for food products in smaller packages. Food choices are also being made by older consumers, who desire and are able to afford more diverse and higher quality foods; and by working women who demand both quality and convenience. The growth of various ethnic populations, the increase in the number of health- and weight-conscious consumers, and the increasing number of consumers concerned about the safety of their food, have also changed the market for food products.

Some other trends to be aware of include:

- *The demand for fresh, in-season, local produce.* Consumers are learning that in-season carrots and beets in the winter are infinitely better than green, imported tomatoes.

- *Color.* Lavender eggplants, blue potatoes, yellow squash and yellow beets—unusual color is *in*.

- *Nostalgia.* Traditional American comfort foods like corn bread, corn-on-the-cob, or unusual varieties of potatoes or tomatoes. There are thousands of varieties of tomatoes in all different colors, shapes, sizes, flavors and textures.

- *Organic produce* has come a long way since the days when people considered it moth-eaten. Now its appearance is top-of-the-line, and people are willing to pay top dollar.

- *Edible and cut flowers.* This movement just keeps growing and growing. (Warning: Before you plant edible flowers, check with your local botany lab, read books on poisonous and edible plants, or check the list of safe edible flowers in Rosalind Creasey's *Cooking From The Garden* to see if what you're planning to grow is safe.)

Marketing for health

Consumers are choosing foods for health reasons, and health and nutrition have become hot items in food marketing. A recent issue of the *Natural Foods Merchandiser* claims that Americans spend $3.5 billion on natural and organic foods yearly—twice as much as they did 10 years ago.

According to a recent *What's Hot. . . What's New* bulletin published by Frieda's, Inc., "(Many food) items will be eaten as much for their health benefits as for their versatility and taste. There is a growing interest in and respect for the notion of food as medicine. The produce department, with all of its delicious and diversified options, is a veritable food pharmacy."

Nutrition labeling has become an important produce marketing tool. An article in a 1992 issue of *The Grower* magazine quotes Elaine McLaughlin, a registered dietitian with the United Fresh Fruit and Vegetable Association: "Nutritional benefits of produce will be the way produce is marketed in the future. (Under the new FDA food labeling regulations), it soon may be easier to promote produce's nutritional values. As never before, consumers may be made aware of the nutritional benefits of eating produce."

Just as you provide recipes or tips on preparing fruits and vegetables for consumers, you might also provide basic nutritional information on fruits or vegetables you produce. Several fruit and vegetable commodity groups, health organizations and government agencies provide free or inexpensive

pamphlets and brochures on nutrition that can be used for point-of-purchase signs or displays, or that can be handed out to customers (see "Chapter Resources").

If you make health claims for your produce, be honest and make only justifiable health claims. Store and display your produce so it maintains its health and freshness.

WARNING: Promoting health in food products is fraught with legalities. See discussion of this topic in "Rules & Regulations," Chapter 25.

Specialty crops

Several years ago, Stuart Dickson's 15-acre Stone Free Farm in the Sacramento Valley of California grossed over a quarter-million dollars selling organic vegetables to restaurants, farmers markets, several produce wholesalers and a small supermarket chain. Dickson claims a large part of his success is due to growing and selling vegetables that are not available from other growers. For example, he sells a mixed tomato pack, including many heirloom varieties, for as much as $25 per 20-pound box. This assortment is such a favorite that he can hold his prices even in summer, when ordinary tomatoes are selling for 30¢ a pound!

Specialties are crops that are not produced and sold in mass quantities. Specialty crops range from *exotic vegetables* like daikon, jicama, radicchio, Belgian endive, bok choy, and a mesclun mix (salad mix) of lettuces; *herbs* such as basil or fennel; and *exotic fruit* such as cherimoya, bitter melon, casaba melons and mangoes.

As a smaller grower, it pays to raise high-value crops, plants that the big wholesalers have overlooked because they require lots of handling or special care. Herbs require much specialized, hands-on care, for instance, as do berries or

Why Specialty Crops Demand Savvy Marketing

ACCORDING TO Anne Buss, saleswoman for Fresh Western Marketing, a grower/shipping company in Salinas, California, the secret of high-value, specialty marketing is to know ahead of time what your market is, and where it's going. "Most farmers see dollar signs in specialty crops," she says, "but if you don't have a market for it, you can get stuck."

Another tip in the volatile specialty market is to be prepared to change with the seasons. Two years ago, baby vegetables were hot; now growers can almost give them away. This year the hot crop is a mesclun salad mix. "Specialty items are only high-priced as long as few people are growing them," Anne advises. "When few growers were raising baby carrots, chefs would pay whatever price it took to get them. Too many growers just go by what sold well last year: 'Such-and-such did well last year and I'll grow it this year.' But most specialty buyers, such as chefs, are constantly looking for something *new*."

Another tip Anne passes along is to have secondary outlets for your specialty crops. Look for several end uses for your product, such as canning or processing or lower-end markets. Mesclun mixes are especially good because each of the salad items can be marketed separately, as well as in a salad mix.

haricovert beans. Other specialty market niche crops are those for which there are no registered herbicides. (See: *Crop Protection Chemicals Reference*, C & P Press c/o John Wiley & Sons, NY.)

Remember, however, that specialty produce doesn't have to be exotic. It just has to *taste* special! Regular commercial varieties such as peaches or raspberries are also specialty crops *if* they are allowed to fully ripen on the tree or vine, specialty-packed and moved fast! Unless you live close to a large population, in fact, it may be difficult to market exotic crops. Items like fresh-from-the-field tomatoes or sweet corn, however, command premium prices anywhere.

Since many specialty crops are highly perishable, handling, packing and shipment to market must be careful and quick. At least in the beginning years of growing these crops, they should be marketed no more than a 24-hour shipping distance from the field.

Specialty crops also require specialty markets where the highest return can be achieved in order to offset higher production costs, which include higher labor costs, lack of registered pesticides, intensive production practices, etc. Specialty crop markets are very specific and must be arranged in advance of planting. They should be custom grown for the particular markets you find. The requirements of many ethnic groups are a dramatic example of the specific nature of specialty crop markets. Chinese people, for instance, do not eat the same kind of daikon radish as the Koreans, Vietnamese or Japanese. Each group has different standards for bitter melons, luffa, asparagus, beans, greens and herbs.

Each year, more information is becoming available on specialty crops. See *Specialty and Minor Crops Handbook* in "General Resources–Books." *Knott's Handbook*, as well as *Commercial Vegetable Production Recommendations* (published annually by Cooperative Extension in many states), although not specifically for specialty crops, have much useful production and handling information. Seek the help of your extension agent in finding any market studies that have been published about your enterprise. Also, it may pay to contact individual extension agents who are conducting variety trials on specialty crops.

Growing and marketing for quality

You never have to worry about the competition if you can beat them on quality.
— Steve Hall, Wayne, Nebraska

Quality builds repeat customer business. While appearance may attract the customers, it is quality and taste that bring them back for more.

Another reason to grow for quality is price. Rick and Christie Knoll, of Knoll's Organic Farm near Brentwood, California, grow special varieties of tomatoes selected for flavor, which they raise dry-land style, using little water. They get about a third of the volume of tomatoes as do their neighbors, whose tomatoes are pumped full of water, but they get three times the price for their tomatoes.

The most important ingredient for good taste is freshness. Keep your products on the vine or tree as long as possible; then get them to the consumer as soon as possible after harvest. Underripe fruit can kill the market; overripe fruit should be processed.

Another key to quality is variety. Comb through specialty seed catalogs, searching for varieties that boast of excellence in flavor. Since the quality of your product comes from the soil, make sure that your soil is well-suited to the product you're considering growing. Many specialty farmers grow their products chemical-free, using a program of natural, enriched soil practices.

Don't jeopardize your top-paying markets by mixing your premium products with lesser-grade products! Develop markets for every grade of your product. Premiums can be sold to high-end restaurants, retail markets, mail order outlets, or specialty distributors. Number ones can be marketed as pick-your-own, or through farmers markets, institutional or wholesale outlets.

Markets for number twos and threes (products which are over- or under-sized, but which are still visually attractive and excellent in food quality) include pick-your-own or farmers market outlets, or as donations to charitable food programs or food kitchens. Use your judgment: appearance is becoming increasingly important in some farmers markets, for example, and you may lose sales by having too many number twos or threes mixed in with your number ones. Always ask buyers what is acceptable to them: if a restaurant chops up your products for salads, number twos may be perfectly acceptable.

By doing your own processing—drying, juicing or freezing, etc.—you can also sell your seconds as value-added, high-end products! Some processing companies *may* accept oversized, undersized or misshapen products for juicing, drying, etc., as long as the food quality is excellent. Nothing should go to waste: culls can be used for composting.

Should you grow organically?

As consumers are becoming increasingly concerned about food safety, and as regulatory laws restrict the use of chemicals on farms, organic food has achieved mainstream respectability. The $1.25 billion organic food market has grown at a rate of 40 percent a year in the past several years. Up to 84 percent of consumers have expressed a preference for pesticide-free, organically grown fruits and vegetables. "Farmers surviving the current shakeout will have to be tuned in to the increasing consumer demands for 'clean' food," claims Frieda Caplan.

Ecological concern is another reason for the trend toward organic and locally grown produce. Ecological awareness is growing rapidly, and if you sell organically grown produce in local markets, you should make this a selling point, educating your customers about the environmental consequences of their shopping. (See "Introduction–Our American Food System.")

Organics are, however, a specialty, niche-market rather than a mass-market item. Organics tend to be sold mainly through specialty distributors, health food stores and by direct marketing methods rather than in mainstream retail stores. Moreover, organic premiums, which range from 10 – 20 percent at mainstream retail stores, and up to 20 – 30 percent or higher through natural food markets or other specialty distribution channels, may level off as larger growers go organic. Organic

ACCORDING to a study done by the Cornell University Farming Alternatives Program, "marketing skills" was cited most often as the most important factor for success in alternative farm enterprises. Of the 160 farmers involved in alternative enterprises in New York state who were interviewed, 28.9 percent rated marketing skills as the most important factor, followed by production skills with 14.5 percent, and business management skills at 12 percent. According to Judy Green, coordinator of the Farming Alternatives Program, "Marketing is an area of tremendous anxiety with many farmers, yet it is critically important for any product outside of the mainstream commodity markets, which already have a marketing structure set up. But with any kind of alternative farming enterprise, you need to open up new areas of marketing."

farming is not something to jump into for quick profits. Rather, it is a long-term commitment to a different way of farming. Many organic growers conceive of growing organically as an essential element in a high-value, quality product.

Education is the name of the game in organic marketing. While specialty crops generally look distinct from other produce, organic products don't have that advantage. *Tell* the customer your product is grown organically, get them to *taste* your product, and *educate* them as to why you feel organic products are better.

Other marketing tips for organic growers include:

- Join an organic marketing association, both to learn and share information about organic growing and marketing, and to get certified. With effective certification, the public will have confidence in the product.

- Make yourself and the members of your association available to the media. Invite them to visit your farm, and explain the things you're doing to reduce or eliminate chemical use, and why this makes for a more valuable product.

- Use labels, stickers, twist-ties and stem tags to identify your product and to educate customers. If your fruit contains "no detectable pesti-

cide residues" and you have lab results to prove it, why not say so on the label?

- Make sure that the market you sell to has educational brochures on hand about organic produce. These are usually available from organic growers' associations. Consider forming associations with other small growers to coordinate production and pool products.

- If you want to sell to mainstream retail markets, you'll need to supply quality and consistency in large volume. Appearance is important: organic produce has to look as good as mainstream products.

Production tips

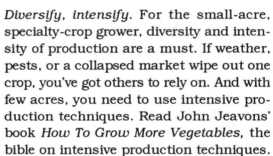

Diversify, intensify. For the small-acre, specialty-crop grower, diversity and intensity of production are a must. If weather, pests, or a collapsed market wipe out one crop, you've got others to rely on. And with few acres, you need to use intensive production techniques. Read John Jeavons' book *How To Grow More Vegetables*, the bible on intensive production techniques.

Aim for consistency, quality, and year-round supply. Extend your harvest by successively planting different varieties with different maturities. Steady production stretched over a long growing season provides regular work for the labor crew, evens out the cash flow, helps capture early- and late-season prices, and provides a consistency of supply for buyers.

Plant 10 percent more than what you plan to market. The first 5 percent should be to ensure quality. Not everything you produce is marketable to a high-end market such as a restaurant. The other 5 percent is for any new customers you may pick up.

Finally, try to make your farm fit the following characteristics of a successful small farm:

- diversity both in production and marketing, such as organic growing methods, specialty crops, direct marketing, and value-added products;

- labor intensive with small-scale equipment;

- good management practices; and

- social acceptance and environmental sensitivity. Since many small farms utilizing direct marketing methods are surrounded by an urban environment, they must be acceptable to their neighbors and to the community. Noisy pesticide applications, middle-of-the-night tractor operations, smelly cows or clouds of dust will not be viewed kindly.[1]

Postharvest handling practices

What happens to produce after it leaves the field is as important to taste and quality as the way it's grown! Improperly harvested and stored fruits and vegetables decline in appearance, flavor and nutrition. Unfortunately, many growers do not pay proper attention to postharvest handling. Many growers still ship produce right out of the field hot, for example, although studies show that for every 18- or 20-degree reduction in field temperature, the shelf life of many fruits and vegetable crops is doubled. According to Michael Boyette, North Carolina Extension agricultural engineering specialist, "Cooling allows you to stay in the market when the guy who is not cooling is out of the market or his product is rejected. A buyer is going to choose your product over one that was shipped hot because he knows a cooled product has better quality, stores better, and can be held longer."

The optimum harvest time for each crop is the first, and most critical, step in proper postharvest care. Pick at just the right stage of maturity, and get your product to market as soon as possible after harvest. If your product is being sold at a farmers market, for instance, the ideal time to pick would be in the cool of the morning before going to market. If evening is the only practical time to harvest, the crop should be placed in cold storage overnight. After crops are harvested, they should be graded according to size and quality and held under the best conditions available.

Pick and handle with care: many problems, such as decay, visual defects and water loss, have their origin in rough handling at harvest. Metal or plyboard bins should be lined with cardboard, carpet, or other padding to prevent bruising.

Storage requirements are specific for different types of fruits and vegetables, and vary considerably. Some crops need to be kept humid, for example, while others need to be dry. Temperature is the most important factor for controlling product quality. High field heat of freshly harvested produce is the major factor contributing to loss of shelf life. If you don't have access to a refrigerated truck,

and have only a *short* haul to the market, use wet newspapers or sheets to throw over the produce to help keep it cool. Picking greens with the roots on helps preserve freshness. Most of the time, however, produce needs to be cooled rapidly after harvest. Postharvest cooling not only protects the quality of the product, but also provides more marketing flexibility by eliminating the need to market immediately after harvest.

"Precooling" is the rapid removal of field heat after harvest. There are four basic methods of precooling produce: forced air, hydrocooling, vacuum cooling, and icing. Forced air cooling can be used for most products that can be cooled by water, and is less costly than hydrocooling. An inexpensive way to set up forced air cooling is to stack your produce on pallets, so that air can circulate, and place fans to suck air away from the produce into refrigeration coils. (For several low-cost cooling systems, see "General Resources–Cooling Units.")

Keep your storage area and packing containers clean and free of diseased produce. Cull diseased

Sebastopol, California, specialty grower Don Stiling

or damaged produce to reduce the chance of disease spreading through the pack.

Use specially designed or protected containers, if necessary, and don't fill them too high. Educate produce handlers or buyers on the special handling and storage requirements of your crop. In addition to giving verbal instructions to buyers, print information about storage and handling requirements on the box or packaging of your product. Insert an additional sheet inside the box on how to store and display the product in stores.

First-rate postharvest handling procedures are critical for the success of your operation! There is much low-cost information available both from your local farm advisor and from sources listed in "General Resources–Postharvest Handling."

Acknowledgments

Richard VanVranken, county agricultural agent, Rutgers Cooperative Extension of Atlantic County, New Jersey.

Paul Vossen, farm advisor, Sonoma County, California.

How One Direct Marketer Sells "An Ugly Bunch of Pumpkins"

Last October, Larry Harper looked at the pile of misshapen pumpkins at his place a few miles west of Columbia, Missouri. "What an ugly bunch!" he thought aloud. The part-time farmer and full-time editor of the *Missouri Ruralist* magazine was about to haul them off and throw them away.

Then a light dawned. He grabbed a marker and a piece of cardboard, wrote "Ugly pumpkins—50¢". . . and sold 300 of them in a day!

—*Rural Enterprise*, Fall 1989

Market Research

Evaluating the Market Potential and Defining the Target Audience for Your Enterprise

The annals of business failures are filled with businesses that attempted to market what they thought would sell, instead of finding out first what will sell!
— Bob Reynolds, marketing consultant, Moraga, California

FOR FARMERS WHO HAVE not had an active role in marketing their products in the past, the process of assessing the market may be somewhat intimidating. Market research need not be complicated, however; it is simply a matter of asking the right questions and looking in the right places for the answers. The basis of market research is simply getting to know your customers or buyers, and knowing why they purchase what they do, or what else they might like to purchase. The more you can talk to customers the better; you will learn something new from each person you talk with.

If you are already doing direct marketing, make it a habit to informally survey your customers. At a farmers market or roadside farm market, for example, you might ask: "If I offered yellow bell peppers in addition to my green bell peppers, would you be interested?"

More elaborate market research may use written or telephone surveys or focus groups, but it still involves the same process: asking people for information.

The goal of market research is twofold:
- to project the volume of sales and the price you might reasonably expect to achieve with a new enterprise; and
- to gather information about potential buyers and competitors that will help in developing a marketing strategy.

Planning your market research strategy[1]

Make sure your research is targeted and cost-effective by following these guidelines:

- Allocate a reasonable amount of time and money to this effort, depending on the risks and rewards involved in your prospective enterprise.

- Develop a list of questions about your market that you must answer before proceeding to develop the new enterprise.

- Define the specific type of data that you need to collect in order to answer these questions.

- Determine which of that data is available from *secondary sources*, i.e., information that has already been collected and published by someone else.

- Determine what *primary research* technique(s) you will use to collect the data which isn't already available. Primary research involves gathering information yourself—by observing customers, taking written or telephone surveys, or conducting personal interviews or focus groups.

Need help? Try tapping business students to assist with marketing research. Your chamber of commerce or cooperative extension office, or local small business and economic development agencies may help you design and carry out your market research. Find a librarian who can help track down the information you need. Local fertilizer, chemical, or seed dealers may be valuable sources of information. Producer groups may provide information about marketing various products.

Secondary research[2]

Secondary research is often the easiest and least expensive way to obtain market information. Types of information you can obtain through secondary research include:

- Population and demographic data such as income level, age distribution, level of education, and household size. This is important in estimating the total size of the market, and in knowing how many of what types of customers you have access to. Population figures can be obtained from the state data center in your state, or from local chambers of commerce or boards of realtors, local transportation departments, planning boards, school district offices and other local agencies. Obtain street traffic profiles from a city traffic engineer. Even small cities and towns have traffic volume maps that show how many people pass by your place of business (or potential business site) every day. National demographics are available from the Bureau of the Census and other public sources.

- Information about your local and regional economy, including the numbers of various types of business establishments, availability of support services, credit sources, and zoning and other regulations which may affect your marketing strategy.

- Production data showing the existing level of production of the product or service you are considering.

- Consumption data showing the per capita level of purchase by consumers for a given product or service.

There are numerous sources of secondary data—public, business, agricultural and university libraries, economic development agencies, and state departments of agriculture.

Secondary research varies in dependability. Researchers may have a "built-in bias" in the results. Ask questions of survey results like: How large was the selection of survey subjects? Were they picked at random? Was the information gathered in an environment comparable to the conditions of your own product? Be a little critical—don't make decisions based on bad data.

Primary research

Primary research is especially important when you are considering an innovative enterprise, a new market, or a local market for which there isn't much published data. Study what others are doing in a similar area. Go to trade shows or association meetings and visit other successful businesses similar to your own. It's far cheaper to learn from other people's experiences than from your own!

Study your own customers. Are they interested in specialty foods, shopping for something they can easily prepare for dinner that evening, or are they looking for low prices and large quantities? Observe what customers do inside your market. Count the number of customers who stop at special displays and watch to see which areas in the market have the highest traffic.

Analyze cash register tapes to find out information regarding volume of sales, how particular items are selling, patterns of selection, times of purchase, etc. Such detailed records are very important when attempting to assess growth over time or change in sales after the introduction of a new sales strategy or product.[3]

Personal Interviews.[4] Personal interviews are the most in-depth, versatile and accurate method. A minimum of only 30 people may be a sufficient sampling, so personal interviews are a good choice when dealing with a limited number of potential buyers. But they take more time and effort, and—if you are hiring someone to do it—money. Another danger of personal interviewing is the tendency of interviewers to hint at desirable answers or to explain a question so that a desirable answer is given.

Personal interviews, incidently, can also serve as a promotional tool. When you are trying to establish working relationships with wholesale buyers, for instance, an in-depth interview allows you to discuss the buyer's policies and preferences, as well as to acquaint the buyer with what you have to offer.

Be prepared with a list of specific questions and with solid information about your product or service. Make appointments for interviews with chefs, produce managers, or other professional buyers. Write a script of the interview, and fill out a form for each respondent. When interviews are completed, compile the gathered information for evaluation. Evaluate personal interviews in the same manner as surveys. (See discussion of written surveys later in this chapter.)

Select interviewees in an unbiased fashion. Also, limit the length of lists and choices—no more than three or four possible multiple choice answers, for example. Leave a token of your appreciation at the end of the interview, such as a coupon, a pint of strawberries, or another small gift given as a "thank you" for participating. Commercial buyers should be given samples of your product and sent a thank you letter as a follow-up.

Focus groups are useful for finding qualitative information, as in taste testings, brainstorming a company or product name change, or getting a feel for a new market. For a simple, do-it-yourself focus group, gather 8 – 10 randomly selected people that you feel represent a cross section of your target market, treat them to lunch and ask them questions and invite discussion.

For a higher-budget project, you may want to hire a nonbiased interviewer—this ensures greater accuracy. A more formal focus group may also involve paying each person a participant's fee and video taping the discussion. Focus groups can yield valuable information about market acceptance without spending a lot of money on market studies.

Customer surveys

A written survey can be used to obtain a wealth of useful information, including:

- a profile of customers—address, age, income and occupation, etc.;
- the nature of the purchase—what they purchased;
- the desirable and undesirable features of your market or product;
- interest in other products and services; and
- how they learned about your business—this information helps you to know where to promote and advertise your product or service.

If you already have a farm market, simply conversing with your customers on a regular basis may be a practical way to keep in touch with them. A formal market survey, however, may be called for when you need more specific and reliable information. If you are thinking of adding a new product to your store that requires a considerable investment, for example, it may be worth your time and energy to do a more extensive market survey of your customers.

The way you select people in your survey may bias your results. Try to have the survey sample be representative of your target market. An in-house survey of your customers may not be adequate if you're looking to expand to a customer base with different characteristics than those of your present customers. Supplement the in-house survey with a more random sampling, such as a mail survey from purchased mailing lists, or from a random selection of names from the phone directory.

The more people you survey, the more accurate your survey will be. One hundred people might be a good cross section of shoppers at most farm retail markets, but a smaller sample can provide useful information also. Provide incentives for people to participate in your survey program, such as coupons, recipe sheets or information sheets.

Designing your survey. In designing your survey, you'll need to decide between an open-ended (unstructured) interview, or a structured format, where there are only several possible answers. The open-ended study is appropriate for the in-person interview, where you may be asking questions about the direction of your business, or types of products you want to offer to customers. The structured survey is good to help decide about particular choices, such as whether to offer jams and jellies in your store.

While an open-ended survey will ask questions like: "What is your opinion about tomatoes available in the market today?," a structured study will ask: "What is your estimate of the quality of tomatoes available in the market today—excellent, good, fair, poor?" Open-ended questions are easier to ask, but they are much more difficult to tabulate and interpret. Try to include at least one open-ended question in your survey; this gives customers an opportunity to say what they like or make some statement about what concerns them.

Before you write the survey, sit down and brainstorm with your colleagues: "What do we want to achieve in the survey? How can we ask questions to achieve that purpose?" Every question should serve a purpose. Include only questions in the survey that you actually plan to use for decision-making. Keep it short—a single sheet of paper printed on two sides is usually plenty.

The lead questions should be easy to answer, noncontroversial, and should create interest. Place more difficult or personal questions like age or income level near the end of the questionnaire. Explain how the information will be used, and provide categories of ages and income instead of asking people to reveal exact information.

Design structured studies as fill-in boxes, or as multiple choice or checklists. Design the survey to focus on one issue at a time, and the questions to focus on one subject or idea at a time. Phrase questions to receive quantifiable answers; not: "How much fruit do you regularly buy?," but: "How many pounds of peaches do you buy each week when they're in season?"

Avoid loaded terms, or emotional phrases, as well as "leading" questions—questions worded in such a way as to imply a particular answer. Instead of asking, "Do you like locally grown produce?," ask: "What do you like about this supermarket?" Give the respondents an opportunity to indicate that the question does not apply, i.e., with a blank for "does not apply," "other" or "prefer not to answer."

Unless you can retail, you seldom get properly compensated for quality.
—Wayne Weber, North Fairfield, Ohio

Include a personalized preamble: "Thank you for doing business with us. Your satisfaction is important to us. Please take a few minutes to fill out this survey." Instead of asking respondents at the end of the survey to fill in their name and address for your mailing list, enclose a separate post card which offers to send those who fill it out notices of special sales and events.

After you have developed the survey form, test your survey on a small number of people to see if the directions and questions are easily understood and how long the survey takes to fill out.

Gathering data. Surveys may be written and distributed, or taken over the phone. Telephone surveys can yield information quickly and can be relatively inexpensive. Include only the most critical questions and keep the questions short. Have a written script in front of you to ensure consistency. Prepare a form for recording responses. Since many people consider home calls an invasion of their privacy, survey buyers at their places of business, and make sure to call at an appropriate time of day.

Written surveys take more time to prepare than telephone surveys, but they yield more information. Usually they are mailed or distributed as shopping bag stuffers and handouts. Mail surveys take at least several weeks for the results to come back, and you cannot follow through on answers as you can when speaking directly with the person.

Enclose an accompanying letter, explaining who you are, why you are conducting the survey, why you'd like to include them in the survey, and that the results are strictly confidential. Also include a coupon or other offer to motivate them to send back the completed survey form.

It costs about $4 in envelopes, stamps, questionnaires, and repeated mailings to get one response by mail, or about $400 for 100 names. Response rate is usually low—about 25 percent. Improve response rate by supplying a self-addressed, stamped envelope, mailing a postcard with a reminder message ten to fourteen days after

---

SPARTY'S MARKET

<u>Customer Survey</u>

Thank you for doing business with us. Your satisfaction is important to us. Please take a few minutes to fill out this survey, and then leave it in the box provided.

1. **How did you hear about Sparty's Market?** Check one.

    __ Radio -What station? _____
    __ Television - What station? _____
    __ Newspaper - Which paper? _____
    __ Friend, neighbor or relative
    __ Sign along highway
    __ Drove by market
    __ Don't recall, been coming for many years

2. **Why do you shop at Sparty's Market?** Check up to 5 reasons that are most important to you. (Read through the list before you answer.)

    __ Convenient location
    __ Quick & easy to get in and out of market
    __ Reasonable prices
    __ Special product(s), please list _____
    _____
    __ Good quality produce
    __ Features locally grown (fresher) produce
    __ Knowledgeable and friendly personnel
    __ Nice experience
    __ Can buy amount I want, (a little or a lot)
    __ Can buy unwaxed and organically grown produce
    __ Other, explain_____

3. **How often have you been to Sparty's Market <u>this season?</u>** Check one.

    __ First trip this season
    __ Once a week or more often
    __ Once in two weeks
    __ Once a month
    __ My first visit to the market

4. **Would you come more often if we had a greater variety of products?**

    __Yes __No

    If yes, what additional foods and/or farm market related products would you like to be able to buy here?_____
    _____
    _____

5. **What do you especially like about this market?**

    _____
    _____

6. **What do you dislike (what bothers you) about the market?**

    _____
    _____

7. **From your viewpoint, does Sparty's Market provide anything <u>not</u> available at the supermarket where you buy your groceries?**

    __Yes __No

    If yes, please explain _____

8. **Would you recommend Sparty's Market to a friend, relative or neighbor?** Check one.

    __Yes. . . Why? _____
    __ Maybe
    __ No. . . Why not? _____

9. **Your age group:** Check one.

    __Under 25 years old
    __ 25 - 34
    __ 35 - 44
    __ 45 - 64
    __ 65 and older

10. **How many members living in your household now?**

11. **How many children do you have under 18 years of age living at home now?**

    Number ___ (Write in <u>0</u> if none)

    If you'd like to have your name added to our mailing list, please fill out the card on the counter near the market entrance.

    Thank you very much for completing this survey.

Courtesy of Mary D. Zehner, extension specialist in agricultural economics, Michigan State University, E. Lansing, MI.

the survey mailing, or by calling participants on the phone.

Interpreting the survey results

Tabulate the answers and analyze what the customers are telling you. If the survey was well-designed and conducted, the sample of names selected carefully, and the response rate adequate, the survey results should accurately reflect the characteristics and behaviors of the market.

Structured questions can be tabulated in each category by percentages. Open-ended questions are more difficult to tabulate. The best way is through content analysis. Read each response and note down the major points; then go over all the surveys and count the number of people who mentioned each point. Then calculate the percentages of these responses.

Be aware that the people who don't return a survey are probably those least interested in the product or service. Therefore, projections of consumer interest may be overly optimistic. Also, just because 80 percent of the respondents claim they will buy from you doesn't mean they actually will!

Look for ways to use the results of your survey for maximum benefits. For example, if you find that eight out of ten of your customers would pay a premium for locally grown produce, send the results of this survey to your local paper or radio station and offer yourself for an interview.

Test-marketing: the ultimate in market research

Test-marketing a new product involves offering your product or service on a limited basis in order to evaluate potential sales. Test-marketing can be expensive and time-consuming, yet it is especially useful in testing an unknown product or service. It is also a useful strategy when evaluating minor changes in your enterprise, or when attempting to tap into a new market with a product or service you are already providing.

Obviously, test-marketing is possible only when you are producing a product or service in at least a minimum quantity. It may be used as a follow-up to the previously discussed market research techniques, to fine-tune sales projections and to project production costs and problems. A grower might conduct a market test as simple as offering tastes of his organic produce to customers at the fair, or as elaborate as a three-month sales campaign in cooperation with a local roadside market.

Some low-cost ways to test-market products are:

- Find someone who distributes similar products, and give them samples to distribute freely to customers, asking for their feedback.

- Ask your family and friends to give you both positive and negative feedback on any new product or idea you try. Similarly, if you are selling to retail or wholesale buyers, send them new product samples and follow up with a phone call to ask for their feedback.

- Use small focus groups to gain feedback on your new product.

- Use advertisements as a type of low-cost market research. Patti Belmonte, a marketing consultant in Olympia, Washington, relates how a client ran an ad inviting customers to "Send blueberries to someone you love." The purpose of the ad was to test-promote the gift pack line they were considering expanding. Although the ad cost $600 and did not pay for itself in cash returns, losing a few hundred dollars on an ad was cheaper than investing heavily in gift packs.

Acknowledgments

Judy Green, coordinator, Farming Alternatives Program at Cornell University.

Dell Christiansen, Detroit Lakes Technical College, Michigan.

Mary Zehner, Michigan State University.

Making A Marketing Plan

The SOS(BAM) Marketing Plan

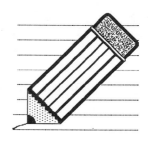

Successful marketing management incorporates the marketing concept into every phase of the business. Therefore, the markets that your business are targeted to determine how your business is organized and operated.

—Timothy M. Baye, in "Beginning Business Planning for Direct Marketers," *University of Wisconsin Cooperative Extension Direct Marketing Newsletter*, Nov. 1988 and March 1989

WITH THANKS TO Dan Block, a marketing consultant in Ventura, California, this section is modeled loosely on his "SOS(BAM)" model for making a marketing plan. The first "S" in SOS(BAM) stands for Situation Analysis: where you are right now, your situation. The "O" section of the SOS(BAM) marketing plan is the Objectives section: "Where are you going?" This section contains the measurable objectives you'd like to achieve with your operation. The second "S" in the model stands for Strategies: "How will you get there?"

"BAM" stands for budget, action plan, and measurement. Budget summarizes the resources needed to implement your strategies. Action plan states when to start the various activities, and who will be responsible for each activity—it is a calendar of events. Measurement is a means of evaluating your programs.

Situation analysis: SOS(BAM)

In the previous three chapters, you've studied yourself and your operation, asked your customers what their needs are, talked to your buyers, observed operations that are successful, studied the competition, read articles that discuss trends in your business, and analyzed your market for potential niches. You've determined who wants (or could want) your product, where these people are (your target market), and who (if anyone) is currently servicing their needs.

The market research you've done determines not only what you will grow, but how you will market it. You are now ready to map out the objectives and strategies of your marketing plan.

Objectives: SOS(BAM)

In the *objectives* section, put down on paper some specific, measurable objectives you'd like to achieve with your operation. List your marketing objectives according to short-range and long-range goals. You may want to increase the number of customers, for instance, or to make people more aware of your brand name. Be realistic and specific. The objectives you choose should fit the needs of your business, your resources, and be realistic in your market area.

Good objectives are measurable and have a completion date. For example: "I want to sell 10 percent more zucchini by August 31." Also, subdi-

SOS(BAM):
A marketing planning model for agriculture

Situation analysis: "Where are you now?"
- Marketing potential
- Customer needs
- Differential advantages of your product
- Competition's strengths and weaknesses
- Your operation's strengths and weaknesses
- Market segments or niches
- Industry trends
- Target market

Objectives: "Where are you going?"
- Must be measurable
- Must have completion time or date
- Must be specific
- Must be attainable

Strategies: "How will you get there?"
- What products your customers want and what forms they will be in
- How you will distribute/sell to your customer
- What price you should charge
- How you will promote products

Budget:
- What these strategies will cost
- What the financial return will be

Action plan:
- When you should carry out the recommended strategies

Measurement:
- Are you making progress toward your objectives?
- Did you achieve your objectives?

vide your goal into increments, so you'll know if you are getting there on schedule.

Make your objectives attainable. Set objectives that make you stretch, but are not so impossible to achieve that they only frustrate you and those who work with you. Each year, review and refine your projections.

Strategies: SO<u>S</u>(BAM)

The *strategies* section in our marketing plan model looks at how you will tailor your product for the unique needs of your customers.

"Where producers used to sell to all who could buy, today's market-oriented farmers incorporate a precise definition of their target market into their plan and focus their time and resources on that target exclusively," says Dan Block. "You cannot be all things to all people. There is no question that you make more money, more efficiently, when you tailor your product to specific market segments. Finding your niche in the market means finding customers who have needs that you can satisfy better than anyone else can."[1]

Most marketing experts talk about the "four P's" of marketing strategy: product, price, place (or distribution), and promotion. You might also add two more "P's": position and people.

Product. In a crowded market, you need to differentiate your product. Perhaps your herbs aren't any different than those of Farmer Jones' next door, for example, but adding a few family recipes along with the product makes it unique! Remember that customers are not simply purchasing material items; they are purchasing a bundle of benefits and attributes, which are sometimes symbolic, and often a result of their perceptions.

Look at your product or enterprise from a number of angles. Why would a consumer want to buy it or partake of it? What makes your product unique in the minds of your customers? Start with the basics, the product itself. If you're aiming for a premium price, quality—appearance, taste and nutritional value—has to be high.

You can also differentiate your product not only by what you grow, but how you grow it (e.g., in-season and without sprays); what you do with it (e.g., processed products); or how you package or market the product (e.g., through local, direct-to-consumer marketing outlets). Some other ways to

© Sibley Orchards, 4121
California Ave., Sibley, MO
64088 (816) 249-5535

add value to your product might include a *service*, such as washing your lettuce, or home delivery of products; *information* such as recipes or workshops; *image:* "country," "healthy," "natural"; or *recreation*, such as a weekend outing in the country.

Price. In order to ask a higher price, you need to deliver more value to your customers than your competitors do. Remember also that pricing should be consistent with your marketing position. Price conveys a message. If your packaging says you're in the high-end of the market, then your pricing should say the same thing. (See "Pricing," Chapter 24.)

Place (distribution). How do you want to distribute your product—through brokers, wholesalers, retailers, farmers markets, specialty stores or other distribution channels? Distribution, too, needs to be consistent with your marketing position: a jam selling through a gourmet store will be packaged and priced differently, for example, than a grocery store jam.

Promotion. What form of promotion should you use to achieve your marketing objectives—advertising, public relations and publicity, personal selling, or sales promotion? What is your primary sales message? What key marketing points must you communicate? Promotion, too, changes with your marketing position, as customers driving a BMW may likely listen to a different radio station, for instance, than customers who come to your store in a Chevy.

Position. Getting to know your customers helps you decide how to place or "position" your product in order to appeal to your target market. The *Shiitake Mushroom Grower's Guide,* for example,

identifies seven possible "positioning" strategies for the shiitake mushroom: unusual, flavorful, exotic, trendy, wild, nutritional and natural. Other ways to position your product might be by quality, convenience, environmentally sound growing practices, artistic design of your packaging, flavor, fragrance, variety, or customer services.

Once you have selected your positioning strategy, it will become the basis of all your marketing decisions. Every detail of production and marketing, from pricing and packaging to presentation, should be consistent with your marketing position. Let's say, for example, that you've decided to position your mushrooms as "exotic" and sell them in a retail market. Your mushrooms would need to be: packaged using graphics, colors and a logo that make them look exotic; placed in the specialty food section of the produce department; and priced higher than a regular button mushroom.

Your promotional materials might include point-of-purchase literature with recipes for "exotic" dishes, or the history of the mushroom in Japanese culture. You might distribute your mushrooms through grocery stores that are known for carrying the highest quality and most uncommon produce.

"Exotic" is only one example of a positioning strategy. Experiment with several ideas, then test them on friends, customers, or a focus group before making a final decision. Always base your positioning strategy on your customers' perceptions and their needs and wants. Your perception of your product may be vastly different than that of your customers!

People. People are the link between production and sales. As Dan Block observes: "The person answering the phone or behind the counter is the most important person in your business. Get a person there who makes people feel good." Take a close look at how you hire and train employees. The more competent your employees are, the more valuable they are to your customers!

Budget: SOS(BAM)

What will your marketing strategies cost? What will be the financial return? Once you've refined your objectives and strategies, you can pinpoint more accurately your *budget* for marketing your new enterprise. Develop a marketing flow chart, detailing how much you plan to spend for each project, and when. Keep accurate records, not only for year-end taxes, but also to compare your estimates with actual expenditures. This will allow you to revise and refine your budget-making process for future projects.

Action plan: SOS(B**A**M)

The *action plan* is the section of your plan for putting down who should implement strategies; when the strategies should be started and completed; and your plans for training employees in how to implement the plan. Prioritize items, and break the big projects into smaller, "do-able" projects.

"Where the rubber meets the road is in implementing your ideas," states Dan Block. "Almost all successful marketing involves doing the 'basics' well. You'd be amazed at what can be achieved by doing things like follow-up calls or quizzing customers about their likes and dislikes. It doesn't have to be glitzy or fancy, just meat and potatoes marketing."

Measurement: SOS(B**A**M)

Is progress being made toward objectives, on schedule, and within your budget? Were objectives achieved? Don't just measure gross sales; the more precise your *measurement* devices, the better. Were deliveries made on time? Are you getting fewer complaints, or fewer returns?

Set monthly goals or even weekly goals, as well as annual objectives. If your yearly goal is to sell $500 worth of mail order gift baskets, and you've sold only $200 by August, you're behind schedule! Setting up "check stops" helps you modify your plan according to unforeseen events that come along the way.

Watch out for the trap! "Just because someone has purchased from you doesn't make them a customer," warns Dan Block. "The first time you give them a shoddy product or bad service, your competitor is waiting in the wings." In a crowded market, losing customers is deadly, because the process of replacing them is difficult. "The sale is the marriage, and service and satisfaction keep the relationship going!"

Service what you sell; go all-out to build bonds and ongoing relationships. Survey customers on a regular basis, both by informal conversation and written questionnaires. After you've made a delivery, call up the customer: "Did you get the order? Any problems with it?"

Conclusion

"A good marketing plan," according to Dan Block, "is a dynamic, living thing. Two months later your marketing plan should be dog-eared and coffee-stained!" Distribute your written plan to employees, and review it regularly with people who are responsible for implementing it. Review your marketing plan often. Feel free to make changes every month; it's a guide, not a bible.

Study past marketing successes and failures, both your own and others'. Matty Matarazzo, a successful fruit and vegetable grower from Belvidere, New Jersey, when asked for his success secret, said: "I'm a good observer." When he was a boy, Matty relates, his father took him to the farmers markets, where Matty would observe how neighboring farmers set up their displays. Then he would imitate those who seemed to sell out most quickly.

Finally, don't get caught in the "paralysis by analysis" syndrome of being too cautious. Marketing is an art, not a science; there are many intangibles that make for success. Listen to your instincts, as well as your research. Guinness McFadden, owner of McFadden Farms near Potter Valley, California, has about eight successful enterprises, ranging from herbs to garlic braids to wild rice, and he's had at least as many failures. "Just about everything I've tried turned out differently than I'd planned it," McFadden says. "Try to be flexible, and quick on your feet. Keep your eyes open and go with the market. Go with what works best, and try to magnify that."

Acknowledgments

Dan Block, D. W. Block Associates, P. O. Box 2720, Ventura, CA 93002; (805) 650-6399.

Section II: Direct Marketing

Is Direct Marketing For You?

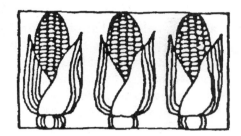

We started pick-your-own in 1967. Before that we were commercial fruit and vegetable growers. We were having a tough time making it, so we started a pick-your-own farm. This way we could sell direct to the consumer. We started out with five acres of strawberries and a half-acre of green beans. It's now 23 years later, we're farming 350 acres, and we raise 32 kinds of fruits and vegetables. All of the products are marketed directly at our farm, either on a pick-your-own basis, through the farm market, or through our restaurant.

—Joe Huber, Huber Family Farm, Orchard and Restaurant, Borden, Indiana

NOTE: This chapter talks about "direct marketing," i.e., selling through farmers markets, roadside markets and pick-your-own operations. It also includes selling directly to local retail stores, restaurants, and institutions. While selling to retail outlets is not strictly farmer-to-consumer direct marketing, the management and marketing skills needed and the intensive labor requirements are similar to those required for direct marketing.

HISTORIANS BELIEVE that cities owe their origin to farmers markets, where nomadic wanderers would stop their trekking long enough to replenish their culinary provisions from the produce hawkers. For many small farmers, direct marketing is an idea whose time has come—again.

"People cut off from the earth tend to be intrigued by its most mundane manifestations," explained a recent *New York Times* article about the direct-to-the-consumer food boom. "The city dwellers want more than just good food or an outing in the country. They want the contact; they want the farmer. Keith Stewart, who has a farm in Greenville, New York, sends a newsletter to his regular customers about life on the farm. 'To talk to a real farmer is meaningful to them,' he said."[1]

Attracted by the lure of a cash business, a higher percentage of the food dollar by cutting out the middlemen, and the opportunity to be in control from "seed to sale," an increasing number of farmers are turning to direct marketing and finding creative ways to do it. The traditional methods of roadside stands, pick-your-own farms, and farmers markets are being supplemented with

---

> *We went from a 2,000-acre farm with very limited opportunities to a 100-acre farm with unlimited opportunity.*
> —Lawrence Teeter, Jr., a Tennessee grain farmer who also sells fruits and vegetables through a roadside market and other direct marketing outlets

mail order sales and subscription farming. According to Morris Fabian, Rutgers University marketing specialist, sales of homegrown products direct to consumers have boomed in the last decade. National sales represent about $1.6 billion, an increase of about 68 percent since 1980.

Even some larger growers have cut down their acreage, added a few direct marketing outlets, and seen profits climb. Lawrence Teeter, Jr., a Tennessee grain farmer who added a roadside market and other direct marketing outlets to his marketing mix, said at a recent farm conference: "We went from a 2,000-acre farm with very limited opportunities to a 100-acre farm with unlimited opportunity."

Direct marketing outlets offer shoppers the opportunity to purchase fresh-picked, good-tasting, seasonal produce from the farmers who grew it. Direct-from-the-farm produce is usually fresher and of higher quality, especially for the more perishable items such as sweet corn, strawberries, raspberries, and tree-ripened peaches. These products are often picked at the peak of maturity only hours before they are sold at farmers markets and roadside stands.

At direct marketing outlets, customers are able to sample new products and varieties not ordinarily found in supermarkets. While supermarkets usually offer only one or a few varieties of a product, direct markets may sell many different varieties of one product, such as apples, peaches, peppers or tomatoes, as well as exotic and heirloom products, organically grown produce, and ethnic foods.

Direct marketing outlets frequently offer products at lower-than-supermarket prices, and customers are able to shop in a relaxed, friendly atmosphere. Whether it's a family outing to pick fruit in the country, or the exciting sights, sounds and smells of a farmers market, direct marketing is fun!

Direct marketing advantages

Some direct marketing advantages are:

Profits! By eliminating or taking over some middle-level marketing activities such as transportation, brokerage and other handling requirements, growers get better-than-wholesale prices by selling direct. In addition, because many direct sales products are exempt from costly packing, labeling and container regulations of wholesale transactions, direct marketers save money on packing and shipping.

Cash flow. While the direct marketer gets paid cash-in-hand, payment from wholesalers often takes 30 days or longer. Immediate payment is especially helpful for small or startup growers whose capital is limited.

Marketing diversity. Since many direct sales outlets are exempt from the usual sizing, standard pack, and container and labeling requirements of wholesaling, misshapen or odd-size fruit can be sold through them, as long as food quality standards are maintained. Thus, direct marketing outlets often provide a market for products that may not be acceptable in the chain supermarkets. While supermarket customers generally select products based on appearance, farmers market or roadside market customers are more liable to choose products based on qualities like uniqueness and flavor. Similarly, home canners are often unconcerned with the size of the product they purchase. Vine- or tree-ripened products which are overripe by the time the wholesaler gets them to the supermarket may be just right for the consumer looking for peak-of-the-season maturity.

Small farmer. Direct marketing is especially suited for the smaller grower. Small lots and variable quality often are prohibited in the wholesale trade; in direct marketing, however, exemptions from grading and container requirements allow the small grower to market his crops "field run," or directly into the boxes or containers in which the products are sold to the customers. Eliminating the need to repack crops harvested in field boxes reduces costly packing fees. Almost anyone with the desire and a few acres can become involved in direct marketing.

Control of marketing. As a direct marketer, the grower becomes a "price maker" instead of a "price taker," dependent on current wholesale prices.

Family labor. Direct marketing is often a family business, a benefit both for the farm and the family. "The family that farms together, stays together."

Flexibility and diversity. A grower may decide to add or drop markets depending on the volume of crops produced. The diversity of direct marketing outlets encourages diversity in production, thus reducing the risk of being wiped out by failure of one crop.

Test-marketing. Direct marketing gives farmers an opportunity to test new crops and receive valuable feedback from customers, such as new ways in which their products can be used or prepared. At a farmers market, for example, growers can talk to customers about their product, exchange information with other growers, and observe new products just coming onto the market. By talking with people about your product and sharing growing and cooking tips, direct selling is a great way to educate customers about new products and increase demand for unusual or high-quality items.

Customer contact. Face-to-face direct marketing enables the direct marketer to make the business more personal and develop more customer loyalty. With middleman marketing, you lose contact with customers.

Public relations. Direct marketers are the "voice of agriculture," representing farming to the public. This is your chance to tell customers about the problems farmers have in dealing with the weather, insects and disease, and the whims of government laws and regulations.

It's fun! There's a reward in direct-to-the-consumer marketing—the pride and fun in selling to the person who enjoys eating your produce. Many growers enjoy talking to people about their products and how they're grown.

Direct marketing disadvantages

Direct marketing went through a period of rapid expansion in recent years, and has now reached the mature stage where further growth will be limited, and existing operations will face intense competition. The conditions necessary for success have consequently become more stringent. Marketing direct to consumers or to specialty stores and fancy restaurants takes special skills and abilities on the part of the marketer, and often takes a favorable location with respect to land resources and local markets.

Some other special direct marketing challenges are:

Volume. The total volume that can be sold through local direct markets is limited by the number of consumers living nearby. Since crops are highly perishable and must be marketed quickly, local demand may be insufficient to absorb your production. Direct marketing is more profitable for small volume, high-value crops, and for those farms located near urban areas.

Time spent in marketing. You and your family need to be at the stand to meet and talk to customers. They want to meet the farmer and the farm family!

Selling cherries at the Davis, California, Certified Farmers Market

Estimating Local Direct Marketing Potential

IF YOU ARE PLANNING to direct market through a farmers market, or your own farm market or pick-your-own operation, utilize the "30-mile marketing" principle. According to Curtis Stutzman, a farming consultant with the Rural Innovation Center in Amana, Iowa, small-business men have found that nearly all of their customers live within 30 miles of the place of business. In fact, 75 percent of a retailer's customers live in a 20-mile radius and the remaining 10 percent come from 30 miles or more. You can use this information to determine your market potential.

Step 1. Get a local map and draw a circle around your farm corresponding with a 20-, 25- and 30-mile radius.

Step 2. Call the county auditor's office and ask for the populations of those townships and cities that fall into your trade area. This census data is also available in the local library or by writing the census office. (The auditor's office may be an easier route since they usually will do the work for you.)

Step 3. Add up the population figures for each of the three main circles that you draw around your farm (with a 20-, 25- and 30-mile radius).

Step 4. Adjust the data for competition or other factors that may contribute to certain areas responding more or less favorably to your idea. Certain parts of your population, for example, may have lifestyle or income characteristics which make them more or less inclined to purchase from you.

Adjust the "30-mile principle" also for other considerations, such as cooperative marketing efforts with neighboring farmers, or major highways nearby that would draw customers from farther away.

Step 5. Take your total potential population (after adjustments) and try to put a figure on how much you can produce without creating surplus. For strawberries, for example, the University of Illinois has calculated that you need 10,000 people to be able to market one acre of pick-your-own. For service businesses, try your local chamber of commerce or the Small Business Administration for population equivalents.

One of the best ways to get started in direct marketing is with farmers markets. Farmers markets allow you to build production capacity and avoid high packing costs.

Personality. Dealing with customers day in and day out requires patience and a friendly, outgoing personality. Direct marketers should enjoy being around people, and be prepared to work long hours, including weekends and holidays. As one subscription farmer said: "The phone is ringing all the time and you have to be polite and friendly. If you're the type who just wants to enjoy the quiet solitude of growing, direct marketing is not for you!"

Marketing skills. In direct marketing, the farmer becomes the retailer and needs to know about merchandising, display, quality control, pricing, packaging, and so on.

Legal restrictions. Direct marketing operations have many legal restrictions, such as licenses, inspections, highway zoning and access restrictions. Check with local, county, state and federal agencies to see what restrictions apply to your prospective operation. Do this at the planning stage. Don't build your farmstand next to the freeway, only to end up tearing it down so the freeway can be widened.

Production for direct marketing. You need to stretch your season with succession plantings of early and late season varieties—some growers aim for a year-round supply! You need to produce unique, high-quality varieties that customers don't find in supermarkets, or standard varieties of just-picked freshness. Direct marketing is for high-value crops. Don't head for the farmers market with a truckload of watermelons and expect to make a lot of money!

Characteristics of Direct Marketing Alternatives

Characteristic	Pick-Your-Own	Roadside Market	Farmers Market	Grocery Stores & Restaurants
Market Investment	Containers, ladders, etc. Locational signs & parking. Building or stand.	Building or stand and parking. Containers, signs, scales, coolers, etc.	Usually rent parking or building space. Containers, scales, bags, etc.	Truck. Boxes & containers.
Grower Liability	Liable for accidents. Need liability insurance.	Liable for accidents. Need liability insurance.	Need liability insurance unless coverage provided by market.	Liability insurance often required by buyers and/or state law.
Prices Received	Often lower than other markets because of transportation and harvesting costs assumed by customer.	Producer sets prices given perceived demand and competitive conditions.	Producer sets price. May be competition from other sellers.	Buyer & seller bargaining with one another.
Quality	Can sell whatever customers will pick.	Can classify produce and sell more than one grade.	Ability to sell may depend on competing qualities available from other growers.	Highest quality needed.
Other Considerations	Balance between number of pickers and amount needing to be harvested sometimes difficult to achieve.	Sometimes other items besides produce are sold to supplement income.	Sometimes other items besides produce are sold to supplement income.	Long-term, steady outlet for consistent quality.
Special Advantages	Average value of purchase per customer may be higher than at other DM outlets. Customer assumes cost of harvesting and transportation.	Attractive displays and variety of produce can draw customers. Can be expanded to meet needs of the producer. Can be tailored to producers' and/or customers' tastes and preferences. Minimal transportation costs.	Central location. Potential for large number of customers. Advertising and promotion done by organization. Low overhead.	Good price for quality produce. Brand recognition.
Special Disadvantages	Location may be critical. Greater costs for liability insurance, advertising & promotion, parking, and sales & supervisory labor. Greater zoning and planning restrictions. Rainy weather may reduce customers. Customers may damage plants. Longer hours. Must get customers to the produce.	Location may be critical. Higher overhead costs. Greater costs for liability insurance, advertising & promotion, parking, and sales labor. Greater zoning and planning restrictions. Long hours. Must get customers to the produce.	Must transport produce. Do not have as much control over promotion. Sell only when the market is open.	Difficult to enter market and develop customers. Frequent deliveries, low volume per delivery. Increased packaging costs (grocery stores). Must rely on retailers to sell product (grocery stores).
Direct Marketing Advantages	Greater control over marketing. Producer sets price. Satisfaction in selling direct to the people who enjoy your produce. Use of family labor. Cash payment. Greater profit potential. Customer feedback and personal promotion of products. Less stringent packing requirements than wholesale.			
Direct Marketing Disadvantages	Limited volume (may need other market outlets). Must deal with all kinds of people. Need for greater variety of marketing skills. Greater time & resources spent in marketing.			

Multi-Level Marketing

LIKE A SALAD, your marketing mix may involve several ingredients. A U-Pick vegetable patch, gourmet herb shop and farm restaurant or organic country vegetable market may combine to create a totally unique shopping/recreational experience that could lure urban consumers out for a weekend drive.

If you are selling at a farmers market, hand out leaflets or tell customers about your farm market or PYO operation, or where they can savor your produce in the restaurants to which you sell. Or, on the way to deliver your major commodity crops to a chain warehouse, you might also set up a route of high-end restaurants and retail stores for your specialty items.

Sammy La Bastida, who farms 500 acres of vegetables near Santa Maria, California, estimates that he sells 5 – 10 percent of his produce through direct marketing. La Bastida Farms supplies a few local restaurants as a "secondary wholesaler," providing the specialty items they don't get from primary suppliers. "We can get it to them cheaper and fresher—hours old, instead of two or three days through commercial channels," says La Bastida. As for expenses, La Bastida says he's "cutting out long-distance shipping and cooling costs, expensive shipping cartons, and a lot of brokers' commissions."

La Bastida also sells at farmers markets in order to make his production and transportation cost-effective for restaurant stops. "We use the same people who sell to restaurants to sell at the farmers markets. And if you're cutting cabbages for the restaurants, you might just as easily cut a few more for the farmers markets."

Many PYO operations also offer products through a roadside market; they often find that the pick-your-own operation actually increases sales at the market, as many customers who come for the PYO option end up purchasing additional amounts of the pick-your-own product at the market, as well as other items.

Special costs involved in direct marketing include liability insurance, advertising and promotion, and sales and supervisory labor. A pick-your-own operation, for example, does not eliminate the need for harvest labor; employees are also needed to supervise and work the checkout stands. Direct marketing is characterized by higher overhead costs, such as farm market structures, cold storage facilities, etc. Direct marketing is a seasonal business, with wide fluctuations in labor requirements and cash flow.

Choosing marketing outlets

The smaller your acreage, the greater the proportion of your product you'll need to sell through high-end marketing channels. The main advantage of direct marketing is that you increase revenues by taking the middlemen's share of the profits. There's a trade-off, however: the more direct your marketing, the greater return per unit, but also the greater the amount of time, work and resources spent in marketing. Taking over the job of the middlemen means less time for farming and a lot of time on the phone, delivering to restaurants or retail stores, or tending store at the roadside market. Time spent talking with customers and answering their questions is just as essential in direct marketing as time on the tractor!

Direct marketing is most likely to be successful for:

• seasonal items such as berries or asparagus, or relatively high-value products such as strawberries, dried fruit, mushrooms, floral and nursery products (including bedding plants), honey and syrups, gift packs, and other "value-added" products;

• small and part-time farmers within 20 miles of urban population centers or on access roads to major tourist areas;

• sideline enterprises for larger farms; and

• auxiliary markets for fruit and vegetable products that are not suitable for conventional wholesale and retail market outlets.

Your involvement in marketing should suit your needs and abilities. If you like merchandising and dealing with people, such as customers at a farmers market or chefs at restaurants, or if you have family labor available to help with a farm stand or farmers market, you may prefer selling direct to customers.

If you only like to grow, on the other hand, wholesale marketing is the way to go. A broker or distributor who caters to the specialty grower and sells to high-end markets can enable you to spend all your time growing and still net a high return. If you do decide to sell through middlemen, utilize as many direct marketing tools as you can in getting close to your customer. Provide your middlemen with information and sales material to personalize and customize your product, so as to build customer loyalty and to get top dollar for your products.

In sum, find high-return marketing channels for your high-quality products. Consider specialized, high-return, nondirect as well as direct marketing channels.

Acknowledgments

Kevin Hosey, Knox County Regional Farmers Market, Knoxville, Tennessee.

© Living Earth Organic Agriculture, P.O. Box 622, Valley Center, CA 92082 (619) 749-0712

Farmers Markets

A farmers market is 'theatre'; customers expect it to be more lively than a supermarket! Display, layout, containers, signage, composition, color, contrast, structures and lighting, as well as the products and service you offer customers and how you talk to them, all come together to tell your story. What makes you unique?
—Leon Sugarman, architect and urban designer, San Francisco

FARMERS MARKETS ARE growing fast. The 1992 National Farmers Market Survey showed that the number of farmers markets across the country continues to grow, and more will be developed over the next several years. According to the survey, conducted by Public Market Partners, over 1,800 farmers markets operated nationally in 1991. This compares with slightly under 1,700 in 1988.[1]

Farmers, shoppers and city planners alike are sold on the concept of farmers markets, and no wonder. At a well-trafficked farmers market, part-time farmers can achieve gross sales of from $300 to $500 per day, while full-time growers often gross up to $1000 a day! Some farmers selling at the Greenmarket in New York City drive over 200 miles to sell there!

Farmers markets differ from other direct marketing operations in that growers usually share insurance, advertising and other marketing costs. Farmers markets may be operated by grower orga-

nizations, by community development groups or by state or local governments. Facilities may range from an open lot where farmers park their vehicles and display products, to enclosed buildings with display counters, lights, heat and refrigeration. Farmers usually pay a fee for the space occupied to cover maintenance and advertising.[2]

Farmers markets often serve as business incubators for startup growers, giving young businesses a chance to get off the ground without the overhead expenses of a traditional business. Also, many large farm operators who sell most of their produce through conventional outlets use farmers markets to dispose of produce that does not meet the requirements of conventional outlets. Such products include undersized or oversized fruit, and fruit too ripe to withstand the rigors of the conventional marketing system.[3]

Consumers enjoy a wide selection of farm-fresh produce at lower-than-supermarket prices. Produce is available in large quantities for canning, and consumers also find in farmers markets an opportunity to support local agriculture and meet the farmers who grow their food.

Farmers markets are also important social events. People stop and talk, or exchange recipes. Money spent at farmers markets generally tends to stay in the community, benefiting farmers and townspeople alike. Farmers markets are being used to regenerate downtown areas.

Advantages

Sellers at farmers markets enjoy all the benefits common to direct marketing, such as cash payment, and the pride and fun in selling to the people who enjoy eating their produce. In addition, there are special advantages in selling at a farmers market:

Startup. For the beginning or small farmer with little access to established marketing channels or small amounts of produce to sell, the following advantages of farmers markets offer a golden opportunity to get started in farming:

- minimal marketing startup costs, requiring only a truck and selling area;
- exemption (at most markets) from standard size and packing regulations;
- little or no packaging, advertising and promotion costs (since farmers markets are usually well established and centrally located); and
- prices substantially higher than wholesale.

Personal promotion. Farmers markets allow you to talk with and educate people about your farm and your growing techniques, and to pitch your product face-to-face with the buyer. One Southern California farmer couldn't sell his exotic chocolate fuyu persimmons wholesale, but when he took a truckload to the Santa Monica Farmers Market, at least 85 percent of those who tried his samples purchased a bag!

Customer feedback. Farmers markets are the ideal place to experiment with new varieties, and get customer reaction before committing to planting on a bigger scale. By chatting with customers, you can gain new product and marketing ideas, suggestions for packaging your products or new ways to use your products, and immediate response to new products. You also can learn from other producers at the market, as growers share ideas and experiences. Doug Richardson, the only commercial banana grower on the continental U.S., planted 40 varieties of bananas on four acres near Ventura, California. By going to farmers markets, he found which varieties achieved the greatest response, and soon expanded his banana acreage to 12 acres, focusing on those varieties which were best received in the farmers markets.

Miscellaneous. Insurance, advertising and other marketing costs are usually the responsibility of the market rather than individual growers. Parking space, restrooms and other facilities are usually provided by the market. At most farmers markets, the sponsoring group already has worked through many of the regulations and restrictions—zoning, sign, health department, business license and site insurance—which might take considerable time and effort to comply with if you tried to market at home.

Disadvantages

Farmers markets share the common direct marketing disadvantages of limited volume and the need for other market outlets, greater time involved in dealing with people, and a higher proportion of your time spent in marketing. Consider the value of your time in selling the produce. Be prepared for long hours spent in loading up, travelling to the market, unloading, setting up, and the reverse at the end of the day. There may be waste, unless you have secondary markets lined up. Cold, rainy days, or even bright sunny days, may keep customers away. Depending on the market where you sell, there may be space limitations, product limitations, a few irritating rules, bureaucratic policies, and politics you have to deal with. Volume per sale will be small compared to wholesale.

Also, producers may be required to rent stalls for a year when they need them for only a few weeks. At most markets, the producer can sell only produce grown on his farm. Market hours are controlled by the market organization and may not be ideal for producers; advertising, or lack of it, also is controlled by the market. Markets that are poorly located may not attract consumers.[4]

Special considerations

You need to pay a rental fee; sellers are usually charged a flat fee or a percentage (usually 6–10 percent) of their gross sales. You'll need to coordinate production with marketing, and estimate demand when picking the load to take to market. You should have a variety of produce to sell, and be close enough to a market so that transportation time and costs are not excessive.

Rules and regulations vary from state to state, so check with the market manager as to which apply to you. Ask for a written copy of the rules and regulations. There may be requirements regarding weight and measure specifications, labeling, sales tax reporting, vehicle permits, and provisions for the food stamp and Women, Infants and Children (WIC) programs. Also check to see if you need to carry individual insurance for accidents at the market or for food product liability, or if the market covers these. Some markets require that you sell only what you produce, while other markets may allow you to sell other growers' items in limited quantities. In many markets, processed foods may not be sold. You may also need a health permit in each county in which you sell your product.

Check out the markets

Visit the markets. Ask your county extension agent or state department of agriculture personnel about markets in your area. Talk with the market manager and some of the sellers and patrons to get a feel for different markets. Check the prices and what kind of volume the growers are moving. How well you do depends more on whether there's a need for your product at the market than the market's overall volume. Are too many other growers offering the same product or variety of products? Ask the manager about items needed for that market, and consider adding them to your product line, or seek another market where there's less competition for your products.

Study the market's clientele. Are they the right market for your products? It may be worth traveling some distance to a market farther away in order to obtain a premium price for your products.

Study the market rules and learn the costs of participating—stall fees, promotion fees, and insurance assessments. Consider whether the market's hours of operation meet your work schedule. Evaluate services offered, such as stall size, rainy-weather shelter, restrooms, and water for drinking or washing produce.

How much advertising and promotion does the market do? Is it timed to coincide with the time your product is available? Look for signs of active promotion, such as posted signs and banners, and flyers placed on windshields and store windows. Don't waste your time and resources in a market that is not actively promoted.

Consider alternatives. Could you consign your produce to a regular participant? Check market regulations to see if this is allowed.

Suitable products

Farmers market product trends are toward diversification, unusual products, organic products, and value-added, processed products which can increase profit margins.

Offer a selection of mainstay products that are higher than supermarket quality: in-season, tree- or vine-ripened, fresh-picked and organic. Having mainstay products encourages one-stop shopping. Carry some non-mainstream items as well, such as cut flowers, herbs, or specialty items. A few unusual items will attract people to your stand, and having something new each week encourages repeat visits by your "regulars." Do not have so many items, however, that you have little of each—remember, the higher the heap, the better it sells.

Try to have crops available as early in the season as possible; if you consistently supply desired produce before other growers, consumers will learn to look for the products they want at your stall.

In larger and more competitive markets, you may want to specialize in a fewer number of high-value items like honey or mushrooms. If you offer only a few items, however, create diversity by offering a line of products. If you specialize in almonds, for example, offer raw, roasted, smoked and blanched almonds, almond butter, etc., in a variety of packages and sizes.

Fresh quality produce is the most important drawing card at farmers markets. It's OK to offer oversized or undersized products if the food quality is excellent. If products have cosmetic blemishes, are overmature or not up to the usual quality, however, reduce the price and sell them as seconds. Do not sell anything you would not use yourself. It is better to take home any picked-over "junk" food produce than to move it at bargain basement prices. Price cutting may cause ill will between buyer and seller, and between the price cutter and other sellers. A reputation for price cutting will soon develop, and patrons will try to bargain even for first-quality items.

Try to bring enough produce to last throughout the day, so that there's enough left for your last few customers. Develop secondary uses or outlets for what's left over. The aim is not to sell out, but to keep repeat customers.

What to bring

Prepare a list of things to take. Your list might include:

Shelter. Patio umbrellas, or a canvas patio (open-sided) tent provide shelter for yourself and your produce from sun and rain, as well as help make a colorful display. Be careful about color choice, as colors affect food appearance (see "Display" in this chapter).

A lightweight folding table and a tablecloth. Remember to leave a space at the edge of the table where customers can set their parcels while getting out their money. Make sure your tablecloth is plastic, or a material that you can keep clean.

A plastic spray bottle of cold water. Spruce up your products throughout the day to help keep them fresh. Bring a water jug for yourself also, so you don't have to leave your stall to find a drink of water.

A cash box with change to start the day. Suggested amounts of change to bring to the market: If you estimate your gross will be under $200 for the day, bring about $80 in pennies, nickels, dimes, quarters, singles (ones), fives and tens; if you figure your gross will be from $200 to $500, bring about $150 in change; over $500 a day, bring about $160. Keep the cash box out of sight to avoid tempting the light-fingered. You might also utilize a carpenter's apron with deep pockets for holding bills and coins so that you can make correct change on the spot. This helps increase the speed of sales, and you don't have to turn your back on customers to go to a change box.

Signs. Use lots of them! Use cards and markers to make up display signs beforehand. Off-white paper is preferable to white paper, as white is glaring and tends to show flyspecks. Blue, green or red markers are preferable to black. Color-code your signs—use neon red for tangelos, green for avocados, etc. Department store-type metal sign-holders with slots allow you to replace the signs as needed for product or price changes. A green chalkboard along with several colors of chalk works well for posting a customer price list.

Be creative in your product signs. "Sweet, Ripe Kiwis"; "Savoy Cabbage, Crisp & Crunchy"; "Walnuts: Crack 'Em Yourself," etc. Describe your product—let people know that it is crunchy, tangy, tart or sweet. Provide useful information: "Good for soups" or "2 lbs. of these apples make an 8-inch pie," etc.

Scale. For the items you sell by weight, a simple spring scale hung from a bracket will suffice. It needs to be certified by the County Sealer of Weights and Measures. Consider purchasing an electronic scale. It will cost upwards of $600, but its greater accuracy will pay for itself if you do large volume. Most produce items can be sold by the piece or by volume, however.

Salespeople. Things go better by twos. Having a partner makes it easier to wait on customers and allows you to take a break.

Containers suitable for your produce. Look for used crates, baskets, or grape lugs (flats) from your local supermarket, and wash them thoroughly before using. If you are growing organically, be aware that organic certification rules forbid using crates and boxes with chemical fungicide residues from commercial packers.[5]

Lynn Bagley, director, Marin County, California, Certified Farmers Market

Farmers Market Selling Tips: A Profile

J ERRY RUTIZ, a grower of mixed vegetables near Arroyo Grande, California, became one of the top salesmen at the Santa Monica Certified Farmers Market by following the oldest principle known to marketers: giving the customers what they want. "If a customer is looking at my basil," says Rutiz, "I ask, 'Is there a variety you'd rather have?' . . and they might answer, 'Yes, cinnamon basil,' or 'Yes, purple basil.' "

Rutiz, who sells 20 to 25 items at three farmers markets each week looks for specialized varieties that the supermarkets don't carry, such as Chantnay carrots ("a sweeter, crispier carrot than you get in the grocery stores"), and Blue Lake greenbeans ("better tasting, more tender").

"I try to find out what the customers want and no one else in the market is growing," Rutiz continues. "I also ask the manager what is lacking in the market. Once she told me no one was growing brussels sprouts, so I grew that. This usually works for a few years, until other growers catch on and start growing it—then I try something else."

At least a third of Rutiz' products are unusual crops, for which little growing literature is available. "Experimentation gives me a challenge. If I planted lettuce year after year, I'd get bored. I'm trying new things all the time and it keeps me interested.

"Most of my varieties are not available in the supermarkets, so I don't have to follow their prices!" adds Rutiz. "I figure what it costs me to grow and market a product, and then I set my price. If I can't get the price it takes to make a profit, I stop growing it."

Wooden baskets are nice display containers, but they are expensive. Line the wooden containers with paper or plastic bags and then hand these removable bags to the customer, saving the wooden container for reuse. This reduces handling time and damage to soft produce from pouring it into a bag. Paper bags are preferable from an environmental standpoint, but plastic bags for moist items may be a necessity. Use larger paper sacks for easier carrying of small individual items, and have large grocery bags for customers who buy a substantial amount of products. See-through mesh bags not only allow customers to see the quality of your product; they also allow air circulation and are great for hot days.

For cost and environmental reasons, allow customers to bring their previously used bags for the produce that they're taking home. In order to avoid potential liability problems that might occur should a used bag be contaminated with chemical residues, however, use new bags for customers who do not bring their own.

Having your farm name and logo printed on bags is an excellent low-cost way to keep your image in the customers' eyes. Your state department of agriculture may have a program for cooperative purchases of printed shopping bags.[6]

Educational materials. Recipes, pamphlets and flyers. Especially helpful if you're selling anything new or unusual!

Miscellaneous. Bring pencils, pens, calculator, a sales and tax record book, and business cards. Do as much bunching, bagging and pricing as you can beforehand. Be prepared for the morning rush of buyers. The more you do in advance, the smoother your day will be.

Bring yourself! Try to grow a diversity of crops so you can come to the market year-round. Regular attendance at the market is important, as shoppers get to like you, look for you, and depend on you!

Display tips

Attractive displays are a great aid in selling produce. Look over other growers' displays and borrow from the best ideas. Produce should be kept in the shade to help maintain quality and provide a pleasant shopping environment. The display should be off the ground so that customers do not have to bend over to inspect the produce. Elbow to eye level is a good rule of thumb to use for proper display height. Tables, platforms or truck tailgates may be used to display produce. Prop boxes at a slant toward the customers.[7]

Quantity. Abundant displays attract attention. At a New York City Greenmarket, one grower displayed green beans in a small bowl, which she refilled from a basket in her truck. The effect was that few people saw her green beans. In contrast, another grower made a mountain of radishes and the splash of color drew people from across the street.[8]

Color contrast helps attract customers' attention. Choose the color of your awning carefully. A blue covering can make peaches look green, while a yellow shade can make them look good. Darker colors attract heat.

Use creative display ideas. A "waterfall" of potatoes created by an inclined board covered with spuds of all shapes and colors; wicker flower-gathering baskets used to display a colorful collection of peppers, eggplants and squash; or buckets of flowers lined up according to the colors of the spectrum, creating a rainbow effect from a distance, are a few examples of crowd-capturing, profit-making, creative display ideas.[9] Other excellent display ideas are simpler, such as interspersing product displays with leaves, herbs or flowers, or stringing balloons or chili peppers around the canopy or entryway.

Develop a focus. If your focus is herbs, for example, fill up your space with herb plants, potpourri and sachets. Get out in front of your display and look at it critically, from a customer's point of view. Everything should be clearly visible, alive and enticing. If it doesn't command attention, change it.

Signs. An attractive wooden sign with your farm name and logo painted on it helps your customers come back to you week after week, and makes it easier for them to refer friends to you. For the same reason, insist on setting up in the same location throughout the year. Make sure your farm sign is well above your display so customers can see it above a crowded booth, and put your farm name also on your apron or cap.

Picture of your farm. Talk with customers, and hand out brochures about your farm and farming

© Napa Valley Farmers Market, P.O. Box 436, St. Helena, CA 94574 (707) 963-7343

practices. Make customers feel part of your operation! Whenever Tom and Denesse Willey, of T & D Willey Farms in Fresno, California, go to a farmers market, they bring along their big full-color farm photo. Beneath the portraits of Tom and Denesse against the gorgeous layout of their farm is a description of their farm and sustainable farming methods. While customers wait in line at the Willeys' booth, they read the sign.

NOTE: See also the "Display" section in "Merchandising," Chapter 17.

Pricing

Quality and uniqueness. Use market competitors' or local grocery store prices as a starting point, but remember that customers come to farmers markets for quality, freshness, flavor and uniqueness more than for price. If you have something that is unique, such as organic produce or specialty products, or highly perishable items such as sweet corn, don't be afraid to ask a price (a premium of 10 percent or more) which will reward you for your effort and initiative in providing it.

Post prices. Many shoppers are in too much of a hurry, or are hesitant to ask about prices, and they may bypass you if you do not have prices posted. Have cards and markers on hand for price changes, or use a green chalkboard. Signs should state item price and unit, e.g., Santa Rosa Plums, 35¢ per pound. Use easy-move pricing: round numbers like 75¢, not 79¢; $1, not 99¢.

Methods of pricing. There's an art to selling—should you sell by the pound, by the bag, or by the

---

unit? By the pound means more time and hassle at the market; it also takes time and expense to bag each product beforehand. In general, give prices by the unit whenever possible. This makes the checkout move a lot quicker, since you don't have to weigh products. Study your market. Some ethnic groups may be accustomed to open-air markets where they can pick out their own produce. Other markets may attract customers used to supermarket convenience who prefer packaged produce.

Adjust prices according to the market. It's easier to lower prices than to raise them, so don't start too low. If you're selling too slowly, however, and a lot of customers are complaining about the prices (a few folks are chronic complainers; don't worry about them), it may be time to reduce your prices.

If you're selling out too quickly, on the other hand, increase the price next time. The goal is profits, not how fast you can sell out. Unless your goal is to get rid of excess produce, do not lower prices toward the end of the day just to sell out; customers will learn to wait for end-of-the-day basement prices. Develop other outlets or uses for unsold produce.

Selling tips

The friendly interchange between farmer and customer is the heart and soul of a farmers market. People go to farmers markets seeking a more personal shopping experience than grocery stores offer, part of which is getting to know the farmer who grew the food. It is that relationship that will make them come back again and again.

When I visited the farmers market in Santa Monica, California, one grower was explaining to customers why one variety of persimmon needs to be very soft when eaten, while another variety should be hard; another grower was telling customers the difference between apple cider and apple juice; while yet another grower was talking about the fine points of cooking with exotic mushrooms. At the Redondo Beach market, "Cactus Jeff" Notias, an ex-bartender from New York City who got hooked on growing exotic cactus, was giving customers lessons on how to care for their cactus plants!

Selling your produce yourself is ideal—no one sells it like the farmer who grew it! But if you'd rather grow than sell, hire enthusiastic employees.

Selling styles. Should you "hawk"? Ever since folks first called out, "Come and get it!" a couple of million years ago, there have been hawkers and hawks. Modern farmers are not deficient in this aspect, as farmers fill the air with shouts of: "Delicious and nutritious!," "Give peas a chance!," or (in the case of a farmer selling honey) "Pure and sweet, just like the ladies!" At its worst, hawking creates a low-vibe, carnival atmosphere. At its best, it lends a festive, joyous mood to the market. Use your discretion; don't drive your neighbors crazy and customers away!

The most popular growers are those who provide entertaining conversation, a bit of education about their produce, and some indication that they are interested in their customers, without getting too familiar. "You have to like selling to people," explains New York City Greenmarket director Barry Benepe. "You have to like to chat. You can't be a wallflower."[10] According to Vallejo, California, market manager Brooks Kleim, "Two growers can have markedly different styles, yet be equally effective. The desire to serve the public seems most important."

Exhibit hustle and enthusiasm—show your eagerness to serve the customer. Customers will forgive having to wait for a good product if they feel you're doing your best to serve them. If a long line does build up, talk to the people and have samples for them to try as well as pamphlets to read about your farm and products while they are waiting. Thank customers for waiting (acknowledge their wait). If long lines are chronic, hire more help during peak hours and consider other ways to speed up the checkout process.

When things slow down, use the time to restock the display, bag more produce, clean up around the table, and move the excess cash from your apron or cash box.

Educate your customers. Prepare to answer questions about your products, such as when peak supplies are available, or what quantities to buy for canning and freezing. Make sure your helpers are also well-informed! Providing information about varieties, growing methods, storage, cooking, serving and nutrition helps build customer trust and loyalty.

Farmers Market Startup Tips

REACH OUT TO all elements of the population. Include farmers who cater to a mix of ethnic groups, income levels and lifestyles. Each of these groups has different buying habits. At many farmers markets, customers may purchase the most unusual vegetables, as well as "seconds" at substantial savings.

Develop a policy to discourage dumping of large quantities of produce at low prices. You might require vendors, for example, to stay within 10 percent of local retail prices and to keep the quality and uniqueness of their products in mind when determining prices. Such guidelines prevent price wars within the market and prevent undercutting by hobbyists who are not concerned with making a profit.

Require that all products sold at the market be grown locally by members. Disallowing "imports" promotes local agriculture and aids the regional economy. Assure safety and high standards by requiring members to obtain any applicable state licenses. Food processors should have a certified kitchen, and growers who claim to be organic must be registered by state law.[11]

Make opening day a smash. The Marin Certified Farmers Market opened in July, 1983 with 30 growers. Within two months, over 60 farmers were selling their produce there. The reason, feels director Lynn Bagley, was the work that went into the market prior to opening day.

"If you start out successful, it builds," she says.

Bagley did everything possible to let the public know about the event, such as holding a series of public meetings, and organizing volunteers to call every other household in the zip code area. Volunteers put signs over all the major highways, and two TV stations did features on the event. The local paper ran features and front-page stories, as well as continuing stories throughout the season. This set the tone for the market's importance, and on opening day all the sellers were sold out within two hours.

Work with your local community to build a farmers market which will meet their needs. Involve representatives from city government, local business merchants, nonprofit organizations, farmers and the community in the planning of your farmers market. Let everyone understand how a farmers market will benefit the community. Point out that farmers markets help promote community spirit and involvement. You might allow different nonprofit groups, such as a hunger group, a local chapter of the American Heart Association, or a 4-H club, to set up information tables at your market. Invite a local community food bank to collect unsold produce from farmers at the end of the day for distribution to low-income citizens.

Point out to townsfolk that farmers markets benefit communities by making nutritious and relatively low-priced fresh fruits and vegetables more readily available to people. This is especially important in low-income areas, where families often skimp on purchases of life-sustaining fresh fruits and vegetables. Set up a booth to give free samples of various products, along with nutrient information for those products, and information about healthy eating habits. For information about the Women, Infants and Children (WIC) Farmers Market Nutrition Program, a federal program which provides low-income, nutritionally-at-risk mothers, women and children with coupons redeemable only at farmers markets for fresh fruits and vegetables, see Chapter 31, "Sharing The Bounty–Feeding The Hungry."

The Seeds of Hope Farmers Market Project unites church groups and farmers to create and sustain local farmers markets. For information write to Dr. John O'Sullivan, Farm Management and Marketing Specialist, North Carolina Cooperative Extension Program, N C A & T State University, P.O. Box 21928, Greensboro, NC 27420-1928; (919) 334-7957.

Farmers Market Promotion Tips

Asked why the markets she has directed have succeeded so well, Ms. (Lynn) Bagley responded without hesitation: "Relentless marketing, attention to detail, hard work, an obsessive personality and learning how to beg, constantly, in a ladylike way."

—*New York Times*, June 20, 1990

*H*OLD SPECIAL EVENTS. Invite restaurants to stage a cooking demonstration at the market, home economists to give demonstrations on home food preservation, or master gardeners to give gardening tips. Sponsor baking, gardening or music contests. Other ideas for special events include Ethnic Days, Farm Days for school children, or an April Flower Festival. The possibilities are endless!

Work with the media. As a festive, community-oriented group, your farmers market has a real "in" with the media! Use any excuse to send out a news release: the manager being hired, the site being chosen, or farmers getting together to organize. Make contacts with the food editor, the community events editor, and the calendar and metro sections of your paper. Radio and television are also effective. If your farmers market is registered as a nonprofit group, public service announcements are sure publicity-getters.

Contribute a recipe each week for the local newspaper's food page, focusing on food that is in season and plentiful at the market. These might be contributed by members on a voluntary basis, and the member's farm name can be mentioned in the article. You might also write a gardening column with tips submitted by the market's grower members.

Develop a group ad. The Medford Growers and Crafters Association takes out display ads stating the locations and hours of operation, and growers tack on individual ads, which cost $20 each. The small grower ads are charged at the organization's contract rate, which is 25 percent less than the individual rates.[12]

Publish a cookbook. These are also great fund raisers.

Stretch the farmers market concept. A number of new and different ideas are being added to the traditional farmers market model in an attempt to expand sales and better serve the consumer and farmer. At the Knox County Regional Farmers Market in Knoxville, Tennessee, a 27,000 square foot barnlike structure accommodates some 70 permanent stalls for farmers, plus additional places for craft and food purveyors. Plans call for including facilities for produce wholesalers, a garden center, an agribusiness park, and an ag educational center.[13]

If you are certified organic, display your certification sign prominently; don't just assume that passersby know you are organic! Hand out educational brochures about sustainable growing practices, and encourage the market manager to have a booth in the market with information about organic farming to help educate consumers.

Samples. If your produce is suitable, offer samples. A taste is worth a thousand words, and many of those who try will buy! Lots of growers hesitate to give away free products, but if giving away $50 in samples makes the difference between a $300 day and a $900 day, it's worth it!

Provide sliced vegetables, melons, or fresh berries in clean, covered dishes. Have a napkin holder and a toothpick holder handy and encourage customers to try something. Provide a trash can for dirty napkins and toothpicks. At the Santa Monica market, Lori Nichols has a large sign over the sugar snap peas which reads: "Free sample—taste one. Edible pods: crisp, sweet. Eat the whole pea!" "We've gotten excellent response," Lori says. "People expect them to be tough, because they're big like green beans. But they're surprised to find they're tender and stringless."

NOTE: Check with market regulations to see if sampling is allowed.

SELL WHAT YOU SOW!

Self-promotion. Wear a name tag and have your farm name where the customers can see it. Put up banners and a colorful canopy to attract customers to your booth. Make some flyers describing your farm and produce to put on windshields and in store windows a day or so before the market opens. This will spread your name around and encourage customers to come to your booth. Hand out business cards at your booth. Develop weekly flyers to put in each bag of groceries with recipes and news about your upcoming crops.[14]

Does it pay? Check the bottom line

Some farmers like to go to farmers markets for the pleasure of talking to customers and for getting feedback on their products, and fail to keep tabs on costs. Yet they may be losing money without knowing it. Keep track of how much you take to the farmers market and your costs of producing, transporting and selling your products. Be sure to include labor costs (your own as well as hired labor), and your personal expenses for lodging and food. Subtract the value of unsold food at the end of the day.

Compare your costs with revenues to determine your net income at the farmers market. Compare this with what you might have made selling the food through other marketing outlets. Are the farmers markets profitable for you? Don't forget to consider the nonimmediate returns, like the benefits of using the farmers market as a test market for new crops, or making contacts with customers who may come to your roadside market, etc. But the bottom line is: watch your bottom line!

Acknowledgments

Ransom Blakeley, direct marketing consultant, P.O. Box 449, Dryden, NY 13053; (607) 844-4714.

Randi McNear, manager, Davis Farmers Market Association, Davis, California.

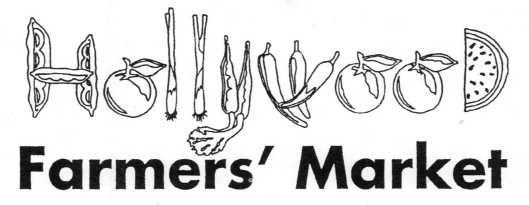

Roadside Markets

CHAPTER

8

ROADSIDE STANDS OR markets offer a welcome alternative to the sterility of supermarkets. You can start off with a simple table or open-framed wooden stand, selling a few seasonal items such as pumpkins or apples under a shade tree, and then expand as sales warrant. Roadside markets may have permanent, year-round, air conditioned facilities with modern refrigerated display cases, fluorescent lighting and computerized checkout systems, and offer a wide array of products, including nonfood items for customer convenience. Operators of larger markets often purchase some of their products from other farmers, as well as from conventional wholesale outlets.

Twenty to thirty years ago, the typical roadside market customer was a housewife who purchased bulk quantities of produce for canning or freezing. Today, many women work outside the home and do not have time for these activities. As a result, roadside marketers are losing an important part of their consumer base. To maintain a profitable volume of sales, therefore, roadside markets need something special: a rural recreational or entertainment experience, lower prices, specialty products not ordinarily found in supermarkets, or fresher, higher quality produce. Roadside markets are often combined with pick-your-own farms, nature trails, tours or festivals.

According to Linda Stanley, marketing director for the North American Strawberry Growers Asso-

ciation: "You need an edge. Parkesdale's Strawberry Market in Plant City, Florida, sells every kind of berry product you could ask for, but the $1.50 'real fresh berry topping' sundae is their most memorable treat. Just imagine a giant, fresh, whipped cream topped sundae and you will know why a tour bus stops by every five minutes. What is *your* specialty?"

With the one-on-one contact with the customers that you enjoy at a roadside market, you can teach them how to can or freeze, or utilize recipes using specialty products. This information is generally not available in supermarkets!

A roadside market is not a convenience store. Shopping at a farm market is an experience—the longer the customer stays, the more she usually buys and spends. Picnic tables, playground equipment, farm tours, restaurants or snack bars, bakery products, crafts, food preservation demonstrations, and local historical displays all encourage customers to stay longer, enjoy themselves, and make more purchases.

Repeat customers—happy and satisfied customers—are the key to success in a roadside market. This means hiring friendly employees, offering quality products, free recipes, picnic tables and a suggestion box. It is important to make your customers' buying experience an enjoyable one so they will return again and again.

Advantages

* reduced marketing costs such as transportation, shipping containers, and wholesalers' handling charges;
* chance to use family labor; and
* attractive displays and variety of produce can help draw customers.

Disadvantages

* higher operating costs including costs of physical facilities (such as interest, taxes, depreciation, repairs, parking lots, utilities and insurance);
* sales labor needed for operating the stand;
* higher costs for advertising, promotion, and consumer packaging materials; and
* zoning and planning restrictions.

Special considerations

Special considerations include getting customers out to the market, and overcoming customers' perceptions of roadside markets as being less clean and having lower quality produce than supermarkets. You'll need to allocate your time between labor and marketing; diversify your crops to meet the need for a year-round inventory; comply with building codes and local ordinances; and develop merchandising, advertising, promotional and customer-related skills.

Farm markets generally try to project an image of natural wholesomeness, fresh flavor, economy, and rural values. Sometimes there may have to be trade-offs between projecting the farm image or using modern equipment, such as replacing baskets with shopping carts or the cash box with a computerized cash register.[1]

You'll need to have regular hours of operation. Some roadside markets operate seven days per week for 8 to 12 hours per day year-round, while some stands are open only Friday, Saturday and Sunday for 5 to 8 hours from June to late October. The highest customer traffic occurs on weekends, particularly on Saturdays.[2]

You may need to hire a manager. The person responsible for managing crop production should not be responsible for the day-to-day management of the roadside market.

A roadside market is not something to get into without considerable research and consultation. Depending on how big you get, roadside marketing may require considerable capital investment and sales force, advertising and promotion costs. Use farm advisors as much as possible in developing the roadside market plan, or hire a consultant. Talk to other market operators and visit as many markets as possible before committing yourself financially.

Unless market research warrants starting big, start small and see what kind of traffic you can draw. It is better to start small with plans for expansion rather than make a major investment in new facilities immediately. Most small businesses take three to five years to become self-sustaining. Sales are difficult to predict, although traffic patterns, surrounding population, and the number and quality of already existing markets where consumers can buy fresh produce, can provide some guidance.

 ## Rules & regulations

Before deciding on a location, consult local, county, and state authorities on regulations governing roadside markets. Some of the rules and regulations that may apply to your roadside market or stand include health permits, licenses, sales taxes, weights and measures requirements, sanitary requirements, zoning and right-of-way regulations. Approval of your plans may take six months to a year or more, so become familiar with the regulations and then plan accordingly so that your enterprise goals mesh with local rules and regulations.

Do not assume that a roadside market will be considered just another farm building. The definition of the building, either as an agricultural or commercial structure, will vary considerably based on location, products sold at the market, and source of the products (that is, whether they are farm or nonfarm products). Building size, restroom facilities, parking, type and size of signs, standards for entrances and exits, and driveway design and construction are examples of items that may be regulated by local ordinances. Check also with the highway department to make sure you are not constructing your market too close to a road which may be widened or rerouted in the future. Contact agencies such as departments of health, highway, sewer and water districts, etc., to familiarize yourself with regulations before investing large sums of money.[3]

Suitable products

The most important factors influencing purchase of produce at a roadside market are freshness and quality, appearance, nutritional value, price, ability to purchase desired quantity, and whether or not it's grown locally. Apples, peaches, strawberries, melons, cherries, tomatoes, sweet corn, green beans, pumpkins and squash are some of the popular crops sold at roadside stands.

Encourage larger purchases by providing a larger selection of products. An assortment of products generally attracts a larger number of repeat customers than a display of only one or a few items. If only one or a few products are available for sale, such as apples, provide more than one variety. You might also offer alternatives in processing or packaging, such as cider or apples by the pound, peck or bushel.

One way to increase variety is by presenting products in different ways, such as jams, jellies, chutney and pickles. Suggest additional uses for each product through recipe handouts. Offer "add-on" items: if you are selling berries, for example, you might also offer toppings and pie shells.

Extend the season by succession plantings, choosing early and late varieties, and by reselling produce purchased from neighboring farms or the wholesale market. (In some states, you may need to obtain a resale license, depending upon volume purchased—contact your state department of·agriculture market enforcement branch.) Cultivate contacts with neighboring farmers for fill-in orders when you run short.

Offer supplementary items such as herbs, potted flowers and plants, seeds, honey, nuts, cider, and homemade crafts to extend your product line. Sales can also be increased by offering complementary products such as pickling cucumbers and dill, and lettuce and salad dressings. If you are selling fruits and vegetables for home canning and freezing, sell canning accessories such as jars, lids, freezing bags, pectin and citric acid, as a convenience to the customer. Consumers who can and freeze purchase three times more fruit and vegetables than consumers who buy produce for immediate consumption.

Location[4]

Since direct market shoppers usually become aware of a roadside stand when passing by or through word-of-mouth, choosing a favorable location may be your single most critical decision in setting up a roadside market.

Some factors to consider when evaluating a site for your roadside market include the number of potential customers (nearby population density and composition), zoning regulations, and the traffic flow. Consider also the number of competing businesses in the area and how they compare to your operation. In addition, consider the level of customer interest and whether it is sufficient to support several stands. Often several markets can benefit from the competition and operate profitably in the same general area. But in order for several stands to operate in close proximity, there must be considerable traffic flow.[5]

The more successful stand sites are located within 15 miles of a city and are easily visible from the road. Normally, a level stretch on the right-hand side of the road heading toward the city has the most promise as a market location. You might consider locating farther away from a city if the potential site is located on a main highway or a well-traveled road. If the site is near a busy tourist attraction, for example, customers will stop by for fresh produce on their way or on their return. Call your state department of transportation for an estimate of the number of motorists who drive by your potential site. There is an inverse relationship between sales and the speed of passing traffic. Roadside stands are generally more successful when the average speed is 45 miles per hour or less.[6]

Since part of the appeal of a roadside stand or U-Pick is the excuse to get out to the country, you may be able to draw customers to an out-of-the-way location as long as you do ample promotions to let people know where you are, and have the products or special attractions to help create interest in your farm and attract customers for repeat visits.

The population characteristics of nearby communities should be determined. Numerous studies suggest that the folks who patronize roadside markets are generally younger, have larger families, and have a mid-range income (i.e., $18,500 – $74,000 yearly for a family of four). They may be characterized as "typical Americana."

A potential site should have access to water and electricity, as well as proper soil and site drainage. Some clay soils and soils with high organic content swell and shrink as moisture content changes, making it difficult to maintain the site. Good drainage is another consideration; muddy parking and pedestrian walk areas discourage prospective customers.[7]

Visibility and safety are also major considerations. Customers should be able to see the market in time to stop safely and conveniently. Potential customers may not stop at a roadside stand with hazardous entrances or exits. Locations that are along level stretches of highway, at the top of a long sloping hill, or on the outside of curves provide good visibility up and down the road. A wide turnoff or hard shoulder should be provided for roadside stands on faster highways. Regulations permit-

ting, place a sign along the road that lets travelers know they are approaching your stand, e.g., "Farm Market 100 Yards On Left."

On-farm roadways should be maintained in smooth and fairly dust-free condition. Post prominent speed limit signs (10 – 15 miles per hour) at the entrance and in the parking areas.

Plan for expansion so that future additions can be made with minimum expense or disruption. Expansion of the sales building away from the road rather than parallel to the road allows for simultaneous expansion of the parking area, so that expansion of a sales building will *not* reduce the ratio of parking-to-sales area.[8]

Your market location should be light, gay, even showy. Strings of bright-colored pennants flapping in the breeze, for example, draw attention. Pictures of fruit and vegetables on display not only verify what is happening, they whet the appetite.[9]

Location: on-site or off-site?

You will need to decide whether to sell at your own farm, sell to other roadside stand operators, or to obtain retail space within a commercial business district. Transportation costs are reduced or eliminated if the stand is located on or near the site of production. If the stand is on the farm, you can sell your products without special packaging, container, or grading requirements. You can keep the stand open for business on slow days without having to spend all your time watching the stand.

You may want to locate the market on or near your farm especially if you wish to capitalize on the down-on-the-farm atmosphere. The closeness of labor, supplies, utilities and management, and lower land costs are other excellent reasons to consider the farm area for the market. Smart marketing can enhance the potential of an out-of-the-way site by promoting a visit to the country. On the other hand, poorly maintained roads, complicated directions, and inadequate parking may outweigh the advantages, making an off-farm location more attractive.[10]

Facilities & buildings

Many roadside farmers sell their crops from picnic tables, or under tents or awnings when first starting. If you want to have a permanent building, try refurbishing your barn, shed or other existing

Nita Gizdich, Gizdich Ranch, Watsonville, California

structure. Essential facilities include a sales area, adequate parking and roadway access. Some optional facilities are a cool storage area, restrooms, playground and a picnic area.

Study your market's location. A design which incorporates existing buildings and blends in with the natural surroundings creates a unique market. A small, inexpensive structure is all that is needed for markets offering only a few crops in season. Permanent buildings are required for large-volume markets open from spring through fall or year-round. The buildings or stands must be neat and attractive, large enough to handle the expected volume of produce, have adequate display space, and room for customer movement. You should plan a market that fits your needs and a structure adaptable to expansion.

Plan the interior of your stand and the amount of space you will need for storage, displays and aisles; then calculate the stand's exterior dimensions. One rule of thumb is to allow 1/3 preparation area and 2/3 display and sales space in your market. Strategic location of the plumbing and cold storage area will permit you to expand at a minimal cost in the future.

Structures with open fronts or sliding doors are conducive to large displays and allow for convenient delivery of produce. If you display produce outside, use an umbrella or awning to protect it from the weather.

See *Facilities for Roadside Markets* (listed in "Chapter Resources") for a more complete description of roadside market structures and facilities, as well as for many other topics presented in this helpful booklet.

© Pioneer Fruit Stand, 4495 Suisun Valley Rd., Suisun, CA 94585

Parking

Problems with parking and traffic flow are among the major complaints about roadside markets. Even a good market will lose customers if parking is unsafe, inconvenient or inadequate. Provide ample space and smooth flow for parking, so that customers can go in and out easily and safely.

Make sure your parking is far enough from the road so as not to be a hazard. On-street parking is dangerous because of its proximity to fast-moving traffic. Construct separate entrance and exit driveways. Entrances and exits should be at least 30 feet wide and intersect the highway at a 90 degree angle for maximum visibility and safety. They should not channel traffic into busy intersections. Check with the highway department responsible for your road for regulations regarding entrances and exits.

Organized traffic patterns can make a big difference in the number of cars that can park at any given time. Steps you can take to fully use parking lot space include setting up definite entrances and exits, setting up one-way traffic flow and marking off distinct parking spaces for cars. These elements improve safety as customers enter, move through and leave the lot.[11] A parking lot attendant during busy times is advisable.

Angled parking allows a one-way traffic flow. One-way aisles are safer for pedestrians walking to and from their cars. Perpendicular stalls, on the other hand, divided by a center lane with two-way traffic, make more efficient use of space and provide for the greatest parking capacity. Two-way aisles within the parking lot should be 25 feet in width. Allow space also for cars to circulate around the parking lot.

Provide an area approximately 10 by 18 feet for each parking space. Marking rows and parking spaces with ground limestone or hydrated lime gives a neat and orderly appearance, enhances safety, and prevents haphazard parking. Enclose the parking lot with concrete parking blocks, railroad ties or hay bales in order to protect customers and keep cars at least five feet away from buildings and walkways.

To estimate the parking area size, allow 15 parking spaces for each 100 cars on a peak business day. If 200 cars are expected during the busiest day, for example, provide space for 30 cars. Another way to calculate the parking area size is that each projected $100 in daily sales requires one parking lot space. Still another way to project parking space requirements is that each square foot of sales area requires four square feet of total parking lot area.[12] For a pick-your-own operation, allow one acre of parking for every five acres of crops that ripen at one time.

The parking area should be level and firm. If dust is a problem, consider graveling or paving your parking lot and roadways. Graveled surfaces require regrading periodically to fill in any potholes. Asphalt surfacing requires less maintenance and is advisable in heavy traffic areas. Marketers report that paved lots pay benefits, but wait a year or two before paving to see if business warrants the expense.

Market layout

An effective and efficient market layout can attract customers, induce them to buy more, and reduce labor costs. Market layout design should be based on product mix, available space and the marketer's goals, as well as customer flow and labor efficiency. Arrange sales, work and storage areas so that employee and product movement does not disturb customer traffic. Professional advice and good planning will pay big dividends in market layout design.[13]

To plan an efficient market layout, the expectation for the market should be defined. For instance, the length of the market season and the product mix through the season should be estimated. The volume of produce to be sold affects the areas required for preparation, refrigeration and other storage needs.[14] Determine the sales area size by listing the products to be sold, their seasonal availability, and the amount of display space needed. Use this information to estimate the maximum amount of display space needed and when this need occurs. The booklet, *Produce Handling for Direct Marketing* is helpful for planning the types and sizes of displays appropriate for various commodities (see "Chapter Resources").

Design your market layout so that customer traffic flows one way. Congestion hurts sales and is created more quickly when traffic moves two ways. Make baskets and carts available near the entrance.

Make sure aisles are wide enough to accommodate peak-day crowds and shopping carts. The aisles should let customers easily pass by someone restocking a display or by another customer stopped at a display.[15]

Arrange traffic flow so that customers are encouraged to shop the entire market. One way to do this is to disperse demand items throughout the market in strategic locations so as to guide the customers to your various displays. (A demand item, such as a large bulk display of in-season sweet corn or strawberries, brings customers to the market and is commonly featured in advertisements.) Alternate demand items with related items (e.g., salad dressing to go with the salad vegetables, or popcorn to go with cider) so that the customer is led from one demand item to another and is drawn past as many items as possible. Display one demand item near the entrance so that customers will want to buy something as soon as they walk in. Impulse items, such as jellies and jams, nuts and gift packs, can add significantly to sales and should be placed at the end of layouts or near checkout stations.

Spread out your sales areas. People don't want to come out to the country and feel all bunched up as if they were in a department store. Use specials to pull customers into corners and into slow turn-over sales areas. Consider having movable displays which may hold seasonal items or impulse items; these can be moved around the market to increase visibility of certain products. Emphasize your farm-fresh image by locating fresh fruits and vegetables near (although not *in*) the entrance.

Scales and bag supplies should be strategically located throughout the market. Utilize information signs throughout the store to direct customers to departments and restrooms; to provide business history and philosophy, product guarantees, product information and use; or to announce specials.

Cleanliness, simplicity and good visibility are key rules. Maintain clean, sanitary, and well-lit facilities. Involve your community in your market by arranging some space in a corner or aisle, or on a wall, for community groups to set up displays. Allow for rearrangement of displays; customers enjoy changes in the market surroundings from time to time.

Finally, ask a friend to take a fresh look at your business. Solicit comments and suggestions regarding your signs, parking lot, visual layout of the farm store, displays and so on. A second pair of eyes can work wonders!

Fennel

Market decor

Market decor and style help set the mood of the market. Make your customers enjoy being at your market and want to come back. Items to consider are soft mood music, colors, smells, employee dress, and the way the produce looks. Although important, mood and decor should not hamper the market's efficiency.

The rustic and simple image goes well with the farm theme. Avoid an extravagant or expensive look. Pay special attention to two areas of decor: the entrance (the customer's first impression of the market), and the floor, because customers look at floors more than ceilings.

A neat, clean, well-organized market helps greatly in attracting customers, and implies that the merchandise will also be top quality. Make sure you always have fresh paint on buildings, manicured landscaping, and clear instructional signs.

At Machado Orchards near Bowman, California, the market's bathrooms are kept immaculately clean and are provided with fresh flowers and facial tissues. They are also decorated with old-time farm photographs. The bathroom mirrors are rimmed with old lug boxes refurbished with shellac. "People make a special stop at our stand just to see the bathrooms," says market owner Bobbi Machado.

Make your market unique. Differentiate your market from your competitors. The addition of a cupola (small dome), an enticing entryway, or carefully chosen color combinations, for example, can help turn ordinary buildings into distinctive landmarks that will help draw passersby off the highway and into your market. Impart a taste of the farm with special farm equipment, antique boxes and milk containers, picture albums, a display case with photos of your growing/harvesting process, or a pamphlet about your farm.

Appeal to your customers' senses of sight, smell and taste. While properly displayed produce is a visual feast, tantalizing aromas are also an effective marketing tool. Keep a pot of cider on the stove to waft enticing aromas through the market. Ripe cantaloupes, strawberries, or the tangy fragrance of a freshly sliced sweet onion can also stimulate sales. One farm marketer reports that she sells 60 percent more cookies on days when they are baking. She leaves the kitchen doors open so that the customers get full benefit! Taste is also important: make samples available so customers can taste the produce.

Equipment

The amount and type of equipment needed varies with the type of stand or market. A simple stand needs only a money box or a cash register and a produce display. Standard equipment in larger roadside markets includes items from refrigerators to product containers.

- *Cash registers.* A cash register is a good investment because it keeps a running total of the day's receipts, sales tax (if applicable), and number of customers. This can save a lot of bookkeeping time and provide valuable management information. If you code different items, you can also determine the amount of each commodity sold.[16]

- *Scales.* These are needed whenever products are sold by weight. They need to be certified by your couny sealer of weights and measures section. Scales should be available to customers for their own use in order to minimize misunderstandings. A spring scale with a metal basket (costing about $300) should suffice for most small markets. For larger markets, a digital computer scale offers greater convenience because it directly computes the purchase cost.[17] Some growers say that a computer scale, which costs $600 or more, will pay for itself the first year. "You're constantly giving customers the benefit of the doubt when the marker falls in-between," one grower said. "Computer scales are right on the ounce."

- *Product containers* such as shopping carts, baskets, boxes and bags. Shopping carts and baskets encourage larger sales per customer.

- *Display tables and shelves.*

- *Cold storage equipment* such as a walk-in cooler or refrigerated case for larger markets; cold chests or refrigerators for smaller markets.

- *Proper lighting* is important for the attractive appearance of your produce. The source of light affects product color. For example, tomatoes appear to change color as they are moved from

Mobile Markets

WHY NOT TAKE your show on the road? With mobile markets, operators sell off the back of their trucks, or sell door to door where permissible. This method has low overhead costs, but you might encounter legal restrictions and required licensing.

Check on zoning permits regarding signs and structures. If a permanent sign isn't allowed, use movable structures and "A-frame" or sandwich board signs. A good place to advertise is on your car or truck, with either door signs or roof signs. This can overcome zoning regulations and sign bylaws altogether, and still get your message out to the public.

Keep a notebook with you and list the number of customers during each hour. Write down the total amount purchased and any comments. You may find that the bulk of your customers come to your booth or stand during the lunch hour, or from 10 a.m. to noon. Perhaps they will come from 3 p.m. to 6 p.m. It may not be profitable to keep the stand open long hours unless you are in an area where there is constant traffic that will stop.[18]

According to a recent article in *The New Farm* magazine,[19] Jim Crawford, owner of New Morning Farm near Hustontown, Pennsylvania, delivers up to five tons of fresh fruits, vegetables and other farm products twice weekly, from June through November, to five Washington, DC neighborhoods.

Crawford concentrates on high-demand vegetables that customers can find in any grocery store, such as tomatoes, beans, peppers, sweet corn, summer squash, and fall brassicas. "If I have to spend time educating the public about (unusual specialty crops), it's probably not worth the effort," he says.

Advertising his business chiefly through leaflets which tell potential customers "who we are, what we are doing, and when and where we will be selling near them," Crawford adds these tips when choosing an off-the-truck marketing site:

- Select areas of sociable, friendly, family-oriented neighborhoods.
- Avoid congested areas, where your presence could be a nuisance to traffic or people.
- Don't pick commuting areas, despite their high-volume appearance. Commuters are always in a rush and rarely give you a second glance.
- Conform with any permit requirements or other regulations in your marketing area. Check with city hall before selecting locations.
- Try inner-city as well as affluent or ethnic neighborhoods. If sales don't increase after two or three tries, move to a new neighborhood.

sunlight to tungsten to fluorescent lights. *Deluxe cool white* fluorescent lamps are recommended since the light they emit appears most like natural daylight. To maximize lamp efficiency, paint walls and ceilings a light color to reflect light from the lamps. Most utility companies employ lighting specialists who can help with lighting design.

- *Checkouts* must be easily identifiable, clean and uncluttered. They should have room for scales, bags, a display of impulse items, and a cash register. Consider also how many people can wait in line without crowding other areas of the market and how many items purchased can fit on a checkout counter.

Storage and handling

The back room should include cold storage, space for preparing produce, and a storage area for nonrefrigerated stock. Locate the back room close to the sales area to minimize clerk travel. Design the preparation and storage area layouts to allow for efficient produce handling. Often employees will not only store and prepare produce but also assist customers and operate checkout areas. If your employees have several responsibilities, they need to be able to see the customers from the produce preparation and storage areas.[20]

"Self-serve" selling

"Self-serve" selling has proven successful for some operators when sales volume does not warrant full-time sales personnel. Wagons or small portable stands or tables are all the equipment you'll need. Stock the display area with available products, and let consumers buy on a self-serve basis and leave payment in a cash box. This method, of course, depends on the honesty of your customers. Bolt down and lock your cash box, and have a small slot on top for payment.

One special consideration in self-serve selling is keeping your fruits and vegetables fresh. For some vegetables such as winter squash, potatoes and carrots, just providing shade may be sufficient. For items that need refrigeration, such as lettuce, peas and broccoli, keep them chilled with crushed ice, lay wet newsprint over them, or keep them in a refrigerator.

Back room equipment should include a sink, table, and materials for product preparation and trash disposal. For specialty products, additional equipment may be needed, such as a cider press and bottling equipment or ovens for baked products.

Because fresh and flavorful products are the prime qualities attracting customers to the roadside market, it is extremely important to use proper product handling and storage. Perishables should be protected from the sun, from overheating, and from drying out. Try to give as much attention to products' individual storage needs as possible.

Temperature control is an important aspect of postharvest handling. Tomatoes, for example, should be kept cool (50 – 60 degrees F), but not refrigerated. Check the temperature of your coolers daily, and keep a daily check on how long each item has been in storage. Keep a chart on the cooler as to when items have been put in storage, or mark cases daily. If you see five slash marks on a case, for example, you'll know it's been there five days. Clean and sanitize all refrigeration and display equipment regularly.

Safety and security

Basic safety and security precautions include an alarm system, a well-lit market and parking lot area, and a fire protection plan. See *Facilities for Roadside Markets* for a discussion of these topics.

Try to make daily bank deposits. Always lock the cash register when it is not attended. Keep only enough cash on hand to make change. Put extra cash in a locked safe until you make your bank deposit.

Prepare a written report of any customer-related accidents which occur in the parking lot or on the market premises. Notify your insurance agent.

Acknowledgments

Monika Crispin, Cornell Cooperative Extension.

John Cottingham, professor & agricultural marketing specialist, University of Wisconsin-Extension-Platteville.

Pick-Your-Own

IN U-PICK, OR PICK-YOUR-OWN operations, the customer comes to the farm, does the harvesting, pays cash for the produce harvested, and transports it home. U-Pick operations are a natural to add to a roadside stand. The customer buys peak-freshness produce at low cost, while enjoying a fun farm experience.

University of Illinois horticulturist J. W. "Bill" Courter, the nation's expert on pick-your-own, says: "People will work harder picking your crop than if you paid them! Moreover, PYO customers will buy produce you couldn't sell at a stand, and they'll drive 30 or 40 miles to do it, sometimes as often as once a week!"

Pick-your-own seems to go up and down according to the economy and the times. In difficult economic times, U-Pick savings appeals to customers. As many housewives today work outside the home, they do less canning, freezing and preserving, and are after the convenience of prepicked foods at supermarkets or roadside stands. (An important exception is among ethnic minority customers, who adhere to their home-country customs of open-market shopping, buying and storing in bulk.) Strawberry U-Pick operations, for instance, have declined 20 percent over the last several years.[1] The current trend is that customers are wanting ready-picked berries. U-Pick also assumes greater appeal for farmers in areas where it is hard to find seasonal labor to pick crops.

In order to compete with supermarkets, pick-your-own farms need to offer produce with home-grown freshness and quality, clean and neat picking conditions, along with prompt, courteous checkin and checkout service by well-trained personnel. Many of today's successful U-Pick operations have also added rural recreation attractions—farm entertainment, festivals and events—to attract customers and keep them coming back.

Pick-your-own customers have drastically changed their produce buying habits over the past 20 years. Products are being bought more often but in smaller quantities, as customers purchase fresh produce at the farm during the local season, and at the grocery store during other months of the year. To sell larger quantities of produce, therefore, local farms must be active in teaching customers how to store and use fresh produce. Encourage home preservation and storage through instructional classes, workshops and educational materials. Look for crops that can be dried, canned, frozen or otherwise stored for a period of time.

As with other ways of direct marketing, study PYO carefully and talk with established U-Pick farmers before entering this business. An excellent book on the subject is *Pick Your Own Farming*, by Ralph Wampler and James Motes (see "Chapter Resources").

Joe Huber Family Farm, Restaurant and Orchard, near Borden, Indiana, is proof that a well-planned and managed pick-your-own operation can thrive in modern times. The operation has blacktop parking for about 450 cars, and temporary parking for over 1,500 cars. "We get super crowds in peak seasons, and it takes a tremendous amount of management and supervision to control the people," says Joe Huber. "Be prepared—if you can't park their cars, you're not going to sell them a thing."

Advantages

- reduced need for seasonal harvest labor—transportation, grading, washing, packing, packaging and storage costs are eliminated;
- average value of purchase per customer may be larger than at many other direct market outlets; and
- low capital requirements to get started.

Disadvantages

- customers may damage produce or plants;
- increased costs for accident liability insurance;
- may need alternate market outlets;
- need for a large parking area(s);
- increased costs for sales and supervisory labor;
- lowest prices among direct marketing methods;
- long hours, including weekends, supervising customers—the typical PYO season lasts three weeks or less, so you need to keep long hours during pick-your-own season;
- bad weather may reduce customers—rain, snow or cloudy weather can send your sales into a tailspin; and
- some farmers may not want to invite the public to their farms—as one PYO operator said: "You can't do anything else when you are open. You are interrupted constantly."

Special considerations

Since most consumers are not experienced with harvesting agricultural produce, U-Pick requires top-level field supervision to train and supervise customers in harvesting, to direct or transport customers to and from the fields, to insure that customers don't injure themselves or the farmer's crops and property, and to ensure that customers pay for everything they harvest.

Although PYO prices are in most cases higher than wholesale fresh market prices, PYO may not be a less expensive way to harvest your crops.

While transportation, harvesting and packing equipment costs are reduced, supervisory labor, advertising, insurance and parking lots entail increased costs. On many PYO farms, labor can be one of the farm's largest costs. One kind of labor (field helpers, supervisors, etc.) is substituted for another (harvesters). It may be easier, however, to find competent high school and college students to supervise seasonal PYO operations than it is to find seasonal harvest labor.

Some harvesting may have to be done by the operator. Some customers will not be able to pick the produce for various reasons, so some harvested produce can be made available to sell to these customers at a higher price.[2]

Other special PYO challenges include limited demand in sparsely populated areas, seasonality of production, and the limited number of crops suitable to pick-your-own. There may be an insufficient number of pickers during critical periods of maturity, so some of the crops may need to be sold through other market channels. Unless you extend your season through much of the year, it's wise to consider U-Pick mainly as a supplement to your farm's operation.

Location

Although customers generally will drive farther to purchase pick-your-own crops than for farm-stand produce, location is still of prime importance in PYO operations. The ideal location is easy to find, on or near a good road, and within a half-hour drive of a major population center. Generally, pick-your-own operations situated near a major thoroughfare have the best chance of success.

Studies at the University of Illinois show that 75 percent of PYO customers come from the "primary trade area" around the farm. Some approximate primary trade areas are: vegetables, 10 miles; strawberries, 20 miles; blueberries and raspberries, 25 miles; and apples, 30 miles. This rule-of-thumb does not apply, however, if your PYO operation is on a highway leading to a major tourist attraction. Growers who cooperate to offer complementary products and attractions often sell to customers who live 60 – 70 miles away.

A rough rule-of-thumb, obtained from a study done several years ago, is that it takes 2,500 people to support one acre of U-Pick strawberries. (Since the study that this figure is based on was done several years ago, the figure is probably greater now.) This is not a "linear figure": as you increase acreage, it may require greater promotion and advertising to reach more people. Also, since strawberries are a high-demand pick-your-own item, the nearby population numbers required to support other U-Pick crops may be greater.

Suitable PYO products

Some of the most popular pick-your-own crops include:

- *small fruits:* strawberries, blueberries, blackberries and raspberries;
- *tree fruits:* apples, peaches and pears;
- *vegetables:* beans, tomatoes, sweet corn, greens and peas.[3]

Generally, optimal pick-your-own products are high-value and labor-intensive (such as berries, cherries and grapes); or highly perishable (such as asparagus); and their maturity or ripeness is easy to recognize. The plant or tree is not likely to be excessively damaged in picking, and the produce is easy for consumers to use, prepare, or store. Tree- or vine-ripe quality is a main attraction for pick-your-own. PYO enables the customers to pick these products at their finest and freshest!

To avoid the use of ladders, plant dwarf trees for crops such as apples, peaches or citrus. Avoid extra-expensive crops such as mangos or avocados, where theft may be a problem. Avoid easily damaged plants, such as melons or lettuce. Look for crops such as okra, black-eyed peas or Chinese vegetables that might appeal to nearby ethnic groups.

Develop code numbers for the items you sell. At checkout, note the code number and number of pounds sold. At the end of the season, this will tell you the number of pounds of each item sold, and how much to plant next year.

Plant a variety of crops to make it worthwhile for customers to keep coming out to your farm. Stagger plantings and choose a variety of crops that will ripen at different times. Offer "top-of-the-crop" to your customers, not just remnants that are left over after shipping. Customers will make repeat visits year after year if they feel you are offering them your best.

Whatever else you plant, plant strawberries—especially day-neutral, everbearing strawberries which are greatly in demand yet difficult to grow on a commercial basis. As one PYO grower said, "Strawberries bring people—you almost don't have to advertise!" Another "hot" product for pick-your-own is cut flowers. Flowers are not only profitable in themselves, they also make your farm more attractive.

Another product that can be promoted successfully to customers is homemade jam—its fresh-berry taste is far superior to commercial jam! Promotions may include providing samples of homemade jam for customers to taste at the checkout; offering a free box of pectin with a $15 berry purchase; or offering recipes for using frozen berries.

By utilizing suggestion boxes and questionnaires, and talking to customers, find out what they would like to purchase!

Bob Kirtlan, Silver Bend Farm near Clarksburg, California

Management

PYO personnel are required for supervising people as they check in, obtain containers, receive instructions about prices, farm guidelines and other information. Field supervisors should be trained to answer questions, place customers on rows, and direct traffic if needed. Many customers are older, so anything that makes picking easier and safer such as high yields, dwarf trees, and convenient layout will result in greater sales per customer.

A key challenge for PYO operations is to match crowd flow with availability. Make sure you have enough volume and variety of produce available to please your customers. Nothing will kill your PYO plans faster than having to turn away customers. Plant more than you'll need, and then have a contingency plan for selling unpicked produce to a processor, or at the farmers market or your own roadside market.

Have family or hired labor available if produce begins to ripen faster than customers can pick it. Additional advertising to attract customers, or alternative markets may be necessary to avoid losing valuable sales. Lowering prices is a poor solution, and by-passing a field may be better than having customers pick overripe fruit.[4]

Plan for extra help during peak season to avoid long lines at checkout and confusion in the field. A hotline answering machine is one way to regulate crowd flow, letting your customers know what's available, and what's coming up. Weekends, especially, can be a challenge. A farm market is a good addition to your PYO operation when huge crowds come to the farm. Those out for a Sunday drive can stop for refreshments and buy fresh produce without interfering with the PYO customers. To spread traffic throughout the week, establish a weekend minimum purchase or admission charge (deductible from purchase); develop a club membership system; open new fields during normally slow weekdays; or offer a 10-percent weekday discount or other price specials to select customer groups (e.g., ladies, senior citizens).

Adapt crop cultural practices to PYO. Maintain weed-free fields. You might also place a mat of straw between rows as a knee-cushion for customers. Allow plenty of room for access to the plots and plant far enough apart so that customers can move around easily. Place later maturing varieties or late plantings sufficiently distant from earlier plantings so that pickers are less likely to damage immature crops. Plant crops which require the greatest amount of supervision and/or attract the greatest number of customers closest to the checkout area.

The potential of customer damage to plants can be minimized with proper supervision, posted signs about picking rules, and training for beginning pickers. Many PYO owners report that customers, because they have more time and are not getting paid by volume, are often more conscientious and do less damage than cannery or other paid pickers.

Finally, carry liability insurance. Many PYO operators do *not* do this, yet there are many situations in which customers may become injured on a PYO farm.

Labor [5]

The amount of labor needed for the pick-your-own operation depends on the services offered, the length of the growing season, the distance to the picking site and the types of containers used. Most operations need field supervisors and check station operators. If the farm offers only one crop throughout the growing season, then two or three people can supervise the operation. If the operation offers more crops or services, more employees may be necessary. Often high school or college students can provide the supplemental labor needed.

If possible, have employees wear some type of clothing that identifies them as workers—t-shirts, caps or bandannas, for example, with the farm name or logo on them.

Parking

Set up controlled access to your operation. Try to arrange for customers to come into your place on one lane and out another. Separate entrances and exits to the highway, and one-way farm roads help eliminate confusion and congestion. One-way roads are also safer for pedestrians. Fence in your fields if feasible. Don't let your customers park just anywhere, along the road or in the fields. Potential problems include customers driving over your

GIZDICH RANCH
PIK-YOR'- SEF BERRIES

© Gizdich Ranch, 55 Peckham,
Watsonville, CA 95076
(408) 722-1056

crops, cars stuck or lost, traffic jams, or other unsafe traffic conditions.

Have a designated parking area, with an attendant(s) available in peak periods. A centrally located parking area is desirable for large-volume operations or in fields that are located close together. If the fields are located at a distance from each other, you'll need to provide transportation to the fields. Vehicles which can be used to carry people include pickup trucks, large trucks with seats and steps, or flat-bed, tractor-pulled wagons or trailers. Design wagons so that they are close to the ground; cover the wheels with skirts; and provide railings for people to hold on to. Hand carts with bicycle wheels are one way to haul produce from field to checkout. Review your transportation procedures and equipment on-site with your insurance agent.

A central parking area is also desirable if you have a farm market where you sell ready-picked produce. The checkout stand should be close by the farm market, where customers can pick up additional items on their way out.

Other advantages of a central parking area include:

• Traffic control is safer and easier. Especially when customer volume is heavy, auto traffic around the fields can increase the chances of customers being injured in the fields or orchards.

• Security and theft prevention are generally easier.

• Maintenance and supervision of one large parking lot may be less than for several smaller ones.

Another parking alternative is to locate individual parking lots near each field. This may be appropriate when the volume of picking is so small that the cost of providing transportation to the picking areas would be too high; when widely scattered picking locations are a long distance from the checkout area; or when bulky or heavy produce items such as apples, peaches, tomatoes, etc., are difficult for customers to carry long distances to their cars. Portable stands or inexpensive permanent buildings may be located by the entrance of each field, where customers can check in and be given instructions on where and how to harvest.

Checkin/Checkout

At the checkin point, customers receive picking instructions, containers, brochures or perhaps an orchard (or farm) permit. Posted signs give prices, rules and other information. If sales are by weight, customers who bring their own containers may have them weighed at the checkin. The farm owner or an employee should be present to greet people and answer questions as they check in, and as they depart. (Retired persons familiar with the farm are wonderful for this!)

When the fields or orchards are some distance from the checkin point, customers are directed to a loading area where they can board wagons or trucks which carry them to the picking areas. While customers are waiting to get into the wagons, or during the ride itself, the grower (or driver) can explain how to harvest the crops, give information about varieties, and invite questions.

The simplest checkout system is an attendant with a small table. Movable checkout stands on runners or wheels that can be towed by a tractor may be practical when the parking is at the picking site. For relatively compact or concentrated planting areas, a building may be used through which all must pass to and from the fields. Fencing prevents other entry and exit, and no cars are permitted in the picking areas. A permanent structure combined with a farm market is another alternative. Both of these systems prevent the need for inspecting cars for unpaid goods at checkout.

Keep the checkout as orderly as possible. Always have enough people on hand during busy times so checking out can be done promptly. Don't make your customers wait very long on a hot day!

Theft is always possible in a PYO operation, but most PYO customers are honest. Assume everyone is honest, but remove as many temptations as possible. In cases where close supervision is not

---

possible, some PYO operators have reported success with an honor system in which customers are allowed to take marked bags of produce from a sales area and pay by putting money in a plastic bucket with a lid. As a precaution, large bills are removed often, and the amount of merchandise on display is limited.

It is simpler and more efficient to provide harvesting containers than to allow customers to bring their own. Uniform operator-supplied containers speed the checkout process and provide a place to print information such as the farm name, phone number and location. They are often so attractive and handy that no one complains about paying a slight fee for them. Make sure they are correctly designed for the products they contain.

Deep-volume containers such as buckets, for instance, can damage fruit. Allow customers to bring back containers for reuse, allowing a discount for each tray or container that is returned. (Reusing containers is also more ecological, an important consideration with many consumers!) Wax-coated, or wax-impregnated, cardboard trays are best for reuse, and also hold together better in wet conditions. For sanitation reasons, the grower should always issue new containers rather than allow exchanges of containers.

Sales can be done by volume, weight or count. Cabbage, corn, peppers, pumpkins and squash are often sold individually or by the dozen. Volume sales is the traditional means of sale for crops such as tree fruits, berries, and many vegetables such as beans, greens, peas and tomatoes. Selling by volume speeds up the checkout process: with just a glance, the checkout person can ring up a basket of strawberries, for example, without the time and labor in weighing. Typical containers used for volume pick-your-own selling might include a standard bushel basket, a cardboard bushel box, half-bushel bags, 2-, 4-, or 6-quart cardboard hand baskets, or quart berry boxes.

Volume selling, however, often causes hassles over what constitutes a full container. To help prevent disputes, exhibit at the checkin a model container filled *to the maximum*, and charge accordingly. That way, customers can't overfill the container. If they check out with containers having *less* produce than your model, offer them more. This is much better public relations than asking them to remove excess or charging extra for overfilling.

Selling by weight eliminates the need for providing standardized containers. Weight often is used as a basis for selling fruits or vegetables, especially for any product that lends itself to selling in large containers. Selling by weight allows mix-n-match, in which different varieties are sold for the same price, encouraging more volume and speeding up the checkout. Many growers and customers feel that selling by weight is the fairest system for all concerned.

 ## Pricing

Setting the right prices at pick-your-own is very important, especially if there are several competing operations in the same trading area. Factors to consider in setting prices are last year's prices, prices for other crops this season, competitors' prices, and prices at wholesale markets or in supermarkets. Well-run operations with distinctive or unique features are often able to hold prices moderately higher than those of competitors without losing customers.[6]

Traditionally, pick-your-own prices are considerably less than retail prices. Currently (1992), pick-your-own prices for strawberries are about $1.20 – $1.35 per quart, while grocery store prices for top-quality, locally grown strawberries are about $2.50 per quart. Imported California strawberries range from $1.25 – $2.50 per quart. Pick-your-own prices will be less in rural areas than in suburban metropolitan areas.

According to an article in *American Fruit Grower* (December 1992), pick-your-own strawberry customers are primarily female, mostly from older age brackets and financially comfortable. According to David G. Himelrick, small fruit specialist at Auburn University in Alabama, several surveys of PYO customers suggest that farmers can charge grocery store prices without damaging sales. But they need to emphasize quality and flavor. In two separate surveys of PYO customers, according to the article, only 13 percent of PYO customers said price was the primary reason for choosing PYO. Quality and flavor were far more important in both surveys.

To avoid price squabbles, post prices where they are clearly visible to customers before picking begins. Allow discounts for larger quantities—give

Pick-Your-Own Promotion

YOUR GOAL in promotion is to develop repeat customers. Your own customers should be your *first* concern. "Word-of-mouth" is often reported to be the most important way customers first learn of the farm, and repeat customers are essential. Inform your customers with news about upcoming crops and events. Invite regular members to come ten days before the season's opening for an exclusive picking. Offer a club membership for your frequent customers, with discounts or free bonuses for amounts picked over a specified season total, or offer discounts for each purchase over $30 or $40 worth of products. Discount and bonus programs encourage return visits and larger purchases, and help build awareness and excitement about upcoming crops.

Develop brochures with a map to your farm, hours of operation, crops available for pick-your-own, and a tentative harvest schedule. Include information about other nearby points-of-interest, helpful hints such as how to tell when fruits and vegetables are ripe, weight of a bushel of various produce items, etc.

Develop a mailing list and use direct mail to alert customers at the start of the season. Place a guest book at the checkout, or let customers fill out postcards addressed to themselves, checking the crops for which they would like notification. A chalkboard at the checkout is also a good place to tell customers about upcoming crops and harvest dates.

Use an attractive display with coupons for a season opener. Then run classified ads each week of the season to give customers continual reminders about when and where they can get fresh strawberries or vegetables. Classified ads may be used to alert people about items approaching maturity, give directions to the farm, and state prices and hours of operation. Classified ads will reach people specifically looking for pick-your-own produce. Display ads in the weekly food section of the paper are more effective in reaching people looking for family entertainment.

Radio can be an effective PYO medium, especially when a message needs to be spread fast. If the crop is becoming overripe, for example, well-placed radio spot ads can bring out the weekend crowd. Several short announcements during the day work better than a long spot.

Recorded telephone messages are useful for providing up-to-date information on picking conditions. Start your message on your answering machine with a greeting, the name of your farm and the date; and then give information about what is being picked, hours open, directions to the farm, prices, picking conditions, container information, and another phone number to call if they want to talk with the grower.

Inviting groups of people out to your farm, such as consumer groups, school classes, senior citizens, master gardeners, or food co-ops, etc., is a good way to move your produce in volume. Offer weekday group specials, and send out notices of new varieties useful for canning or freezing.

a price break for ten or more quarts, for example, or more than 25 pounds.

Once set at reasonable figures, PYO prices are usually maintained at the same level throughout the season. Cleanup specials for a last picking where produce is scattered and of uneven quality may justify a reduced price, however. Make this a promotional event so that it does not alter regular pricing policies. Other growers like to keep prices unchanged throughout the year to avoid customers waiting for end-of-season reductions. Or, instead of reducing prices to help clean out your field, offer a free Senior Citizens' Day. Many of your senior friends will show up next season as regular customers.

Supervision

Customers like to pick fresh, neat rows, and this means supervision. Field supervisors assign rows, furnish baskets, and demonstrate how to pick the plants clean. Generally it is easier to *show* people how to pick than to tell them. Establish an orderly system for marking which rows or trees have been picked. You might hand out little flags requesting customers to mark where they finish picking. The number of field supervisors on PYO farms averages about one worker for approximately two acres. Small farms average closer to one worker for each acre.[7]

Use signs to direct customers where to pick up containers, where to pick, how to pick, and to give product prices. This frees your employees from answering the same questions many times. Hand out mimeographed copies of picking instructions with more detailed rules, such as limitations on the size of the produce to be picked; minimum quantities; whether you or the picker supplies containers and whether the picker can take them home; your policy on allowing children to pick; warnings of customer actions that may present a hazard to other customers or damage to property; hours of operation; the method of sale (weight, volume or count); and consumer information.

You can increase sales by having your field staff carry extra picking flats. They might also suggest to pickers that their filled containers be tagged/marked with their name and taken from the field to a cool box and retrieved when the customer is ready to check out. Portable two-way radios enable field workers to keep in contact with wagons or the home base to call for more pickers, containers, or additional help when needed.

PYO is a family activity, and children should be allowed to pick. Children are not only your next generation of customers, but they are your best salesmen, as they will bring Mom and Dad back next time. Encourage children to pick, and let

© Friske Orchards, 11027 Doctor Rd., Charleuoix, MI 49720
(616) 588-6185

parents know that they are responsible for their children. Let the parents know what you expect of children, such as no throwing berries or no running. PYO is a people business, so hire friendly staff persons who love working with people.

Customer service

Customers appreciate good picking conditions: weed-free fields, good yields of high-quality produce, availability of containers (free or for sale), as well as ready-picked produce available for retail sales. Customer courtesies include hand-pulled wagons to carry their bags, carry-out of produce to their cars (especially for the elderly), restrooms and drinking fountains, shade, and a play area or wagon tours for the children.

Never let a customer go home without free recipe handouts or tips on canning, freezing and processing the produce they have just purchased. Ask your home economics extension personnel about appropriate bulletins available. And don't forget to put your name, address and a map to the farm on *everything* you hand out.

Acknowledgments

J.W. "Bill" Courter, University of Illinois, Department of Horticulture (Retired).

Del Mar Yoder, Cooperative Extension, West Virginia University.

The Rural Attraction

Located off I-5 and 15 miles west of Bakers-field, the Al Bussell Ranch attracts two to four thousand people per day in peak season, and is a study in how to farm for fun and profit. In order to entice customers to make a day's outing to the farm, the ranch offers a variety of family-style fun and entertainment, in addition to a broad selection of farm-fresh produce items available in U-Pick or at the farm stand. On weekends, 20 percent of Bussell's business comes from the Los Angeles basin, several hours' drive away. "People want to get out of the smog and traffic and out to the farm," comments Al.

With his easy-going, good-natured humor, it is easy to see how Al Bussell got into entertainment farming. "I used to wait on customers, but I got myself in trouble by smarting off too much," he relates. "Awhile back, we had a lady looking at peaches. Some of the fruit was $7 a box, and some of it was $10 a box. She asked what the difference was, and I told her 'about $3!' She failed to see the humor of that!"

THERE'S GOLD TO BE discovered in good old-fashioned country fun these days. Haul out the scarecrows, scatter some pumpkins around the barn, and you'll be amazed at how many city folks are eager to escape the asphalt jungle for a fun, family visit to your farm! Busy urbanites are seeking places to go for a weekend family outing, where the kids can feed the goats, or find out how bean plants grow.

Tehrune Orchards, near Princeton, New Jersey, draws some 350,000 visitors per year, who come to purchase or pick apples or peaches, and for the farm's many festivals, classes and farm tours. "The main attraction for people coming here," Gary Tehrune explains, "is the farm itself. People come here rather than to the supermarket because they enjoy the farm experience."

Many products and enterprises can be added to a roadside market or pick-your-own (PYO) operation to attract and keep customers, including a bakery or restaurant, festivals and contests, hay-rides, farm vacations and crafts. Rural recreation farming often offers more potential income than "food farming" because customers can almost never get too much of it! As California PYO owner Al Bussell says, "We're in the entertainment business now."

Turning your farm into a rural attraction is not something you can do overnight, however. Start with simple things, like adding a shaded picnic area to your roadside stand or PYO operation. Resist the temptation to herd people through one attraction after another. Remember that the main desire of people escaping from the city is simply the chance to relax.

Farmers who operate rural attractions put lots of time and energy into entertaining their customers. You must like people and be a showman! Since meeting the farmer is part of the attraction for your customers, you should be available to them. Although rural attractions are often quite profitable, they require additional employees, increased in-

---

Let's Pretend!
How One Farm Has Fun

AMIDST THE business of making money in recreational farming, don't forget that it's meant to be *fun*—for the farmers as well as customers. The Pumpkin Patch at the Phillips Ranch near Lodi, California, is a good example. It was developed over 20 years as a labor of love by owners Don and Jeanne Phillips. Admission for school tours is two dollars per child, which includes a free pumpkin and refreshments.

When children come to the Pumpkin Patch, it's showtime. "We tell the children that everything is make-believe . . . 'Let's just pretend and we're all going to have some fun'," explains Jeanne. She introduces children to the wonders of the Pumpkin Patch: Raggedy Ann & Andy; the Friendly Monster Man who chases the Dragon (who is intent on eating the pumpkins) away at night; the Sunflower Princess who grows in the sunflower forest; Peppy Popcorn in the popcorn patch; real-life tom-toms in Indian Village that the children can beat on; the 50-foot long (hay bale) pirate's tunnel; as well as Captain Hook and Peg-leg Pete, who have hidden a treasure chest somewhere in the straw tunnel maze. Each of the 22 full-size papier-mache figures in the patch has his or her own story, which is usually told in rhyme. "Children love those stories," says Jeanne. "And they go back and recite the rhymes to their parents."

Finally, there is an enormous haystack. "You wouldn't *believe* how popular this is with children," says Jeanne. "Maybe a thousand children a day will climb up on that haystack!"

surance coverage, and—depending upon where you live—additional licenses and permits.

Themes and activities

As farms are disappearing near urban areas, people have a great desire to recall what they remember grandfather's farm looking like. The closer your farm resembles Old MacDonald's Farm, the better. Don't forget that the storybook version of rural life is a fantasy without the mud and sweat of real farm life. Your farm needs to be clean, neat and attractive.

Popular themes and activities at rural attractions include farm tours, nature trails, train and hay rides, hay bales or corn stalks, pumpkin patches, antique and craft shows, petting zoos, food booths, apple butter cooking, country bands, pumpkin land and pumpkin painting, scarecrow making, museums and displays of antique farm equipment. Farm animals are a "must" for children. Many customers get to know them by name. Families come out to feed the geese, or to see if Rosie the goat has had her new kid yet.

As time goes on, you'll need to rotate attractions at your farm to provide the variety that keeps folks coming back. In addition to an ongoing selection of farm attractions and fresh farm produce, there's nothing like special weekend themes or festivals to keep customers eager to visit your farm. Variety is also essential to attract customers coming long distances. People are willing to drive one, two or three hours—*if* there are enough attractions to make a worthwhile family outing.

Possible recreational activities are limited only by your imagination and creativity. At Yarnell's Farm Market in Westerville, Ohio, for example, customers not only pick the pumpkins, they paint them in the "paint shop." For a fee, customers are given a brush, a mini-pumpkin, acrylic paints, and old long-sleeve shirts for paint smocks. In the scarecrow-making area, customers are provided step-by-step instructions for making scarecrows, as well as materials such as rags, string, old ties and panty hose, for stuffing full of rags. For a supply of panty hose irregulars write Sue Lynn Textile, Inc., Highway 49 N., Box 516, Haw River, NC 27258; (919) 578-0871.

At the Nita Gizdich Ranch near Watsonville, California, several early-day gas engines are hooked up to run various implements, such as an old washing machine, or machines to grind corn, saw wood, mill flour or pump water. "People are fascinated by the old farm operations," says Nita.

Farm vacations are a variation of rural recreational farming: people pay you to come out and experience rural life. Some may even want to work and learn on your farm. Don't demand too much from your city cousins in the way of labor, however; a few hours of picking apples is sufficient.

Another idea is to "rent a tree" for the season. Figure what the seasonal bounty of the tree will be, then charge the family about 25 percent less than your roadside stand prices. Your profit won't be so much on the tree itself, but on helping make loyal, repeat customers.

Contests

Contests are a good way to arouse interest, create publicity and increase business. Keep it simple: pumpkin painting, going through the cornstalk maze, apple peeling, guessing how many apples are in the barrel, a pie bake-off, or a recipe contest centered around the product(s) you're promoting.

The king of farm market contests is the International Cherry Pit Spitting Competition at the Tree-Mendus Fruit Farm in Eau Claire, Michigan. The annual contest attracts thousands of spectators and is covered by many major U.S. as well as overseas newspapers and TV networks. Popular radio personalities volunteer to work as "spit by spit" announcers, and the *Guinness Book of World Records* recognizes the current world record pit spitter, Rick ("Pellet Gun") Krause, as the record holder with a distance of 63 feet, 2 inches.

Another innovative contest is held at Huber's Family Farm, Orchard and Restaurant near Borden, Indiana. With a different theme each year, such as Thanksgiving, Halloween, American History, or Scarecrows, art class students are invited to build papier-mache, life-size characters. Entries are exhibited in the farm's 50-by-100 foot barn. The public and the media flock to see the exhibit!

The key with contests is good public relations. Give lots of prizes so that nearly everyone can be a winner—a bag of apples to everyone who participates, for example. To protect yourself from charges of favoritism, and to gain free publicity, bring in outside, celebrity judges. Make sure the rules are carefully drawn, and that both participants and judges understand them thoroughly.

Festivals

Fun on the farm means festivals. Farm festivals often attract thousands of people, providing golden opportunities to attract new customers and generate sales. You can also use these occasions to promote your products and market as well as upcoming events at your farm. The key to using farm events for promotion is to send out news releases telling about the event, with enough details to make people want to come. Mail invitations, hand out flyers, and distribute announcement posters.

Festivals can center around a commodity such as corn, peaches or strawberries, have a seasonal focus, or center on events such as blossom time. Fall harvest festival themes are traditionally the most popular seasonal theme, with pumpkins and sweet corn, as well as ornamental gourds and squashes, apples and autumn nuts. Spring is

Al Bussell, Al Bussell Ranch, Bakersfield, California

blossom time: promote U-Pick, cut flowers, pre-made bouquets and tree blossoms. Summer is the time to promote your U-Pick produce, as each crop ripens. Winter is the time to promote cross-country skiing, sleigh rides with horses, holly, pine cones, fresh wreaths, fresh-roasted chestnuts and bundles of firewood and kindling.

When things are slow, think of a special event or festival. It doesn't have to be big to perk things up. Tehrune Orchards has a springtime Kite Flying Festival, for example. Other ideas might include Heritage Days, in which you can promote special recipes from the past, or Canning or Freezing Know-How Days, when you can promote bulk-buying of produce.

Make festivals a regular, ongoing promotion. From May through October, the Al Bussell Ranch hosts dozens of promotional events that help attract customers, such as the "Berry Good Weekend" featuring free whipping cream with strawberry purchases; the Fresh-Fruit Ice Cream Freeze Off, with the winning recipes published in the newspapers; the Fourth of July Weekend, with Uncle Sam walking around and entertaining people; the Great California Tomato Weigh-In; Johnny Appleseed Day; a Senior Citizens' Day; and the Jack-O-Lantern Jamboree that includes a scarecrow contest and magic show. The media especially enjoy the scarecrow contest because it provides interesting photographs.

To create a major happening, the Al Bussell Ranch schedules several attractions simultaneously. Al looks for special interest groups to tie in with to create a special event. During the Memorial Day weekend, for example, a TV station might be on hand to co-sponsor a cooking contest. Meanwhile, a dancing club puts on a square dance demonstration; a farm-equipment dealership co-sponsors a pedal-tractor race for children; and an antique car club puts on a display of antique cars.

If you need help in putting on a festival, get together with two or three other farm families. One might raise strawberries, another apples, while another does pottery, etc., so that together you can have a "Country Farm" festival.

Another way to expand your possibilities is to subcontract out some of your activities: for example, horse or sleigh rides to someone who owns horses, or skiing to a ski rental operation. Bring in a local dairyman to sell dairy products, and recruit

responsible high school students to help park cars on weekends.

Try to arrange most co-promotions on a percentage basis, so that both you and the subcontractors assume some risks. This works well with crafts booths, for example. For free services provided to your customers such as wagon rides or entertainment, you may have to pay subcontractors a flat fee. (See also Chapter 30, "Group Festivals: A Checklist.")

Educational tours

The crowds coming to your farm week after week present a unique opportunity to educate nonfarm folks about farming and the necessity of preserving farm values, clean air and open land—and you can promote your farm while doing it. Open up your farm to garden club tours, church groups, senior citizens, school children and tourists.

School tours especially are an investment in the future of farming! In addition to providing a valuable education for children, school tours are also a good way to promote your farm. The children who come often bring back their families. Admission price should not be exorbitant. Charge a sufficient admission price ($2.50, for example) to provide the staff, equipment, demonstrations and free samples necessary to do a good job and make a profit from the enterprise.

At John and Jean Coulter's farm near Westville, Indiana, the Coulters host as many as 300 school children a day during the last week of September and the first three weeks of October. The Coulters are quick to admit that hosting school kids is good promotion for their business. "A child can be here in the morning and by night come back with his parents and neighbors," says Jean. But there's more to the tours than that. "You can't put a price tag on the smile of a preschooler who has just picked his own pumpkin," says John.

To set up a school tour, schedule reservations with teachers; then send them a confirmation letter, confirming time, date and the number of students, teachers and parents arriving. Enclose procedures: when to arrive, where to park, where to go, how to pay and what is included in the tour. Also include a map to your location. Instruct the teacher to pay before the tour begins, and if using purchase orders, make sure you have a signed receipt and the teacher's paper work. Prepare for handicapped children.

School tour activities might include pick-your-own (make sure a friendly employee is on hand to give picking instructions); a trip to your farm's fantasy land or special children's area; a wagon ride; and an educational demonstration or talk. Talk about the produce or plants the children are taking home, and how to use or care for them.

Provide some free take-home items such as a pumpkin, gourd, ear of corn, etc., as well as farm coloring books or refrigerator door magnets with your farm name and logo on them. (Check with teachers beforehand to make sure what you give out is useful and safe.) Make sure each child leaves with a newsletter of information about upcoming activities, or a brochure about your farm, and a coupon redeemable at your market. Follow up with a letter to the parents thanking them for allowing their child to come to your farm. Coordinate with the children's teachers, or your local farm bureau or extension agent, to develop ongoing ways to weave agricultural lessons into the school curriculum.

Adults aren't a whole lot different. As Pam and Gary Mount explain, one of the most popular activities for customers at Tehrune Orchards is simply watching the apple-washing and sorting operations. "Just show them what you do each day on the farm and they think it's special!" says Pam.

Look for other local ag-related institutions or businesses with whom you can conduct cross-promotions, classes or demonstrations. Your extension agent might come out to give demonstrations on canning, drying or freezing, or you might invite a local chef to give a demonstration on ways to use your products.

At the Museum Orchard at Tree-Mendus Fruit Farm near Eau Claire, Michigan, owner Herb Teichmann loves to educate customers about some of the 170 unusual apple varieties he grows. He regularly conducts applebutter-making and cider-making demonstrations, as well as demonstrations on preserving by drying. "Once people watch these demonstrations, they want to buy apples," he says.

Business

Charging for activities. Some growers consider farm attractions as a way to draw crowds to help move the products they sell—an important consideration for perishable crops that need to be sold quickly. The profit, they point out, is made on the products sold at the farm stand, such as produce, pies and refreshments, or complementary products, such as strawberry hullers, pectin, or jams and jellies.

As Joe Huber says: "We make our money selling pick-your-own, or at the farm stand or restaurant, and we don't charge for the hayrides, tours, or use of playground equipment. We raised five kids ourselves, and we know that our customers can't afford a lot of extra money on entertainment. But we figure if thousands of people are spending even five or six dollars a day, we can make a little money!"

Generally, however, the trend is toward charging for events, and including a certain amount of produce as part of the price of admission. This ensures that you make a profit on each attraction. The idea behind this is that it is cheaper to give away products than time and resources. It costs only pennies a pound to grow a pumpkin, for example, so it is good public relations to give a pumpkin to each customer who pays two dollars to enter pumpkin land. Or on school tours, you might charge each child $2.50, and—after they have completed the farm tour, wagon ride and educational event—let them each pick a pumpkin and an ear of corn.

Rental Agreements:
Another Source of Income

With "Rent-A-Tree" agreements the customer pays a specified sum at the beginning of the season in return for the yield of a certain tree or row in the field. Generally, the grower does all the cultural operations to produce the product and supplies harvesting equipment, and the customer does the harvesting. This marketing method entails reduced harvest labor expense, but involves increased effort in keeping records of individual trees and in modifying cultivation practices to satisfy customers. The Rent-A-Tree idea could also be used for a row of strawberries, tomatoes, or other produce.

One of the appeals of Rent-A-Tree for consumers is that the renter becomes in effect, part of the farming operation. Pride in being a country-gentleman grower and landowner is attractive to many. Tree rental fees can be calculated from the expected production of the tree when sold at going retail prices, or regular pick-your-own prices.

A Rent-A-Tree contract should state what the grower will do regarding tree care, grounds maintenance, etc., as well as the rights, privileges and restrictions the renter must adhere to. The agreement should plainly state that no specific amount or quality of fruit is guaranteed. Weather risks are inherent in farming and are therefore assumed by the renter. Include hours of the day and days of the week the orchard or farm is open for visiting. Also include specific areas where picnicking, hiking and other activities are permitted and the areas where visitors are not allowed to go. Provide an identification card for each tree renter, corresponding with the number on his or her tree.

Some growers use the Rent-A-Tree idea as an added attraction in recreational farming. The renting family is free to visit their tree in the orchard, and use the picnic area or wooded area with hiking trails, as often as they desire. Add on a "farm privilege factor" for the recreational use of your farm. This privilege can also be sold separately on a yearly basis similar to membership in a country club.

In a Rent-A-Garden arrangement, you rent space to urban gardeners. Rent-A-Garden offers savings in food cost, fresh produce, a healthful recreational activity, and "I grew it myself" satisfaction for the gardener. Optional services may include basic land preparation, basic fertilizer application, and some seasonal cultivation and irrigation. Draw up a written contract to clarify rights and duties of both parties.

Yet another example of creative attraction pricing is that of Ann Tennis, of the Country Mill Farm near Charlotte, Michigan. The farm has a three-car, rubber-wheel, 100-foot train to carry customers out to the apple orchard. Customers buy "tickets" to the train ride by purchasing a plastic bag which holds up to five pounds of apples. Cost is $2.50 per bag, and two people can share a bag. Customers may fill the bag up as much or as little as they like. Many people, coming mainly for the train ride, fill the bag only partially full, while others purchase extra bags for additional amounts. Everybody's happy: customers because they get *both* a train ride and apples for their money, and farm owners, because they've sold lots of apples at a good price. "The train is a great attraction," says Ann. "We often hear kids pleading with their parents to ride the train, even if they don't want the apples."

Since it is difficult to get free publicity if you charge for everything, give free admission to your festival with some events free, such as hayrides and children's playground, while charging a fee for other attractions.

Rent facilities. Develop another profit center for your farm by inviting companies and corporations, clubs or churches to use your farm for picnics, meetings, reunions, shows and contests. Not only does this make you money on the event, it also attracts many first-time customers. Many groups are reluctant to pay very much for facilities only, so include activities and/or food as part of your rental agreement.

If you have a beautiful farmstead, take panoramic slides of your farm and send them to advertising agencies, inviting them to use your farm for video-filming or photo-taking. Matarazzo Farms, near Belvidere, New Jersey, hosted a Jolly Green Giant commercial which netted a nifty $2,000 for one-half day's use of the farm.

Promotion

Word-of-mouth will make or break your rural recreation business. Develop an image as a good, clean, fun place to bring the family. Your place should be neat and picture-perfect, like a Currier & Ives painting. That's the image of the farm your customers want to visit!

Your employees, since they are the chief contact customers have with your farm, are your farm's foremost advertisement. Cashiers and field supervisors should have smiles on their faces, be knowledgeable about your products, and be trained in the niceties of customer relations, including handling complaints.

Rural recreation farms enjoy, perhaps more than other forms of farm marketing, a special advertising opportunity—free publicity. At the Starlight Strawberry Festival in Indiana, for example, each grower submits a gallon of his or her best strawberries for judging. The winning entries are auctioned off. Several years ago, the first-place gallon of strawberries sold for $9,400! The proceeds went to a local charity. This has become a major publicity event for the Starlight Fruit and Vegetable Growers Association. "We have lots of gimmicks to get into the media," president Joe Huber explains. "Several years ago we built the world's longest strawberry shortcake—762 feet! Events like this pull so many people from the community, and they come back to your farm throughout the season."

Invite a photographer to take pictures of visitors with your farm in the background—it's amazing how many people want pictures of their children at the farm! Invite a magician to put on a show or a nutritionist to do a demonstration on Saturday mornings or on festival days. Invite the mayor. Invite your customers to enter a picking contest. Paint, carve and decorate fruits and vegetables for lavish displays. Video-tape events and submit them to local cable TV networks for additional free publicity.

Opening day weekend (or your Grand Opening) should be special. Spend time and effort to make it a success. Create some excitement—invite the governor, and send him or her up in a hot-air balloon! Make your grand opening a smash—it sets the tone for the whole season!

Look for opportunities for co-promotions with other businesses, service clubs or organizations. Co-promotions help everyone. Businesses get exposure and a place to advertise their services or products; service clubs raise money which they can reinvest in the local community; and the farm benefits from the added attraction the event creates. By linking up as a threesome with a local newspaper, radio or TV station and a local charity organization, your chances of attracting media coverage multiply. The media feel that co-sponsoring an event with a charity organization helps upgrade their public image.

Acknowledgments

Bob Cobbledick, OMAF, Vineland Station, Ontario, Canada.

Kelso Wessel, professor, agricultural economics, Ohio State University.

Subscription Farming/ Community Supported Agriculture

Subscription farming

How would you like to sell your produce by having your customers order, and sometimes pay, before the first seed is planted? They would come out to the farm to help you plant, care for, and pick the crop, and then thank you for letting them do this! It's called "subscription farming."

Subscription farming sells produce like Rodale sells magazines. City folks or rural nonfarmers sign up in advance to buy a share of your farm's produce for the coming season. Payment can be made in monthly, quarterly, semiannual or annual installments. Customers can come out to the farm to help plant and pick the crop; have it delivered to a central pickup point; or, for a higher price, have it delivered to their doorstep. In order to increase the variety you offer your customers and increase your sales, you might sell additional items from neighboring farmers or from the wholesale produce center. Customers can be found through newspaper ads or flyer-inserts, or through notices on bulletin boards inviting interested consumers to send for a free brochure or come to a meeting in which you explain your concept. You might find customers simply by knocking on doors. Show them color pictures from a seed catalog, your brochure, or a picture scrapbook of your farm. Bring along an attractive basket of fresh produce from your farm and hand out free samples.

Instead of selling by prepaid shares, Lynn Coody, a retired subscription farmer from Cottage Grove, Oregon, sent out questionnaires to her customers in January, requesting them to estimate the number of pounds of each product they would purchase each week during the season both for fresh use and for canning or preserving. Depending on the product, items were specified by the pound or by the number of the items they wanted. Conversion sheets made it easy for customers to estimate their needs for canning of various items. Customers then paid for the product upon delivery. "People really did live up to their agreements," Coody recalls.

Here are a few variations of subscription farming:

Clientele membership club

Families pay a membership fee for the privilege of coming to your farm and picking produce when it is ready. The customers pay by the pound for what they pick. You get a committed group of consumers to buy your produce and you get money upfront. All the money you make after expenses is yours; you also assume all the risks of crop failure—your members don't share this risk with you.[1]

As popularized by the book *How to Make $100,000 a Year Farming 25 Acres*, by Booker T. Whatley, the "Whatley Plan" involves growing at least ten high-value crops maturing at different times to provide a year-round cash flow. The crops are sold to city folks ("farm club members") who, for

> *Our goal is to put the community back in farming, and the farmer back in the community.*
> —Andy Lee, *Backyard Market Gardening*

$25 a year, can come out to pick their own produce at 40 percent below supermarket prices.

Food buyers' clubs

Again, families pay an annual membership fee to join, usually $25 to $50. The grower takes the food to a central receiving point for pickup by the club members. Rather than purchasing a seasonal share, the club members usually fill out an order for each week.[2] A variation of a food buyers' club is selling prepackaged bags of produce to groups such as food co-ops or businesses.

Home delivery

This is a time-consuming way to market, yet house-to-house delivery has intriguing possibilities, especially for products that can be delivered on a regular schedule. Health and travel restrictions, as well as stay-at-home convenience, make many consumers willing to pay extra for home delivery. On a larger scale, you'll need a computer to keep track of individual orders and delivery schedules.

Baskets of fresh-picked, organic and tree- or vine-ripened fruit delivered to customers' doorsteps in the morning make an attractive offer! Add a personal touch by tucking in a small bouquet of fresh-cut flowers! A variation of home delivery is a "Monthly Subscription" mail order package: customers receive a gift basket each month full of farm-fresh produce items.

To speed delivery, it helps to find similar types of customers in a centralized area. "Nine-to-five" working couples, for example, would all be home pretty much the same time each evening or Saturday mornings. You might work out a plan to leave the grocery delivery in a box on the porch, in the garage or just inside the kitchen door. Since the produce is fresh, and delivered quickly, it will resist wilting for several hours as long as it is in the shade. Naturally, you will charge more for this

home delivery service. It's more work than if the customers were coming to your garden and picking up their weekly share. You may be able to trade shares with someone who will do the deliveries for you.[3]

Community supported agriculture

With "Community Supported Agriculture" (CSA), customer involvement is greater than with subscription farming. Members purchase "shares" of the farm's harvest, accepting less if a crop is damaged or fails. This is different than with conventional farming where the farmer bears all the risk. Once or twice a week mature crops are harvested and divided up among the shareholders. Usually the payment is several hundred dollars and the family receives enough vegetables to last them throughout the season and sometimes for winter storage. The share is payable before the season starts, in one or several installments.[4] As with subscription farming, members get a regular supply of fresh produce, while the growers pre-sell their crop before the growing season starts. If shareholders come out to the farm to pick up their produce, prices are usually from 25 to 50 percent less than retail prices for similar quality produce. Prices may be close to or above retail if the farmer makes deliveries to drop-off points or if home deliveries are made.

CSA practitioners hail the concept as a way to revitalize the deteriorating family farm, to promote organic agriculture and to help consumers create their own food systems in the increasingly impersonal and detached world of agribusiness and supermarkets.

Jan Vandertuin, one of the pioneer CSA organizers in this country, describes CSA as a way of life rather than a way to make a lot of money. "With CSA, the emphasis is on community. The consumers feel they are owners. Instead of handing over ownership and operations to the farmer, CSA brings people together around one thing, food. Business is almost secondary."

Currently there are an estimated 400 CSA projects in the U.S., but at the rate they are multiplying, there should be about 1,000 CSA's by the year 2000, according to CSA pioneer Robyn Van En. According to Walter Ehrhardt, who with his wife Sylvia and daughter Beth, runs a CSA at their farm in Knoxville, Maryland, "I really think this is the wave of the future."

CSA advantages

In addition to getting a fresh weekly supply of homegrown produce at a modest cost and the opportunity to help support local farms, shareholders have a say in what varieties are planted and how the plants are grown (organically, for example). Generally, CSA's find that consumers are less concerned about price than they are about freshness, nutritional content, freedom from chemical contamination and supporting their local grower.[5]

Since customers pay in advance, this guarantees the farmer a market for everything he or she grows. Advance payment creates working capital at planting time so the farmer can purchase equipment and supplies as needed. The farmer gets a paycheck weekly through the season, and at some CSA farms the farmer also receives health and life insurance, vacation and sick days. Upfront money means the farmer can devote more time and energy to growing. CSA's also allow for better off-season planning. By allowing the farmer to know ahead of time what he's going to be able to sell, the farmer is better able to match planting to a pre-sold market and thus he can plan better during the off-season and figure what and how much to plant.

A committed consumer group providing a guaranteed income lends financial credibility in case the farmer needs to seek a loan or get a mortgage. CSA arrangements also spread out the risks of farming. At the outset, shareholders sign contracts with the farmer acknowledging that inclement weather, insects or other factors may mean lower-than-anticipated yields. But if there is a crop loss, instead of a single farmer absorbing a $3,000 loss, 100 shareholders would lose $30 each.[6]

CSA and subscription farming also have similar advantages to U-Pick, such as reduced labor costs. Consumers often help with production, harvesting and delivery. By tailoring production to fit the market, crop waste is dramatically reduced. Containers are reused until they wear out. Consumers return organic wastes to be composted.

Produce need not meet market cosmetic standards, so little is discarded.

Finally, both CSA and subscription farming offer an urban-rural link that many feel is the soul of community supported agriculture. As one subscription farmer said: "I did not anticipate the enthusiasm which would be generated by offering my town-dwelling customers an opportunity to come to a farm and learn directly about the sources of their food. My subscription marketing system satisfied the need for good, organically grown food, and the longing that many Americans experience to live in the country and have a part in the production of their food."

Another grower remarked, "We get a real kick out of knowing who'll be enjoying the fruits of our labors. It makes raising crops a lot more sensible if one actually knows they will be enjoyed and appreciated."

Special challenges

One special challenge with CSA's is to educate consumers about the delights of eating in-season produce. Although not being able to eat sweet corn or tomatoes in January may cause some grumbling among customers used to supermarket shopping, the quality and freshness of fresh-picked produce will win them over to the wisdom of eating from the table of the earth.

Another CSA challenge lies in management. Don't commit to more than you can manage. CSA's or subscription farms can become a management nightmare if done on too large a scale. It's quite a task keeping up with all the different maturing varieties and packing dozens of individual orders.

You have to calculate yields, coordinate deliveries, and keep production and marketing records in much greater detail than with most other farming operations.

Subscription farming also requires someone with lots of people skills. There may be a lot of traffic at the farm with customers coming to help or to pick up their shares. The CSA consumer coordinator, for example, needs to have both people and managing skills.

One way to handle visitors is to set up certain days of the week or month as marketing or work days, and ask members to make an appointment if they need to come at other times. CSA's take a lot of time to deal with people, especially at the beginning of the harvest season when you need to show newcomers how to harvest crops that they've never harvested. "At our farm," Lynn Coody reported, "we were harvesting over 70 vegetables and 12 fruits, and it takes a lot of time to teach people how to harvest those crops."

If, however, you sometimes feel farm-bound and desire more people contact than farming usually allows, CSA may be the ticket for you.

What to grow

Selection of crops and varieties is one of the most important aspects of CSA's. As in any specialty market, you must study what your customers' needs are and fill that market. If most of your clients have backyard gardens, for example, you might plant items like pie pumpkins, winter squash, eggplant and honeydew melons that home gardeners don't like to grow because of space requirements or the need for extra tools or skills. You might also plant storage items that people purchase in large quantities like potatoes, garlic and onions, as well as preserving items like tomatoes, corn, beans, apples and hot peppers.

Select only those crops you feel confident in growing. Start planning ahead by planting trial crops and keeping careful note of yields so as to be able to figure exactly how much you'll need to plant for customers. Keep meticulous records of production and yields each year; this will help you plan for the next year.

Send a questionnaire to customers between seasons, asking their preferences and needs for both fresh and preserving items. The question-

naire also helps determine what additional crops you might add to make a profit.

Try to offer as much variety as possible at your pickup site so customers don't have to make a number of stops to obtain their food supply. People are used to supermarket shopping and finding everything they need for dinner from salad lettuce to dessert. One way to increase product variety is to network with other growers in your area to provide products for the customers that you don't offer yourself. If you grow vegetables, for example, consider supplementing your product selection by cooperating with a grower who has maple syrup or a vineyard, etc. The exchange may be in barter or trade, or the supplementary producer may pay the CSA a percentage for marketing.[7]

Customers usually prefer a longer season of freshly harvested crops. For example, it is preferable to have a steady supply of broccoli over many weeks rather than a huge amount all at once.

Since it takes a few years to refine your estimates of your production and customers' needs, don't commit all your produce volume to subscription farming at first. Develop additional markets such as health food or grocery stores, or to a wholesaler or a farmers market to provide an outlet for extra produce.

CSA plan

After figuring costs and a reasonable salary for yourself as the farmer, next figure the cost of shares and how many subscribers or farm members you'll need to meet that amount: 1) Estimate the number of participants; 2) Figure the costs to feed them; 3) Figure the average share per person; and 4) Figure how much production the land can ecologically sustain. If few members are available to join, each member will have to pay more per share. Share memberships usually range from $250 to $1,000 annually. Often, two households will share an allotment. It's best to encourage all or at least partial payment upfront so that members help support startup and indicate their commitment to the concept.

At some CSA farms, part of the share price is an agreement that members work a certain number of hours each season. Shareholders' help will be particularly welcome for labor-intensive planting and harvesting. Such chores can be turned into wonderful social events, allowing members of the community to come together to visit with and entertain one another.[8]

You might also offer shareholders a choice of summer, winter or full-season shares. This allows home gardeners, for example, to supplement homegrown produce with a winter share of storage crops.

Distribution & delivery

Some projects hire someone to distribute the food; some farms do it themselves; and in some projects the consumers are organized to take turns on a volunteer basis. Some CSA projects grow a certain amount of each crop to fulfill the requirements for pre-sold shares, with surplus sold through either wholesale or other direct marketing outlets such as farmers markets. Other projects determine approximate share per family by taking the total daily harvest and dividing it by the number of shares, marking the totals on a blackboard. Shareholders then weigh and pack their own produce according to their shares. A surplus table is provided where people can put back what they don't want. Other customers may pick items they can use, or the surplus left may be donated to a soup kitchen or convalescent home.

If it is not practical for consumers to come to the farm to pick up their shares of produce, one or more drop-off points can be arranged as a regular delivery site. The farmer can deliver prebagged shares to a central receiving point such as a church or community center. Other projects simply take all the produce to a distribution shed and let people take what they need. "This may sound daring," comments Ron Shouldice, executive di-

How To Start A CSA

1. *Determine feasibility.* Find out how a CSA might be helpful to consumers in your area. Talk to others who are interested and plan a community meeting to spread the word. Ask yourself the following questions: How much land is available? What is the population within a five-mile radius? How much labor is available? How much of your time and capital can you spend? Is this the marketing scenario that interests you most?[9]

2. *Determine local interest.* If there is enough positive information in your preliminary survey, talk to people in your community, or try an informal market survey with a brief questionnaire to see what the interest is within the community. How many families can you count on to join and support the farm? Ask for input from poten-

tial members. Give people a list of vegetables that you feel confident you can grow, asking them to mark which varieties they might want, with approximate quantities, and their suggestions for additional items. Additional questions you might include in your informal survey are the number of family members and ages (this will help determine consumption patterns); days they would like to pick up produce (plan on two days or evenings each week, so you can keep produce picked regularly); and if they can suggest friends or relatives who might be interested. Invite people to call you for more information, and when they do, invite them to attend an informational meeting.[10]

3. *Spread the word.* Word-of-mouth is the primary way to let people know about your CSA project. Develop flyers and bro-

chures explaining your idea and take them to the media for free press coverage. Leave copies at health food stores, co-op markets, alternative health facilities, medical clinics, day care centers, etc. Contact social and service groups, emphasizing the CSA's positive social aspects such as land preservation, annual field trips for schools or senior citizens, etc. Emphasize also that your food will be locally grown, fresh and chemical-free.

4. *Set up an informational meeting.* Once you have enough people interested in learning more about your project, invite them to an informational meeting. (Make this a potluck open house!) Explain the concept of CSA, give a farm tour and show slides of your growing methods. Emphasize the benefits members receive, such as the nutritional value of fresh produce, and the superior taste of home-

rector with the Biodynamic Association, "but this has worked consistently well for years. People are considerate of each other and usually the problem is that people don't take enough." Some subscription farms even make personal door-to-door deliveries of the week's vegetables. If you do this, be sure to charge extra for this service, and bring home the customers' compostable material!

Proposal

The *Proposal* introduces prospective customers to the CSA concept, and contains a Commitment Form if they wish to join. Printed as a short flyer or brochure, the Proposal contains sections such as "The Concept," explaining the CSA idea; "The Plan," listing types of memberships available including price, volume and contents of each share, harvest and distribution, work/trade options; "The

Farm," a description of the farm, or, if no land has been purchased, your land requirements; "The Farmer," or a job description if you are looking for a farmer; "Budget," showing salaries, equipment and land costs for the year to show how share-prices are calculated; and a "Commitment Form." For examples of CSA Proposals, send for Robyn Van En's handbook on how to start a CSA (see "Chapter Resources").

Community involvement

The rewards of CSA, for many CSA farmers, are a rich, community-oriented lifestyle; the right livelihood of producing healthy and nutritious food; and the excitement of a social experiment. "The real key is to connect production with the consumer so they can take responsibility for their food," notes Steve

---

How To Start A CSA continued...

grown, fresh foods. Also emphasize price savings with charts that show what the average family will spend weekly for vegetables and fruits, comparing that amount to what shareholders might pay at a CSA farm. Discuss the importance of preserving rural farmland and the need to keep the community's food buying dollars in the local economy. Show the video "It's Not Just About Vegetables" (see "Chapter Resources" for ordering information).

5. *Form a Core Group.* A group of three to eight committed individuals should meet to set policies and solve problems that arise. The Core Group makes sure that the food is being distributed and is responsible for collecting payments, preparing the budget, paying the farmers, dealing with legal issues, and finding more consumers as required.

6. *Draw up a proposal and budget.* This document is an outline of the concept and its underlying philosophy, and an estimate of capital and operating costs, plus a list of intended crops and approximate yields. Distribute it to the persons who have attended your informational meetings and throughout the community to find shareholders.

7. *The Budget* is a detailed expectation of expenses for the coming year, including costs incurred in running the farm. Be sure to budget a sufficient amount to provide a decent living salary for the farmer.

8. *Acquire land, buildings and equipment.* In many cases the farmer already has land, but in some new projects people in the consumer group have land which they may offer to the project. It's not easy to move a farm, so long-term land security

is essential! A community land trust might be set up, or if that's not possible, try to lease the land with an option to buy, or seek a long-term lease.

9. *Obtain shareholders.* The consumers' group includes everyone, including the farmers. There are groups as small as 10 households or (in Japan) 1,000 families. The consumer group is comprised of a cross-section of local, interested people from all walks of life and income levels. Shareholder requirements vary greatly. Some projects honor food stamps. Some expect shareholders to help with harvest and bagging on a rotating basis or to help on potluck/workdays, etc. Other projects may not require work from the consumers, but leave the farm open for people to visit and volunteer their services, either free or as labor-trade in payment of their "share."

Home Delivery: Back to the Future?

HMMM. . .WHAT would you like for supper? Rouge de Hiver lettuce or Arugula salad greens? Simply dial the number for "At Your Doorstep" Farms, say your BankaFoodCard number into the phone or punch it into your computer, then place your order. A sales rep is on the phone in an instant to a UPS-like delivery truck, and your salad greens are at your doorstep within hours.

According to Michael Norton, owner of Kona Kai Farms, the celebrated one-half-acre farm in Berkeley, California, that grosses nearly $200,000 a year selling salad greens to restaurants, home delivery of produce may be the wave of the future. . . again. "Doesn't it make sense for one truck to go to 100 houses, instead of a hundred cars going to one central market?" he asks. Michael's concept is not a new one. Jewel Tea Company used to make deliveries of both produce and grocery store goods until the early '60s, primarily in the Chicago area.

With the proliferation of computers and cellular phones enabling instant communication with delivery trucks, Michael Norton feels that the time is ripe once again for home produce delivery. Michael also points to another factor: time has become a valuable enough commodity nowadays that many people would rather not spend it shopping.

Michael claims that the food distribution network he hopes to set up at his Berkeley location is applicable in any city. Five to ten small growing plots could be located in a city, each supplying nearby restaurants and distributors with their most perishable foods, such as edible flowers or salad greens. A larger plot on less expensive acreage in the nearby countryside could serve as a central supply for foods with longer natural shelf life, such as herbs and root crops.

"What would really get this going, though," Michael enthuses, as he slices into a freshly picked Chioggia beet, "is that once people get a taste of this, they'd realize that the fresh food they could get from such a delivery system requires a lot less time in preparation in order to taste good. Just boil these beets and they're delicious!"

Decater, who with his wife Gloria operates a CSA farm near Covelo, California. "We try to have field days at least twice a year where people can come and work on the farm or just come and get a sense of what the life here is. We like having that connection with them so they can think of the farm as *their* place."

Keep an eye out for opportunities to encourage members to be personally involved in your CSA project. One way to do this is to ask them to bring their leaves, grass clippings and kitchen waste out to the farm regularly and add them to the compost pile. They can also bring their own bags and boxes to pick up produce.[11]

Many CSA groups have a newsletter to let people know what crops are coming on, share recipes, and announce things of common interest. The newsletter and phone chain can also be used to let people know if volunteers are needed to help with an emergency situation. When the weather forecast showed an unusually early frost at one CSA farm, for example, a group mobilized in an afternoon to harvest a crop that otherwise would have been lost.

Acknowledgments

Ron Shouldice, Biodynamic Farming and Gardening Association, Kimberton, Pennsylvania.

Robyn Van En, Indian Line Farm, Great Barrington, Massachusetts.

Mail Order

WITH THE AVAILABILITY of small, inexpensive personal computers, 800 numbers, credit card payment, improved packaging and shipping of perishables, and the availability of overnight delivery service, food-by-mail has begun to boom. Computerized mailing lists allow you to pinpoint the types of customers you feel will be most interested in your products, whether your target audience is your own farm-market customers, or a selected group of "yuppies," senior or ethnic groups.

Mail order is not a game for beginners, however. Before you start, research the basics of mail order marketing, your products, and your potential customers. Go to the library or bookstore and get several books on mail order marketing. *Mail Order Moonlighting* (Ten Speed Press), for example, provides a list of 900 books, tapes, newsletters, seminars and articles on selling by mail. Since mail order is built on repeat business, it may take years to build a substantial income. Plan on going slowly, with mail order being an addition to other existing outlets.

Advantages/challenges

Here are some additional advantages to offering your product by mail:

- *location*—mail order opens up even the most isolated farm to a nationwide marketplace;

- *premium prices*—from one-and-a-half to several times wholesale or even retail prices for the same product;

- *low capital investment*—it is possible to get into mail order on a limited scale at first, to see if mail order works for you.

Special considerations in mail order include packaging, shipping, advertising, and labor costs. You'll need to be computerized to update your mailing list and track when and what your customers buy. High quality in product, packaging and customer service are vital in mail order.

You may also want to consider the ecological effects of direct-mail marketing. In order to conserve paper in using direct mail, you might choose a printer who uses recycled paper. You should also mail to highly targeted lists such as your own in-house list rather than send mail willy-nilly to rented lists hoping for the standard 1-percent response.

Products

The food-by-mail consumer enjoys food and is looking for unique specialty products or quality that she can't get elsewhere. In addition, she likes to purchase by mail. The ideal mail order product is relatively low weight compared to its price, ships well, and has a good shelf life. It should also have at least a 100-percent markup. Dried fruits, nuts, dried herbs and flowers, and processed or value-added items such as preserves and herbal sachets are good examples of products that can be shipped by mail order. Check with your farm advisor on postharvest handling conditions for your product

to see if it is suitable for mail order. Check also with your county agricultural office to find out if any quarantine requirements apply.

Variety is important in mail order. With the costs of shipping, packaging and advertising, mail order is an expensive way to market, and it is difficult to be profitable in mail order on less than a $25 order size. Variety is one way to increase your average order size. Even if you offer only one product, try to offer choices in price, packaging, size and variety.

Mailing list

Many growers get started in mail order by shipping to farm-market customers who request their products by mail. According to many mail order experts, the mailing list is 40 to 60 percent responsible for success in mail order. The best list is your own house list, from customers who have signed the guest book at your farm market or who have placed mail orders with you recently. A 10- or 20-percent house list response is not uncommon, whereas mail order entrepreneurs are happy to get a 2-percent response from a rented mailing list!

Keep close track of what your customers buy, how much they buy, how often, and how much they pay. Customers who were single purchasers during a two-year period, or who never placed an order for more than five dollars, should be placed into a dormant file.

Sales package

Is your sales literature attractive and professional looking? Are the ordering instructions clear and easy to understand? The homespun farm image does not excuse sloppiness; in mail order, you are competing with Williams-Sonoma and scores of other professional mail order companies for consumers' attention. You need to look as professional as your budget and creativity will allow. With food, especially, mouth-watering appeal is important. Try one- or two-color brochures with first-rate drawings at first; as your mail order business grows, you may want to try full-color photographs, as well.

Strong money-back guarantees are critical in mail order, since the customers may be thousands of miles away from you. A good quote from a satisfied customer will also help build confidence in your mail order product. To get testimonials, ask customers for their comments, along with permission to use the quote if they say something nice about your product.

Packaging/shipping

U.P.S. offers several advantages over the U.S. Postal Service, such as guaranteed delivery in satisfactory condition on nonperishable goods; an immediate record of shipment, with an invoice; pickup and delivery services; and automatic insurance up to $100 if they lose or damage the package. Never promise what you can't deliver. Study U.P.S. delivery times and learn how long it takes to get the product from your place to the consumer. Rather than asking customers to study a U.P.S. chart to figure shipping charges, make it simple to order by figuring out an average shipping rate for your product to anywhere in the U.S.

Shipping durability is of prime importance. Plan on your package going through conveyer belts and being bounced and juggled over thousands of miles. Ask U.P.S. for packaging pointers. Get as strong a box as possible, preferably a stock item in a standard size. Ask the rep for a sample; then pack it and send it to a friend and have it returned to you to see how it holds up. Include a notice on the box saying how the customer may get in touch with you in case of damaged goods or goods delivered in unsatisfactory condition.

Spin-offs/catalogs

An alternative to developing your own mail order business is to sell your product through other mail order companies' catalogs. You will have to sell

Most farmers view marketing as sort of a wisdom tooth—if we absolutely have to do something about it, we will! At Pettigrew Fruit Company we were driven to marketing by the most desperate of circumstances; we weren't making any money at all!

—Sally Small, Pettigrew Fruit Company, Sacramento, California

products at a discount, but this option avoids the costs and risks associated with starting your own mail order business. Some state departments of agriculture publish guides listing producers who sell their products by mail. Look in "Chapter Resources" also to locate other producers who sell their products by mail.

Some other mail order spin-offs you might consider:

- Offer your products at discount to corporations or hotels, etc., as mail-order gift packages to send to their clients or employees.
- Offer your regular customers a "Fruit of the Month Club," giving them the chance to send gifts containing a different type of fruit every month of the year.
- Develop a catalog.

Building a customer base

Mail order is built on customer trust and repeat business, not on first-time orders. First-rate quality and outstanding service are vital. Personalize your business by including a picture of yourself and your farm in your brochure and catalog, and include little notes in packages you send out. Throw in a gift certificate, some recipes, or a package of carob-coated almonds—a little something extra with every order. A grateful customer will reorder!

Other customer services you might offer include prompt (same-day) shipping service; custom orders and custom packaging; large-order discounts; special requests (e.g., to send to someone's relative in Canada, etc.); free samples on request; and invitations for customer comments. Also put a bounce-back into every package, even if it's just an extra business card, catalog, or order form.

Mail order promotion & advertising

Don't waste your money on an expensive and ineffectual ad in a gourmet or general interest magazine. Spend your initial efforts promoting to your list of previous customers, through word-of-mouth, and free publicity channels. Keep careful records of inquiries and mail order sales; a computer with a database program is invaluable for keeping mail order records.

Put a sign-up book on your table at county fairs, trade shows, or at your roadside stand to gather names for your mailing list. Make sure your address and ordering information are written on *all* your products and sales literature (not just the order form), and have something to send people when they inquire how to get more, such as an informational sheet or a free sample.

Acknowledgments

Art Seine, Ag Index Marketing, 2640 Cordova Lane, Suite 110, Rancho Cordova, CA 95670; (916) 635-6828.

Leigh Gruhn Nurre, Nurre Direct Mail Consulting & Copywriting, 9323 Tech Center Drive, Suite 1800, Sacramento, CA 95826; (916) 366-6245.

Special thanks to Ron Zimmerman, co-owner of the Herbfarm Retail & Mail Order Farm and Nursery, 32804 Issaquah-Fall City Road, Fall City, WA 98024. The Herbfarm offers over 639 potted herb plants and herbal gifts by mail. In addition, they conduct classes in gardening and cooking with herbs.

Chives

CHAPTER

13

Marketing To Retail Outlets: Introduction

THE KEY IN SELLING to local retail markets, such as grocery stores or restaurants, is to try to find retailers who will work with you in personalizing your product and getting "close to the customer." If you sell to a natural foods store, for example, the produce manager might display a poster of your farm together with information about your growing methods and suggested uses for your product. For this reason, read carefully the information presented in this book on direct marketing, as much of it applies also to local retail marketing.

Suitable products

Concentrate on specialty items that retail stores or restaurants can't get from traditional distributors, or for which you can offer premium freshness and quality, such as fresh herbs, unusual varieties of leaf lettuces and small-scale vegetables like baby carrots and eggplants, or peppers and tomatoes of different colors and shapes. Don't look only to the exotics or specialty items: organic produce and field-ripened vegetables or tree-ripened fruits are

also high in demand by restaurants and natural food stores.

Offer alternative, split or small-volume packages. Arugula, for example, normally comes 24 bunches in a crate. Offering restaurants a 6- or 12-pack of arugula in a small mushroom basket allows chefs to use the product fresher.

Keep tabs on trends in the marketplace by reading magazines such as *Bon Appetit*, *Gourmet*, and trade publications like *National Restaurant Association News*. Develop multiple sources of information. When there's no product around, buyers may encourage you to grow lots of something, but they're telling *all* their suppliers that. And if lots of farmers start growing it, this brings on overproduction and market gluts—so keep in touch with what other growers are doing.

Use sequential plantings and choose varieties to make sure you have a steady supply all season. Stay in constant communication with buyers as to what's up and coming so they can plan ahead, and you can move your crops when they're harvested.

Never compromise on quality. A one-time sale is not worth ruining a reputation. Don't throw in a

© Capay Fruits & Vegetables, Capay, CA 95607 (916) 753-1636

few number twos with the ones, for example. Separate them and offer a price break. Check with your buyer. With restaurant accounts, some product seconds can be chopped up for use in salsa, pizza and salads. Restaurants may be glad to take your smaller tomatoes, your large squash, or your misshapen cukes, for example, if the quality is otherwise good.

Potential markets

Potential local retail markets for various specialty products include garden centers, nurseries, florist shops, local grocery stores, gourmet shops and health food stores. Other avenues include selling to restaurants, nursing homes, hotels, campgrounds, or other nearby farm markets who are looking to sell farm-fresh produce that they don't raise themselves.

Contact your state department of agriculture and your local agricultural extension agent to find out about organizations to which your potential customers belong. For example, you might join your local grocers' association, chefs' society, or restaurant and hotel associations. Many of these organizations have a separate category of membership for suppliers. You might also inquire about renting their mailing list of members. Ask food editors for the names of cooking schools. Join growers' associations and attend meetings. Plan to give some information in order to get some, especially with competitors. Ask your current customers who else might want your produce.

Collect printed information associated with your specialty product or target market. Look for newspaper or magazine articles, new store openings, and local grocery store flyers that give you ideas about possible prospects.

Develop referral sources. There are many people who are familiar with your target market. For example, local cooking schools would know the stores where its students usually shop. An area vocational institute with a chef training program might know local distributors, restaurants and chefs in your area likely to try your specialty products.[1]

Getting the accounts

Make a round of phone calls to potential buyers and explain what you are selling. Ask if the restaurant or retail store buys locally, and what crops they might be interested in buying. Ask if you can pay them a personal visit and if so, when is a convenient time.

Start close to home—you'll find that local people are more interested in giving you a chance than someone in a distant metropolitan market. Saturate your local market, and then move towards the larger metro areas. Practice your presentation on smaller accounts so that you'll be well-rehearsed when you approach your major prospects. It will be a lot easier to deliver to restaurants or retail stores that are next door to one another than to drive all over the county to scattered buyers.

Whether it's a fancy restaurant or a retail store known for its top-of-the-line produce department, go after the top markets in your area. Convince them that you can get them the best product they've seen—and then deliver what you've promised. Do this even if you are able to sell them only a few products—as they find that you are dependable, you can increase the order size. Once you've established yourself as a supplier to "the best," use them as a reference. This gives you a real "in" when selling to other markets.

When you visit potential customers, determine the products you can supply which they are having difficulty getting elsewhere, or that are different, fresher, or better than those currently being purchased. Give the buyer a reason to buy from you; let him know how your products are different or better, and about the services you offer such as frequent deliveries and split packages, etc.

Bring a fact sheet to leave with the prospective buyer that includes a product list, prices, a calendar of harvest dates for each crop (to serve as a

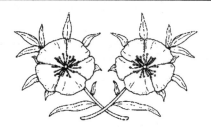

Finding Clientele With Disposable Income: A Lesson From The Floral Industry

When you're approaching new accounts, start at the top and work your way down. Go to the most chic flower shop in your city. Find out which florist does the country clubs, the trendy restaurants and the society parties. That's where you will find your customers.

"The appeal of local growers will be to the higher-end stores," says David Porterfield, owner of Porterfield's in Topeka, Kansas, and retail advisor to *Florist Review* magazine. "You need to find the people who are using specialized products and are willing to pay for them. I can't imagine the FTD-type store would be a good outlet. I don't think the local grower can really compete at a store used to buying carnations for a dime."

Linda White Mays of Sundance Nursery and Flowers in Irvine, Kentucky, says she is swamped during July, traditionally the slowest time of year for florists. That's because her customers do the flowers for the many events associated with Lexington's thoroughbred-horse business. "You've got to find the shops that have clientele with disposable income," she says.

—"Florists Want Local Flowers," *Growing for Market*, November 1992. (See "General Resources—Periodicals & Newsletters" for ordering information.)

ready. Leave your business card and product list. Follow up with a phone call after your visit and again as new crops come in. If a retail store buyer seems reluctant, offer to sell products on a consignment, trial basis.

Be prepared to support your price, explaining that your product is a unique, hard-to-grow variety, etc. Later on, take buyers out to the farm during the growing season and let them see how much is involved in the production of your product. It is very important to be dependable; be sure you can deliver what you've promised. Don't take on more regular customers than you can handle.

Find out as much as possible about how your buyers operate. Find out the quantities they use per week, how often they order, payment terms and the prices they pay, and their preferences for packaging and grading. Find out the best time to make deliveries. Learn how to make out proper invoices, and to whom your invoices should be submitted, and who is authorized to sign for deliveries.

Use the personal visit as an opportunity to evaluate prospective buyers. Is it a reputable, stable operation that likely will pay on time? Cash flow is important; it may not be feasible for you to deal with buyers who don't pay in cash or within 30 days. Will your deliveries be taken into storage immediately and handled properly?

If it is not possible to visit the restaurant or retail store personally, send a personalized letter to interested buyers that includes your product list and a questionnaire. Then follow up with a phone call confirming orders.

Try to get produce managers at independent retail stores interested in your product. Independent retailers (i.e., companies with less than 11 stores) are much more likely to introduce new or local products into their stores than the major chains. Give them a sales pitch; send or bring them samples; and then ask for the names of their suppliers.

Payment and terms

Before you make any deals, be sure you understand the terms of payment. Contracts may be formal written contracts for the growing season, or informal agreements, with the store or restaurant letting the grower know ahead of time the volume they can take. Check out prospective buyers thor-

reminder later in the season when they might need the products), and a questionnaire asking weekly requirements for each crop they are interested in purchasing. Try to get the buyer to go over this with you on the spot. For restaurants or retail stores that sound promising, tell them you'll be back in touch later in the season before your crops are oughly before extending credit. Ask prospective buyers to fill out a credit application (get these at any stationary store), and ask for references of other farmers or suppliers they deal with. Then call these suppliers to find out if the restaurant or retail store pays its bills on time. Also ask for one bank reference. If everything does not check out, insist on C.O.D.

Discuss the need for a delivery charge on less-than-minimum orders, and the need for on-time payment. It is your responsibility to determine the terms of payment. Don't leave it up to the buyers to determine when and if you'll get paid.

Be sure that the restaurant or retail store lives up to its agreed-upon schedule. Offer an incentive for early payment, such as a 3-percent discount for payment within 10 days, and a 5-percent discount for C.O.D. If their normal payments are 60 days or more and you can't live with that, don't accept the account.

Don't forget to have buyers sign for each and every delivery. Make sure your name, full address, phone number and the delivery date are on your invoice, along with complete details of what you sold to the store.

Make sure you get paid at least what the buyer would have been charged by their regular wholesale supplier. Since your produce is fresher, better and/or more unique than they can get elsewhere, you should bargain for a better price—10 percent more for standard items, up to a third or more for unique items they can't get through other suppliers.

Is it profitable? Take a close look at the distance you travel making deliveries, the volume of produce you are able to move through retail outlets, the time you spend in making phone calls and deliveries, and finally, the comparative value of your restaurant and retail store accounts compared to other markets. Be sure you are making money!

 ### Delivery

Upon arrival at the store or restaurant, find someone from the produce department or kitchen and tell them that you are there. Have a multiple (3-copy) shipping invoice ready for signature and have an employee sign it. (Leaving the invoices off with your delivery saves you the paperwork of billing customers.)

If some of your product does not meet a buyer's standards, whether upon immediate inspection or later on due to spoilage, the retailer may ask that you replace it "next time around," or to credit their account. Offer to do this.

Sell before you sow!

Make contact with potential buyers in the winter months to identify packing, quality, container, and variety requirements, and to become acquainted with buyers. It's a lot easier to sell to a chef, a retail store buyer or a purchasing agent in the winter or early spring than in August when the fruit is on the vine. If you go in with a ripe product, you're at their mercy, because they know you've got to sell it fast. Winter or spring is a better time to negotiate price. Tell buyers that you'll grow a product for them, and it will cost them such-and-such a price if the product meets agreed-upon standards.

When possible, however, showing product samples to buyers is a great idea. While you are making delivery rounds, stop by a few extra restaurants or retail stores that are likely prospects for next year or that might be added to this year's route. Call them ahead of time: "I've got a truck delivering near you; could I drop by a sample of our tree-ripened peaches?" Particularly with prospective buyers who are reluctant to buy from you, court them with quality. Prove that your product looks and tastes great!

Working with other growers

Some of the challenges of selling to restaurants or natural food stores—small volume, time spent in selling and delivery, having enough variety to build up your accounts, etc.—can be overcome by working with other growers. Grow the crops which you grow best, then work with other growers to supply the crops you don't grow. When Ina Chun and John Mero began selling edible flowers to restaurants in the Bay Area from their farm in northern Sonoma County, California, they soon found themselves picking up produce from neighboring farmers. Now their distribution services have become a major part of their business.

Selling To Restaurants

CHAPTER

14

Chefs who were once judged by technique, by their ability to deftly mix flour and butter and cream into sauces that would glorify and embellish, are now judged by their ability to enhance, not disguise. A great chef now provides the freshest and best ingredients—berries off the bushes for only hours, mesclun ripped from the earth when the flavors of the greens combine in the most felicitous way. Ever more conscious of the importance of ingredients, chefs meet with farmers early in the season to discuss what seeds to plant. During harvest, they make pilgrimages to visit the farmers who supply their restaurants.

—"In '90s Cuisine, the Farmer Is the Star," by Trish Hall, New York Times, July 8, 1992

IN MANY OF TODAY'S top restaurants, diners are being served dishes made with fruits and vegetables they've never seen before. The sorbet is made with prickly pear; the salad is a symphony of edible flowers; and greens have foreign names like mizuna and radicchio. The flood of new produce items has given topnotch chefs a whole new palette. Because of the upsurge of interest in gourmet cuisine and health consciousness, the competition for tasty new meals is intensive in the restaurant industry. Chefs are increasingly willing to buy directly from growers in order to find products that are difficult to purchase from distributors and purveyors. Moreover, it's often easier to sell spe-

cialty produce to a chef than it is to other customers. Professional cooks know good food and they will go out of their way to get it!

Chefs stress that they welcome sales calls from farmers, but are rarely approached. Michael Batterberry, editor and associate publisher of *Food Arts*, a magazine for chefs, says: "Most chefs jump at the opportunity to have things grown to order. It's much easier than it sounds to develop a working relationship with a chef."[1]

Although many restaurants buy directly from growers hoping to get a lower price, chefs working for high-end restaurants are often willing to pay top dollar for hard-to-find items. For a top-quality producer, prices may be high enough to justify the expense of delivering produce directly to restaurants. During a recent "A Taste of the Carolinas," Neil Clark, chef from the Greensboro/High Point Marriot, told growers: "Serrano chilies, which we use in a lot of our dishes, are ridiculously priced because we have to fly them in. The more we can get locally, the better for everybody—the restaurant, the consumer and the grower."[2]

Products must be of top quality and freshness, and available as needed, sometimes in small quantities. Other restaurant concerns are for price, consistency and reliability of supply and delivery, and for specialty produce not available in wholesale markets.

SELL WHAT YOU SOW!

> *Chefs can't find a good tomato through brokers. Bring them a great-tasting tomato, and you've got a real "in."*
> –Ina Chun, Ocean Resources, Graton, California

Advantages

Restaurant accounts give you a steady market throughout the production season. Advance orders allow you to harvest only what is already sold. If you can establish a solid relationship with a restaurant, you can peg a price on a product and stay with it.

Many restaurants will pay top dollar for your product. A minimum of 10 percent over wholesale terminal prices for standard items at mainstream restaurants; much more from upper scale restaurants for specialty items that they can't get wholesale.

Personal contact with the owner, manager or chef allows for greater flexibility in products grown. Dealing with creative chefs gives you a marketing edge in your other marketing outlets. You can learn techniques about growing and marketing a new kind of produce by selling to a restaurant first; then you can hit the mainstream market and make good money for a couple of years until other farmers figure it out. Restaurants are a "people" business. You'll find lots of joking and camaraderie among the kitchen crews.

Selling to restaurants sometimes brings brand name recognition. Restaurants like to emphasize locally grown produce, so they often mention the names of their farm suppliers on the menu. In turn, mention that you supply such-and-such restaurants in your promotional literature.

Disadvantages

Selling direct to restaurants is not practical unless you live fairly close to a large population center or tourist area. Most restaurants have limited cooler space, and require frequent (daily, or thrice-weekly) delivery. The limited volume may not be high enough to justify direct delivery; burnout rate among growers selling to restaurants is high. In order to get your restaurant orders up to a level that justifies delivery, you need to sell a variety of products. Consider going in with your neighbors so you can offer a wide variety of produce, and set up a delivery route with multiple restaurants on one trip. Or look for high-end brokers or distributors who cater to restaurants.

Product liability insurance may be required by state law and/or the individual buyer you are selling to in case someone gets sick and blames your produce as the culprit. The premium could outweigh the profits. Check with your state department of agriculture regarding required insurance in selling to restaurants.

Researching the market

Restaurants which feature regional specialties, specialty salads, homemade soups, vegetarian dishes or unique cuisine are good prospects for direct-farm sales. Make a list of all the restaurants that can be served easily from your location, say within a 50-mile radius, or are along a delivery route in a city one or two hours drive away. To find restaurants, look in the yellow pages, dining guide surveys in newspapers, or restaurant guidebooks in libraries or bookstores. Contact your state department of agriculture to find out if they have a directory or other programs that link growers and chefs.

Check for restaurant buyers in directories of chefs' or restaurant associations. To find the names of these associations, look under "Associations—Food" in the yellow pages or check in *Gale's Directory of Associations* at the library. Or call restaurant owners, chefs or retailers and ask if there is an association to which they belong. You can also find contacts by attending restaurant association trade and food shows. When you contact restaurant associations, inquire about presenting information on the benefits of locally grown produce at one of their meetings. Take slides to show them, along with samples of your freshest and finest products.

Another great way to meet restaurant buyers is through a tasting festival. (See "Group Promotion," Chapter 30 for a discussion of tasting events.) Be sure to invite hotel and hospital cooks.

Target a range of food providers including "white-tablecloth" restaurants, county fairs, caterers and family restaurants. Family style restau-

rants may not pay as much as the more upscale restaurants, but they use more volume. The bargain basement or fast food outlets, however, will be looking to pay only the cheapest prices. Take a look at menu prices. If the restaurant charges less than $6.99 for a meal, it is unlikely they can pay you enough to make selling and delivering to them cost-effective, unless they order in large volume.

Also include bakeries on your list—they use lots of fruit—as well as chain restaurants, country clubs and hotels. Some of the chain restaurants will not buy from you—they often have strict centralized buying procedures and contracts with large suppliers—but some of them do have local buying authority. Choose restaurants that are neither so big that you can't realistically supply their needs, nor too small to meet your minimum order requirement. Some small restaurants don't use very many vegetables!

Getting the accounts

Start lining up prospective restaurant buyers as much as a year in advance. Call first and arrange for an appointment, as visitors to the kitchen are not welcome during rush hours. (2 p.m. to 4 p.m. is generally a slow period.) Ask to speak to the executive chef. If the executive chef isn't in, find out his or her name and a good time to call back. Chefs are busy people, and restaurant cooking is a high-stress job, so dealing with chefs can often demand the utmost in persistence and diplomacy.

When you visit restaurants, bring samples and a cutting board with you. Prepare your product for them and let them taste your great produce. Espe-

cially with a new product that requires special preparation, make sure that you train the chefs in how to prepare it; otherwise they may prepare it incorrectly and not order it again!

Stress the five-day-a-week delivery service you offer; the special varieties; the freshness, uniqueness, and vine-ripened flavor of your products; or the extra care and personal attention your products receive. Order extra copies of seed catalogs to leave with chefs.

Payment and pricing

Make sure that payment terms are clear; some restaurants are notorious for not paying their bills. Restaurants go bankrupt more often than other ventures, so be very cautious in extending credit, especially to small restaurants, or restaurants that are new to the market. (See previous chapter for tips on getting paid with restaurant and retail accounts.)

With the exception of less-than-minimum orders, it's probably best not to insist on C.O.D. with restaurant buyers; you'll spend too much time chasing down the bill-payer when you are making deliveries. And since some restaurants allow only a certain percentage of the budget to be paid in cash, this makes it harder to raise your total volume. Ask what the restaurant's normal billing schedule is. Two weeks, 30, 45 or 90 days is common; if you can live with that, accept it.

Establish a consistent price throughout the season rather than fluctuating up and down. This makes it easier for chefs to plan menus and pricing. Set prices on a consistent basis a little above the wholesale average for the year. If tomatoes are $12 a case on a yearly average, you should be able to get $13 or $14 for yours.

One way to increase the price you can get from restaurants is by offering convenience packages. Giving produce to restaurants in small-quantity, split packages saves them money. If they buy 24 bunches of carrots at a time, for example, the carrots may turn rubbery in a few days, and they'll end up wasting 30 percent of the product. New Jersey grower Matty Matarazzo sells a convenience package of 6 bunches of carrots, 12 bunches of radishes, and 6 bunches of arugula to restaurants, each wrapped separately in moist newspaper. He is able to command prices 50 – 80 cents a pound over wholesale.

Establishing a working relationship

Try to establish an ongoing working relationship with the restaurant, either as a supplier for a specified commodity or as their "restaurant gardener" to supply a wide range of their needs. Work closely with the chefs. Ask specific questions about their expectations and then do your best to meet them. Find out what they need, what they want the produce to look like, and what amount they want. Most chefs have certain specifications and you should grow to those specifications. If chefs know your harvesting schedule, they can plan their menus around it. Circulate a newsletter to let chefs know about upcoming crops so they can plan their menus.

Try to get the restaurant buyer to be as specific as possible about the quantities they need and what, if any, substitutions are acceptable. It may not be OK to arrive with broccoli when they want cauliflower, for example, or to arrive with more than they ordered when they have only limited cooler space. Most restaurants expect delivery at least two or three times a week. Some will set up a standing order of so much per week, but many will expect you to call the day before each delivery to take their order.

Figure out how much it takes to make a stop worthwhile; then establish a delivery charge for less-than-minimum orders. Small orders that don't even pay for delivery can kill a good business. Request that orders be made by 5 p.m. the day before delivery. Also let buyers know that you need a certain number of hours or days notice for special orders. Offer to call buyers at a specified time each week to discuss the week's order.

The restaurant will probably not want to set up any kind of contract with you, at least for the first year. Verbal agreements are more common, but later on, try to get a written contract if possible. A contract or agreement may specify kinds of produce to be delivered, amounts and delivery times, prices and terms, as well as trucking fees and reliability. Contract growing provides a steady supply of high-quality produce for the restaurant and a stable market for the grower.

Make sure you are dealing with someone you can trust—you'll be left in the lurch if a restaurant pulls out on you! Chefs often move from restaurant to restaurant, or place to place, so center your business around the establishment and not the chef. Get to know the sous (assistant) chef in case the executive chef moves on.

Delivery

When your first crops are ready to harvest, contact the restaurants you'll sell to, and confirm the date, time and quantity of delivery. Be prompt with deliveries and supply exactly what you've promised. Reliability is a must. If you don't show, it means panic in the kitchen and missing items on the menu. They may not buy from you again!

Ask where to go when you bring your produce, and when to deliver. Don't deliver during lunch or dinner-time rush; most restaurants will want delivery between 9:30 – 11:00 a.m. or 2:30 – 4:00 p.m. Your customers will often appreciate additional efforts like placing your baskets directly in their walk-in cooler and rotating the stock (putting your new delivery behind or under the older crates already on the shelves). Making sure your produce is put away properly helps ensure its quality. Often restaurants don't need or want produce delivered in standard packs; ask them how they want it

Ina Chun, of Ocean Resources in Graton, California, making a delivery to the Chez Panisse restaurant in Berkeley

delivered. Restaurant personnel may also be willing to help you out by giving you baskets, boxes, and five-gallon plastic buckets.

Keep in touch and make it easy for the restaurant to reach you. An answering machine will allow them to call you for special orders. List what's available and then ask them to leave their order on the answering machine. If you have a fax machine, fax them your price/availability list with check-offs for their order.

Service what you sell

Since affordable labor is one of the biggest problems faced by chefs, they are glad to buy food products in a semi-prepared form, such as presliced vegetables, prepeeled potatoes, prewashed greens, or tomatoes and potatoes sorted according to size. The less time spent preparing produce in the kitchen the better. Chefs use big tomatoes, for example, for slicing, and little tomatoes for salads.

Let's say you are supplying cherry tomatoes to a restaurant: you will win the gratitude and loyalty of the chefs by conscientious grading to make sure all the tomatoes in a flat are of equal ripeness. The flats that come through regular commercial channels often require re-sorting to pick out green and overripe tomatoes.

Knowing what happens to your product after it leaves your hands also lets you think of ways to enhance its value. One way to do this is to eat at the restaurant—hopefully with the bill on the house. You can find new ways chefs might use your produce, ways to sell less-popular varieties in other markets, or ways to use cosmetically inferior, though otherwise good, produce. Build value-added into your premium price, rather than as an additional cost: charge $12 for washed greens, for example, rather than $10 for the greens plus $2 for washing.

Chefs also want information about how to store and handle products, shelf life, and ways in which the products can be used. Some may also appreciate recipe suggestions.

Increasing the order size

A perennial problem with selling to restaurants is that it's hard to make their small-volume, frequent deliveries cost effective. It may not be feasible to ask for a minimum-size order right off the bat, but if you can't build up your order size with certain restaurants within a few months, drop them.

Work your way into a restaurant by offering them a hard-to-find specialty item; then build up the order by educating chefs about what other products you can supply. If you've got a restaurant that buys your mushrooms, for example, give them a free bag of your edible flowers, along with some suggestions on how to use them in salads. In addition, provide recipes suggesting additional ways to use the products you already supply. "We go from restaurant to restaurant, chef to chef, and ask them what they do with certain products," explains Matty Matarazzo. "Then we go to the next restaurant and pass along these additional ideas about how to use the products. Next thing you know, the restaurant is ordering 50 to 100 pounds weekly of the product."

Product diversity is a must. "Products like tree-ripened peaches or baby vegetables are like gold to restaurants or high-end supermarkets," Matarazzo explains. "They can't get these products wholesale. So I tell them: 'Look, it's not economical for me to come out to your place to deliver just these few items. I'll sell you my squash blossoms or my snow peas if you'll also take my green beans and corn.' But if I only grew one crop, I'd be at the mercy of what they can take of that one product."

Promotion

Help the chefs communicate your local, home-grown quality to restaurant customers. You might make signs or table tents the restaurants can display at the counter, such as: "We're proud to use local produce from Full Belly Farm." Table tents can be an effective way to promote your product. The front view of the tent can be a nice picture of your products on a plate, with the description of your products and farm on the back. Table tents can be expensive to print, however.

Probably the most effective and the least costly restaurant promotion you can do is to educate the

The Grower-Chef Relationship

ACCORDING TO Ina Chun, a specialty grower and distributor with her company, Ocean Resources near Graton, California, selling to restaurants represents the state of the art in growing: "It's an incredible feeling to grow all this great produce and know you're getting it to where it's really appreciated."

For chefs, cooking from the garden represents the ultimate in cooking. According to Alice Waters, owner of the Chez Panisse restaurant in Berkeley, California, buying direct from Bob Cannard's farm near Glen Ellen has had a dramatic impact on restaurant operations. After the cooks visited Bob's farm, they became fully committed to cooking seasonally and planning the menus around what's fresh. "We cook from the garden now," Alice says.

One of the most enjoyable aspects of selling direct to restaurants is the ongoing dialogue with food professionals. Feedback from chefs allows the farmer to upgrade his products and services.

Always communicate if there is a problem. If you are short on a product, call the restaurant to let them know so they can cover themselves on the menu. If your products are frost- or insect-damaged, for example, chefs still may be able to use the products as long as the damage is cosmetic only. Discount the price and sell them as seconds.

Chefs often are unfamiliar with the new specialty crops coming into the marketplace and are usually grateful for recipes, cooking suggestions and nutritional, storage and handling information. Be tactful—chefs can be prima donnas!

Winter is a good time to sit down with chefs, show them seed catalogs, and plan varieties and quantities. Regular review meetings allow you to discuss what you grew that was right, and what you grew too much or too little of. In addition to quantity and variety, the meetings can decide how things are grown, picked and packaged. Salad greens for example, can be plucked either as small, tender edibles, or allowed to mature for greater color, tone and texture. Size is important—green garlic, for example: how many big ones to be chopped up for cooking, and how many small ones to be used as vegetables?

Chefs are accustomed to buying from brokers, and it will take them awhile to understand the lead times you need in order to grow crops. Give them a harvest calendar of upcoming crops so they can plan menus and purchase from wholesalers the items you can't supply.

Taking chefs on a tour of your farm is a good way to impress upon them the farm-freshness of your products, to give them a sense of how things are grown, or why you can't get certain products to them at certain times of the year.

restaurant staff about your produce. Bring them a brochure that describes your farm and your products. When you're at the restaurant, make it a habit to speak with the waiters and waitresses as well as the chef. These people are your frontline sales staff. Restaurant customers will ask, "What's good today?," and most often will buy according to the recommendation. Hold a meeting with the restaurant staff if possible.

Acknowledgments

Dale Riggs, area vegetable specialist, Cornell Cooperative Extension.

David Visher, U.C. Davis Small Farm Center.

Selling To Retail Outlets

WITH THE COMPETITION among supermarkets to obtain the freshest, the finest and the least expensive produce, opportunities to sell direct to retail outlets are opening up for small growers. Produce departments are becoming the major focus of supermarkets around the country. Studies show that their highest profit margin (about 25 – 30 percent) comes from the produce section. In addition, the quality of the produce section is a major factor influencing shoppers' choice of markets. Consequently, retailers are scrambling to expand produce sections. In 1980, retailers offered an average of 75 produce items; by 1986, that figure had risen to 225 items.

Although chain stores generally are supplied through a central warehouse, the competition to supply fresh quality produce has caused many chains to give produce managers the option of buying certain items directly from farmers. Many local independent grocery stores also are relying less exclusively on large terminal markets or food brokers, and are buying from local suppliers. Markets are using local produce as a selling tool, featuring local farms in their advertising promotions, putting out "Farm Fresh" signs and making special displays.

Direct sales to a retail outlet can succeed for farmers who have sufficient, consistent production to provide for the retailer's needs. Farmers must convince the retailer that they will be reliable and dependable in supplying quality produce over the harvest season.

Advantages and special considerations

Major advantages in selling direct to retailers are:

- the small capital investment required to get started;
- the potential, in the case of supermarkets, to sell large volumes of produce;
- the opportunity to capture a greater share of the price by eliminating brokers' fees. Upscale markets, especially, may be willing to pay top prices for specialty items they can't get through conventional distribution channels; and
- the potential for brand name product identity.

Special considerations in selling to retail stores are:

- increased transportation costs, strict grading standards, handling and storage requirements, stiff competition;
- increased delivery time and costs. If you are selling to smaller stores, there may be low-volume sales per customer and frequent deliveries required. Produce often must be delivered three, four or even five times a week! Supermarkets, on the other hand, may require a very large volume. Can you meet this demand on a consistent, reliable basis?
- increased packaging costs—each retail outlet may require specialized packaging; and

- dependence on the retailer's ability to sell the product. How will the retailer display and promote your product?

Barriers to entry are similar to those of the more traditional wholesale markets, and include volume and pricing requirements, and the seasonality of produce.

Retailers' concerns

Bernardo Vera, produce manager at Food-4-Less in Santa Rosa, California, says: "I wish more growers would come in. I don't have time to go out looking for them, but if the growers would bring me samples, I'd buy. I'm pleased with the quality of local produce, and you can't get it any fresher—picked this morning, delivered this afternoon." Particularly appealing, says Vera, is that "local growers can be extremely price competitive."

Retailers *do* want your produce, but they also express some concerns in purchasing from local growers:

Consistency and reliability of supply. "If ten cases are ordered, then ten are needed, not six!" Don't commit to what you are not able to do. If you are doing something new, then wait until you have a good grasp of quantities, harvest times and driving times before you make commitments. According to one produce manager: "The worst case for us is to take on a product and get it selling, and all of a sudden it's not available. We're pretty understanding about production problems as long as you let us know ahead of time. If we're expecting 200 cases of your product, and have the display section cleaned and ready, and then you don't show up, this can make us look pretty bad. But if you let us know ahead of time, that gives us some options."

Timeliness. "If a farmer says that he will deliver at six a.m., then he shouldn't drift in at nine!" If you are late even once, this can create a problem for the retailer, and they will remember your mistake! Deliver on your promises. If this is not possible, then call ahead to let them know.

Quality. "Beautiful samples, but something totally different is delivered." The goods delivered should live up to the quality of the samples displayed in negotiations. People buy produce with their eyes, so appearance is all important for a retailer. This means produce must be fresh looking, with no insect holes, slime, or dirt.

Cooling. "Local lettuce and other leafy vegetables, and berries, don't last." A frequent complaint from buyers about local growers' produce is that it lacks shelf life; smaller, local growers can't afford the hydrocooling facilities used by larger commercial growers. Harvest in the cool of morning and deliver your products as soon as possible, preferably in a refrigerated truck.

What to sell

Shelf space is crowded, and the way to get your produce in the retailers' doors is to get them something that's better than what they've got already, or items that they can't get elsewhere. Upscale, gourmet markets, especially, are willing to pay more to get farm-fresh, ultra-premium products, or specialized items which they can't get from their regular suppliers.

Local producers have some built-in advantages they can emphasize in selling to retail outlets: pride-in-product, greater care in growing and handling, and shorter delivery time. Look for other ways to differentiate your product: Is it grown organically? Is there an interesting farm story you can convey on the label or point-of-purchase sign?

The key to commanding premium prices in selling to retail stores is to offer them unique, smaller-volume items in a nonstandard premium pack. Tom and Denesse Willey, growers from Fresno, California, offer a "retail pack" of potatoes with several different sizes. The pack appeals to retailers with very limited shelf space, as well as to customers who often prefer several different sizes of potatoes for different uses.

Emphasize uniqueness with special packaging and labeling. Tomatoes, for example, come in a standard 20- or 25-pound box. New Jersey specialty grower Matty Matarazzo delivers a 10-pound package of near-perfect, uniformly sized tomatoes in a "cell-pack" that gives each tomato separate protection. The lid folds back so the box can be used as a display box. For his premium tomatoes, Matarazzo gets $1.10 per pound! "Stores often balk at the price I ask, but the alternative, special packages make it acceptable to them since they can also command a higher price," Matarazzo explains. "You also need to label it differently—'premium tomatoes'—for example."

As with restaurants, a critical challenge in selling to high-end retail outlets is to make your volume per delivery sufficiently large to be cost effective. See "Increasing The Order Size," in the previous chapter, "Selling To Restaurants."

Finding market outlets

Retail outlets can range from high-end specialty or gourmet stores, to independent grocery stores, to chain stores. Like restaurants, high-end specialty outlets are willing to pay premium prices for high quality. They use relatively small amounts of produce, however, and will not accept inferior or even average quality. Since it is difficult to sell sufficient volume through smaller stores, try to get a few large-volume outlets in your accounts.

Be prepared in dealing with supermarkets to meet their standards of volume, price, quality,

Mark Mulcahey, produce manager of the Good Nature Grocery store in Walnut Creek, California

standard pack, shipping and labeling. Poor packaging is often a shortcoming of the small-grower specialty trade. Does your packaging hold up alongside the professional packaging of the larger commercial growers? Shipping boxes, for instance, should be in good condition and have your farm label on them.

Supermarkets may want a lot of produce—250 boxes of zucchini a week would not be uncommon. You should have enough volume and commitment to merchandising before attempting to sell a stock item to a major retail operation. Supermarkets may accept smaller quantities of specialty items, though, or items of a different variety in order to supplement their regular line.

The independent retail stores are easier to sell to: they are more rooted in the community and often feature specialty or local products as a selling edge over the larger chains. Natural health food stores, gourmet shops and fruit stands are even more likely to carry specialty or local items, since they like to cultivate a personal relationship with the grower.

Many specialty stores also will put up point-of-purchase material about your farm and help you personalize your product. People who come into these stores are not just buying food; they are buying ambiance or atmosphere, something new, different and exciting—they're buying the farmer and the farm story along with the product!

Other marketing outlets are farm markets who are looking to sell farm-fresh produce that they don't raise themselves, yet have difficulty finding from conventional channels. Don't regard these markets as an outlet for poor quality, however; sell them only the quality of produce you would sell from your own farm stand.

Study your prospective markets. Visit the stores and talk to the growers who supply them. What do the markets emphasize in their ads? Some stores emphasize low price—don't sell to these. The best chance to get top dollar for your top-quality products is to target top-of-the-line stores. The "bargain markets" will tell you that if you can match their cheapest price, they will buy from you. But with small acreage, you have to get a consistently high price for each product you grow.

Donna Sherrill, of Sherrill's Orchards near Arvin, California, comments: "I would give samples to produce managers. If they were really excited about it, then I knew they were the right ones. But

Personalize Your Product

THE SUCCESS of Frieda's Finest, one of the nation's leading-edge specialty wholesalers, is proof that the personal touch in selling produce is effective not only in natural food stores but in mainstream markets as well. An ability to create consumer demand for the unusual has helped Frieda Caplan make success stories out of items like kiwifruit, horned melons, cherimoya, baby squash, jicama and spaghetti squash.

Work closely with retail produce buyers to promote new or exotic items, Frieda advises. In 1972, for instance, Frieda sold one of her first big orders of jicama to Big Bear grocery stores in Columbus, Ohio. At first sales were slow, but Frieda sent the store dozens of recipes and encouraged produce managers to set up sample tables. After a couple of months, jicama became Big Bear's number one selling specialty produce item.

In order to distinguish superior-tasting, nonspecialty items from mass-produced products that may look the same, Frieda advises sticking a tiny decal on each piece. Go all out on your packaging. "Identifying a specialty product is not enough," says Frieda. "Customers like to be romanced, so tell a story on your packaging; give a little background of your farm or the history of the product. This gives the customer a warm feeling."

Communicating with consumers is the major focal point of Frieda's marketing efforts. Her bright purple packages describe the nature and flavor of the items and provide cooking and storage tips. Each Frieda's label contains an invitation for the consumer to write her with their comments on the product or suggestions for recipes. "Informing the consumer as well as the produce personnel is critical when it comes to exotic produce," notes Caplan. "Shoppers are reluctant to choose unfamiliar items. Our labels take the fear out of purchasing a new product."

When Frieda introduces a new product, she routinely sends free samples to interested retailers. "The retailers have to be convinced themselves, before they can sell it," she says.

---

if they said, 'Oh, yeah, this is nice,' then I would say to myself, 'He's not my guy.' I'm a small grower. I don't ship that much but what I do ship is top quality. I'm proud of it and I want the guy who's selling it to be proud of it, too."

Sales call

The first step in selling to retail stores is to approach the produce manager. In the case of chains they may refer you to a higher-up supervisor or set you up with an appointment with the district buying office. But go to the produce managers first, as it is usually their recommendation that gets products into the stores. According to Frieda Caplan, "The single key to success is the produce man in the store. Unless he's convinced, specialties haven't got a chance."

Especially in the introduction of new or specialty items, the buyer may wish to see your willingness to invest in promotion and the education of the consumer. Be prepared to present a merchandising program to help promote your product with point-of-purchase materials, free samples for tastings, and in-store demos. Another way to gain an entree into stores is to guarantee sales—offer to take back any products that don't sell.

Coming to terms

Find out what a prospective buyer's payment schedule is and hold him to it. Usually, the large grocery store chains pay within 21 to 30 days. In most cases, smaller chains and locally owned stores pay within 10 to 15 days. Drop any accounts

© The Farmery, 875 River Road, Fulton, CA 95439
(707) 546-FARM

that let payments go too often beyond your agreed upon time.

If the buyer is hesitant to try your product, offer to consign a small amount. Follow through several weeks later to check sales. If you are guaranteeing sales with an offer to take back unsold products, the easiest way to handle take-backs is to subtract them from your delivery total. When you wholesale products, the standard discount to retailers is 40 percent. For example, a bunch of dried flowers that retail for $10 would be sold wholesale for $6. When you consign your stock, the retailer has no cash tied up in it, so the standard discount is less, usually 25 to 30 percent.

Think creatively: by dealing directly with chain stores, Matty Matarazzo, of Matarazzo Farms in New Jersey has sold his "Jersey Fresh" tomatoes for $12 to $15 per 25-pound box, rather than for $8 to a broker. Matty approaches the retailers early in the season, when tomatoes are selling wholesale for $22 a box, and offers to supply the retailer with tomatoes for $14 a box over the entire season. At the height of the season, when wholesale prices dip to $8 a box, Matty is still getting $14 box under his season-long contract. "Buyers are willing to pay more for my tomatoes because they have developed a reputation for quality," Matarazzo explains.

Keep steady prices throughout the season, instead of jumping around week-to-week following market prices. "Wild price fluctuations don't build customer trust," one produce manager said. "If your carrots are 60 cents a pound one week and one dollar the next, people don't know what to expect."

Buyer-supplier communication

Communication is very important in building a good supplier/retailer relationship. One grower has described marketing as a process of talking and asking: "Is our produce good enough? Is it getting to you on time? Is there anything we can do to improve our packaging? Is there any other product you would like to have available," etc. In turn, check out how the store personnel are handling and storing your produce.

If you have a huge crop coming, it's important to communicate this to the people you sell to. Giving your buyers advance notice of a surplus allows them to arrange promotions around the crop. This way you won't be stuck with a surplus. Equally important is letting your buyers know of a threatened shortage of a crop they are expecting.

Be upfront with your buyers about quality control also. Let's say you've had a bad stroke of weather and your peaches don't look good—sell them as seconds for a lower price; don't try to pass them off as first quality. As one produce buyer said: "I've been burned by farmers trying to sell me less than top-quality products, and I'd be hesitant to buy from them again."

Let the retailer know you welcome feedback. Another produce buyer explained how one farmer put rubber bands on his spinach. "I called him and explained how much this hurt the produce. This was much better than just dropping him—he appreciated the information."

Use nonverbal methods as well, such as flyers shipped along with your product, or information printed on your shipping cartons, to inform retailers about special handling or storage requirements for your produce.

When you are finished for the season, set a date with the buyer to review the past season and learn what his needs are for the coming year. This will help you plan your crops and build a solid relationship.

Delivery

Find out from each store their delivery schedules and instructions. If you are selling on consignment, buyers may ask you to drop by in person once a week to help straighten out your display and freshen up your product.

Doing In-Store Demonstrations

While handing out samples, Donna Sherrill chats happily with customers. "The customers are fascinated," she says. "They may be hesitant to take a sample at first, but once they've tasted it, they start asking questions: 'Are you really the farmer? Is it really yours?' Demos open doors!"

FOOD PRODUCT sampling in grocery stores is a promotion device which is growing rapidly. Producers are able to reach the consumer directly, and consumers are able to see, taste and smell new products before purchasing them. Demos allow you to tell customers that your product is grown naturally, for example, or that it comes direct from your farm. Sales typically go up by as much as four times during in-store promotions. As one store manager said: "You can tell people all day that you have the best quality, but until they taste it, how can they know?"

Particularly with new or unusual food items or relatively high-priced "value-added" products, demos are crucial to introducing your product. According to Mary Moss of T.J. Farms near Chico, California: "Most people don't want to pay a premium price for a bottle of salad dressing unless they can taste it. One store we sell to demonstrates our salad dressing, and they sell heavily. But unless they promote it, it just sits on the shelf."

The purpose of demos is to get repeat customers, so look to get your return over a period of months instead of during the demo. Don't waste your money doing demos at places that cater to tourists, since these are not good prospects for repeat customers.

To conduct an in-store demonstration, first contact the produce manager and convince him of the need for a demo. Set up the dates (the best times are from 2 p.m. to 7 p.m. on Fridays and from 10 a.m. to 6 p.m. on Saturdays) and the projected amounts of your product to be used. Most produce departments will require you to provide the product at no charge. Often a store will expect a discount on the product sold that day, such as a 15-percent markdown, as an introductory offer for customers to try the product. Request a free advertisement or co-promotion with the retail buyer in conjunction with your demo.

Do your homework; it's no use doing a demo until you have experimented with your product in your home kitchen, and you can answer questions about cooking with it and offer recipes. Take along small paper napkins, a waste basket, a plate for serving, a cutting board and knife, or whatever your product requires to serve samples.

Hire professional people to give demos only as a last resort. "Hired people don't know anything about the product except what they've been told," as one grower said. If you must, hire a farm employee or relative instead of a professional food demo person. Some stores, however, have a policy that only professional demonstration service companies are allowed to conduct demos in the store. These will cost several hundred dollars a day (including food costs), and are probably cost-effective only for stores in which you have the potential for a very high volume of sales.

If you can't do demos yourself, make an offer to replace all of the product the store uses to demonstrate your product, and make sure you educate the demonstrators about your product.

Tie-ins. You can get more out of your promotion dollar by sharing the costs with another food producer selling a related product—preserves with muffins or breads, for example.

You can tell a lot by making the first few deliveries in person. Does the buyer leave your produce out in the sun, or do they hustle it back into the cooler? This lets you know if they value your product and your business.

When you deliver your product, try—in a tactful way—to make sure it gets refrigerated immediately, rather than left sitting in a storage room. Donna Sherrill unloads her apple cider herself and marches it right into the cooler. She inspects each store's inventory of her product. If any product doesn't look fresh, she replaces it for free, either taking it off the invoice, or giving the manager a credit slip toward the next delivery.

Sherrill also makes sure that each store employee gets a sample, from the box boys to the cashiers to the produce managers. "These are the people who are selling my product," she explains. "Especially in gourmet markets, the customers know the sales personnel, and they ask: 'What's good today?' "

Support materials

Service what you sell! Provide support materials. Go into chain stores and investigate what kinds of signs they have, and provide something similar for your product. Another alternative (an expensive one) is to ship in cartons that can also be used as display cases.

The more support material you send, the better: camera-ready advertising material, pictures of your product, and descriptions of the product. With thousands of items to sell, store people don't have the time to do this; make it easy for them to sell your product!

Since few stores are willing to provide separate display boxes or containers, providing your own point-of-purchase materials represents another opportunity to distinguish your product. Be sure to ask your grocers what they prefer and what gets used in the way of point-of-purchase materials. Each store has different needs—one may use recipes, another may prefer product information sheets.

One problem in providing support material to supermarkets is that it often gets lost in the warehouse. One remedy is to include your point-of-purchase material in the box rather than separately. Even so, produce managers are often too busy to set it up. So you may need to put it up yourself, or hire someone to do it. Another alternative is to sticker each of your product units with your individual logo. Stickers convey the image that someone cares.

After you've made deliveries, visit your accounts later to see how they've displayed your product. Is it displayed prominently or tucked in a corner? Is your point-of-purchase material displayed with the produce or stuck somewhere on a shelf?

Acknowledgments

Paul Vossen, farm advisor, Sonoma County, California.

Matty Matarazzo, RJM Marketing, Belvidere, New Jersey.

Dry It! Pie It! Or Put It In Cider!

Making Profits With Specialty Food Products

CHAPTER

16

Picking and packing signal the end of the busy season for most fruit and vegetable growers, but for Elizabeth Ryan, they're only the beginning. When harvest is finished at Ryan's 35-acre Breezy Hill Orchard near Staatsburg, New York, she takes much of her crop inside—to be squeezed, cooked, baked, bottled and packaged. The result is a diversified product line that has turned her booth at New York City's Greenmarket into a one-stop gift shop and bakery, and increased her profits at the same time.

For example, while apples might whole-sale for $2 to $8 a bushel, Ryan earns up to $12 a bushel for her crop by retailing juices, jams, pies, apple butter, cider and a host of other fruit-filled products. She has also created ready-to-eat salad packs that sell for much more than the individual vegetables, herbs and flowers in them ever would. And in winter, she's busy potting herbs and forcing perennial flowers for sale in spring. "We're using everything to its fullest capacity," Ryan says.[1]

DRY IT, PIE IT, or put it in cider—"value-added" products make sense. Value-added, or processed products have a higher return than raw products. Fruit that may be worth cents-per-pound as a fresh market product may be worth dollars-per-pound as processed jam, sold in an attractive container. Value-added products can also open new markets for your commodities, create brand recognition for the farm, and add variety to the operation. At many vineyards the pruned vines are plowed back into the soil, but at McFadden Farms near Potter Valley, California, farm workers braid the vines into Christmas wreaths. "One year," says McFadden, "we made more money on the grapevines than we did on the grapes."

Advantages

Here are some additional benefits of doing value-added products:

Creates additional products to sell. Direct marketers can enhance profits by adding products that complement a single product line. For instance, an apple grower can sell processed and prepared products such as apple juice, apple cider, apple sauce, candied apples, apple fritters, turnovers, crepes, pies and muffins, as well as bulk apples. Each additional product you have available increases the amount of money a customer might spend at your farmers market stall or roadside market.

Uses less-than-perfect produce. Value-added is a way to get high prices for lower grade or excess crops. According to Dave Moss, of T. J. Farms near Chico, California, who produces salad dressing from his kiwis: "We can process $500 of second grade fruit and make $50,000 of finished product."

Uses excess produce. Processed products usually have longer shelf life than fresh-market products. This allows you to maintain your price and not have to get rid of produce in a flooded market.

Generates off-season work. By saving produce in your freezer, you are able to use labor at a time of year when you might not otherwise have a need for farm labor. This helps keep good employees.

Special challenges

Making your own value-added products may involve considerable investment in facilities, added labor, numerous legal restrictions and governmental regulations, and a whole different set of production and marketing expertise than that required to produce and sell fresh fruits and vegetables. You will be dealing with buyers who are unfamiliar with your product, so you will have to educate them about your product. Considerable capital investment may be required, and the failure rate for value-added products is high.

You may find that adding value-added products to the product line at your roadside market, and perhaps selling through other local independent retail stores, may be a natural progression for your market and can add a profitable supplemental income. As you attempt to sell beyond your local area, however, you are playing in a whole different

ball game. The specialty food marketing business is competitive and complex. Approximately three new products come and go in a typical grocery store each day, and 74 – 94 percent of new products last less than a year. Mary Ellen Mooney, of Mooney Farms in Gridley, California, which manufactures kiwi jam and processed sun-dried tomato products, explains: "Grocery items are a lot more restricted in the chains than produce. Lettuce is lettuce, but there are 400 different lines of jam out there and lots more competition."

Before attempting to enter the world of brokers, distributors, and slotting fees, seek further expertise such as the book, *From Kitchen To Market* by Stephen Hall. (See "New World Bookshelf," p. 301.) According to Hall, a beginning gourmet food business might incur minimum startup costs of approximately $25,000 – $100,000 each year for the first three to five years. Since success often takes at least three years for the beginner, Hall suggests having an independent source of income to start a successful gourmet food marketing business. Unless done with considerable planning and sound judgment, value-added products are a good way to lose your shirt!

Products

The first question to ask with a value-added product is: "Will this product meet a specific need in the marketplace?" The gourmet field is crowded. Look for something that is unique. Make sure that what you're doing is different (not just better) than what anyone else is doing.

The "storybook" gourmet company starts with an old family-favorite recipe: "I've been making this for 10 years and the neighbors just love it." Or you may have lots of surplus product on hand—let's say kiwis—and decide it's a good time to make kiwi jam. Study trends, and figure how they might work into new food products. Subscribe to food trade publications, such as food and cooking magazines, business magazines and gift publications to find out what's happening.

Look into ways you might cooperate with another company: if you make jelly, for example, you might approach another small company with a complementary product such as specialty breads.

Quality control is crucial for a high-quality, high-profit product. Work only with fresh, high-quality ingredients. Work with vendors with a reputation for high quality. Hire people with manufacturing experience. Work with small batches so they are fresh.

Developing a new product

Developing a value-added product consists of four phases: a look-and-see stage, a market-application stage, a working-dollars-and-cents stage, and a test-marketing stage. In the *look-and-see* phase, you look at your existing operation to find raw products which might be turned into value-added products. Uniqueness is crucial; look for gaps in product lines already offered to the public. Some examples are smaller or larger packages, fresher or more direct access to the market, or health angles such as "wheat-free" for allergy sufferers.

In the *market-application* stage, you define the whole process of getting your product into the hands of consumers. Is there a market for the product? Is the product something retailers and consumers would be interested in? Bring samples—ask potential buyers to try it. Value-added products need a clearly defined target market: don't try to market a gourmet product in grocery stores, for example, or a grocery store product in gourmet specialty stores. You also need to assess food and drug laws applicable to your product.

In the *dollars-and-cents* stage, you evaluate the technical and production cost requirements for your product, as well as how much extra equipment and labor will be needed. You need to consider not only the ingredients of the product, but shelf life and packaging.

Both for your cost analysis and to refine your planning, develop a process flow diagram that describes and explains each step in processing your product. Questions you might ask include: 1) How will raw materials be delivered? In what form? Size? 2) How will ingredients be stored? Frozen? Refrigerated? Dried? 3) What must be done to ingredients before use? Measuring? Cleaning? Thawing? Weighing? 4) How much time is necessary for preparation? Cooking? Cooling? Packaging? and 5) How will the finished product be handled and stored? Frozen? 6) How will the product be packaged? Transported?

Ask your local home extension agent for help in locating sources that can help you find the information you need, such as nearby colleges or universities that have a school of food science, or write to the Institute of Food Technologies, 221 North Lasalle Street, Chicago, IL 60601; (312) 782-8424. Companies that produce ingredients or materials for your value-added products are also good sources for technical information.

Finally, *before* you invest a lot of money in production facilities, *test-market* your product by recruiting friends or family members for a taste panel; by handing out samples to passersby; by doing in-store demos; or by selling the product at farmers markets, craft shows or fairs. (NOTE: Certain sales outlets may require value-added products to be processed at an approved facility—check to see what their requirements are.) This will give you an idea of how the product will sell. Consumer feedback also will help you refine and improve the product and packaging. Ask for comments on taste, prices, packaging and varieties. Be willing to adapt your product to meet consumers' preferences and make it more marketable. An easy, low-cost way to test a new product is to

Dave Moss, of T.J. Farms near Chico, California, displays an assorted nut gift pack

contract a test batch. That way, if it doesn't go, you haven't spent a lot of money on equipment.

Processing facilities & equipment

In the startup phase, try to rent production facilities and equipment rather than building your own. You might rent a restaurant or bakery kitchen during its off-hours. Also check your yellow pages for organizations or associations such as the Lion's Club or Rotary, or even fairgrounds, which might be willing to rent their kitchen facilities when they are not using them. Contact local health authorities to notify them of your cooperative arrangement with the facility.

Look for used equipment in order to save on startup costs. Call other food manufacturers to locate used equipment suppliers or check the yellow pages ("Equipment Manufacturers—Used"). Look for auctions selling used equipment. Contact supermarket chains or restaurant supply stores and ask to be put on their mailing list for auctions. Investigate leasing equipment rather than buying it—leased equipment is a tax write-off.

Another way to produce your product without investing a lot of money is to contract with an existing processor to process, package and label your product to your specifications, with your company logo on the package. The advantages of using a co-packer include elimination of capital costs (no plant to build or equipment to purchase); utilization of seasoned experts; help with compliance in meeting federal, state and local regulations; and technical services. Teaming with a co-packer also may allow you to obtain a price break by going in together to purchase larger quantities of products than either of you might use individually. One way to locate co-packers is to ask your state department of economic development for a copy of a "Manufacturers Directory," and check it for "Food Processors" in your state.

The co-packer alternative allows some flexibility to test the waters before diving in head first. This option may be less expensive in the short run, but some of the control over product quality and day-to-day management will be taken out of your hands. If you subcontract your processing, work only with a manufacturer who is known for first-rate quality.

Packaging

In the gourmet section of an upscale supermarket a 10-ounce package of beans was priced at four dollars. Four types of beans, some maize, and Mexican seasoning were interlayered attractively in a show-through plastic package, with a trendy art-label and a fancy blue ribbon wrapped around it. These beans would ordinarily sell for 60 – 70 cents a pound in bulk, showing that the trick of imaging is in the packaging!

Packaging is vitally important in marketing gourmet products. Package your product similarly to other products on the market for your product category. Go to stores and see how similar products are packaged. Consider how customers will be using your product and what packaging features are desirable.

The first purpose of packaging is food safety: does your product need to be vacuum-packed, for example, in order to maintain food quality? Check with a specialist at a university food science department, or an extension home economist (nutrition and food safety specialist) to find out what types of packaging are appropriate for your product.

Another consideration in choosing packaging is the aesthetics of your product: if your product is attractive, like a colorful three-bean salad or an antipasto, you may choose show-through packaging like glass or cellophane. If your product is not so attractive—crushed garlic or kiwi jam, for instance—perhaps a gorgeous label will make your product attractive.

Packaging types for specialty food products range from plastic- or wax-lined cardboard to wood, cellophane, glass and metal. Try to find a good looking and reasonably priced container. As a rule, your product must be able to fit and stack on standard store shelves.

Choose a container which is easy to get and is not going to be discontinued. If your distributor isn't sure, call the mill and ask. It is wise to start with stock items (such as jars and lids) rather than special orders. At first, choose minimum orders to limit your startup costs.

In addition to the inner packaging that holds the product, an outer "jacket" protects the product in shipping and handling. To conform to unofficial trade standards, the outer container should hold no more than one dozen of your product.[2] Most value-added products travel long distances, so use sturdy, protective outer packaging. This may be of wood, plastic or cardboard, etc.

Every detail of production and marketing, such as pricing and packaging, should be consistent with your marketing position. If you are manufacturing a gourmet food item, the package and label should convey quality and elegance. For customers to pay $3 – $5 for a jar of jam, it has to look beautiful! Pick a theme and use it consistently throughout your labeling and advertising: gourmet, country or generic? Gourmet packaging, like clothing fashion, changes from year to year, so keep abreast of changes. Browse through the gourmet sections of stores and ask the clerks: "What's selling?" If your product is aimed a notch or two below the gourmet image, packaging (and prices) won't need to be so fancy.

Rules & regulations

There are strict regulations for any food processing operation. Enforced by the USDA, FDA and state and local agencies, these regulations are designed to keep processed products safe and properly labeled.

Manufacturing license. You need a state manufacturing license from your state health department. The FDA recommends (and state health departments may require) that products be tested prior to any public consumption.

Commercial location. It is not legal to manufacture food products in a home kitchen for commercial sales. Your processing facility and procedures have to meet "commercial standards." Check with your state health agency to obtain a license for your commercial kitchen. Check also about county zoning requirements before building a commercial kitchen on your property. The regulations governing "good manufacturing practices" are published by the Office of the Federal Register. A copy of the "Current Good Manufacturing Practice in Manufacturing, Packing, or Holding Human Food," Part 110 of the *Code of Federal Regulations*, can be obtained from the Food and Drug Administration or from your nearest college or university that receives the *Code of Federal Regulations*. These regulations set forth the requirements for establishing and maintaining sanitary conditions in your commercial kitchen. Your state department of health also should be able to advise you concerning FDA regulations, and they also should give you handouts detailing food processing guidelines and requirements for your state. NOTE: Products containing meat fall under strict USDA standards which often require expensive facilities.

Product liability insurance. You'll also need product liability insurance that is specific to your value-added or processed product. Value-added or processed products are not covered under most general farm policy programs. Make sure you have insurance from the very beginning, even when handing out samples. Most distributors and sales people will ask that you provide them with a current certificate of your product liability insurance coverage, and that the certificate name them as an additional insured member. While standard coverage is generally a minimum of one million dollars, some distributors will ask for two million.

Costs will vary from company to company, so shop around. Start with an independent agent who can check out different sources. If you are setting up your own manufacturing facility, you will have to pay for workmen's compensation insurance, as well as offer some sort of group medical insurance to your employees.

Most food safety issues can be handled easily if the manufacturer uses the proper manufacturing procedures and exercises common sense. Tamper-resistant closures may or may not be necessary, for example. Even food-borne diseases can be minimized by proper handling and care during the manufacturing process. It is also important that the product maintain its appearance, texture, taste, etc., beyond the date on the package (if applicable). Once the shelf life date passes, the product is viewed as old, stale, or deteriorated in quality. Finally, have a food scientist check your process for the safety of your product. Most universities that have a food science department will have a food microbiologist on staff. Or ask your local extension home economist for a referral.

Labeling laws

All value-added or processed fruits and vegetable products that are to be shipped across state lines must comply with FDA labeling regulations. There also may be state department of agriculture regulations that apply to processed foods sold locally within a state.

The recently passed Nutritional Labeling and Education Act (NLEA) provides direction to meeting FDA nutrition labeling guidelines for processed foods. The most sweeping changes ensuing from the NLEA concern nutrition labeling. Your label must adhere to guidelines for statement of ingredients and net weight; product name (to identify what the product is, i.e., "Raspberry Jelly"); manufacturing statement (name and address of manufacturer); nutrition labeling; and the physical aspects of labels.

You may fall under the "small business exemption" of the NLEA guidelines for nutrition labeling, however, if one of the following conditions is met: 1) sales of all items (food and nonfood) by the company are not more than $500,000 per year; or 2) sales of all items (food and nonfood) by the company are greater than $500,000 per year but

food sales are not more than $50,000 per year. Other exemptions also exist and may apply in certain situations. NOTE: If nutritional claims are made on a product, it is *not* exempt from NLEA guidelines even if your business meets any of the above exemptions.

Although you may fall under the gross sales exemption, there is a provision allowing for voluntary nutrition information displayed alongside fresh produce. Contact FDA offices for guidelines. Companies planning to expand may still want to prepare new labels which comply with NLEA's guidelines. In addition, remember that all current labeling information (net weight, manufacturer, etc.) is still required.

For up-to-date information on federal labeling regulations, request a copy of the booklet, *Food Labeling Regulations*, from the Industry Activities Staff, HFS-565, Center for Food Safety and Applied Nutrition, FDA, 200 "C" St., SW, Washington, DC 20204. Make your request on a company letterhead and include a stamped, self-addressed 9-by-12-inch envelope. Another FDA publication, *A Food Labeling Guide*, is available from the U.S. Government Printing Office, Washington, DC 20401; (202) 205-5251.

Copies of new regulations also can be obtained from the Superintendent of Documents, Washington, DC 20401; (202) 783-3238; FAX (202) 512-2250. (Document #069-001-00045-9.) The price is $4.50 per two-volume set. Specify Federal Register, Volume 58, No. 3, January 6, 1993. Copies of the new regulations may also be available from regional U.S. Government bookstores.

There are also several private industry guides available to help food processors comply with the new labeling regulations (see "Chapter Resources–Specialty Food Products"). These publications are intended as guides only; final authority is the wording in the Federal Register and its interpretation by the FDA and USDA plus any additional documents published by either agency related to the new labeling regulations.

The laws that govern package labeling are complex, confusing, and subject to change. Since it is very expensive to reprint labels to make them conform with NLEA regulations, do not spend money on labels until you have had your mock-up label reviewed by an expert!

Sources for a food labeling consultation include food law attorneys, or universities that have departments of food science. In addition, many food label printing companies have on-staff advisors who can answer questions about food labeling laws. Check industry journals for these.

To find out about state laws concerning labeling, contact your state department of agriculture, county agricultural commissioner, county extension agent, or your local food inspector.

Pricing

Pricing should be consistent with your marketing position. If you discount your product too much or if the price is too low, the customers will wonder if there's something wrong with it! Provide a good markup at each support level so that your distributors as well as yourself can make a profit. This means leaving enough markup for promotion, advertising, discounts and in-store demos.

Another factor to consider in pricing is where your product will be marketed. The same one-ounce dried tomato package that sells for $1.79 in grocery stores might sell for $2.95 in gourmet shops. If you are marketing your product through your own roadside market or local farmers markets, you may have more flexibility in your pricing than if you are marketing through others' retail outlets, especially if your product is unique. If your product is being marketed alongside competitors' products in other retail outlets, however, your prices will need to be in line with competitors' prices.

Getting started in marketing

In addition to grocery stores and supermarkets, value-added products are sold through specialty or gourmet food stores, gift shops, lunch counters, department stores, fairs, natural food stores, mom and pop shops, delicatessens, the "HRI" trade (hotels, restaurants and institutions), mail order catalogs (your own or others'), conventions, and local businesses or corporations. In addition, they can be sold through prisons, camps, schools, club stores (large volume, membership grocery department stores), and government commissaries. (Call your state department of economic development for tips on selling to the government.) Another

sales outlet for value-added products is to act as a supplier for other large mail order companies.

Start small and build a solid local base before attempting to sell to larger or more distant markets. Test market your product at farmers markets. Supply local gift shops and independent retail stores with a specialty item that they can't get through normal distributors. Rent a booth at the local county fair. It is difficult to get a distributor or broker to carry an unproven product; you need to establish a demand for your product yourself. The idea is to get "visibility"—testimonials, publicity in local papers, proof-of-sales, etc.—which will entice large distributors to carry your product. Similarly, before you can sell to supermarket chains, establish a track record. Start with small specialty independent stores who will accept back door drop-delivery, in which you deliver and merchandise the product, including pricing it, placing it on the shelves and replacing it.

Mary Ellen Mooney is co-owner of a six-figure company, yet she recalls loading her car ("until the bottom scraped") with kiwi jam and making deliveries herself. Even now, with distributors delivering the product, 75 percent of her buyers know her personally. "Establishing those first contacts builds a lot of customer loyalty," she points out. "You go door to door and beg and plead and stand on your head," explained one grower. "Anything to get one or two customers to try it. Then you say, 'Hey! So-and-so is selling a case a week. Why don't you try it?'"

Representing your product yourself in the beginning stages also helps you learn what is required of you and your product in order to compete on a much larger scale. In establishing their Hillbilly Soup, Dan and Vondel Rush relate how they hit the road with a station wagon full of their product.[3] "We just drove into a town and started calling on store managers. We guaranteed our product to sell within eight weeks, or we would buy it back and pay the freight on the returned product. That kind of warranty left store owners and managers with little risk. They stocked a few packages of the soup, and it sold." The Rushes followed up by telephone and mail, and most supermarkets became repeat customers. Before long, Hillbilly brand soup mixes occupied regular shelf space in stores in a dozen states. (Don't make this type of offer if you can't afford to take the product back.)

Even harder than getting your value-added products into grocery stores is keeping them there. Support your product by doing in-store demos, doing cooperative ads with stores, offering discounts for large-volume orders, and providing stores with recipes and point-of-purchase materials. Spend your money on attractive labels rather than fancy point-of-purchase materials. Simple one- or two-color, gummed, one-sided, pull-off recipe sheets will work fine.

Make regular rounds of your accounts, asking "How's it doing? Do you need more?" Provide retail store managers with display stands to group all your items together—this way, all your products stand out rather than being scattered throughout the store amongst other items.

Mail order is another way to sell your value-added product. At each step, ask: "Does this pay?" Techniques that work in supermarkets may not work in gourmet shops. Determine your costs for each promotion and find out if it is cost-effective. Once you've built a solid, enthusiastic local following, you may be ready for the big time of brokers, distributors and fancy food shows.

Brokers and distributors

When you are ready to expand beyond the territory you can deliver to and service yourself, you are ready to work with distributors or brokers. Since sales is a game of "It's not what you know, it's who you know," brokers can be vital for getting certain hard-to-get accounts.

Food brokers represent food processors and sell food products for them in return for a commission on the products sold. In addition, the broker arranges for delivery of the product, either through a distributor or directly from the processor. Brokers often demand an "exclusive" within a given geographical area, giving them the right to collect commission on all products sold in that territory. This arrangement protects the broker when it it is not possible to tell who may have been directly responsible for the sale.

A food broker never takes possession of the product, meaning that the company owns the product until the customer buys it. A broker is not responsible for collecting payment. It is up to the company to determine if they want to sell to any given account and to specify credit terms.[4] Since brokers work on commission, they must sell products or they will not get paid. A broker may sell to HRI markets, other brokers, distributors, chain store distribution warehouses or individual retailers. Look for a broker who sells to the markets that are of interest to your company. Brokers' commissions can range from three to 15 percent of your F.O.B. (wholesale) price, depending on the type of product and the services they perform.

Sales representatives, or manufacturer's reps, differ from brokers in that they are employed by the company whose products they sell. Unlike brokers, sales reps don't rely on distributors for delivery of the product; the manufacturer sells directly to the account. Sales representatives are paid a salary and/or a commission, and they sell to brokers, distributors, retailers, or food processors. You need to be a big company to hire "reps" on salary; paying independent sales reps on commission avoids putting them on your in-house payroll.

Distributors differ from brokers in that they buy the product from you and in turn sell it to someone else, whereas a broker never actually takes possession of your product. Distributors are specialized according to the market they serve—retail stores, HRI's, etc. Match your production capabilities to the distributors' volume requirements and the type of market they serve. Distributors' markups can range anywhere from 15 – 50 percent, depending on the range of services they do: selling, delivering, and merchandising your product, i.e., setting it up in a display, along with point-of-purchase materials, and checking and restocking it on a regular basis. To sell through distributors, you need to establish a distributor price and a wholesale price and create a large enough margin for the distributor to make between 10 – 35 percent profits, depending on the services performed.

Finding a broker or distributor

In deciding whether or not to use a broker, you must judge your own potential as a salesperson and the market you are trying to reach. You may be able to get certain accounts on your own and find it necessary to go through brokers to get others. Although you can sell to distant markets by telephone, there are limits to the area(s) you can

Trade Shows:
"Where The Action Is"

TRADE SHOWS allow you to meet a large number of potential buyers at one place and at one time. You can accomplish in several days at a trade show what it might take months to do through traditional business channels. At a trade show, you can learn sources of supplies and find how to do things and what pitfalls to avoid. Try to attend at least one trade show each year—this keeps you up on your knowledge about your competition, new products on the market, and helps you make contacts.

Evaluate the right kind of trade show for your product. Don't go to the Fancy Food Show unless you have a gourmet product! First, define your trade show objectives: to introduce & publicize new products? To sell products to consumers? To develop retail store sales leads? To find distributors to sell your product? Collect names & addresses for mailing lists? This will help determine the type and size of trade show you want to attend. Target your trade show: obtain a list of booths and attendees and determine which trade show matches your market.

Types. Consumer trade shows are a chance to make money by selling large volumes of your product and increasing product awareness amongst consumers. *Professional trade shows* which are open only to commercial buyers are useful for signing up new distributors and establishing new accounts. *Specialty trade shows* (e.g., restaurant or deli expos) provide a chance to generate sales leads. In addition to food shows, check out trade shows that your product might fit into, such as gift or craft shows, souvenir or antique shows, home shows, and sporting good trade shows.

In the beginning, start out by doing fairs, local conventions or regional trade shows. Not only will a modest display be drowned out in the midst of big company exhibits at a major food show, but you may not be ready to fulfill the volume requirements of buyers you meet at major food shows. Most trade show buyers come from within a 500-mile radius, so don't go to a distant market unless you can distribute there and follow up on the leads you obtain. Major national shows are also expensive—up to $3000 when floor space, transportation and other expenses are considered. Regional trade shows are often held in conjunction with association meetings; you'll pay approximately $350, plus transportation and room costs.

Checklist. Things to consider when planning for a trade show include:

- supply—do you have enough supply to fulfill orders you might take at the show?
- product information to give to prospective buyers, along with a pricing schedule;
- samples of your product to give to prospective customers;
- recipes, business cards, display materials, and press kits (consisting of brochures, news releases and black and white photos of your products); and
- show "specials"—offer a discount on items ordered at the show.

Look for techniques that draw in potential buyers. Find out if you can cook your product on-site, for example. The aroma of fine foods, samples to give away, and ongoing demos are a lure for passersby.

Push what is unique about your products. Lots of people sell herbal potpourris, for example, but stress that yours come with a little cloth sack so you can simmer your potpourri loose or in the bag.

Greet people and tell them what you are selling (e.g., "We have a complete line of herb products"). Develop a few "click phrases" that best describe your product. Find out what the retailers sell, where they're from, etc. Don't be hesitant to ask questions ("Do you think you could use a product like this in your shop?"), or to ask for an order. Know facts, figures, prices, discounts, sales specials, and so forth. Qualify prospects by determining need, decision making power, and budget.

service yourself. Therefore distributors are indispensable in selling to distant markets.

To find a distributor or broker, ask the places you're trying to get your product into for their recommendations of four or five brokers they use regularly and who carry similar, complementary products. Or, ask buyers for their recommendations: "Who could carry this?" Attend commercial gourmet trade shows and ask other people marketing a similar line of products who their brokers and distributors are.

Look for a broker or distributor who is familiar with your type of product but doesn't have something similar enough to conflict. Don't get too big a broker, though; you'll simply get lost amongst his clientele. Ask for—and check—references.

Since brokers and distributors like to take on large accounts, it is sometimes difficult for startup companies to find one to take them on. Brokers and distributors are afraid of missing out on a hot product, however, so it is not hard to get an appointment, especially if you can point out that you're already doing business with several accounts they service. Distributors see a lot of sloppily presented products each day, so try to gain an edge with an already-tested product and professional packaging.

Working with brokers and distributors

Distribution is your lifeblood; work continually to get distribution of your products. It's not easy to get good distribution—someone who will service your account on a regular basis, putting products on the shelf and keeping recipes on the rack. A distributor may be representing 40 or 50 products, and he will push the ones that sell best for him. Ask for an up-to-date listing of all sales and services that brokers, sales reps or distributors perform for you. Give them sales goals to meet and contact them regularly.

Watch every percentage you pay in middlemen's fees! By checking references of prospective distributors or brokers, find out whether services rendered are worth the additional fees. "Don't let middlemen gobble all your profits," advises Mary Ellen Mooney. "At least in the beginning, try to avoid paying more than five percent in middlemen's fees. Call the stores or distributors and ask for names of brokers, and find a small broker who can deal with you." You may find, for example, that instead of paying 40 percent to a distributor, you can find a broker who, for five percent, can send the product to a chain warehouse which will distribute the product.

Make it easy for retailers, brokers or distributors to sell your product. Provide them with samples, signs, and information to make them knowledgeable and enthusiastic about selling your product.

Don't leave it all to the distributors. Keep making sales calls. Make sure that your distributors check on your products in stores at least once a month. Keep close check on your sales volume for each account. If orders start to slip, make a visit to your accounts to find out if your shelf space is well-stocked. If things aren't moving, call your distributor and find out why.

Each phrase of a contract is negotiable. Feel free to modify a contract so as to specify the conditions necessary to make it work for both of you. Make it fair for both sides, and if your brokers and distributors do a good job, reward them. Avoid exclusives in those areas in which you may want to promote and sell direct to stores yourself. Make agreements with brokers so that commissions come out of paid sales only—the broker or distributor doesn't get paid until you get paid. A broker typically should be able to double orders over what you were obtaining in any given area.

Acknowledgments

Darice Bauerle, The Food Processing Center, University of Nebraska, Lincoln, Nebraska.

Mary Ellen Mooney, Mooney Farms, Gridley, California.

Merchandising

CHAPTER

17

The local fruit-stand operators always had a line of chatter going. In between the hawking and calling out for more of this and a crate of that, they had a way of teasing and flirting and selling, selling, selling.

— *Barry Ballister's Fruit and Vegetable Stand,* by Barry Ballister

PRODUCE MERCHANDISING, in our modern world of supermarkets, is a lost art. The old time produce clerks, according to Barry Ballister in his book, *Barry Ballister's Fruit and Vegetable Stand,* were "each one an encyclopedia of knowledge and experience."

"I teach our clerks as much as I can and as much as they can absorb," Ballister says. "They are taught recipes, varietal differences, fruit and vegetable preparation, and are constantly briefed on new items. They are taught places of origin, taste qualities, seasonality, nutrition, and a wide spectrum of tips that will help their customers select and enjoy our fruits and vegetables. We know the specific qualities of every apple, and our displays carry little cards that indicate the hardness of each

variety, its sweetness or tartness, its best use, and how well the apple keeps. We can tell our customers that three pounds of apples make a flat eight-inch pie and five pounds make a high nine-inch pie."

This chapter can only present the first-grade basics in the art of produce merchandising. To get your high school diploma in the subject, read Barry Ballister's book (see "New World Bookshelf," p. 301). To get your college degree, visit his roadside market, Sunfrost, in Woodstock, New York!

Packaging

In addition to extending the shelf life of a product or protecting it during handling, shipping and storage, properly used containers provide information to consumers including commodity, grade, weight, size/count, and the name and location of your farm. In addition, containers can describe the produce, tell how to use it, attract the attention of the customer, and add to the appeal of the produce.

Merchandising

Well-designed packaging and labels act like constant, ongoing, point-of-purchase advertising. Your package should grab the customer: "Look at me! Try me! Pick me off the shelf!" Product packaging has been called the silent salesperson in marketing a food product. Once your products have been placed on display, there is often no person there to sell them—just the package and label. Spend a lot of time, effort and necessary expense on your package and label.

If you hire a graphic artist to help with design, shop around. Ask to see samples and get price estimates. A label that costs $3,000 from a glitzy advertising firm may not be more effective than a $100 or $200 computer-generated label done by a local desktop publisher. Personalize your product. Use a picture or drawing to convey a visual image of your farm. Keep the design simple. Use large, bold, and simple lettering. Sources of information on design can come from publications like *Packaging Digest*, *Food and Drug Packaging*, *Specialty Packaging Digest*, *Showcase Magazine*, *Food Distributor Magazine* and *Gourmet News*.

Packaging should reflect your farm image, as well as meet the industry standards for the type of product it contains. Look at and evaluate your competitors' packaging; decide on the label requirements; evaluate your cost; and, finally, test your packaging. Test a sample to measure the effect on your product and the potential loss of shelf life; then test-market with your potential customers and ask how they like your packaging.

Package for the market. In a roadside stand you'll not need such fancy packaging as in a high-end tourist gift shop. Check with buyers purchasing your products to see how they want your product packaged. Find out if a fancy box is worth it and if the time and money spent on fancy labeling and packaging are worth the extra price for your market. With retail store herb packages, for example, you might use labels to educate shoppers about your product and see-through plastic bags that allow them to see what they're buying. For restaurant wholesalers, on the other hand, who already know what the various herbs look like and are more concerned about the quality of the product than with flashy packaging, a simple paper bag might suffice.

Offer to custom pack depending on individual buyer needs. For example, you might ship commodities in multiple packs, dividing the box or

Donna Sherrill, of Sherrill Orchards near Arvin, California, serving samples of her delicious apple cider

package into compartments for different varieties. Package new or unfamiliar items in small packages so shoppers don't have to buy a whole bagful of your product to find out if they like it.

Appearance—a beautiful box and an attractive label—is especially important with high-end specialty products. Tim Korn, a grower from Glen Ellen, California, who sells salad greens through specialty distributors, packages his salad mixes in white boxes with a stunning, full-color picture of the farm. "When you see a stack of these boxes in the marketplace, they really stand out!" he says.

Packaging supplies. The best way to find a good supplier for packaging and labels is to look at other food products; then call the producer and ask: "Who did your labels? Who did your packaging?" Check in food or farm industry trade journals or the yellow pages under "Boxes." Check also the *Thomas Register of Manufacturers* (at your local library) under "Packaging," "Bottles," etc. Food trade shows are another place to find suppliers.

Ask prospective suppliers if they have any experience in producing boxes designed for food storage; get price quotations; find out if they produce in the quantity you need; and look at sample boxes. If you are thinking of having them do the art work, ask to see samples of their work.

Packaging for direct markets

Several types of containers are used in direct marketing. One type may be used for harvesting, transporting, and/or displaying, with produce placed in another container for the consumer to carry away. Among the containers usually not released to the customer are baskets, hampers (tall baskets), field crates, buckets and bulk bins. Some of these have considerable rustic and nostalgic appeal if they are kept clean and can add to the ambiance of a farm market. Using this type of container means labor is required on the sales floor to transfer produce into take-home containers.

A second type of container is designed to be sold with the produce. Common types include brown paper bags, colorful shopping bags, plastic bags, boxes with handles, pulpboard trays, and plastic or wooden berry boxes. Wooden baskets, cardboard boxes, and mesh bags also are used. New baskets, while attractive, may be expensive.

Have your farm name and logo imprinted on the carry-out containers as a reminder of where the produce was bought. There is a one-time charge for making a printing die. Shop around, as there is much variation in the cost of both dies and containers.

 ## Labels

Include your farm name and address on all your labels and packaging; this helps keep your name in the mind of the buyer and makes it easy for buyers to find you. Other standard information includes the item name (with variety), product ingredients, and net weight, liquid measure or count as required.

Other useful label information includes a description of the product, the growing method or organic certification, instructions for handling and storage, and perhaps a recipe. If the commodity has been processed (e.g., canned items, baking mixes), provide an ingredient list. Labels are strictly regulated by both state and federal laws. (See the "Labeling Laws" sections in Chapters 16 and 25.)

If you are selling through other retailers, include a Uniform Pricing Code (U.P.C.) on your label. Many grocery stores won't carry your item unless it can be scanned. Contact the Uniform Code Council, Inc., 8163 Old Yankee Road, Suite J; Dayton, OH 45458; (513) 435-3870.

"Test small" when producing labels. Order a small number and see if the label works before buying a large quantity. Label costs can vary greatly depending on the size, number of colors used, complexity of design, and volume ordered. Since prep costs rather than paper are the major costs in printing, adding colors will cost you more than increasing volume. Look for printers who specialize in printing labels. A specialty label-maker will be less expensive than a general printer.

Your labels need to have paper stock and adhesive that will withstand the requirements of storage and distribution. Talk with your label company and discuss the types of environments to which your product will be subjected—for example, will it be frozen, or placed in a produce department where it may be subject to moisture? This will affect the type of label required.

Labels don't have to be expensive. In fact, the homespun image may work best for your farm. Consider the uses of your labels and packaging and the audience for which they are intended. For the farmers market stall or startup roadside stand, in which your customers know and like your products, a rubber stamp, waterproof pen and "crack and peel" stick-on labels may be sufficient to identify your product. You can produce your own labels and have them printed at your local copy shop at a fraction of the cost of pressure-sensitive labels. This will work, for example, if you are using plastic bags or zip-lock bags with a fold-over, stapled label at the top. Typeset your label at one of the quick-print shops which offer use of computers with a laser printer. Use your farm logo for the main visual element and add additional drawings, borders, or illustrations. Dover books, available through bookstores and print shops, contain many copyright-free designs.

If you are selling through other retailers, or if you are aiming for the higher end with value-added or specialty products, however, you'll need a more professional looking label. Many label companies have graphic designers on staff. Whether your label is glitzy or homespun, make sure it is visually pleasing, easy to read, and communicates your message.

Be sure to register your trademark. Do an initial search to make sure no one already owns the name you want to use. Most universities can help you to find if there is a trademark already existing that may be in conflict with your proposed trademark. Having to change your name later in order to avoid a lawsuit costs a lot of money and may hurt product recognition. Trade marks protect the name or symbols (logos) only, not the food recipe. General information on Patents and Trademarks is available from the U.S. Department of Commerce, Patent and Trademark Office in Washington, DC; (703) 557-3158.

Produce merchandising tips

The decision to display your produce in bulk or prepackaged depends largely on your clientele, as well as on the produce item. If your clientele consists of commuters who want in-and-out convenience, selling by the count or by prepackaged units makes sense. Ready-to-use items such as fresh herbs might sell well prepackaged. Home canners, or ethnic groups accustomed to open-air markets where they can pick out their own produce, may prefer buying in bulk.

Bulk displays. Generally, the trend in farm markets is toward bulk displays. Bulk displays are often prefered at on-farm markets over prepackaged fruits and vegetables because they allow customers to select the type, size and quantity of produce they desire. Bulk displays require less labor and materials and—especially when using wooden baskets—contribute to the farm-fresh look. For produce such as melons, straw bedding or foam padding may be used to protect produce from damage. A challenge with bulk displays is that produce may become bruised or marred with continuous customer handling. Therefore, bulk displays may not be desirable for small or delicate produce. Some items, such as Jerusalem artichokes, tend to dehydrate in a bulk display and hold up better when cello-wrapped.

Prepackaging. Prepackaging produce helps some products maintain freshness, enhances appearance, allows for quicker shopping and is conducive to neater displays. Prepackaging, however, is associated with supermarkets and detracts from the image of roadside markets. Prepackaging with film bags or prewrapped packages is not used extensively because most farm markets do not have the equipment for it.

Unit pricing. Selling by volume or unit rather than by weight generally saves time, both for the customer and salesperson. Unit pricing makes the checkout move more quickly, and allows you more time to talk to customers. Selling by the unit is especially convenient for larger items like pumpkins, watermelons, eggplants and sweet corn. For pick-your-own operations, selling by volume or count allows the customers to know the approximate value of their product before leaving the vineyard or field.

Weight. Selling by weight is popular because people are used to buying by the pound, and consumers feel they are getting full value for the price. It also avoids the controversy in pick-your-own sales of over-filling the containers. Selling by weight requires the use and inspection of accurate scales.

If products are sold by the piece, they should be grouped by size and priced accordingly. If sold by the pound, products do not need to be arranged by size, although this may make a more attractive display. As products deteriorate, they should be removed from the display and temporarily offered at a reduced price. If this is not effective in selling the deteriorating produce, they should be discarded to prevent detracting from overall market appearance.[1]

For certain vegetables and fruits, keep the quantities small. Snow peas, for example, may be as high as $4 per pound. This will make customers reluctant to buy. It is better to offer such items in more manageable units, such as a quarter pound for $1. Similarly, with strawberries, blueberries and raspberries, sell pints instead of quarts. Customers will pay more for two individual pints than they will for one quart.

Individuals and smaller families often cannot use large quantities before the product loses its freshness and flavor. Better to have your customers come more frequently for smaller orders. Don't sell them so much that they can't use it up before it loses flavor.[2]

Cash register savvy. Make sure your cashiers know how to handle cash properly. If two or more employees are working in the stand at one time, designate one as the cash handler. Take the customer's money politely, and place it on the shelf above the cash register while making change. This prevents any misunderstanding concerning the amount of money the customer gave you. State the item price and what the customer gave you ("$6.27 out of $10"); then count out the change. Count aloud the coins to the nearest dollar and then the bills to the total amount given to you by the customer. "That's six twenty-seven, 28, 29, 30, 40, 50, 75, seven, eight, nine, ten dollars." Give the customer the change, thank her, and put the money in your cash register.[3]

Serve only one person at a time. Trying to serve more than one, especially while making change, leads to confusion and misunderstandings.

Display tips

Use the racks or tables as your canvas and the rich colors and textures of the produce as your paintbrush to create displays that are both visually satisfying and inviting.
— from the *Organic Produce Merchandising Manual*

Fresh produce is responsible for creating the image of a store. Proper presentation of products increases sales. Shoppers receive a positive impression if products are top quality, clean and tastefully displayed. Remember that high-quality products are the strength of roadside markets!

A lively and well-stocked produce department entices the customer to buy and increases sales and profits. Think of yourself as an artist, with several palettes of colors to choose from: *visual*—color, contrast, shapes, sizes, scale; *smell*—herbs, flowers, fruits (avoid rotten smells!); and *touch*—soft, firm, texture. Sketch out your plan on paper first. This can save hours when you are setting up your displays. The drawing should show the layout of the sales area, the location of display fixtures or tables, a list of the fresh items you are going to display, and the location and amount of space allocated to each one.

Display fixtures. The types of display fixtures you use depend on the market facilities. If you are selling in a temporary location such as a curb or tailgate market and facilities must be removed at the close of the selling period, then portable fixtures are the answer. Folding tables may be all that is needed. For more permanent locations such as roadside markets, display fixtures may be constructed of wall racks, flat-top tables, shelves,

Red Hook, NY

© Greig Farm, RD #3, Box 473B, Red Hook, NY 12571 (914) 758-1234

benches with sloping tops, step displays, tables on wheels, wheelbarrows and carts.[4]

Make displays that look like they came from the farm. Wooden crates or boxes work well. Baskets are beautiful; slant them toward the customer. Even an attractive tablecloth can add to your sales. Stair-stepped displays create an array of depth, color and texture; however, they may not be easy for the customer to reach or easy to restock. Utilize vertical space by hanging products from slings or hangers. (Caution: keep products below eye-level, so customers can reach them easily.)

Stocking. *"Pile it high and kiss it goodbye!"* Full, well-stocked displays make customers want to come and get it! Customers don't like taking the last of something from a bare, picked-over display; they want the best. A cornucopia of produce conveys abundance, prosperity and quality. Never overstock, however, to prevent the risk of crushing tender items on the bottom or (in an air-cooled case) of blocking proper air flow. For most products, avoid piling them higher than 6 – 8 inches—they may bruise or tumble. Avoid steep pyramid displays, for instance, where products continuously roll off the top. Stock fully, but not so picture perfect that customers hesitate to disrupt the display by removing produce. Removing one or two packages from a full display may even help customers start buying.

Make it easy for the customers to reach for the produce. Your display should be no more than an arm's reach in depth, and between knee- or waist-level and eye-level in height. Don't put your merchandise on the ground. Instead of placing your boxes flat, try slanting your produce to give the customer a more pleasing visual sense of your product. Give customers a clear view of all displays. Use low fixtures in the center area (pallets, tables, baskets, etc.) and place tall displays and high shelves at the outer limits or walls of the market.

Organize products in related groupings. Such groups might include dessert items such as melons, salad items, cooking vegetables, herbs, citrus, soft fruits, apples and pears, tropical fruits, bakery items, and luxury items such as flowers and decorations. Displaying compatible products together serves as a suggestion for additional purchases and uses of the product. These might include salad dressing with salad greens, popcorn or doughnuts with apple cider, and impulse items (jams, jellies, flowers, crafts and gifts) for convenient sale near the checkout.

Merchandise exotic specialty crops together as a group. Displaying them side by side with ordinary varieties makes customers wonder why they should spend the additional money for them, while placing them in a separate section helps emphasize the products' premium or exotic quality and makes them look different and interesting.

Place high demand items in strategic locations throughout the market and/or on display fixtures. Large displays attract attention, so use bulk displays to generate sales, especially for high-volume seasonal crops such as apples.

Color and texture. Use color and texture to enhance eye appeal. People enjoy food with their senses, so displays must be eye- and sense-appealing. Mix a row of radishes between the mustard and kale, tomatoes between the lettuce or cucumbers, or intersperse peaches with blueberries to create dazzling color displays. Bright, vibrant color contrasts within produce groupings lead to tie-in sales. Some good color contrasts are: RED next to yellow or dark green; ORANGE with light or dark green, brown or purple; LIGHT GREEN with yellow, purple or brown; YELLOW with red, light or dark green, brown or purple; DARK GREEN with red, orange, yellow or brown; and WHITE, which contrasts with all colors.

If you do not have a lot of variety, create a color mixture with packaging, or by arranging cut flowers between the produce. Additional color can be added to the display by ringing it with fresh plants or flowers, or by using bright shade awnings or signs. Be careful, however, that the reflection from surrounding colors does not cast an unwanted hue

(such as blue) on the natural color of your produce.

Contrasting textures and sizes of produce is also an effective merchandising tool. Zucchini, gold zukes, cucumbers and other cylindrical veggies should be stocked in different directions if next to each other. Don't overlook the power of the sense of smell, especially when your customers are hungry. The fragrance of apples, ripe cantaloupes and strawberries, or the tangy aroma of a freshly sliced sweet onion can stimulate sales. Taste and smell go together, and product sampling of new and seasonal items is a good sales technique.[5]

Creative touches can enliven a produce display, e.g., carrot wheels, fresh flower bouquets, edible flower arrangements, garden-like groupings of lettuce and greens, baskets within the displays, or hand-stacked potatoes and yams. Enliven your display and avoid monotony with the use of tilted tables, barrels, produce baskets, buckets, paper sacks, burlap, pallets, bulk bins, etc. One inexpensive way to decorate your roadside stand is to nail baskets to walls at a tilt. In addition to creating a charming country look, the baskets will provide more space to display impulse items.

Seasonal themes work well on dry tables, such as fall squash and yam displays, or summertime berries, figs and soft fruits. Do a complete rearrangement of your department when the produce seasons change. Do not imitate supermarkets by trying to provide out-of-season products such as tomatoes in January. Produce has its best flavor, holding qualities and overall value in season, when it is available at its greatest volume and lowest price.

Price signs. Prices should be clearly marked on or near the display. Most shoppers are in a hurry and will not search out the produce manager to find out how much an item costs. In making your pricing signs, use card stock that contrasts pleasantly with the product, such as yellow for blueberries, or buff for other products. Use red or orange

Sage

Point-Of-Purchase (P.O.P.): Where Profits Are Made

IN A RECENT MARKETING study conducted by West Virginia University and the State Department of Agriculture, russeted Golden Delicious apples grown in West Virginia were displayed side by side with shiny and smooth Washington State apples. When signs were placed over the local apples urging shoppers to "Taste A Real Apple," emphasizing flavor over glossy perfection, the russeted apples outsold the smooth ones (62 percent of sales). Without the poster, the russeted apple sales averaged only 47 percent of the total. The sign's appeal to taste appeared to be the critical factor!

Point-of-purchase (P.O.P.) materials increase sales! Building up the purchases of customers once they're in the store is where profits are made. Most purchases are unplanned—few people go into a store with a list and stick to it 100 percent. The goal is to get consumers to try a new or unusual product or buy larger volumes of produce. If consumers don't know how to cook patty pan squash, for example, they won't buy it. However, consumers will try a new product if you give them preparation information and recipes for how to use your product.

P.O.P.'s may include:
- *Tent cards* are small, V-shaped cards that can be placed on counters, tables and shelves.
- *Posters* are especially useful during in-store promotions and in trade show exhibits.
- *Shelf-talkers* are small card-signs posted under or hung from a shelf above the product.
- *Product information tags ("hang-tags")* are affixed to the product. This ensures that they will be displayed along with the product.

Other point-of-purchase materials include gummed, tear-off *recipe pads* and *brochures*. Point-of-purchase material can provide descriptive information such as price and suggestions for use. It can also include recipes, information on storage, handling, company history, ingredient description, or coupons for free offers. Brochures can personalize your market by giving a history of the market, local points of interest, cultural practices used in growing your product and announcements of product availability.

Tie in media promotional campaigns with in-store signs. A newspaper ad, for example, can be shrunk down and displayed next to the item being sold or next to the cash register; or the ad can be enlarged and placed in the entrance way or reproduced and handed out as flyers.

Use signs to make sure customers know about everything you carry. Use large, highly visible, banner-type signs to announce something special (such as strawberry season or freshly juiced cider). Use brightly colored "SALE" or "SPECIAL" header cards to attract attention to a promotion. Industry or commodity groups often supply members with P.O.P. material.

Point-of-purchase sales should not stop with printed material. Train your sales people to say to customers: "Did you see the special we have on such-and-such a product?" or "That's a good buy today." These suggestions can boost sales.

markers to do the lettering. Avoid stark black on white. White card stock shows fly specks, and is glaring in bright sunlight.

Use point-of-purchase signs and educational materials throughout the department to promote your products and educate the consumer. The more educated consumers are about your produce, the easier it is to ask higher prices for specialty, locally grown or organic products.

Produce handling

Handle with care. Proper care in handling and placing produce on displays is essential to minimize damage and injury. Many items can be handled similarly, but some require special attention. Produce is very perishable. Each item must be handled carefully from the time it arrives in the store until it is sold. Items should be displayed in ways that will increase sales and maximize shelf

Sampling:
Once They Try, They'll Buy!

I consider sampling to be the most effective marketing method available.

—Jay Conrad Levinson in *Guerrilla Marketing*

SINCE THE TIME the first watermelon was "plugged" on the back of a wagon, customers have expected to have someone personally offer them a taste and a sales pitch. In today's supermarket world, however, tasting is a forgotten art, and product sampling is an "extra" that will lure customers to your farmers market stall, roadside market or local retail market where you are giving "demos." Get some paper plates, a knife and some paper napkins and start sampling and selling!

Once they try, they'll buy. If a picture is worth a thousand words, letting customers taste the luscious quality of your products is worth at least ten thousand words! For products like green beans that are hard to sample in-store, give the customers a few to take home, with cooking tips: "If you like it, come back!" Studies show that free samples increase sales at least 30 percent, and probably more. You might even include samples in your press releases to editors!

Product sampling is especially important for introducing new products, or new varieties of a product. Over a display of apples with nine different varieties, for example, you might set out a sign, "Sample One." This makes it easy for customers to find out which one they want.

Sampling is not only the best advertising you can do; it's also inexpensive. Hand a customer a small paper cup of cider, and they'll probably want to purchase a gallon—that's cheap advertising! In traditional food merchandising there is an adage that for every 10 percent of oversupply, prices need to be lowered 30 percent to move the product. So rather than creating an oversupply in the market, give some excess produce away as free samples!

Regulations may require you to give samples on a disposable utensil without anyone's hands touching the sample. Use toothpicks, spoons, or wooden ice-cream sticks. Provide a place next to your table for samplers to throw away these utensils. Check with your county health department for health regulations concerning sampling.

NOTE: See also the discussion on doing in-store "demos" in "Selling To Retail Outlets," Chapter 15.

---

life. Some products deteriorate faster than others. Green peas, asparagus, strawberries, raspberries and sweet corn deteriorate quickly. Sweet corn loses about 50 percent of its sugar in a single day if it is displayed at 70 degrees F., while corn cooled to 33 degrees F. loses only 5 percent of its sugar.

Group compatible items according to temperature/humidity requirements. Wet and dry items always need to be separated. Since moisture loss is the major cause of produce breakdown, it is vital to store items appropriately to reduce moisture loss problems. For most products, maintain cool temperatures, preferably 32 – 35 degrees F., and high relative humidity in the range of 90 – 95 percent. Moisture loss is easiest to recognize in vegetables because it causes wilting and shrivel-

ing. Use iced displays where applicable, or mist the produce to slow the rate of moisture loss and help keep products fresh.

Avoid direct sunlight and excessive air movement. Fans or strong breezes cause dehydration. Closed markets should have means to exchange just enough air to eliminate unpleasant odors and excessive moisture. For guidelines in protecting product quality while storing or displaying produce, see the appendices starting on page 279, as well as the "Postharvest Handling" section in "General Resources."

Working display items. Restock displays frequently, rotate products as needed, and remove damaged, decayed, or unsalable products promptly. Cull the produce section every morning and throughout the day—this means removing from the rack any wilted, shriveled, yellowed or decaying items. Unsightly produce left on your stand not only detracts from sales, but it leaves the customer with the notion that you sell rotten produce. A good rule for knowing when to cull or not cull is to judge whether you would buy the item in that condition for that price. If leaving items out on the stand will bring down the overall image of your department, they should be pulled.

Many items such as greens and lettuce can be "worked" or rinsed and cleaned up and put back out on the stand. Although it takes labor to do this, highly perishable items can have shelf life extended to help curb what otherwise would be a complete loss.

Wash down cases and racks regularly with hot soapy water or a disinfectant made of one teaspoon of household bleach with one gallon of water (rinse well). This reduces produce breakdown from bacterial buildup.

Acknowledgments

Alden Miller, University of Massachusetts.

Harold Love, Agricultural Economics Department, University of Kentucky.

Monica Crispin, Cornell Cooperative Extension.

Customer Service

When observing those who are successful in agricultural marketing, one notices a common thread throughout. They are more concerned with what their customers want, rather than what they grow or have to sell. In addition, they like people and they enjoy serving people—and serving people is really what marketing is all about.

—Dan Block, agricultural marketing consultant

"**F**ARMERS ARE JOINING the rest of the economy in appreciating that there is a substantial number of customers who are demanding quality and service and are willing to pay for it," observes Vance Corum, an agricultural marketing consultant from Oakland, California. Vance sees the "new" farmer changing from being interested solely in production to being more service-oriented toward customers.

Whether you are marketing your products through wholesalers, retailers, or directly to consumers, your success depends on repeat customers. Studies show that it is five times as expensive to find new customers through advertising as to retain old ones! A customer's value is not in what she might spend on any one occasion but in what she might spend over a lifetime if she becomes your loyal customer!

Let customers know you value their business and that you will go all out to keep them happy. Give them personal attention and find out what it takes to make them want to come back. Give

incentives to return, such as frequent purchaser coupons.

Customer service

You do not make money from high-quality tomatoes. You make money from satisfied customers.

—Matty Matarazzo, Matarazzo Farms, New Jersey

One reason farm markets enjoy customer loyalty is personal service—one of the few things customers *cannot* buy at grocery stores. "A lot of farm markets think they are a grocery store," says Linda Stanley, marketing director of the North American Strawberry Growers Association (NASGA). "But this is silly! Farm markets are as much recreation as food." Your farm market, for example, might provide a place for customers to sit down and relax, especially for older citizens. Other extras you might provide include food samples for your customers to taste, doughnuts or popcorn, and a pot of hot apple cider on the stove, permeating the market with its tantalizing aroma.

Customers expect the basics at direct markets—fresh, high-quality produce sold at reasonable prices; safe, attractive and clean facilities; convenient checkouts; reliable, informed, helpful staff; and well-stocked displays. Offering extras, however, will set you apart from the rest. Especially in areas of heavy direct marketing competition, your marketing advantage may be primarily in customer relations and services. Do customers who come each week get bored with your regular offerings? Is your product, service or pricing so easy to match that a competitor can easily outdo you in a single promotion? Remember, you must *earn* customer loyalty every single day.

Remember the "80/20" rule of business: 80 percent of your business comes from 20 percent of your customers! *The most effective way to increase gross sales is to increase the average sale per customer!* It takes little more time to check out a $30 order than a $3 order, so go all out to increase your sales per customer.

Go the extra mile and provide information on types and varieties of produce and recipes for customer use, a picnic area, a call-in ordering service, and acceptance of credit cards. Washed produce is welcomed by travelers or picnickers; you might provide a produce-washing facility for customer use. You might also offer free carry-out for bulky or heavy purchases, and free delivery for large orders within a 20-mile radius.

Treat your customers as invited guests. For example, you might offer your regular customers a free box of berries, or the chance to pick for a week at your pick-your-own operation in a "preferred customer only" pre-opening special.

Some other things you can do to increase sales per customer include:

- Tag on a "tie-in" suggestion for just about everything you sell: "Would you like some of our homemade tomato sauce to go with those avocados?" Or: "What *else* can I get for you?"

- Make shopping carts available for customers. In addition to being a great convenience, they greatly increase the average sale per customer.

- Plan ahead, and help your customers do likewise. Inform them as to what items are coming and what are the best varieties for home canning or freezing. Post a schedule of items expected in

the stand, U-Pick operation or farmers market stall.

Finally, as customers leave, express your sincere thanks.

Cleanliness is an important part of merchandising. Lots of folks feel that direct markets are generally less clean than supermarkets—this is a notion that you must strive mightily to overcome. Keep your facilities sparkling clean. Encourage your employees to maintain a clean and healthy appearance and neat attire. Eating, smoking and gum chewing by staff should be avoided in the sales area.

Listen to your customers

A woman whose name has become synonymous with specialty produce gained her position in the industry largely by listening to customers. "The kiwifruit story shows the power of one customer," Frieda Caplan says. "Look what happened when a customer in a Safeway store asked for Chinese gooseberries." In 1962 a buyer from Safeway called Frieda wondering if she had ever heard of Chinese gooseberries, some kind of fuzzy fruit a shopper had requested. Upon investigation, Frieda found she could import the product from New Zealand growers. She began to promote the item, renaming it kiwifruit. "We encourage retailers to tell us when a customer asks for something, no matter how strange it may sound," Frieda concludes.

It pays to listen to your customers. A satisfied customer will tell five others about you; an unhappy customer will tell ten or more other people. Sixty-eight percent of customers who quit patronizing a store do so because of poor employee attitude.

A key indicator of a business' customer service level is its return policy. Do you offer prompt replacements or refunds to dissatisfied customers? Another way to keep customers is through prompt and efficient handling of customer complaints. Ninety-five percent of customers who are dissatisfied will buy from you again *if* their complaints are answered quickly.

Make it easy for your customers to communicate with you. Provide postcards or evaluation pads (with pens or pencils available), similar to

Ten Commandments For Customer Service

by Frank Cooper

1. The customer is never an interruption to your work! The customer is your real reason for being in business. Chores can wait.

2. Greet every customer with a friendly smile. Customers are people and they like friendly contact. They usually return it.

3. Call customers by name. Make a game of learning customers' names. See how many you can remember.

4. Remember, you are the company! As an owner and/or employee, the way you represent yourself to your customer is the way your business will be perceived by that person.

5. Never argue with customers. The customer is always right (in his or her own eyes). Be a good listener; agree where you can, and do what you can to make the customer happy.

6. Never say, "I don't know." If you don't know the answer to a question say, "That's a good question. Let me see if I can find out for you."

7. Remember, the customers pay your wages. Every dollar you earn comes from the customers' pockets. Treat them like the boss.

8. State things in a positive way. It takes practice, but will help you become an effective communicator.

9. Brighten every customer's day! Do something that brings a little sunshine into each customer's life. Soon you'll discover that your own life is happier and brighter.

10. Always go the extra mile! Always do just a little more than the customer expects you to do.

This article appeared in *Rural Enterprise*, Summer 1992. Frank Cooper has written and produced several books, videos, and tapes regarding customer relations. If you are interested in learning more, please contact Frank Cooper at P.O. Box 3206, Everett, WA 98023.

---

those offered on the back of restaurant checks, for constant evaluation of your services. Place a large suggestion box near the checkout stand for customers to place them in. Use phrases like: "How can we serve you better?" Find out what customers like about you, don't like about you, and what they wish you would offer them. The customers' wish list is your key to new sales opportunities!

Train employees who work at the checkouts to make a practice of asking customers for their comments and suggestions and then writing them down. Finally, *act on customer suggestions*. This *really* shows customers that you care about what they want. Serious consideration of customers' comments leads to higher customer satisfaction and higher average sales per customer.

Ellen Todd, manager for the Greig Farm market near Red Hook, New York, has developed a customers' "Wish List." Customers are encouraged to ask questions about products in the store or to request products they don't find available. The manager then telephones the customer or responds by letter. "The 'Wish List' has given me increased information on what my customers need, want or miss," Ellen says.

Educate the customer

As the produce industry moves toward the year 2000, it will not only sell produce. It will educate consumers on produce use, preparation, safety, convenience and nutrition. Consumers will demand such marketing.
—Roberta Cook, U.C. Davis marketing specialist

Educate your customers about your products. Whether you are selling to a wholesaler, chef or farmers market customer, the more the customers know about your product, how it is used, and what goes into producing it, the more they are willing to pay a premium for top quality.

Know your merchandise. If you are a retailer, know what your market carries, the location of each item carried, and information about what you sell, such as how to use your products, nutritional facts, and special values. Be an expert on your merchandise. Read trade magazines, and convey your enthusiasm about your products to your customers—it's catching. A retail market introducing organic produce, for example, might put out a newsletter to its customers with articles about organics and about their organic farmer-suppliers. The store might also carry point-of-purchase educational brochures about organics beside the products, and encourage growers to sticker their products with organic labels.

Other steps you can take to educate the customer include:

• make educational brochures and flyers available (special recipes for low salt, low fat, low sugar, low cholesterol, or high fiber foods, for example);

• conduct on-farm demonstrations and workshops;

• submit educational articles to your local newspaper food editor;

• demonstrate a recipe on television or answer questions about fruits and vegetables;

• present educational slide shows at local service clubs;

• print product information on labels, such as nutritional content, storage tips and recipes;

• publish a newsletter; and

• invite people out to your farm for tours.

Michael Abelman, owner of Fairview Gardens in Goleta, California, produces some 100 organically grown crops on his 12-acre site, and he has worked at being accepted by his urban neighbors. One way he does this is by selling produce to them at his roadside stand. He is also developing an educational center at his farm, where he holds classes, puts on tours, and hosts open-house/field days for the community. He also is establishing a library and resource center in a barn. "Farming in the urban environment does present some difficulties," he says, "but it also provides unique opportunities—an opportunity to sell organic produce directly to the public, and an opportunity for the public to learn what organic farming is all about."

Take time to train your sales staff in the use of your products. If a customer is looking at the cabbage, an employee might ask: "Do you use sugar when you can sauerkraut?" After the ensuing discussion about canning, the customer may go home with 20 pounds of cabbage to make canned sauerkraut!

To educate your employees and your customers, you'll first have to educate yourself. As an expert in your field, you'll soon be consulted by all kinds of people—and perhaps even be invited to speak at the local junior college or garden club on your chosen topic. These contacts will bring some of your best customers.

Nutritional knowledge is a basic to produce retail selling. You should be able to answer many

Customer service par excellence: serving customers at the Sacramento Certified Farmers Market

Boulder County Farmers Market

© Boulder County Farmers Market, P.O. Box 18745, Boulder, CO 80308 (303) 532-2591

customer questions concerning food. Study books like the USDA's *The Food Guide Pyramid* (published by the Human Nutrition Information Service, Home & Garden Bulletin #252, available from Consumer Information Center, Department 159-Y, Pueblo, CO 81009). Other useful books on nutrition and food composition include *Nutrition Handbook* by Jane Brody; *Vitamin Bible* by Earl Mandell; *Nutritional Almanac* by John Kirschmann; *Barry Ballister's Fruit and Vegetable Stand* by Barry Ballister (see "New World Bookshelf," p. 301); and *Laurel's Kitchen* by Laurel Robertson. These are available in book stores and health food stores. At the Sierra Nut House in Fresno, California, customers find that owner JoAnn Arvanigian is a storehouse of knowledge about nutrition. "Did you know," JoAnn asks, "that pecans are very high in vitamin B6, or that sesame seeds are the highest source of calcium? Customers really want to know these things!"

Customer relations

The customer is always number one and comes ahead of everything else. Tasks such as straightening the displays, talking on the telephone or talking to other salespeople rank second in importance to attending to customers. Nita Gizdich expresses her philosophy about customer service at the Gizdich Ranch: "As customers walk in the door, we hit them with kindness, and we always give them something free as they leave, such as a bottle of juice, or a piece of pie!"

Simple greetings or a friendly word and a smile are just as important as the product in making the sale and attracting repeat business. Take time to talk to customers. Greet regular customers by name. Learn the names of family members, likes and dislikes, how frequently the customers entertain, whether they like to try new recipes and so on. Each customer has to be treated individually. Some customers may appreciate additional information while others may consider suggestions a type of salesmanship and want to be left alone to shop.

Staff your phones with friendly and capable personnel. If you don't have a product customers are asking for, tell them where they can get it. This builds goodwill, and people come to rely on you for information.

Farmers who are not "people persons" may find they are not good salespersons. The solution for many direct-marketing farm families is to assign the job of dealing with customers to the most outgoing members of the family. Don't let shyness prevent you from becoming a topnotch salesperson, however. Simple human warmth and the sincere desire to serve the customer are more valuable selling traits than having an extroverted personality.

Take the time to train your employees in all aspects of selling with an ongoing staff training program. Develop a manual on how to do "demos," deal with customers, product information, and so on. Every employee should be kept informed on what products or services your store offers, where they are located and when they are available, as well as on ways to use the products.

Using Recipes To Keep Customers Coming Back For More

ONE OF THE MOST productive ways to educate buyers and promote your products is with recipes. Recipe sheets and booklets, according to Linda Stanley, marketing director of the North American Strawberry Growers Association (NASGA), can sell produce by the bushel, and keep people coming back for more.[1]

You can use recipes to promote the healthful aspects of your product as well as to teach inexperienced cooks how to use farm-fresh fruits and vegetables. Use fairly simple but unique recipes that use at least one or two of your products. Offer a variety of recipes and include your farm name on each one. "Once customers use and trust the recipes they've received on their visits to the farm, they're likely to become loyal, repeat customers," Stanley says.

Looking for innovative ways to use your product in recipes? In her book, *Cooking From The Garden*, Rosalind Creasey suggests an "adopt a chef" program: "Work with your chefs to develop new uses for your products and to find out what other products the chefs or consumers can use."

Joe Quieirolo, for example, who sells produce to Mudd's Restaurant in San Ramon, California, worked with the chef there and showed him that his Yellow Romano beans needed less cooking than regular beans. The chef began using a lot of them for the restaurant, and Joe was able to expand his market for Yellow Romano beans to other restaurants.

Handling customer complaints

Keith Adler, professor of marketing at Michigan State University, relates that his grandfather sold only Red Haven peaches at his roadside market. "Yet a woman came in and asked for her money back for a bag which were not Red Haven peaches. My father said: 'You know, they don't look like my peaches, but I'll give you a new basket.' The woman came in weekly for the rest of her life."

Customer complaints should be recognized as constructive criticism that can be used to improve your business. When customers complain, it usually means that they want to continue doing business with you.

Listen to customers carefully. Allow them to blow off steam. Show empathy and concern; show that you value their business. Ask questions to obtain details and solicit solutions. The fault may be the customer's; perhaps the customer neglected to cool the produce properly. Give them another dozen ears of corn anyway, saying: "Try to get it into the refrigerator right away, and if you eat it within a day, I think you'll be more satisfied."

Propose a solution to the problem and apologize for the inconvenience caused to the customer. Take action immediately to remedy any causes underlying the complaint.

Food safety and the direct marketer

According to an article in a recent issue of the *University of Wisconsin Cooperative Extension Direct Marketing Newsletter*,[2] recent consumer surveys reveal that Americans want improved safety in the foods they eat and are willing to pay more to obtain it. According to the author, Mary E. Mennes, many shoppers choose direct-marketed foods because they perceive them to be fresher and safer than those they might buy in the supermarket. "Safety should be one of the product qualities that you consistently deliver," she advises.

The direct marketer is in an excellent position to build consumer trust in the food system. Since most of your business is conducted directly with the buyer, you have an excellent opportunity to provide clear and accurate information about the safety as well as other characteristics of the foods you sell. Suggestions for food safety include:

- Check refrigerator temperatures regularly. Be sure that refrigerator temperatures are no higher than 40 degrees F. and that freezers are at 0 degrees F. or below. This protects product quality as well as safety.

- Refrigerate all perishable foods properly. For example, even though natural cheeses taste better at room temperature and will keep for short periods of time that way, they are still a perishable food and should be held at refrigerator temperatures.

- Clean display tables, cases, and shelves. Keep food display areas clean, free of spills, dirt and insects. Discard spoiled foods.

- Provide plenty of waste containers and empty them often.

- Keep all equipment in the sales or storage areas clean.

- Help your customers keep foods safe. Many direct marketers sell to a traveling public. When travelers buy fresh produce, they may want to eat some right away. Provide a way for them to wash the produce or offer to do it for them. If you are selling foods that need refrigeration, offer ice for sale and inexpensive coolers. Plastic storage bags, paper towels and other items might be useful—and profitable—tag-on sales items.

- If you have picnic tables, benches or other areas where people can sit down to have a snack or eat a meal, keep them clean. These popular areas need regular attention.

- Know your products and be honest about their qualities. If someone asks about pesticide use on a vegetable or fruit, know the answer. Be able to explain what might have been used in growing the item, why it was used, and how it breaks down. If you are growing produce yourself, follow application rules precisely. If you sell produce grown without the use of pesticides, be honest about other qualities (such as shelf life) as well.

- Help people learn more about food safety. Cooperative extension offices have several inexpensive fact sheets or publications available on food safety and storage subjects. Many industry associations also provide handy leaflets that deal with specific products. Train your employees and family members who are involved in your business to understand and practice sound food safety principles.

Acknowledgments

Bob Cobbledick, OMAF Vineland Station, Ontario, Canada.

Section VI: Wholesale Marketing

The Wholesale Picture

When a grower sells to a packer, he's fighting the whole marketing system. From the farmer to the packer to the broker to the wholesaler to the retailer—that's a lot of middlemen between the farmer and the consumer. And the farmer always seems to be at the short end of the stick.

—Bud Weisenberg, seller at the Santa Monica Certified Farmers Market

HIGH-VALUE MARKETING is the name of the game for the small farmer: growing high quality crops and selling them through specialty marketing channels. The resource that limits most direct marketers, however, is time. Spending all day at the farmers market or at your pick-your-own operation doesn't leave much time for growing. The main advantage of wholesale outlets such as supermarket warehouses, distributors, shipper-packers, terminal brokers, chain warehouses and cooperatives is that they allow you to sell a lot of produce in a short time. You don't have to spend so much time delivering, promoting and selling your product as in direct sales. As one grower

remarked, "You just drop off your watermelons at the loading dock along with your invoice."

Then there are some growers who may not be successful at direct marketing because they lack the desire, enthusiasm or personality that it takes to deal with the public on a daily basis. Also, many growers live too far from cities to market the majority of their produce directly to customers.

For the above mentioned growers, specialty brokers or wholesalers can be vital in marketing their product to more distant markets. Many wholesalers possess years of marketing experience and numerous marketing contacts. Wholesale contacts are also useful for market diversity. In slow market conditions, a long-standing relationship with a broker or wholesaler can prove invaluable in moving your products.

There is an increasing number of produce buyers, brokers and wholesalers who are willing to handle specialty products and pay higher prices for them. Wholesalers are increasingly more open to purchasing products from local growers.

As Michael Grabowski, director of marketing and sales for General Produce Company, a Sacramento-based food service distributor, explains: "As with any kind of marketing, find a need. Our company sells over $800 worth of edible flowers per day, a product that five years ago didn't exist! Don't grow something you can't sell. Research your market and find out what's in demand!"

There *is* a demand for local products, Grabowski emphasizes. "It costs me $2 per carton to bring products up from the Imperial Valley (in Southern California). Buying local products is a good way for me to cut costs."

One of the biggest challenges that smaller growers must meet in selling through wholesale channels lies in meeting market requirements. As Jim Catchot, buyer for JC Produce, Inc. in Sacramento, told growers at a recent marketing conference: "There're lots of opportunities for local growers to work with us. But don't just call us up and say, 'I've got five acres of cherry tomatoes.' We need to work with you over the growing season so we can know what and how much will be available and plan for it."

It is not advisable to sell exclusively through wholesale outlets, especially with specialty crops which are more subject to market changes than commodity crops. If you haven't guessed right about which crops to plant, you can get hurt. It's a real art to target the right item with the right quantity at the right time. A wise back-up to selling your crops to specialty distributors is to line up secondary markets, such as roadside stands or retail stores.

The problems with traditional wholesale marketing

The traditional wholesale marketing system is geared to move large volumes of produce huge distances. Without having sufficient volume to ship directly to wholesale firms, smaller specialty growers find themselves at the periphery of a market geared to serve large farms. It doesn't make sense for the specialty grower to sell the bulk of his or her products through marketing channels in which products are sold alongside those of large-scale commercial crops. While thousand-acre farms can survive on pennies-on-the-carton profits, the smaller grower cannot.

To begin with, you may be selling your crop wholesale for about 50 percent or less of its retail value. Then you must add on transportation costs, which are usually high. And because wholesaling packaging standards are high, you may need to spend another 5 percent of your sales to pack your produce in new, expensive boxes. In addition, wholesale grading standards for size, color and shape are usually strict. Produce that is only slightly blemished, slightly misshapen, or under- or over-sized by fractions of an inch may be rejected. When you get through grading for size and appearance, you may lose up to half your crop. The remainder of your crop will have to be sold as seconds (if you can find a market), or wind up in your compost pile.[1]

Then, there are wholesale standards for ripeness. Tomatoes, for example, have to be picked at exactly the right degree of ripeness (actually greenness) called the "mature green" stage. If you miss the "critical window" for ripeness, your fruits will not be accepted.[2] "The least bit of tip burn on a few lettuce leaves or a few flea beetle bites on the spinach can cause a whole truckload to be rejected," states Andy Lee, author of *Backyard Market Gardening*. "Then what do you do with it?"

Perhaps the major problem with wholesale marketing is the lack of control over the market. You wind up risking your all on only one or two major crops. According to Andy Lee: "One day you may get a decent price for your crop, the next day the price falls dramatically, because one or more of the large commercial growers has flooded the market. There are many sad tales about $14 per crate on Tuesday but only $2 per crate on Wednesday."

All in all, Andy Lee claims that wholesale commercial growers often earn 10 percent or less per acre of what is possible in small-scale market gardening. "Many large-scale commercial vegetable producers are averaging less than $500 per acre in net income from their fields," he says. "Market gardeners can earn that much in their backyard with just one hundred tomato plants. The more you produce, the less you get paid per unit. It's the law of supply and demand."[3]

In addition, a low volume of produce means relatively high marketing costs for the small farmer due to diseconomies of scale. Certain services are as costly for low volume as high volume. Long distance telephone calls to a broker, for example,

---

144

cost the same whether they involve a few crates or a few hundred.

Finally, another important consideration of traditional wholesale marketing is the social and ecological aspects of long-distance shipping. Long-distance shipping of fruits and vegetables is an expensive, wasteful system that necessitates the shipping of immature, unripe produce of little flavor and questionable nutritional value. (See "Our American Food System: The Great Debate" in the "Introduction" of this book.)

The wholesale market distribution system is a present day reality, however, and for many growers—especially larger growers—wholesale marketing is a necessary component of making a living.

A recommendation. For the smaller, specialty grower looking for optimum return, it does not pay to use *conventional* wholesale channels as your primary marketing outlet. Look for brokers, distributors or wholesalers who handle high-value products and can give you the price you deserve for your products. Some brokers or distributors may specialize in certain kinds of produce, such as ethnic, organic or other types of specialty items, which they find more readily available from small growers.

Try to develop local rather than long-distance wholesale market outlets, and utilize direct or direct-to-retail marketing outlets, such as small independent grocery stores, specialty stores or even other growers' roadside markets. Many grocery stores as well as major city supermarkets are responding to consumer requests for more locally grown produce and are more willing to accept field-run grading standards. In some cases, they will even agree to guarantee a season-long wholesale price.

Another way to thrive as a small-scale wholesale grower is to sell your crops to other growers who have an established direct-to-retail market. Or you might consider setting up a small distribution service or growers' collective yourself. For the grower who already is selling to supermarkets, restaurants, grocery stores, etc., it is mutually beneficial to purchase wholesale from other growers. (See the "Informal Cooperatives" section in Chapter 22.)

The wholesale marketing system

According to Roberta Cook, agricultural economist at U.C. Davis, "the system of produce distribution has evolved into a highly sophisticated, efficient, yet hard-to-understand marketing mechanism in which only a pro may recognize the distinction between brokers, commission merchants, merchant wholesalers, jobbers, purveyors, and shippers. It is a very complex mosaic," Cook admits. "All you can do is learn the basic system and take precautions, like subscribing to *The Red Book* or *The Blue Book.*"

Most wholesale produce marketing is very competitive and rapid due to the large number of handlers and the large number of items that are available in the marketplace. Marketing facilities and services include box and crate manufacturers and assemblers, loading docks, common carrier transporters, cooling facilities, and the terminal

Kimura Trucking, in Parlier, California, provides overnight shipping to the Bay Area and Los Angeles for Central Valley growers

markets. Loading docks make it easy to bring in a load of palletized product to be reloaded onto refrigerated tractor-trailers. *Common transportation carriers* provide the service of transporting your product in a consolidated load for a fee, to be delivered to a wholesaler in a terminal market, usually in a large metropolitan center. The wholesalers usually house the product in cooling facilities until the shipping point destination is determined. They also palletize products and re-load them into refrigerated tractor-trailers to be shipped to intermediate or final destinations.[4]

Terminal markets are colorful and bustling centers of free market enterprises. Information on quality and quantity of different items available for sale is conveyed rapidly. For new and/or established growers, the terminal markets, as represented by the produce wholesalers, facilitate ease of access to retailers (grocery stores, supermarkets, restaurants, hotels, etc.). The wholesaler, acting for the retailer, is the grower's closest link to the consumer. The grower gathers information on consumers' eating habits through the wholesaler, and often schedules the timing and type of production on his advice.[5]

Only 35 – 40 percent of produce sales are currently handled through terminal markets, as corporate chain stores and independent retailers increasingly purchase through a central wholesale supply organization. Large-volume chain stores and retail cooperatives primarily use terminal markets only for fill-ins, or to obtain specialty items not readily available—which may represent an important opportunity for the smaller grower.

Wholesalers in these markets increasingly cater to smaller supermarkets.

Wholesalers, or dealers, vary according to the clientele they serve. They may specialize in servicing restaurants, hotels, cafeterias, hospitals and other public institutions. They may also supply independent grocery stores, co-ops and markets. They may order direct from a grower, buy at an auction, order through a shipping-point broker, or call a local broker to handle the details. Wholesalers may perform such functions as receiving, re-packaging, storage and distribution to the end-user.

Wholesalers' markups can range from 20 – 40 percent, depending on services performed. Some wholesalers specialize in certain types of produce such as ethnic foods or organic or specialty items. Usually they buy by the truckload or pallet and sell by the pallet or case. With certain low-volume specialty items they may deal in smaller quantities.

Commission merchant (CM). While a *dealer* buys or contracts for the purchase of farm produce for resale at a designated price, a *commission merchant*, or shipper, buys on consignment, i.e., on trust rather than paying cash, with the understanding that he will sell the product for a commission and get the best price he can. The CM differs from the dealer in that the price at which the produce will sell does not have to be specified. But the CM is obligated to find the best price at which the produce can be sold. The CM may also perform such services as packing, hauling, precooling, palletizing, storing, and distributing.

Brokers are firms or individuals who arrange to have the packed product moved from the farm to the market. They negotiate sales on behalf of either buyers or sellers and make arrangements such as transportation; they rarely physically handle merchandise or take title. Wholesalers who want a small amount of produce or a small number of specialty items frequently rely on brokers. The broker's commission is usually about 5 – 10 percent. Another common method of payment is per unit—normally 15 – 30 cents per box shipped.

As a go-between, the broker's job is to match the producers' products with customers' needs. Brokers can be helpful in providing you with information on the needs of particular customers, which can vary by firm and by market area. Some customers, for example, may prefer small prepack-

> *The key to growing potatoes successfully is in the marketing of the crop. I cannot emphasize it enough: Know your market before you plant the first potato. Have your buyers lined up.*
> —Jack Kennedy, vegetable grower, Clear Lake, Iowa

aged packs of produce while other firms may prefer bulk packs.

Brokers can be particularly helpful in gaining initial access to major metropolitan markets. They can save you a lot of phone calls in trying to find customers for your product, whether your product is a high-value specialty product or an off-size product that needs to be marketed as number twos. Specialty brokers are often instrumental in the promotion of a new, specialty product. Although most brokers deal in relatively large volumes, some specialty brokers deal in smaller volumes.

Shippers. Some growers sell their product directly to buyers located in major growing areas through the services of shippers. Shippers locate buyers, normally chain stores and wholesalers in major metropolitan areas. As in the case of a grower selling to wholesalers, similar marketing protocol follows: shipper and buyer agree to a price on the delivered product; the shipper handles transportation costs, arranges for transportation, cooling, or special handling; the shipper charges a commission, and pays the grower the net price after all deductions are made. If necessary, lower price adjustments at the receiving end are worked out to deal with quality dissatisfaction. Shippers may also assist the grower with production cost and financing and may agree to suffer varying financial loss in the event of unsatisfactory crop yield. Shippers may also grow their own product but will consolidate with other growers in order to augment their market share.[6]

Large commercial produce operations are frequently state-licensed in the categories of wholesaler, broker and commission merchant, since they may be involved in all of these transactions at some point.

Restaurant purveyors satisfy the needs of chain and individual restaurants. Small growers may find it advantageous to contact these wholesalers since their production can be catered to specific needs of well-paying clients, and the volume of products required is often less.[7]

Specialty distributors, who purchase your product for distribution to high-end restaurants, natural food stores or gourmet shops, can be one of your best buyers for high-end crops. Specialty distributors not only pay top prices for your product, they are experienced and knowledgeable in handling specialty products. For some resourceful growers, selling through specialty brokers or distributors leaves them free to spend most of their time in production, while getting top dollar for their crops. According to Don Stiling, a farmer who grows specialty salad mixes and tomatoes near Sebastopol, California, the prices he gets for his specialty products range anywhere from one-and-a-half to double what the same items would command on the commodity market. "This is close to what I could get selling them at the farmers market," says Stiling, "and I don't have to spend the time in marketing."

Specialty distributors may handle only limited volume, however. In addition, the high-end specialty trade is a highly crowded, competitive market that demands the highest quality product and packaging. There are relatively few specialty distributors, and therefore the supply-demand issue is very critical. The market can become easily glutted. You can't just grow anything and expect to get high-end prices. Specialty produce changes from year to year depending on what's fashionable.

Miscellaneous wholesale outlets

Private packing facilities provide grading, packing and cooling services for growers. In addition, they may also harvest, field haul, finance production, manage field operations, provide certain supplies, deliver to buyers, and lease production equipment.[8]

Processors. Another marketing option is to sell to fruit and vegetable processing plants. Good managerial capabilities are essential for a producer to provide the required amounts and qualities of produce to a processing facility. Processing often requires different varieties than are used for the fresh produce market. Crops should not be plant-

ed without an assured contract with a buyer. Generally a contract is made by the grower to provide the processing plant with a specified amount of quality produce over a certain period of time, thus providing an assured market for the grower. Processors may control the production practices through contracts and field representatives, and may provide supplies as well as production and harvesting assistance.

Selling to processors offers growers the opportunity to market large volumes with reduced marketing effort. Prices for selling to processing plants may be lower due to less risk, however, and quality standards may be stringent.[9]

To find processing companies, look in the yellow pages under "Processing" or "Canning" or "Juices"; check directories such as *Organic Wholesalers Directory and Yearbook*; talk to other farmers; or check for company names on labels of processed products in stores.

Schools and institutions such as government agencies, military bases, prisons, company cafeterias, summer schools and camps, hospitals and convalescent homes are worth looking into for higher volume, mainstream items. They are not a prospect for your specialty or high-end items. Institutions may have very specific needs, such as packaging and uniformity of product. Also, since they generally require a high volume and often ask for a full line of products, they usually are not a viable market for the smaller grower with only a few items.

Some institutions, such as schools, are coming under increasing public pressure to buy more local products, however, and if the persons in charge of purchasing have a particular interest or preference in buying local produce, they may be very receptive to a sales call from a local cooperative. Don't be afraid to write letters to your local newspaper, call your local board of supervisors, or in other ways call upon community influence to persuade local institutions to buy local produce!

Every school is required to provide a feeding program for children. Contact the school's food service staff to find out what products they buy on the open market. Likely candidates are fresh fruits and vegetables or simple processed products such as applesauce.

If you find that you cannot supply a sufficient quantity and/or diversity of products for bulk sales to institutions, contact other producers in the area to see if they are interested in selling cooperatively.

Bulk sales of certain commodities must conform with state and federal marketing orders if they exceed a maximum volume limit.

Marketing research for the wholesale market

How to find wholesale buyers?

The method with which to market your products will depend on the contacts you develop, availability of facilities, the market conditions, and the risks you are willing to take. Talk to as many knowledgeable marketing experts as possible to determine who may be interested in handling and marketing your products, including marketing agents, point-of-shipment buyers (shippers), wholesalers and brokers.[10]

One way in which to select a wholesaler is by word-of-mouth. Many wholesalers have been in business for a number of years and their reputation will precede them. Check with other growers in the area and see whom they recommend.[11] Also talk to your farm advisor, as well as to local trade associations.

"Work backwards" in the market you'd like to sell to. Call a few restaurants, for example, and ask them who their suppliers are. With retail chains, try to get produce managers at independent retail stores interested in your product. Independent

---

Market Windows

In the fast-changing, competitive world of wholesale marketing, product timing is critical. The strategy is to identify a "market window" and attempt to produce for that window. Market windows represent opportunities in production not yet fully exploited by other growers—for example, the production of uncommon products. Currently, the production of specialty lettuce represents an area of potential growth. However this marketing window will close as competition from other growers increases, as in the case of kiwi and avocado production. Determining when to market involves gathering firsthand information from various sources, including point-of-origin sales persons, field agents and wholesalers.[12]

---

retailers (i.e., companies with less than 11 stores) are much more likely to introduce new or local products into their stores than the major chains. Give them a sales pitch, send or take them samples, and then ask them for the names of their suppliers.

"Walk the market" at a wholesale terminal, visiting different houses and talking to buyers. Major terminal markets have lots of different kinds of buyers, and you'll quickly learn who specializes in what, and where your product might fit in. Take along a few samples and/or pictures of what you grow.

The *Progressive Grocer's Marketing Guidebook* is a source for finding phone numbers and addresses of retailers. Other sources include the trade directories of the United Fresh Fruit and Vegetable Association and Produce Marketing Association as well as *The Packer* newspaper and *Produce News*. Check the directories of local trade associations.

Names and addresses of grocery stores, health food stores and department stores can also be obtained through purchased mailing lists. Names are sold by the thousand (usually between $50 and $100 per thousand). You can purchase them for a particular area or by size. Ask your library for a copy of *Direct Mail List Rates and Data* published by Standard Rate & Data Service, 5201 Old Orchard Rd., Skokie, IL 60076. Or contact American Business Lists, 5711 South 86th Circle, P.O. Box 27347, Omaha, NB 68127; (402) 331-7169; FAX (402) 331-1505.

The Red Book or *The Blue Book* are excellent sources to find phone numbers, addresses and contact people for wholesale buyers. *The Red Book* and *The Blue Book* are two industry credit rating services for both buyers and sellers which are updated on a regular basis. The books contain names and addresses of wholesale houses, chain store warehouses, grower/shippers, brokers, shippers, buyers, truck brokers, etc., throughout the nation. Instructions on handling claims, rules of transport, state laws and regulations also are covered. Organic specialty brokers and distributors are listed in *Organic Wholesalers Directory* and *Healthy Harvest*.

Check under "Fruits & Vegetables–Brokers," "Fruits & Vegetables–Growers and Shippers," "Fruits & Vegetables–Wholesale," or "Flowers," etc., in the yellow pages of major cities. Phone directories for major U.S. cities are usually available in local libraries. Cities of 100,000 or more are likely to have produce wholesalers which service independent stores and restaurants. Call them to get the names of their buyers.

Getting the accounts. When you have obtained your list of contact names, call the buyers, explain what you are selling and ask for an appointment to talk to them about your product, or better yet, ask to go in and see them. Buyers are busy people—letters do little good. When you meet with buyers, ask them about their marketing requirements (see "Meeting Marketing Requirements" in this chapter) as well as current sources of supply, weekly purchase volume, preferred transportation methods, prices paid, payment schedule and ordering procedures.

To develop next year's market, or to supplement your current buyers' list, take your prospective buyers *samples*, especially when introducing a new product to the market. Then they can taste the product and in turn take samples to *their* customers.

In researching buyers, consider their payment policies. Some firms will pay weekly; others pay on the last day allowed under the applicable law—or later. If cash flow is a concern, choose those buyers who offer prompt payment.

Unless you are marketing with other growers to combine loads, look for handlers who take consolidated loads. You may not have the volume or want to take the risk of shipping full loads to distant cities. Ask wholesale buyers if there is a broker or marketing agent they work with who will accept consolidated loads.

Consider transportation. You need to get the product to buyers in good condition and at a good price. For example, in shipping highly perishable products such as berries, you may want to choose major cities with direct flights, since your product won't keep well in flight-transfers or long truck hauls.

The video camcorder is a useful tool for promoting to buyers you cannot visit in person. The idea is to send a duplicated VCR recorded tape to buyers who may be interested in your products. Your 10-minute tape should describe some of the more technical aspects of your business, number of employees, types of products produced, delivery, and methods of growing. You also might mention other buyers to whom you sell.

Wholesale market reports. Most wholesale marketing report information can be categorized as current price reports; production (supply) information; and summary (year-end) reports which can be used for analysis, such as making a market window analysis. If consumption of a particular crop is rising in a particular market area, and supply is not rising along with demand, this could identify a "market window." You should correlate the information received from the Market News Service with the experience of several buyers in determining the profitability of various marketing opportunities. Most wholesale marketing report information is geared for volume marketing of major commodity crops, however; the marketer looking for high-value markets needs to target low-volume, niche markets.

Meeting market requirements

Wholesalers complain of nonprofessionalism amongst many small growers—that they often fail to follow industry wholesale standards in quality, pack, grading and delivery. Since each market will have different standards, ask your buyers' preferences for product characteristics (variety, grade, size, degree of ripeness, etc.), volume, type of packaging preferred, and then pack accordingly. Be consistent.

Quality, even in the wholesale marketing system, is your most important product. Shipping a high-quality product can minimize spoilage losses throughout the marketing system. Businesses handling produce operate on low margins, so their buyers want to minimize losses caused by spoilage. A group of Lake County, California, grape growers, for example, were marketing flame-seedless grapes through wholesale marketing channels. Their product was beautiful and clean, with nice color and in big bunches. While a normal lug was 23 pounds, they were packing their grapes in 16-pound lugs wrapped as a specialty pack, and getting the same price as other growers for 23-pound lugs!

Product shelf life is different in selling to the wholesale market than in direct marketing. While growers may take fully ripe fruit to the farmers market, products are generally picked greener for the wholesale market. An exception is if you can find distributors who are able to get the product to retail shelves within 24 hours. Most produce needs to be cooled promptly to take out the field heat and to be refrigerated during storage and transport.

Grading. Assorting your produce by quality, size and maturity is called grading. There are USDA grades for most commodities as well as industry and individual buyer standards. You need to know all the grades and standards that apply to the crops you sell.

Grading standards make long-distance produce sales possible by allowing buyers to purchase the exact type of produce they want without seeing the product. The high cost of purchasing grading equipment and building a packing house, however, is a deterrent for most small growers and serves as an incentive for establishing a cooperative.

Don't try to increase your volume by adding lower-grade quality produce to your packs. Mixing poor quality with number one quality may cause a

Characteristics of Wholesale Marketing Alternatives

Characteristic	Wholesale Terminal Market	Cooperative & Private Packing Facilities	Wholesaler	Broker
Market Investment	Truck or some transportation arrangements. Specialized containers required.	May be substantial but low on a per unit basis.	Depends on arrangements. Usually minimal costs to producer. Specialized containers required.	Depends on arrangements. Usually minimal costs to producer. Specialized containers required.
Prices Received	Producer usually price taker.	Prices received by growers depend on costs and revenues.	Producer usually price taker. Price agreed to at time of sale and current prices.	Producer usually price taker.
Quality	Must meet buyers' standards.	Federal inspection may assure buyers of quality.	Must meet standards so that produce can be handled in bulk.	Must meet standards so that produce can be handled in bulk.
Required Volume	Usually larger quantities needed.	Depends on qualifications and products sold.	Usually large quantities needed.	Usually large quantities needed.
Transportation Cost	Depends on grower's distance to market.	Sometimes firms provide equipment.	Depends on prior arrangements.	Depends on prior arrangements.
Harvesting Cost	Normal.	Sometimes firms provide machinery.	Normal.	Normal.
Other Considerations	Good place to gather market information. Can move large quantities at one time. Many buyers are located at market.	May provide technical assistance. Firms help in planning of growing and selling. Share equipment.	Good wholesaler can sell produce quickly at good prices. Long-term buyer/seller relationship. Wholesale buyer assumes the market risk.	Good wholesaler/broker can sell produce quickly at good prices. Long-term buyer/seller relationship. Large number of buyers are exposed to seller's product. Grower retains responsibility for quality until delivery.
Wholesale Marketing Advantages	Opportunity to move large volume. May be less marketing time required. Quality product usually receives a better price. May be lower promotional and educational costs.			
Wholesale Marketing Disadvantages	Strict federal, state or industry marketing orders standards for grading and packing. Grower anonymity: little control of product sales, often resulting in lower prices.			
Special Considerations	May require large volumes. Needs consistent supplies. May have to establish a previous record as a reliable source of supply before larger clients are willing to buy.			

loss of sale on all the product, or a low-grade price for the whole shipment, and will hurt your reputation with the buyer. Find separate outlets for your number twos and number threes.

Grading standards can be vastly different for wholesale than for direct-to-consumer selling. Go by grading standards rather than your own judgment as to what is the best produce. The most perfect specimen from the viewpoint of immediate consumption may be unacceptable after it has been shipped, handled and stored.

To find information on grading standards, contact your state department of agriculture, as well as your local extension office. A set of U.S. vegetable standards is available free from: Fruit and Vegetable Division, Standardization Section, FPB, FVD, AMS, USDA, P.O. Box 96456, Room 2056 South Building, Washington, DC 20090-6456. Most importantly, discuss quality standards with potential wholesale buyers, since many wholesalers, brokers and chain stores prefer to buy according to their own specifications.

Volume. Since buyers prefer to deal with as few suppliers as possible, they frequently look for suppliers who can supply a significant portion of their needs. Can you supply and transport sufficient volume for your market? Low-volume needs of some buyers for specialty crops, on the other hand, may not be economical. You might consider teaming up with neighboring farmers in order to meet minimum volume requirements. Look for

For all of our long hours, farmers are lazy when it comes to marketing. There's always so much to do on the farm, marketing seems to stay on the back burner indefinitely. . . This is a mistake! The most beautiful crop in the world doesn't mean much if you can't sell it, and sell it at a profit!
    –Denesse Willey, T & D Willey Farms, Clovis, California

buyers whose product and volume needs you can most profitably fulfill. Target buyers who can be supplied consistently throughout the growing season. Buyers for the most part are not interested in a one-time-only delivery. Pay close attention to planting schedules and variety selection. Extend availability by successive plantings and/or by using crop protection where possible and economically practical.

Acknowledgments

Curt Moulton, King County Cooperative Extension, Washington State.

Ann Thorp, Produce Ltd., Oskaloosa, Iowa.

Getting Your Product To Market

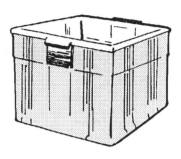

CHAPTER

20

IN THE WHOLESALE marketing system, getting your product to market in the quickest, most reliable, and safest way possible is no less vital than any other step in the process of profitable marketing.

Packing

The first consideration in packing is a high quality product—uniform in size, color, condition, and overall quality. Sort out all physically damaged and misshapen produce. Buyers like to know exactly what they will get when they order produce.

Clean and neatly packed produce reflects a quality product and helps bring a premium price. Pack in standardized containers which hold an established number of the requested items at a predetermined minimum weight. Standardized containers clarify the quantity of items being sold and the price per pound to be paid. Shipping without standardized containers may lead to a significant miscalculation of the total amount of money to be exchanged in a transaction.[1]

Follow the standard package count for each product—e.g., 24 heads of lettuce in a box. Distributors buy on the basis of 24 heads of lettuce to a case, and that's what they expect to get. Easily-bruised products like tomatoes need to be placed in single- or double-layer packages rather than in a loose pack.

Shipping containers

The shipping container must protect the product and maintain product quality; be easy to handle; stand up under stacking, cooling, shipping, and storage conditions; identify the product and the packer; and carry information required by law. In addition, packaging offers a promotional tool for your product and farm name. It is ideal to have the product come in a salable package, because less handling means better shelf life.

Generally, packaging standards are quite stringent for wholesale marketing. The containers must meet industry standards for size, volume and strength, and they must be suitable for storing on standard pallets. State or marketing order standards may apply to your product. Packaging standards are established by the USDA and enforced by the County Agricultural Commissioner's Office of Market Enforcement. These offices are located in terminal markets.

To find the standard wholesale pack requirements for different products, look in *The Packer's Produce and Availability Merchandising Guide*, or *Knott's Handbook* (for vegetables). Your local extension agent can furnish you with the USDA regulations for interstate transport. Information on containers, net weights and other data on weights and measures for many products is also available in *Weights, Measures, and Conversion Factors for Agricultural Commodities and Their Products*, Agricultural Handbook #697, June

---

ORGANIC FRUITS & VEGETABLES

1992. It is available for $11 from ERS-NASS, P.O. Box 1608, Rockville, MD 20849-1608; (800) 999-6779.

Packaging requirements vary with each commodity. Also, commodities being shipped across state lines may require different packaging than for in-state shipping. Many specialty commodities have not been assigned official containers but are sold in containers as determined by the practice of the trade. Contact your wholesaler or Market Enforcement Office before packaging unusual or exotic products.[2]

Use uniform, sturdy containers (heavy-duty bags and boxes) that will hold up in shipping. Look for distributors who can supply standard pack boxes at price breaks. Check the yellow pages under "Boxes—Used." Go in with other growers in your area to save money on large-scale purchases.

Many vegetables are packed in cartons made of waxed fiberboard. Waxing is essential when the produce is packed wet or with ice in order to give added strength to the boxes and to reduce moisture loss from the product.

Features to look for in shipping boxes include:

• *Protection.* How well do the boxes protect your product? Certain products may require holes cut in the carton to provide ventilation of product heat or respiration and to allow circulation of cold air to the product. Product bruising can be reduced by adding pads, wraps, sleeves, or excelsior. How well do the boxes hold moisture? Some products may require plastic film liners or bags to help retain moisture.

• *Stackability.* Are the boxes both fitted for, and strong enough, to stack one on top of another without crushing any produce?

• *Storage.* Do the boxes save storage space by folding when not in use?

• *Presentation.* Do the boxes catch the buyer's eye?

• *Size.* If possible, make sure the boxes fit your product, and fill them full so that the handler feels he is getting his dollar value.

Wood crates allow free air circulation around the packed product and are still popular with some shippers due to the strength of wood and its resistance to high humidity during precooling, transit, and storage.[3]

Attractive packaging helps market products. In specialty, high-end markets, it may pay to spend a little extra to have your farm logo or a striking color label put on your shipping boxes. As wholesale buyers walk through the market terminal, they first glance at the boxes of produce, then check out the ones that catch their eye. If the product looks as good as the packaging, they buy!

Specialty markets particularly may demand more upscale packaging. Some of the new packaging boxes, in fact, may be so attractive they can double as display cases. While some growers have a farm logo or graphics printed on their boxes to help make their product stand out, Tom and Denesse Willey of T & D Willey Farms near Fresno, California, affix a 5-by-8-inch label on each of their wooden boxes. Each label carries a striking full-color photo of their farm, and the Willeys include extra labels for the retailers to use as in-store displays above their produce.

Some products are prepackaged in smaller units before being placed on trays in the shipping carton. Apples, for example, are often wrapped individually, while carrots are often placed in 1- or 2-pound bags. If you prepack, make sure that the additional packaging does not interfere with efficient cooling of the product, and make sure that your pricing reflects the added cost.

Make sure also that your prepackaged consumer packs, such as 3-pound bags of apples or 5-pound bags of potatoes, carry a U.P.C. code. Most chain stores are scanning nearly all of the items they carry. If quality is equal, a supplier who uses U.P.C. codes has a better chance of selling his or her products.

Labels should be correct, complete and highly visible. They should contain the name of the product and the name and address of the grower, as well as a count of how many units are being shipped. Quite often size, variety, commodity and grade are shown on the container by means of check-off boxes which can be marked with an "X." If the product is organic, include the legally required wording to assure the buyer that the produce is organic. Contact your state department of agriculture for labeling requirements for your product.

Labels, in addition to satisfying legal requirements, can also help promote your product and farm name. With new or unusual products especially, additional point-of-purchase materials with recipes, storage, handling suggestions, etc., should be included to enhance consumer awareness and increase sales. See also "Rules & Regulations–Labeling Laws," Chapter 25.

Packaging for the environment

It is predicted that the '90s will be called the "decade of the environment." According to *The Produce News* (June 14, 1990), "The biggest environmental concern of most consumers today is solid waste disposal. As waste disposal and landfill problems have attained crisis proportions, people are discovering that the problems are more serious than once thought."

It makes economic as well as environmental sense to use environmentally sound packaging. If you are shipping to most traditional wholesale markets, however, you will be required to follow industry packaging standards for your commodity. If possible, use recyclable material, such as unwaxed cardboard. If you are marketing directly to local markets, such as to restaurant or retail outlets, or to nontraditional markets where industry packaging standards may not apply, pack in reusable boxes such as wooden crates or hard plastic, which can be sanitized and reused. Ask your buyers or distributors to cooperate with you

in your recycling efforts by saving your boxes for you to pick up for reuse.

Generally, products made of a single material are easier to recycle than packages made with different types of materials. Waxed cardboard can't be recycled, so if your products need to be hydrocooled or iced, it may be hard to use environmentally conscious packaging. Most waxed cardboard boxes are used one time, then sent to the dumpster. Let's hope the industry comes up with a solution soon!

One alternative to waxed cardboard boxes is a wooden crate lined with butcher paper or moisture absorbent, nonbleached newsprint paper. This works with certain products such as chard which are dunked in water before packing. Glue rather than staple your labels onto boxes; staples cut produce workers' hands as they reach into the box to take out your produce.

Ron Mansfield, owner of Goldbud Farms near Placerville, California, sells his tree-ripened stone fruit to specialty distributors, shipping his fruit in old-fashioned wood crates with plastic panapack cups. Ron feels this combination offers the advantages of strong protection for the product and recyclability. The wood boxes are used at least three or four times over the season; each time they are used, a new peel-off sticker is placed on them, with product information, bar code and count.

Fortunately, the natural country look of roadside markets is "in," and some grocery stores and supermarkets often market products right out of the containers. Colora Orchards, near Colora, Maryland, ships its peaches to local stores in fresh, clean wooden boxes with hand cut-outs on the box sides for easy handling and with their farm name stenciled on the sides of the boxes. When customers began asking for the boxes to take home, the chain store owners offered to purchase the boxes for resale to customers.

For products that can take some amount of stacking, such as apples, melons or winter squash, use bulk bins whenever possible. For items that can't withstand stacking, use wooden lug crates with plastic liners that can be reused.

If you use recycled products, let people know—this creates a positive image for your farm! For a series of reports on recycling topics, as well as for their newsletter *Wastelines*, write to: Solid Waste Alternatives Project, 1525 New Hampshire Avenue, NW, Washington, DC 20036; (202) 745-4870.

Another resource for information on ecological packaging is the *Preferred Packaging Manual,* available for $50 from the Coalition of Northeastern Governors (CONEG), 400 N. Capitol Street, NW, Suite 382, Washington, DC 20001; (202) 624-8450. In a nutshell, the "preferred packaging" guidelines they recommend are: 1) *Eliminate.* Whenever possible, eliminate the package altogether; 2) *Minimize.* Minimize the packaging; 3) *Refill/Reuse.* Design packages that are either consumable, returnable, or refillable/reusable; and 4) *Recycle.* Use produce packages that are recyclable.

Transportation

Retail consumers buy produce based on appearance, so don't slack off in finding the shipping method that will get your product to the buyer in the freshest condition.

In selecting a shipper, ask for recommendations from your buyer, produce houses or other growers. Check who is experienced in shipping similar types of produce and who handles and delivers well. Ask for references and talk to their clients. Do they deliver on time and in satisfactory condition? Is the company properly licensed? Do they carry transportation insurance to cover losses due to accidents or equipment failures?

Shipping should be arranged in advance of harvest since trucks may be difficult to obtain during the peak of the season. Arrange transportation directly with the carrier or through a transportation broker or freight forwarder. The buyer usually selects and pays for the transportation directly. In some cases, you pay the transportation cost and include it in calculating the final product selling price.[4]

Trucking.[5] The most widely used means of transporting fresh produce is by refrigerated truck-trailer. It is a very flexible mode: products can be shipped from any growing area to any market in the continental U.S. For current trucking cost information, contact a local truck broker. Also, the Federal-State Market News Service quotes average trucking rates between major shipping and destination points.

Depending on the destination, the produce may be in the hands of the trucker longer than anyone else in the distribution system. So take care to find a reliable trucker with well-maintained equipment. To find a trucker, talk with other growers or the buyer you are selling to, or look in *The Red Book* or *The Blue Book* for truck brokers. Usually brokers handle the billing for a trucker and retain a percentage brokerage fee.

You may also want to contract with local truckers or trucking firms to move your product on a steady basis to regular buyers. In some cases, the buyer provides trucks.

L.T.L.'s. For smaller shipments, look for shippers who will ship L.T.L.'s (less-than-full loads), or try to find a broker who can fill out the load for you. Make sure that the products being shipped with your product have compatible storage and shipping requirements. There are trucking firms that specialize in L.T.L.'s.

You may also try to fill out a load yourself. Locate other growers or vendors of similar produce who have compatible delivery schedules and ship your loads together. Look for possible shipping partners by asking your destination or receiving point person, farmers market contacts, your local extension office, or produce supply houses.[6]

Backhauling. Consider how produce is being delivered to food service and grocery accounts in your own area. If it is being trucked from where you want your produce to go, backhauling could be an option for you. A backhauler will want to know where to make the pickup, where to make deliveries, whether your schedules are compatible, and how much you will be shipping.

F.O.B. (Free-On-Board). If your terms are "F.O.B., your warehouse," then the price includes the cost of transportation. The customer pays the freight and takes title to the merchandise when it leaves your warehouse. This means that the customer will be responsible for taking up the issue of any damaged or missing goods with the shipping company. The shipper should promptly pay the buyer for any damage that occurs in shipping. However, he cannot deduct missing or damaged merchandise from your invoice. If the buyer claims the produce has been received in poor condition, the supplier is left in a vulnerable position. Even with a federal inspection, it is difficult to prove products were damaged in shipping.

"F.O.B., customer location" means the price does not include the cost of transportation. In the event merchandise is missing on delivery or is damaged enroute, then you must seek recourse with the shipping company. Title passes to the

Buying Your Own Equipment

PURCHASING YOUR own trucking equipment may be practical if you are doing a large volume of local shipping. Long-distance trucking puts you in the trucking business both in purchasing equipment and in coordinating deliveries and arranging backloads. If your volume warrants doing your own trucking, however, there are many options for refrigerated vehicles, ranging from an insulated "slip-in" box for a pickup truck or a new or used insulated cargo van.

Reefer systems installed in a cargo van cost from $2000 to $3000, depending on cooling requirements and options. A good forced-air cooling system can cool down your produce in 30 – 60 minutes, so the expense may be worth it if that's what it takes to protect your product. An industrial cold plate to fit an average pickup truck box costs roughly $2000 and with good maintenance it will last an estimated 15 – 20 years. Industrial cold plates may be purchased through firms specializing in truck cooling systems.[7] Another low-end option is simply to pack ice in styrofoam igloos—this is for short hauls only!

When shopping for a used cargo van, slip-in box or other insulated vehicle, search for farm sales and auctions in agricultural magazines under "Equipment Sold" or "Auctions," as well as local used truck dealers and truck rental firms. Also call local packer/shippers or warehouses who may be upgrading to bigger or newer equipment and want to sell their old equipment.

If you build your own storage and packing facilities or refurbish existing buildings, design your facility to minimize handling. A loading dock, for example, which enables you to load by the pallet instead of carrying the produce in and out of doorways, is a good investment.

---

customer when merchandise is delivered, signed for and in good condition.[8]

Bill of lading. Keep good records of what you ship, and make sure you have a bill of lading stating the number of boxes, size and/or weight, and destination signed by the trucking company as proof of the condition of the goods at the point of departure. Sometimes a federal inspection stamp is required on the bill; your county agent can tell you when, where, and if you need it. The bill of lading, which is signed when the produce is delivered, also serves as your proof of delivery when billing by mail. Send an invoice as soon as delivery has been confirmed. Also, line up alternative places of sale in case any load is rejected.

Protecting your product in shipping

It doesn't matter how good a crop is, or how well it's harvested, packed, and precooled, if it doesn't reach the consumer in good condition. To avoid losses during transport, you must know the specific requirements for protecting the product you are shipping.[9]

Cooling and insulation requirements vary widely depending upon product perishability and the distances and time in shipping. Consult with your extension agent, a local university horticulture expert, other growers, a produce warehouse or experienced shipping firm personnel to learn the storage and handling needs of your product. Then select the optimal ways to protect your product in shipping.

Several key factors to consider in transportation product protection are:

- *Mechanical damage.* Ship in well-designed containers and stack the product so that it will not be damaged in shipping. Mechanical damage can occur in loading or unloading produce, or in transit.

- *Temperature, humidity and ventilation.* Maintain the proper temperature for the product being shipped. Fresh produce needs to be kept cool and frozen produce needs to be kept frozen.

Some products are subject to chilling injury or moisture stress. Products should be stacked in the truck so that air can circulate uniformly to all parts of the load.

• *Compatibility with other commodities.* Never store or transport produce that emits a lot of ethylene (this includes many fruits) with produce that is sensitive to ethylene (this includes many vegetables).

If you are shipping by truck, look for a truck line that uses forced-air cooled trucks or other industry-standard temperature control methods such as heaters to prevent freezing in winter, or uses modified atmospheres for highly perishable products. Portable temperature monitors (Ryan Recorders) should be placed within loads to verify maintenance of proper temperature during shipment. Equipment, like the produce itself, should be cooled prior to shipping so that heat doesn't transfer to the produce. The truck should be clean and free from offensive odors and residues that might contaminate fresh produce.

Loading checklist. Develop a loading checklist: Is the trailer precooled and the reefer (refrigeration unit) running? Is there a way, such as air-bags or side-bars, to secure products if the truck is less than full? Are there any leakages caused by damage to the trailer which can create "hotspots"? Is the trailer clean and well-swept, with ribbing on the floor so that air can circulate underneath the products?

Handle the product with care. Arrive at the market at the proper time. Unload the product and

© Oregon Organic Brokerage, Inc., 541 Willamette, #311, Eugene, OR 97401 (503) 687-9535

place it in the buyer's designated place according to his individual storing requirements. Have the proper person inspect the product upon delivery and complete the needed paper work for the transaction.

For specific transport requirements, consult the USDA Handbook #669, *Protecting Perishable Foods During Transport By Truck,* available from the U.S. Government Printing Office.

Acknowledgments

Curt Moulton, King County Cooperative Extension, Washington State.

Ann Thorp, Produce Ltd., Oskaloosa, Iowa.

Making It Pay

Wholesale Payment Practices,
Pricing, and Grower-Buyer Relations

WHOLESALE MARKETING is commonly associated with dumping your crops off at the grain elevator or terminal market. The attitude of "leaving it to the other guy" when it comes to marketing invites financial heartache, however. In wholesale marketing, as in direct marketing, it pays to make yourself as knowledgeable as possible about the marketing process in order to protect yourself and make sure you get what you deserve for your product.

Wholesale pricing

In the wholesale market there is no established market price at which commodities are sold. Prices vary from dealer to dealer, from one location to another and from one hour to another for different quality levels and packaging. Supply and demand as well as negotiation determine the grower price, which is usually within some range of prevailing prices. Production from major growing areas, however, tends to be sold at a relatively uniform price (for the same quality). This price can serve as a guide point for pricing locally produced items.[1] The wholesale market usually is a buyers' market—there are fewer buyers than sellers. It takes a skillful seller to identify the buyers willing to pay the highest prices.

In the wholesale market, more than in direct-to-consumer marketing, prices bear little relationship to costs. In a national market, profits can be affected by factors beyond your control. A big green bean crop in western North Carolina can drive

prices so low your beans may be hardly worth picking. Or a whitefly infestation in another area can turn your fall lettuce crop into a gold mine.[2]

Definite marketing arrangements should be made before planting, with prices to be negotiated near delivery time. Growers should learn to ask questions of prospective buyers such as: "What is the price range you have been paying for a specific grade of commodity during the season I can grow it? What delivery schedule do you want and how much volume per delivery? How do you want it packed?" and so on.[3]

The key to good pricing is good information. You should know the break-even price and the related volume that you must sell to achieve it. In addition, you should know prevailing market prices, the product quality relative to others available on the market, and the purchasing options of buyers. Since supply fluctuation may create marketing opportunities or problems, you need to be aware of the general trend in supply over the season as well as temporary supply aberrations such as heavy rains in major production areas, disease outbreaks, delivery interruptions or harvest labor problems.

The Market News Service of the USDA Agricultural Marketing Service includes wholesale prices and market conditions at major shipping points and terminal markets across the country. The "shipping point" price includes grower price plus packing and brokering charges as well as loading on a truck or rail car. It is listed as F.O.B., which stands for free-on-board, and means the price does

Price and Payment[5]

The price of products is determined by its grade (U.S. Extra Fancy, U.S. Fancy, etc.) and the quantity entering the market. An example of a typical price breakdown is as follows:

A standardized box of eighty Washington Delicious apples (24-pound net weight, 45-pound gross weight) is sold by the grower at $18 F.O.B. Freight cost is an additional $2 per box to be assumed solely by the buyer or by both grower and wholesaler. The wholesaler sells the box to the supermarket at $23 per box (usually no more than an 18-percent profit). The market in turn sells the apples at 99¢ per pound (as much as a 100 percent markup). If a broker is involved in the transaction, subtract an additional 15 – 35¢ per box from the amount received by the grower.

If the supermarket refuses the box of Washington Delicious apples, then the responsibility for the loss becomes solely the grower's. However, the wholesaler usually will attempt to move the product by way of another buyer. In that case, a price adjustment may be necessary and is usually due to lower product quality.

Payment to the grower is made by the wholesaler usually within three weeks after receipt of the product by the wholesaler.

not include the cost of transportation. "Terminal market" prices are what the *wholesaler* (*not* the grower) received when the item was sold to a retailer or distributor. This includes the grower price plus the packing, brokering and shipping charges and wholesaler profit.[4]

Check also USDA *Federal Crop Reports*, as well as "Shipping Point Trends" in *The Packer* newspaper for prices and market trends. Another way to check prices is to call a terminal market for their daily price reports.

You might go into retail stores and ask the retailer what he or she is paying for the product you are planning to sell. Talk also to growers of similar

products as well as to other people in the industry. Wholesalers and brokers may be good market news sources. They generally have excellent contacts in the major producing areas. Never sell on the information of only one person!

Remember also that for specialty produce, or organic or vine- or tree-ripened products, there may not be a market price established yet. Prices depend on what consumers, and buyers, are willing to pay for a new item. And this in turn may depend on the extent to which you are able to educate buyers and consumers about the benefits of your new product.

Wholesale payment practices, misconceptions, and tips

Farmers used to being paid cash-in-hand at the farmers market are in for some surprises in wholesale marketing. Most wholesale transactions in the fresh produce industry are made on credit. Although many state regulations require most wholesale transactions to be paid within 30 days of delivery of the product, and federal regulations require most wholesale transactions to be paid within 10 days of delivery (for products sold across state lines), payment practice is generally longer than this. If the buyer pays his accounts on a monthly basis, for example, the grower may not receive payment until six weeks or more after he delivered the product.

Consignment sales are based on trust; i.e., the grower assumes all price and product risks until the product is sold, and is paid after the sale according to the volume and the price at which the buyer is able to sell the product. For the smaller or startup grower, it is better to seek upfront payment. Try to arrange for payment upon delivery until good working relations and credit have been established. While high-volume growers can absorb the inherent risks of consignment sales, smaller-volume, high-value crops are too valuable not to ask for straight payment. Upfront payment helps cover your initial investment and will save you costly delays in collection time. An exception may be if you find a broker with a superior reputation and track record.

Since prices for perishable, fresh fruit and vegetable crops fluctuate daily, the prices quoted to the farmer at the time of delivery to a wholesaler

VERITABLE VEGETABLE

or broker may be different from the prices existing when the product reaches the market and the broker or wholesaler is paid for the crop. If the market price declines after delivery of the product, the buyer may ask for a "price adjustment" on the amount he had quoted you. The buyer can't legally insist on this, but it may be necessary if you wish to continue to do business with him.

Since wholesale prices are more market-driven than direct-to-consumer marketing, you may want to consider lowering your prices or offering quantity discounts in order to move a large volume. Make sure that delivery requirements and payment terms (such as a 2-percent discount if paid in 10 days, C.O.D., etc.) are specified in your verbal or written contracts with buyers.

Include a statement on your invoices that all claims against damage must be made within 48 hours of receipt of shipment. Your invoices also might make reference to a 2-percent discount if paid in 10 days and a monthly interest on unpaid balances over 30 days. This encourages fast payment.

Payment fees to a broker based on percentage, rather than on a per-carton basis, are probably more advantageous to the grower. A broker selling on a percentage basis has an interest in getting a higher price, while a broker selling on a per-unit basis will be more willing to ship at lower prices.

The high-end specialty market is extremely market-driven, causing prices to fluctuate greatly.

Yellow Wax beans which are $3 a pound when the market is hot may fall to 50¢ a pound when the market drops. This usually indicates that a glut of product has just entered the market. Keep abreast of changes in the market and expect prices to change accordingly.

Since it is the job of specialty distributors and brokers to keep in touch with the ever-changing market, they can be a gold mine when it comes to advising you about what to plant for the upcoming season. But no one has a crystal ball on the dynamic world of specialty produce. When the prices for any commodity are high one season, the next season everyone has the commodity and the prices go down. Then the following season, supply will be short and prices will go up. It's hard to know what growers have planted in the ground, and the market is different each year. Reduce your risks with a diversity of both crops and markets. Be aware that wholesalers and retailers generally benefit in a low-price market. It is often to their advantage to promote increased production.

How to protect yourself in the wholesale market

Since produce commodities are a highly perishable product whose quality and value can deteriorate rapidly, it is to everyone's advantage in the produce business to market products as quickly as possible. There is often no time to draw up written contracts and oral contracts are an accepted way of doing business. Trust is expected and usually maintained at all levels.

Protection for smaller growers in the wholesale market, however, can often be tenuous. Theoretically, the broker's license is in jeopardy if he deals dishonestly, but in practice there are some deals which are not fully protected. The value of one shipment may not be worth going through the legal channels of trying to collect.

Also, remember that with any goods shipped without a firm sales agreement (e.g., on consignment), there is no guarantee of sale. It is possible that the grower could be billed for handling without any sales income! If a broker buys and sells on consignment, there is some economic incentive to place the consigned items in less favorable markets, especially if a flat "brokerage fee" or "commission" is charged.

How to protect yourself in selling on the wholesale market?

Check out the buyer. The first step is to get to know the buyer or handler you are considering dealing with. Be sure that the handler or buyer is properly licensed! If you sell to someone who does not have a license, you have little recourse for collection if they fail to pay you. The federal government, under the Perishable Agricultural Commodities Act (PACA), regulates trading of fruits and vegetables. PACA requires buyers and sellers of fresh and frozen fruits and vegetables to live up to the terms of their contracts, and it establishes rules for timeliness of payment, evidence of proper behavior in rejecting shipments, etc. PACA requires every licensee to prepare and maintain records which fully disclose all transactions involved in the business. PACA also provides for collecting damages from anyone who fails to live up to contract obligations.

Handlers of produce who buy and sell more than 2,000 pounds of produce in any day, as well as retailers who buy more than $230,000 worth of produce in a year, are required to be licensed by PACA. Ask to see the buyer's identification card issued by PACA or a state market enforcement branch, or call the offices for this information. Growers selling their own product are not required to have PACA licenses unless they also sell interstate or also sell produce that is grown by other farmers.

Under PACA regulations, sellers must ship the quantity and quality of produce specified in contracts. Buyers must accept shipments that meet contracts and pay promptly after acceptance. Prompt payment means within 10 days unless there is a prior agreement to extend the time that payment is due. For consigned shipments, receivers must issue true and correct accountings and pay net proceeds promptly. If the act is breached,

the guilty party can have his/her license suspended and incur heavy costs.

PACA can be contacted in Washington, DC or in major regional offices: PACA Branch, Room 2095 S., Fruit and Vegetable Division, AMS, USDA, P.O. Box 96456, Washington, DC 20090-6456. The phone numbers are (202) 720-2890 or (202) 737-4118 (for complaint information); (202) 720-2189 (for license information); and (202) 720-6873 (for trust information).

Is the buyer in sound enough financial condition to handle the type of arrangement you are proposing? A credit check of a buyer is important before you complete a sale. A payment dispute in the middle of the growing season and over a long distance can be expensive to settle. Request prospective buyers to provide you with three trade references and one bank reference. Also ask them about their payment schedules.

Check the buyer's reputation with other growers. If you are visiting his warehouse, look at the labels on a few boxes to see who else is selling to him, and then give these growers a call.

Check the credit ratings of prospective buyers in *The Red Book* or *The Blue Book*, especially when selling long distance. These books contain the text of federal regulations and federal legislation governing fresh fruit and vegetable marketing and a summary of state regulations, as well as a description of customers and rules of the produce trade. These credit services list most buyers of interstate produce and their weekly credit ratings, along with company names, addresses, phone numbers, contact persons, volume and products handled.

Check also the credit offices of the local terminal market association for information about the business reputation of the prospective buyer. Each major terminal market has an association that has credit information on all its members. Many local terminal market members are not listed in national listings such as *The Red Book* or *The Blue Book* or PACA listings. While terminal markets do not issue credit ratings, they often publish weekly bulletins to members, with a "These checks have been returned" section.

Payment policies vary between firms. Some firms will pay weekly; others pay on the last day allowed under the applicable law. If cash flow is a major concern, those buyers who offer prompt payment should be targeted for sales.[6]

Product Quality: What The Grower Can Do To Improve Returns

THE PRICES that growers receive are largely determined by the interplay of supply and demand in the marketplace. Often small growers are frustrated by returns that are lower than expected; prices quoted or prices received by neighboring growers are frequently higher than those they receive. While this may be an indication of an unfair transaction, more likely the difference is due to the frequent shifts of supply and demand in the produce market. Because the number of buyers and sellers in the fresh produce market changes rapidly, the price a handler is able to negotiate for a particular grower can change substantially on a daily basis. If the grower harvests produce when an abundance of that crop is available on the market, handlers may decide to sell at a lower price rather than jeopardize the quality of the produce by waiting for prices to rise. Growers should discuss with their handlers the proper time to harvest, since by harvesting when the market supply is expected to be low, they may significantly increase returns.

Growers often feel that the grading system penalizes them, resulting in less than expected monetary returns. Growers need to know the criteria for various grades and follow growing, harvesting, and postharvest practices to ensure that their produce meets their grade objectives.

Growers need to attend to the handling of their own produce to ensure that it reaches the handler in optimum condition. Packaging, temperature, and transportation conditions significantly affect the quality of produce from field to consumer.

(Reprinted from *Regulations Governing Contracts Between Growers and Handlers of Agricultural Produce: A Primer for Small-Scale Producers*, by Desmond Jolly and Karen Lopilato; University of California Cooperative Extension, Division of Agriculture and Natural Resources. Leaflet #21425.)

Start slowly in a new relationship with a broker, trying one or two shipments. Insist from the start on timely payment. Occasionally, a buyer may start out making prompt payments, and then test you to see if you accept slow payment—don't. Accounts that pay late are a costly option. If a firm is late in payment or fails to pay, insist on prepaid arrangements in any future dealings.

Since trading in fresh fruits and vegetables is such a competitive and rapidly changing business, one can never completely rely even on firms with which business has been conducted satisfactorily for many years.[7] As with direct marketing, develop secondary or alternative marketing options as insurance against failure of sales to any one outlet.

Insurance. Consider taking out insurance such as crop insurance to protect against unpredictable natural disasters, or cargo insurance to cover losses because of accidents or equipment failures in shipping.

USDA inspection. If a buyer claims that the product received is less than the agreed-upon grade, and you feel the produce was damaged in shipping, call the USDA's Fresh Product Inspection Branch to request an inspection. The inspector will determine if the shipment meets the minimum requirement as labeled. A failed grade will necessitate renegotiation of the price to be paid or rejection of the shipment. If the shipment passes inspection, you can then sell the salvageable produce through a commission house and file a complaint for reimbursement (from the shipper) of the balance.

State regulations. In addition to federal regulations governing interstate shipment of produce, there are also strict regulations governing produce produced and sold within many states. In California, for example, brokers and dealers are required to keep records of dealings with farmers regarding price, date of delivery, quality and other significant details. Handlers or buyers violate state law if they make false accounts of sales; false charges for services; false statements about the conditions, quality or quantity of produce; false statements about market conditions; fail to pay for produce on time; refuse to allow the examination of records; or engage in any other unfair or injurious practice. Check with the market enforcement branch of your state department of agriculture for details of state regulations governing contracts between growers and handlers of produce.[8]

Filing complaints

If a buyer fails to pay his bills, or otherwise fails to live up to his agreements, you may file a complaint with PACA or the market enforcement branch. At the same time, file a trust in order to secure your payments in case the creditor files for bankruptcy. Under the trust provision of PACA, there is some chance of recovering money owed if a firm goes out of business or files bankruptcy. The trust notice must be filed within 30 days of the date when the bill is past due. There are also state market enforcement departments to ensure grower protection for products marketed within the state. (Call your state department of food and agriculture for this number.)

For transactions on an interstate basis, contact the PACA regional office nearest you. For transactions in which the farm product is both produced and sold within your state, contact your state market enforcement branch. For transactions in which the products are produced locally and sold out of state, contact either your state market enforcement branch or the PACA office.

Keep complete records of all transactions in case there is an investigation. Any enforcement officer called in to mediate a dispute will need verification of the shipment.

Protecting yourself with written contracts

Know the reputation of your buyer when you are conducting business by verbal agreement. Similarly, don't abuse the trust given you. Although verbal agreements sometimes do hold up, written contracts are more easily enforceable than oral contracts. Disputes between parties as to the terms of the agreement are minimized with a written contract. New producers, for example, might consider tentative verbal agreements to be oral contracts in which the buyer promises to take products upon delivery. When the delivery date comes, however, the buyer may announce that the products are no longer needed—if the products arrive, for example, when there is an excess supply in the marketplace. Do not produce on the basis of a tentative agreement!

Written contracts are easier to compose than most farmers realize. Be sure the written contract clearly specifies all elements of the transaction such as who covers shipping costs, the date payment is due, the date the transaction takes place, quality of product that is acceptable, the product's condition at the time of delivery, and the price and quantity agreed upon. Call or write your state market enforcement branch for a model contract for the type of transaction you are considering. For transactions in which it may not be expedient to ask for a written contract, be aware that the terms on an invoice constitute a contract.

Relations with buyers

Try to establish mutually beneficial, long-term relationships with buyers. Each of you may need the other to stay in business. You can benefit during a market glut by having a reliable product outlet. The buyer can benefit during a crop shortage by having you as a reliable product supplier.[9]

Look for buyers who are reliable purchasers, pay on time, negotiate reasonable prices, and are easy to deal with. Established relationships require less of your time per transaction than new relationships, so they save you money. Some danger of losing touch with the market may exist if you rely on a few established buyers, but if you keep this in mind, you can avoid those dangers. Knowing what is happening in the marketplace at all times is very important to help establish a mutually respectful relationship with your buyers.[10]

Live up to what you say you will do; make a realistic assessment of what you can supply, and then follow up with timely and consistent deliveries. Samples shown to buyers should accurately reflect the quality of delivered goods. Late or skipped deliveries cause shorts in orders going out

The Personal Touch In Wholesaling

THE KEY TO marketing high-value products wholesale is the personal touch. Whether you are selling to a distant specialty broker or to a big buyer like Kroger in Chicago, try to establish a personal relationship with your buyer. Give them as much information about your product as possible and suggest how they might market the product to retailers and consumers. Give them product information to educate their sales staff, and flyers and point-of-purchase materials for their salespeople to take to the chefs and produce managers. Don't put your valuable produce in a clone or no-name box even if you are selling through middlemen. If someone likes your product, make it easy for them to find you!

Especially with high-value, specialty products, you have to educate buyers and consumers about your product in order to make them willing to pay a premium! To most wholesalers, "a pear is a pear," or "a raspberry is a raspberry." A Washington state grower raising Meeker raspberries, for example, needs to educate buyers that his product has a more attractive color, longer shelf life, and is a larger berry than Willamette raspberries grown in California. Next time you are in a supermarket, go to the gourmet section of the produce department and study Frieda's Finest products. Frieda Caplan has built her company by educating wholesale buyers and consumers about specialty produce.

Another example: a California supermarket chain introduced organic products to its produce section recently and spent a lot of money in advertising. Yet the experiment failed. Why? There was no effort to educate consumers about the benefits of organic produce. Natural health food stores in the Bay Area, meanwhile, command high prices for organics primarily because of the extensive product literature they carry in the stores about organic products.

Whether you are selling to a retail store, a restaurant or a wholesaler, try to make the first delivery yourself. Find out how the product is received, if it is taken into cold storage right away, and how it is displayed—if it's getting buried by someone else's product, for example. Check on your packing: if the product appears overripe, perhaps you need to pick it a little sooner.

Use the off-season to arrange regular year-end reviews and planning sessions with your buyer. These meetings can help prepare the buyer about what prices to expect for the coming season and give them time to plan advertising and promotion for the product. Off-season meetings are a time to review all aspects of the supplier/buyer relationship, such as volume the buyer can handle, varieties that sell well or poorly, packaging, delivery and so on. Keep good records so that you are able to tell each buyer how much they purchased from you

the previous season, the sizes, prices and types.

If there's a new product that you'd like to try, ask your buyer to give you feedback as to whether or not they think they can sell it. Perhaps your distributor has gotten feedback from one restaurant chef that they want more bitter greens in the salad mix, while another wants less fennel or less sorrel. Then you can tailor your harvest to suit these clients. Discuss even small details like a prospective logo-change with your buyers. Get the customer involved so they feel a part of your operation.

Invite buyers out to the farm for a tour. This gives them a chance to see for themselves the extra care you put into your products. It also gives them a chance to ask questions. If they see someone spraying, for example, they will ask what he's using. This gives you a chance to educate the customer about all aspects of your operation.

David Weiss, a raspberry grower near Seattle, Washington, was selling to D'Arrigo, a specialty distributor on the East coast. He visited the distributor in Boston and also invited the distributor to visit his farm. Now when D'Arrigo salespersons are out selling to high-end restaurants, they are able to say: "These raspberries are grown by Weiss Berry Farms. They are hand-harvested and are grown without spray."

Westmoreland Berry Farm and Orchard

© Westmoreland Berry Farm & Orchard, P.O. Box 1121, Sr. Rt. 637, Oak Grove, VA 22443 (304) 524-9171

for wholesalers, orders coming in for retailers, or gaps in the menu for chefs; so deliver when promised. If you have any problems with quality of an upcoming product or delays in delivery, etc., let buyers know as early as possible. This allows them to plan accordingly and protects your ongoing relationship with the buyer.

When you are shipping a product, phone or fax the buyer with information on the quantity (number of boxes) shipped, the time it left, the type of label on the boxes, the time it is expected and a reconfirmation of the price. Call immediately if there are any delays in transit, and call again at arrival time to confirm delivery and acceptance of the shipment.

If you are delivering a product yourself, first check in with the receiving person in charge. They may want to spot-check your product. If some of your product does not meet their standards, the wholesaler may ask for them to be replaced immediately—do this.

Buyers often request a 7 – 10 day notice before delivery of large loads. This allows the wholesalers to make arrangements with their retail buyers for shelf space and/or promotion of the product in order to move an oversupply of products, or to alert consumers of the seasonal arrival of a product.

Communication with the buyer should be frequent, accurate and honest regarding availability, delays and changes. Be accessible to your buyers during regular business hours. If you can't be at a phone, buy an answering machine.

Take time to meet your buyers personally whenever possible. If you find it necessary to switch buyers, give your present buyer sufficient notice so he can find a replacement supplier.

Sell to buyers with non-overlapping territories, and don't try to undercut them by selling direct to their clients. Distributors purchase your product based on what they feel they can sell. If you try to sell direct, it undercuts them. In the long run, this hurts your reputation and your business. Communicate openly with your distributor, broker or wholesaler. If you would like to sell direct to a retail outlet in your distributor's area who is not one of your buyer's customers, check with your buyer first; they will probably want exclusivity. If they demand exclusivity for an area, request a solid commitment for a specified volume and regularity. Don't play "price games" by selling the same product, same volume, to different buyers for a different price. If you vary price according to volume, set a formula and stick to it.

Acknowledgments

Paul Levingston, California Department of Food and Agriculture.

Curt Moulton, King County Cooperative Extension, Washington State.

Louis Valenzuela, U.C. Cooperative Extension, San Luis Obispo.

Cooperatives

Getting Along To Get Ahead

If we're planning on surviving, small growers are going to have to work together.
  —Kevin Moran, Mountain Organic Growers, Asheville, North Carolina

MARKETING COOPERATIVES are owned by a group of farmers who produce similar products. It is important for the co-op to have an identity: one co-op might be identified as the "organic" cooperative, for example, while others might center their operations around herbs or cut flowers. According to Curt Stutzman, an agricultural consultant from Amana, Iowa: "Where farmers have banded together into cooperative groups, the success rate of the individual enterprises is much better than in areas where producers are working independently."

Marketing cooperatives can be an effective solution for growers who produce more than the local retail market can consume, but who are not big enough to supply the demands of wholesalers or grocery chains. They may be essential to survival for farmers in rural areas far from cities.[1]

The co-op can perform such functions as harvesting, grading, packing, storing, cooling, shipping, promotion, and selling, as well as purchasing farm supplies and farm business services at volume discount prices. Cooperatives distribute net earnings to grower members in proportion to the volume of products which members market through the co-op. Most co-ops retain some net earnings (profits) for reinvestment or "rainy day" financial periods. Generally, the cooperative mar-

kets all of a single product or product line harvested by its members. A co-op is democratically controlled, usually on a one member, one vote basis. The members elect a board of directors who in turn determine policy and hire management. This contrasts with investor-owned corporations in which the number of votes is based on the number of stock-shares owned.

Advantages/disadvantages

Cooperative advantages

Time. As with other middlemen types of marketing, a cooperative frees the member farmers from selling. While you are out in the field, the co-op sales manager is on the phone selling your product. If you would rather spend most of your time growing and not marketing, look into cooperatives.

Marketing power. By working together as a cooperative, small producers can meet minimum volume requirements of large volume buyers, and they can deliver a more sustained and consistent supply of produce than one small grower can provide. Buyers prefer to deal with one supplier (the co-op), rather than calling 20 or 30 growers to obtain the produce they need. Although sales through the co-op may bring prices lower than some members might obtain through personal sales, co-op sales volume often will be higher and at more stable prices.

The ability to sell to a larger market also makes it possible for individual grower-members to grow

---

ORGANICALLY GROWN CO·OP

greater quantities of fewer items, concentrating on what they grow best, instead of trying to grow a little of everything. Also, growers can plan together to avoid flooding the market for a single crop, which lowers the price for everyone.[2]

Through a cooperative, members can reduce marketing costs by eliminating duplication of effort in packing, selling and transporting goods, as well as share some costs such as cooler space. By pooling resources, the cooperative can hire staff with expertise in marketing. The sales manager, by being constantly in touch with the marketplace, can relay information back to growers, coordinate supply and demand, and help prevent problems of oversupply. Cooperatives can also save money in buying supplies by obtaining group-purchase, larger-volume discounts.

Market development. While an individual farmer may be able to sell to only one store or a few, a cooperative can gain wider market access. Competition is fierce for supermarket shelf space and many growers have gained access to this market through cooperatives. Sunkist, Blue Diamond, Tree Top, Ocean Spray and Blue Anchor are examples of the power of cooperative marketing.

While effective product promotion is often beyond the resources of individual farmers, a co-op can perform in-store demos, distribute recipes and point-of-purchase materials to retailers, develop media promotions, and participate in trade shows and exhibits.

Cooperatives, by spreading out costs over a number of members, make it possible to develop capital-intensive, value-added products, something individual farmers often can't afford to do. The Blue Diamond cooperative, for example, offers almonds packaged in tiny airline packs or huge bakery packs, or converted into almond paste.

Miscellaneous advantages. Cooperative groups act as mutual support mechanisms. Farming is an isolated profession and it helps to be in touch with other growers to share ideas and information.

Because the co-op is a group of producers rather than a private individual, it is often easier to obtain free media promotion. It is also easier to find help from county extension agents, university or vocational school faculty and rural development groups. Financial assistance from various public groups is also more readily available to a group.

Large volumes derived from pooling supplies permit you to divert canning, freezing, and drying grades and varieties to processors. Processors need large guaranteed quantities throughout the seasons. Pooling supplies of small growers will generate a volume that will encourage processors to locate in your area.[3]

Cooperatives also offer important legal and tax benefits. Cooperatives pay federal corporate income taxes only on net earnings that are not allocated to members. With investor-owned corporations, both the corporation and the stockholders are taxed on net earnings. A cooperative provides members with limited protection from antitrust laws. For example, if growers get together informally and decide how much each is going to charge a grocery store for cucumbers, the growers could be prosecuted for illegally fixing prices. Members of a cooperative, however, can do essentially the same thing without fear of prosecution. In addition, a cooperative that is formally incorporated gains the limited liability protection of a corporation. NOTE: Capper Volstead antitrust protection and Subchapter T IRS tax rules apply to members of a firm operating as a co-op regardless of whether the co-op is incorporated or an unincorporated partnership.

Co-op disadvantages. Since cooperatives are generally geared to serve larger-volume markets than individuals can supply, they usually sell wholesale with all the drawbacks of wholesale marketing. Chief among these is lower profits for your products. Andy Lee, author of *Backyard Market Gardening*, claims: "The producer winds up getting 15 – 20 percent of retail prices. You have to sell wholesale, pay the manager of the co-op, and put everything in new boxes."

Another potential cooperative disadvantage is that democratic decision making can be notoriously slow—depending upon membership of the co-op. This can be a major drawback in the produce business, which often demands on-the-spot decisions.

As with other middlemen marketing, selling through a co-op puts you in less direct contact with customers. This can be disastrous if the co-op goes broke! The failure rate for co-ops is high, so do your homework before joining a cooperative. Talk to other members in the co-op—what kind of prices do they get? Are they able to market satisfactory volume through the co-op?

If the co-op is a new venture, find out: Is there a purpose for the co-op, a unique marketing niche to fill? What resources are available in terms of financing, producers, and people capable of setting up and running a business? Co-ops take time to develop, and the farmer is often the last to enjoy the benefits, as profits are frequently plowed back into development of the co-op.

Management challenges

The single biggest challenge for cooperatives is cooperation. One co-op founder described a co-op as "a group of farmer-bosses." Cooperatives may be difficult to manage, with so many different and strong personalities, each one wanting to make decisions.

To get off the ground, you'll need to hire a professional sales coordinator, preferably one with experience in wholesale marketing. Often, however, startup co-ops are reluctant to pay sufficient salary to attract a well-qualified manager, so they end up with inexperienced management.

Often the board is composed of farmer-owners who find it difficult to give hired managers the power to implement co-op goals and policies. The board of directors should create policies, give clear directions, and then give management the resources and clout to carry them out.

Quality control is critical. Strict standards should be enforced. Inferior produce mixed in with top quality not only may bring an overall lower price for the load, but may hurt the reputation of the co-op.

Another potential problem lies in the conflict of interest that may exist having farmers as members of the board of directors. They should recognize that the co-op is a separate business, and policies should represent the co-op's best interests. On issues such as grading standards and production

© Finger Lakes Organic Growers Cooperative, Inc., P.O. Box 549, Trumansburg, NY 14886 (607) 387-3333

allocations, all members need to be treated equally. Farmer/board members need to recognize that in the long run, keeping the co-op viable and profitable is in the farmers' best interests.

Marketing agreements

One study shows that most marketing cooperative failures have been caused by: 1) competition from other production and marketing areas; 2) insufficient volume of farm products flowing through the cooperative; and 3) lack of sufficiently strong marketing agreements.[4] It is important to lay a strong foundation, with bylaws, schedules and commitments from growers about what they are going to grow, how much they will sell through the coop and when they will deliver it.[5] A comprehensive and legal contract with grower-members (marketing agreements) should be standard operating procedure.

Marketing agreements should contain a commitment from farmer-members to sell a specified volume of product through the cooperative. Farmers agree to plant a specific amount of acreage of certain varieties with approximate planting dates. Such commitments can be critical to the success of the co-op. Marketing agreements give the co-op salesperson an idea of volume and times of expected supply, and they help ensure that there is enough income to maintain the operation and to provide sufficient volume to meet sales commitments. Generally, the more that growers are required to sell a high percentage of their crops through the co-op, the better off the co-op is. Many cooperatives require members to sell all of their product to the co-op.

Total crop commitment to the co-op, however, leaves farmers in a precarious position if the co-op should fail. One compromise is to allow growers to seek additional noncompeting outlets such as farmers markets, or even retail or wholesale accounts which are not co-op customers, as long as growers meet their volume commitment to the co-op. This allows the co-op to plan its marketing and meet its commitments to buyers while allowing growers additional marketing options.

Starting a cooperative takes money, and members have to be committed to pay sufficient fees to maintain the co-op. Since the vitality of the co-op is dependent on grower participation, make membership fees high enough to attract only the seriously interested, committed growers who want to sell most or all of their crop through the co-op. A grower investment encourages growers to participate in order to protect their investment.

Miscellaneous tips

Inadequate capital is a frequent cause of failure with many co-ops, especially while starting up. Utilize services from existing companies rather than trying to finance the complete range of marketing services yourselves. Leasing or purchasing equipment is usually advisable for the first two or three years as the organization gains experience. Seek adequate long-term investment capital at competitive rates. New cooperatives with small volume but good growth potential often need a one- or two-year waiver on interest and principal payments or a capital grant equal to overhead costs.[6]

Learn to cooperate. Encourage teamwork, letting grower-members take charge of individual tasks according to their talents and interest. Complaints and criticisms should be resolved before they become major problems. This requires the constant attention of management and regular member meetings.

Learn to share information. The combined experience and knowledge of a dozen growers is much greater than that of one grower. Invite experts to come to your site, and send growers or managers to conferences to learn as much about marketing as possible.

Informal cooperatives

Marketing associations exist to help market and promote growers' products, with no centralized site for packing. According to Paul Vossen, who acted as the advisor for the Sonoma County Agricultural Marketing Program (SCAMP), larger cooperatives with a packing operation often develop bigger, more centralized operations, with a full-time manager and other labor costs, plus expensive machinery. Ensuing debts often lead to the co-ops' failure.

Marketing associations are supported by yearly membership fees or an assessment on products sold through the association, with funds going toward marketing rather than machinery. As well as promoting farm products by type of product, marketing associations can also promote farm products by growing region. (See also "Group Promotion," Chapter 30.)

Another way to control the size, expenditure and legal restrictions of co-ops is to get together as a small, informal group of growers, with perhaps three to six members, and help each other market products. Dale Riggs, vegetable specialist at Cornell Cooperative Extension in New York and a former restaurant grower, reports that one thing she would do differently is cooperate with other growers a lot sooner. "I started out growing 36 crops in order to supply the needs of restaurants, and then I whittled that number down to four crops which I grew best, and worked with other growers to supply the crops I didn't grow." Riggs and her neighbors made an arrangement so that if one sold at farmers markets and another to grocery stores, they would trade boxes or crates of produce with each other, and each would sell and collect for the other. "No one can grow everything well," says Riggs. "I really think cooperation is the way to go." NOTE: Before you cooperate with fellow growers in any fashion, consult with a corporate attorney to make certain that what you are doing complies with state laws of incorporation and taxation.

Acknowledgments

Alan Borst, agricultural economist, USDA Agricultural Cooperative Service.

Edmund Estes, Department of Agricultural and Resource Economics, North Carolina State University.

Business Smarts

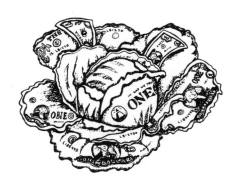

Only 15 percent of farm families really know their cost of production. This is partly because, in general, farm families tend to regard farming not as a business but as a way of life.
— Mike Stanton, associate director, Farm Bureau's Market Master Program

FARMERS WEAR lots of hats, not the least of which is the bookkeeper's green visor. And even though a business suit may not be your everyday apparel, you *do* need the skills and talents of a businessperson.

Study business. Browse through the business section of your bookstore or library, and read books like *Homemade Money* (see "New World Bookshelf," p. 301) and *Small Time Operator.* Other small-business books are available through the *Home Business Booklist,* P.O. Box 101, Bridport, VT 05734; (802) 758-2300. Call local junior colleges and adult extension classes to find out what courses are being offered in small business and management topics.

Be professional. If you are a retailer, for example, do you use your farm market logo to promote your market on all your receipts, produce bags, and the uniforms of your sales staff? If you make sales calls on middlemen buyers (wholesalers, distributors, etc.), do you use business cards, printed invoices, product lists and all the other marketing tools of a professional businessperson?

Pause and reflect. Try to learn from everything you do. Let's say you've sold out faster than anyone else at the farmers market. Did you sell out quickly because you were priced too cheaply, or did you really have better products than your competitors? Or were your products presented better?

Financial planning

Financial planning will help you get a clear picture of the current status of your business and help you determine how specific business goals can be achieved. Decide where you want to go and devise activities to get there. Should you expand your market, sell through a distributor, or establish a restaurant route? Keeping separate sales and expense records for different enterprises allows you

---

to determine the profitability of each enterprise and make sounder decisions about future ones.

Your financial plan should include a minimum of four components: the operating statement (sometimes called the income statement, or profit/ loss statement), projected operating statement (budget), a balance sheet and a cash flow statement. These should be prepared monthly, quarterly or annually, either by yourself or with the help of an accountant.

The *operating statement,* like a wide-angle photo of a landscape, includes a summary of all the income and expenses generated by the business during a specified time period, commonly a year. Making various types of comparisons of income and expenses over a certain time period allows you to gauge the business' financial soundness over the specified time.

Operating statements developed for future time periods are commonly called *budgets.* The accuracy of the operating budget depends on a realistic estimate of sales and expenses.

The *balance sheet* is like a "snapshot" picture of the financial state of the business at a certain date. Showing assets, liabilities and net worth, or how much of the business you own as opposed to what you owe creditors, helps determine your business' financial health.

The *cash flow statement,* like a moving film picture of your business, takes a closer look at the day-to-day, week-to-week, and month-to-month financial status of the business over a specified time period. The budget looks only at the "average" income and expenses for the time period. Even if the overall picture looks rosy, however, there may be within that time period financial valleys, or periods of low sales and high expenses in which low cash-in-hand makes it difficult to pay bills. By anticipating times of low cash flow, you can prepare for them and keep your business afloat.

 ## Recordkeeping

Good recordkeeping practices are essential. Besides providing information needed for financial statements and planning, records are needed: 1) to fill out tax returns; 2) to fill out employee records and forms such as income tax withheld and social security; 3) to apply for credit; and 4) to determine the true costs of producing and

marketing a product, event or project. It is only by keeping good records of production costs, labor costs and marketing costs for each enterprise that you can know which are money-makers, and which are not. Another way of tracking costs of goods sold for products you raise yourself and sell at your own farm market is to set up a separate account for the market and charge that operation for the farm produce provided to it at the going wholesale prices.

Among the many kinds of data useful in helping to analyze your business, records should be kept for inventory; the number of customers daily and sales per customer; gross margins by department, category or key products; operating expenses; accounts receivable and payable; and payroll. Daily and weekly records from previous years with notations as to weather, market conditions, advertising and promotion expenses are also helpful for planning purposes. When choosing a recordkeeping system, make sure that it is simple to use, easy to understand, reliable, accurate, consistent, and able to provide up-to-date information.

Take a look at the business resources listed in "Chapter Resources" for recordkeeping systems. Farm Credit, some commercial banks and Cooperative Extension also have recordkeeping books which can be adapted for your purposes. Some states also offer regional farm business analysis programs; call your local extension office to find out if this service is available in your locale. There are also many recordkeeping systems available for use on home computers. Even if you utilize the services of an accountant to prepare year-end financial statements, keep daily, weekly and monthly records yourself. Keep all receipts, bank statements, and other records necessary to enter into your recordkeeping system.

Develop a habit also of keeping written records of certain kinds of nonfinancial information. Let's say you are selling to a number of restaurants: make it a practice to jot down notes such as "Restaurant A prefers delivery between 9 and 10 a.m.—presentation, appearance important!"; "Restaurant B—volume important," etc. Or if you're selling at a farmers market, you might keep a written tally of how many people in the day request certain kinds of products.

Investigate your own operation. Step back and see what is going on. If you own a farm market, for example, watch your customers. Where do they go in your market? Are they missing any table or display? Do they pick over produce and reject it? Visit and compare other successful marketers in the same manner. Keeping organized written notes helps you learn to spot emerging patterns and to recognize potential problems and opportunities.

If you are selling to distributors, restaurants or grocery stores, etc., and are using invoices for accounts receivable, be sure to keep these files organized where they can be easily accessed when repeat customers phone in orders. Use the information from previous orders to remind customers of what they bought last time and additional products they had requested.

Interpreting the numbers (making your recordkeeping pay)

Take the time to interpret your financial data. Don't just mechanically add up the rows and columns, neglecting to find out what the numbers mean about your business and how they can help in planning. Look at what the numbers say! Each of your financial statements is tied to the rest, and something that happens in one of them can affect your whole operation. For example, the price of baskets goes up, yet you've sold the same amount of green beans. Gross sales stay the same, yet net sales are down. By interpreting the numbers, you can see that to cover the higher price of baskets, you need to increase your selling price to keep net sales up. Similarly, if the minimum wage goes up, a "ripple effect" will spread throughout all your financial statements.

One of the advantages of keeping financial records on your own is that they allow you to keep an up-to-date check on the financial health of your business. This allows you to make adjustments and decisions while you can still seize opportunities or avert disasters. While financial statements give you an overall picture of your business, you

Phillips Farms, located near Lodi, California, sells a variety of fruits and vegetables at the Vallejo Certified Farmers Market

---

also need to know other vital bits of information, such as sales and expenses, on a more frequent basis. If you don't have an up-to-date idea of costs and margins, for example, it may be too late at season's end to find that you've been selling your corn for too low a price.

Computers

The increased ability of small computers to manipulate an enormous volume of information with lightning speed, pinpoint accuracy, and at an increasingly low cost, makes the computer a practical farm tool.

By using a financial management or database program, for example, you can keep a sales tabulation by day, by employee, or by commodity. These kinds of figures can give you instant feedback on questions like: Are certain commodities generating more revenue per acre than others? Do I have too many people in sales? The computer, in addition to being an invaluable accounting, recordkeeping, and farm management tool, is also a useful marketing tool. Since reaching a lot of diverse markets with a variety of crops involves much more information than that which is involved in traditional marketing, the computer is especially useful for farmers catering to specialty markets.

Among the many functions a computer can perform with great speed and accuracy are:

- *Financial activities*—preparing profit-and-loss sheets, income tax forms, billing, accounts payable and receivable, checkbook maintenance, bookkeeping, general ledger, etc.
- *Information & management*—product sales, crop yields, daily sales, inventory control, ordering and purchasing, payroll, etc.
- *Financial planning*—determining future sales, helping prepare tax returns, budgeting, cash flows, etc. Through the use of spreadsheets, computers can give quick and accurate answers to a variety of "what if" questions. Computers also enable you to boost profits and eliminate unprofitable ventures by making separate profit-and-loss statements ("enterprise accounting") for each crop.
- *Marketing*—a computer can be used to develop a customer database. You can also use the word processing and desktop publishing capacities of the computer to generate catalogs, mailing labels, flyers, newsletters, recipe sheets and sales literature, as well as packaging labels and tags. In the use of mail order, the computer has opened up a whole new market for the grower.

Remember, however, that computers don't make decisions. They only process information—the better the information, the more useful the output will be for managing and making decisions. Computers don't solve small business management and marketing problems; only *you* can do that.

Personnel management

Well-trained, courteous help is even more important in a farm market or pick-your-own operation than in a supermarket. Repeat business is the key to success in most farm markets, and helpful, friendly clerks can be as important as product quality and value in bringing customers back.[1] Your employees are on the "front lines"; they represent you to the public. In a farm market, for example, staff deal more with customers on a day-to-day basis than the market owner does. They convey a market's attitude and are responsible for the market's public relations. Not to have a warm, friendly, knowledgeable staff is to severely restrict your market's potential! Make every effort to select and train employees to be extra friendly, cheerful, patient and helpful. Train employees to sell and not just take orders!

Finding good personnel. Determine your personnel needs. How much labor do you need and when? How much do you need during various seasons? Can anything be done to reduce the labor needed, such as custom hiring, shifting enterprises or adopting labor-saving practices? Work out a labor estimate worksheet using your own farm records, especially payroll records, and enterprise budgets available from your local extension office.[2]

To attract and keep good employees, examine the work environment and working conditions you offer them. Do you offer competitive wages? Do you offer a flexible work schedule, opportunity for training, or some type of incentive program? What potential does the job hold for the employee: future role in the business, chance for growth, responsibility?[3]

SELL WHAT YOU SOW!

© Ecology Action, 5798 Ridgewood Rd.,
Willits, CA 95490-9730

Write up detailed *job descriptions*, including job duties, work hours, salary, required experience and skills, as well as the characteristics of the persons you are looking for to fill the jobs. A job description not only serves to help you select the right person, but once the employee is hired, it can be used as an ongoing tool for communication with the employee about job responsibilities. Match present employees with the tentative job descriptions. Perhaps the job can be filled "in-house."

If you need to recruit workers, some possible sources of employees include: friends and relatives of current employees, neighbors, high school and college students, school teachers (during the summer season), housewives, retired people and handicapped people. Classified ads are another source, both by placing an ad yourself and checking the ads already listed. Call local vocational ag teachers or extension agents who may know of prospective employees. State employment agencies can provide you with prescreened applicants. If you advertise for help, be specific about job and employment requirements, or much time will be spent screening applicants who are looking for something else.

Interviewing time can be saved by having each prospective employee fill out a written *employment application*. Only those individuals who meet your criteria need be interviewed. During the interview, tell the potential employee about your business, yourself, other employees, and the job. Describe in some detail your business and its long-term goals. Outline duties and responsibilities of the job and those of the manager. Ask the applicant to talk about himself and past job-related experiences.

Ask some open-ended questions: What are your strengths and weaknesses? What are your most and least favorite things to do on a farm?[4]

Select the candidate who best fits the job description. Do not change the job description to fit an employee you like but who does not fill the job requirements. Recruit based on the needs of the business. Also, do not hire an overqualified or underqualified employee. Either you or the employee is apt to be dissatisfied. Also remember that you can train a potential employee, but you will find it next to impossible to change an employee's personality. New employees must fit well into the existing labor/management team.[5] Trainability is important. Many times the inexperienced person can be trained to do a job better and more efficiently than a more experienced person who will not submit to retraining.

Verify the information obtained in the interview. Call previous employers, school teachers, or others who may be familiar with the applicant. (A telephone call is preferable to writing reference sources, since they may be hesitant to put anything negative in writing.) When a decision has been made, notify all applicants of the decisions and thank them for their interest, time, and trouble. Keep a list of qualified applicants for possible open positions in the future.

Training. A good training program improves productivity and safety, increases innovation, and acts as a motivating force by letting the employees know that you care enough about them and the job to train them. Supervising unskilled workers can be harder, and more time-consuming, than doing it yourself. As a manager, you make money on what your subordinates get done.

All employees who deal with the public should know what varieties of produce you market, when products are available, cleanup specials, how to handle and store fruit and vegetables, prices of goods, how each item is packaged and sold, suggested uses, harvest dates, and growing and pest control practices used with each product. In addition, discuss with them how to greet people in a pleasant manner; how to be congenial and helpful; and how to give clear directions to get to your place of business when people call on the phone. Keep employees regularly informed about advertisements, harvest schedules and any other plans that affect your operation.

Business Smarts

Building A Winning Team

SHARON LOVEJOY, owner of Heart's Ease herb shop near Cambria, California, advises business owners to "cuddle your employees."[7] "A business is only as good as the people who represent it," she says. "We try to have monthly meetings at my home or a restaurant in which every employee gets a chance to speak or gripe. Employees bring up problem areas and hand in lists of suggestions for new stock or a possible change in operating procedures. Our meetings also give us a chance to praise publicly anyone who has done something out of the ordinary, or who has simply continued doing a superior job. We give incentive bonuses, vacation bonuses, 35-percent discounts on our store items, Christmas gifts, and a birthday party and gift in honor of each employee. Let your customer and your employees know that without them there is no chance for you to have a successful business."

Set a team mission. People *do not* work for money alone; they also are motivated by a sense of growth, belonging and self-worth. Team spirit comes when employees feel they're working for a goal, a mission. The book *In Search of Excellence* suggests team building by fostering a "loose-tight" management style, i.e., being fanatical about a few core values (best customer service, largest selection of produce, etc.), while at the same time encouraging independent areas of responsibility at all levels of the organization.

Communicate to the employees what your goals are, both verbally and by posting them on a bulletin board. Better yet, allow employees to contribute to helping create team goals. This way, they will be even more committed to implementing them.

At Tehrune Orchards, near Princeton, New Jersey, most of the recipes used in the bakery originated from employees. "We've found," say owners Gary and Pam Mount, "that it really pays to seek out and utilize your employees' talents!" Before each major event, such as its annual Apple Day Festival, Tehrune Orchards holds regular planning sessions with its employees. "By helping in the planning, employees feel more involved," explains Gary.

Appreciate and challenge your employees. Provide an environment where an employee can grow. Nothing succeeds like success. Give your employees some kind of task that they can succeed in and then tell them that they've succeeded. As they master one task after another, keep telling them how successful they are. People who feel good about themselves produce good results.[8]

Always look for ways to give positive reinforcement. If your employees do something right, praise them. If they do something wrong, teach them how to

Dr. Bernard Erven, extension specialist at Ohio State University, has developed a helpful five-step method for training a farm worker:[6]

1. *Prepare* the learner. Take them on a tour of the farming and selling operation, explaining how each area or activity fits into the overall scheme of things, and how it relates to the task(s) they will be doing. Encourage team building with a "buddy system" of having another employee show the new employee around—where tools are, what they're expected to bring to the job, etc.

2. *Tell* the learner about each step or part of the task. Talking through the task before starting to show it helps the worker get an overview.

3. *Show* the learner how to do each step or part of the task. In demonstrating the task, explain each step while emphasizing the key points and more difficult parts. Get the learner involved by asking for questions about what you are showing.

4. Have the learner *do* each step of the task while the trainer watches and then without the trainer watching. Ask the learner to explain each step as it is done. If the learner omits steps or parts of the task, re-explain the steps and have the learner repeat them.

5. *Review* each step or part of the task, offering encouragement, constructive criticism and additional pointers on how to do the job. Be frank in the

Building A Winning Team *continued...*

do it better. Use positive reinforcement. It has to be immediate and specific. Reward people with comments every time you catch them doing something right.[9]

Just as you give immediate praise for jobs correctly done, give immediate *reprimands* for a job wrongly done. Identify the problem with the correction immediately. Reprimand the behavior, however, not the person. Do it quietly and not in front of other people. Never attack a person's worth or value. Be consistent. Reprimand even if everything else is going well.

Encourage participation. "What problems are you experiencing? What's preventing you from doing this?" "We need to set up some standards for apple picking. How can we measure this?," etc.

Communicate openly. The more employees feel they are treated openly, honestly and respectfully, the more they'll produce. If they have been hired for a seasonal job, and you'll have to let them go after harvest, tell them so.

Set goals. Make it clear what employees are responsible for and accountable for—write guidelines down, if necessary. It is only by spelling out clearly what you desire that employees know whether they're doing what you want them to do. Goals need to be achievable. Give employees something they can achieve, as well as whatever resources are necessary to do the job.

Encourage employee contact. Encourage "family times" by arranging Sunday get-togethers, or treat your employees to a picnic at the park, a day of swimming or ice skating, or a raft trip down the river.

Manage your own time. If you run a market, for example, don't get trapped into physical jobs for more than two hours a day (i.e., cashiering, stacking, etc.). Your time is better spent training, observing, planning and running the market.

Set up an incentive program to reward employees for superior performance. An incentive plan pays an employee in cash or goods above and beyond the normal basic wage and benefit packages. David L. Hunter, associate professor of agricultural economics at the University of Tennessee, offers these tips on setting up an incentive plan:

• Base payments on things over which the employee has control.

• Make the computations which determine the amount of payment simple and easy to understand.

• Make payments in a separate check as soon as possible after employees meet the requirements.

• Put the incentive plan in writing.

• Never use the incentive plan as a substitute for reasonable wages, working conditions or living arrangements.

appraisal. Encourage the learner toward self-appraisal.

Periodic appraisals. Schedule regular evaluation sessions to let employees know how they are doing, how they have excelled, as well as constructive suggestions for improvement. "You're doing fine in this area, but this is the area I really want you to work on!" Don't be vague; make your standards measurable. "We need so many boxes this month or such-and-such standards of quality." Writing out your standards clearly in an employee handbook lets the employee know that your standards are company policy, rather than a personal reprimand.

Acknowledgments

Forrest Stegelin, Agricultural Economics, University of Kentucky.

James Bell, Department of Agricultural Economics, Virginia Tech., Blacksburg, Virginia.

Pricing For Profits

Every salesperson hears a prospect say now and then, "Your price is too high." But what the prospect is really saying is that his desire is too low. The key is to increase the prospect's desire rather than arguing about price. Establish the benefits, create more desire for them, and minimize the price compared to the benefits.
—Adapted from the *Master Salesmanship Newsletter*

ONE OF THE APPEALS of direct marketing is the opportunity to become a "price setter" rather than a "price taker." Yet for most direct marketers, determining the proper selling price is one of the most confusing aspects of running a retail produce business. The aim is to sell products at a price which will cover the costs of producing and marketing the product and return a worthwhile profit, while ensuring satisfied, repeat customers. Remember, your objective is to make the largest total profit, not the largest profit per item nor the largest sales volume!

The best selling price is always a compromise between what you need to cover costs and what the customer is willing to pay. Generally, the *lower* price limits are determined by your costs for producing and marketing the product, while the *upper* limits are determined by demand, competitors' prices, the types of buyers targeted, and your profit goals. Prices also should reflect the quality, uniqueness, service, and convenience provided.

Direct market prices have traditionally fallen somewhere between wholesale and retail grocery store prices, although the trend is to charge at par with retail prices. The key in asking for, and getting, higher-than-supermarket prices is to offer something special, such as freshness, rural entertainment, higher quality or uniqueness in variety, that customers can't buy in the supermarket. Customers may pay a premium price for fresh-picked sweet corn, for example, but they will be willing to pay no more than supermarket prices for a less perishable product such as Irish potatoes which they can easily obtain at the supermarket. Finally, since customers often overlook the fact that produce sold by the direct marketers is of superior quality, you must *communicate* this quality difference to your customers.

Pricing strategies

Charging what the market will bear allows you to make high profits in times of high demand and limited supplies. Unless the quality or uniqueness of your products justifies your premium prices, however, customers will soon go elsewhere.

Going rate. While it is good to know competitors' prices in order to know if your prices are out of line, you should not set your prices solely by what others are charging. Perhaps you are offering products and services that justify a higher price than your competitors are charging. By knowing what your products are worth and charging accordingly, you won't have to change prices every time competitors', grocery stores' or wholesale

Joe Huber: How A Savvy Farm Marketer Sets Prices

JOE HUBER IS OWNER of Joe Huber Family Farm, Orchard & Restaurant, located near Borden, Indiana. Over 350,000 people visit the farm each year to enjoy the roadside market, restaurant, pick-your-own attraction offering 48 different kinds of fruit and vegetables, and a children's mini-farm with miniature tractors and plastic figures like "Peter Pepper," "Wally Watermelon" and "Sunny Sunflower."

Joe keeps meticulous, computerized records of costs for each crop he grows. "Nothing is left to guesswork," Joe says. He figures everything involved in bringing the product to the market; then he marks it up an additional 40 percent. If a head of cabbage costs Joe 40 cents to grow, cut and trim and bring it to the market, then the retail price will be 56 cents.

Costs are pro-rated by percentages among each crop being raised, including fixed costs such as liability insurance, and variable costs such as entertainment. Admission to Huber Farm's activities is free but costs are built into the products. For the wagon used to haul customers to and from the pumpkin patch, for example, Joe figures the cost of the tractor and labor involved, and then builds this into the cost of the pumpkin.

You won't find "loss leaders"—products priced at or below cost in order to lure customers to the market—at Joe's farm. "Production costs are too high," he says. "We have to make a living on each crop!" Joe's prices are often above supermarket prices but customers seem willing to pay the premium. "A lot of farmers try to beat the competition, but they aren't going to survive in these times. Production costs have skyrocketed, and you can't just go by supermarket prices."

Joe spends a lot of time talking to customers, educating them about his produce. "We stress a homegrown product," says Joe. "Customers seem to accept that if they want a fresh product, they must pay a premium price. They can get a bruised, wilted, shriveled up, 10-day-old head of lettuce at the grocery store; but ours is hours-old! People are willing to pay the price for quality!"

market prices change. Steady customers appreciate steady prices.

Break-even analysis. The first step in proper pricing is to know your costs. Otherwise, you may find yourself in the situation of selling items for $4 when they cost $5. The goal is not to move produce, but to make profits. If you can't sell a crop for more than your production and marketing costs, don't grow it! Cost consciousness starts with good recordkeeping in all parts of your business. Keep account of costs and returns for *each* crop separately—this way, you can tell which crops are profitable and which are not.

The "break-even point" refers to the gross sales or volume you need to sell to cover costs, without making a profit. Break-even analysis is a useful tool for determining the right price with respect to a given volume, or the volume with respect to a given price, necessary to cover all costs. From the break-even point, you can calculate the selling price and volume of sales needed to make a certain profit.

Break-even analysis can help you assess your chances for success before you spend any money. For example, if the analysis shows that you must have sales of $400,000 per year to break even, this may be impossible for a market located in an isolated rural area. However, if the analysis shows that it would take sales of $40,000 per year to reach the break-even point, you probably can be more confident about being profitable.[1]

Cost-plus pricing involves estimating the cost of each item, including production, marketing and overhead expenses, and adding a percentage for profit. Do not overlook hidden costs such as waste and spoilage. By using cost-plus pricing, you can try a number of different profit margins and come up with an optimal selling price on a per unit basis. If by lowering prices, for example, total sales can be increased by more than enough to offset the lower

How To Price For Quality

IT IS LESS COSTLY to do better marketing and promotion than to cut prices! Train your sales force to be friendly, hand out recipe sheets to stimulate sales, spiff up the appearance of your market, change the style or location of your displays, or expand your parking area, rather than cut prices.

Offer a unique, high-quality product that customers can't get elsewhere. Stress quality and uniqueness. Perhaps your sweet corn is raised without chemicals or spray, for example, or you grow unique varieties like "Wonderful," "Sweet Sue" or "Gold Cup." Don't mention prices in ads or on highway signs. Make customers want to come and see or taste the product. Once they've tasted fresh-picked corn at a roadside market, they'll never want to go back to 10-day-old supermarket corn again.

Small-unit pricing. For expensive specialty items, price in small units. Instead of $6.50 a pound, make it $3.50/half-pound or even $1.90/quarter pound! Smaller unit pricing makes it easier for the customer to buy and try out a new or expensive product. Similarly, try selling expensive items like strawberries, blueberries and raspberries by the pint rather than the quart.

Price competitively for common items, but slightly above the market for unusual or hard-to-find items, where competition is less intense. This is particularly true for items where quality differences exist. Even when yields are great, maintain your price. You will not stimulate additional purchases with a lower price. People will only buy what they need.

Some customer grumbling is to be expected: "Your competitor is cheaper." If only one customer in twenty complains, so what? Smile, and repeat the classic line, "He knows the value of his produce; I know mine," and use the opportunity to explain your growing methods, uniqueness, freshness and so on.

Show the customer your quality. Give samples. Cut slices, "Here, try one!" Especially with a new product, give out educational literature or recipes, or do demos to show customers the advantages of your product and how to use it. If people in your marketplace wonder, "Why should I pay 25 percent more for organic products?" for example, include some educational material along with your product, provide testimonials from satisfied customers, or give samples.

Finally, if and when you do make upward price adjustments, make them a little as needed rather than all at once.

profit per sale, then it may pay to do so, assuming production is able to support a higher volume. On the other hand, a higher margin and profit per sale may generate greater total profits due to a lower break-even point, even though total sales are less at a higher price.

Margins and markups. A common misconception among managers is that 50 percent added to cost yields a 50-percent profit. Unfortunately, it gives only a 33 1/3-percent profit. It is important to know the difference between profit (or margin) and markup. A 35-percent markup yields a 26-percent profit margin; a 25-percent markup yields a 20-percent profit margin, and so on.

Margin (or profit percentage), generally used by the food industry, is a percentage of selling price, or the amount (percentage) of each sales dollar that is above the cost of providing the product and of making the sale.

The formula for selling price is:

Selling price = Cost of goods ÷ (1.00 - desired margin percent)

Example[2] If corn costs $.90 per dozen to produce and a 30-percent margin is desired, the selling price is $1.29.

That is:

selling price = $.90 ÷ (1.00 - .30) = .90 ÷ .70 = $1.29.

Markup is a percentage of cost, or the amount (percentage) of the unit cost that is raised to achieve the desired selling price.

Markup amount (in dollars) =
     cost x percentage of markup
Selling price = cost + markup (in dollars)

Example[3] If corn costs $.90 to produce and one wishes a 30-percent markup:
markup = $.90 x .30 = $0.27
price = $.90 + $0.27 = $1.17.

Markup or margin percentages should be sufficient to cover all overhead costs including return to operator, capital, labor and management *and* the desired profit level.

As a guide, the average direct market attempts to operate on a 28- to 30-percent gross margin, or a 40-percent markup. Generally, items which require higher storage costs (such as dairy products requiring special refrigerated systems) are marked up higher, while fast-turnover items are marked up less. Markup percentage for fresh produce may be high even though it turns over quickly, because potential spoilage rates are high.

Market considerations

While setting prices at a markup of cost is useful in setting limits for the least amount you can charge for your product to cover costs and make a profit, you should also take other factors into account to determine the price of your product. Market considerations include:

• *Competition.* Regardless of costs and desired margins or markups, prices must be competitive with other sellers.

• *Quality and selection of product or produce.* A premium price requires a quality product. Customers may be willing to pay a higher price for an item but they must feel that the difference is worth it. Blemished or overripe items are usually offered at a slight discount. Discount pricing may be offered for large-volume sales.

• *Uniqueness of product.* How many other products are there like yours on the market? The more unique your product is, the more you can set your own price as long as the price is fair in the eyes of the consumer. The more common your

product is, the less leeway you will have in setting prices.

• *Company image.* What is your image? Are you a discount seller, a gourmet producer, a "country" product? Decide on your image and make sure your price matches that image.

• *Location of the market.* If the market is located in a high-income area, prices might be higher than if it is in a low-income area. A market located on a road with a high volume of traffic may be successful with lower prices provided there is sufficient sales volume.

• *Season of the year.* The first fruit or vegetable of a season may be able to command a premium price, while end-of-season products may have to be priced low in order to sell.

• *Customer response.* How do customers respond to price changes? If your prices are slightly above your competition on high-demand items like sweet corn or cider, does this cause a major decline in sales?

Frieda Caplan, founder of Frieda's, Inc.

© The Just Tomatoes Company, P.O. Box 807,
Westley, CA 95387 (209) 894-5371

Evaluating your price

Trial and error. Pricing, although influenced by the interaction of supply and demand, is nevertheless set by people. In setting prices for a perishable commodity, particularly one with a very short marketing season, direct marketers cannot consider all of the supply and demand factors because these usually are available only after the growing season. Thus, trial and error may be the best pricing strategy: if the product moves quickly or slowly, then the price is too low or too high. Price adjustments can be made to change the pace and volume of sales.[4]

Your price is too low if: 1) you run out of product before you run out of customers, or 2) you have no complaints.

If you have slow product movement, lots of customer complaints, low sales per customer, a lot of "lookers" or walkouts, it *may* be that your price is too high. Before you lower prices, however, ask yourself if you can do more to build the value of your product in the customers' minds.

Finally, sellers should watch the image of the business by keeping prices fair. To do so, they must know the costs of doing business. Knowledge of costs will help keep the business profitable. Knowledge about customers will help in deciding what and how much to produce and how best to market it. Production costs and competitors' prices will establish the lower and upper limits for pricing. Only the business operator, however, can control the quality, the volume to offer and the price to ask.[5]

Why low price policies don't pay

We have never been high-priced; we've just been realistic about what it costs to operate.
—Frieda Caplan, Frieda's, Inc.

Don't get caught in the "I can do it cheaper" syndrome. As a small company, you don't have the means, volume or experience to market products more cheaply than Safeway. Historically, most roadside markets have generally charged below supermarket prices. Too often, direct marketers tend to place too much emphasis on the need to reduce their price in order to increase sales. The trend, however, is to emphasize higher quality (e.g., fresher, field-ripened) produce available at roadside markets rather than "cheap food."

Customers seek quality first—then price. Roadside market or farmers market customers want freshness, ripeness and flavor above all else. Many are willing to pay a premium price for fine quality.

Price influences how your product is perceived. Many customers equate higher prices with higher quality and lower prices with lower quality. So don't take the profits out of your products by pricing them too low. Some growers have found that they can sell more products by setting prices at the high end of an acceptable range.

Gail Hayden, manager for several Bay Area, California, farmers markets, tells the story of how five peach growers brought peaches to the market, creating an oversupply. The growers were trying to sell their peaches for $1.00 a pound. "Although the growers wanted to lower prices, I advised them to *raise* prices," says Gail. She explained that farmers market shoppers were looking for varieties of peaches they can't find in supermarkets. Some growers lowered their price to 80¢ a pound, and *did not* sell out; some raised the price to $1.20 a pound and *sold out!*

Cost-cutters usually go broke in the long run. Being known as the cheapest or always having a sale attracts the bargain hunters, customers who will go down the block when they find something selling for one cent cheaper, rather than the qual-

Break-Even Analysis

BREAK-EVEN sales volume covers all costs related to the production and marketing of a commodity. Break-even, by definition, includes no profit to management, but covers salaries of management, return-to-operator labor and return-to-operator capital investment. Profit is the amount of money returned above total costs, including the necessary return to the operator, capital, labor and management.

In doing a break-even analysis, first figure costs, including both fixed and variable costs. Fixed costs (also called overhead expenses) are costs that vary little regardless of the level of sales. Many fixed costs are part of the general overhead of being in business. They include depreciation and interest, land, taxes, insurance, and salaries. Allocate fixed costs to each crop: this might be according to the number of acres, hours of use, or production tonnage, for example. If you have one acre of specialty tomatoes on a 10-acre farm, your fixed costs for your tomato crop are one-tenth of your total fixed costs for your entire farm operation.

Variable costs vary with the volume of your product. They include seed, fertilizer, pesticides, labor (wages), packaging, postharvest handling, delivery/freight, advertising and promotion, an allowance for waste and spoilage, and so on. Remember to include a fair return for your and your family's time. The cost of marketing for direct marketers—when time is calculated in—is frequently one-third to one-half the cost of production and harvesting. Add your total variable expenses to your total fixed expenses to find the total expenses for each type of produce you sell.

NOTE: Some costs, such as marketing costs or utilities, can be *either* fixed or variable costs, depending on whether or not they are associated with the volume of production of the product. Since it is often difficult to determine the extent or effect of advertising and promotional expenses on overall sales, some companies find it easier to allocate promotional costs as a fixed cost.

Calculate the break-even point (B.E.P.) from the profit equation, with profit set at zero:

Profit = 0 = (P x Q) - (VC x Q) - FC

Where:

P = Selling price per item, pound, bushel, etc.

Q = Quantity sold

VC = Variable costs per unit

FC = Fixed costs

Break-even analysis can be used to calculate the *quantity*, *sales volume* and *price* needed to reach the break-even point.

Quantity. The formula for *quantity* (Q) needed to reach the B.E.P. is:

$$Q = FC \div (P - VC)$$

A direct marketer expects to sell 200 bushels of apples in the coming year at $15 per bushel, when it costs him $13 per bushel to grow and get the apples ready for sale in the market. If the direct market outlet has overhead costs of $300, how many bushels does he have to sell to break even?

Q = FC ÷ (P - VC) = $300 ÷ ($15 - $13) = $300 ÷ $2

Q = 150 bushels = break-even quantity.

Sales volume. Break-even analysis also gives the marketer a means to determine a sales volume (150 bushels) that is consistent with his expected costs ($300 of overhead and variable cost per bushel of $13) and selling price ($15). To see if this works, apply the profit equation:

Profit = (P x Q) - (VC x Q) - FC
= ($15 x 150) - ($13 x 150) - $300
= $2250 - $1950 - $300 = 0.

The level of profits is exactly equal to zero. But what if he sells the 200 bushels he expects? How will he do?

Profit = ($15 x 200) - ($13 x 200) - $300

= $3000 - $2600 - $300 = $100.

The sale of the 200 bushels that he forecasts would net him a profit of $100. The analysis also tells him that he can be 25 percent below his sales forecast before he starts losing money. Such information can greatly assist a manager in assessing his chances for success.

Selling price. Break-even analysis also can be used to establish a selling price.

The process begins by taking the break-even point (B.E.P.) formula and rearranging the terms

from: $Q = FC \div (P - VC)$
to: $P = (FC \div Q) + VC$.

Now it is possible to determine a selling price (P) that is consistent with the expected overhead costs, variable costs, and sales volume. Using the numbers from the previous example, we get:

$P = ($300 \div 200) + $13 = $1.50 + 13

= $14.50 = the selling price per bushel.

Thus, a selling price of $14.50 is necessary for the firm to reach its break-even point given its overhead cost ($300), variable cost per bushel ($13), and level of projected sales volume (200 bushels).

However, if the expected sales volume is lowered to the break-even quantity (150 bushels), reaching the B.E.P. would require a selling price of:

$P = ($300 \div 150) + $13 = 15.00 per bushel.

Thus, there may be a number of selling prices that will work. What is important to remember is that there is a three-way relationship between selling price, quantity sold, and costs that can give you the desired level of profits. By using break-even analysis, it is possible to find a selling price consistent with these values.

Although break-even analysis is a handy method of establishing price, recovering costs, and generating profits, it does have a few potential weaknesses. Standard costs are often based on historical costs, which may be different from present costs if changes in costs have occurred. One of the advantages of direct marketing, however, is that your price is not established until you've put up signs at your farmers market stall or your farm market. Unlike contract wholesale marketing, you are not locked into a seasonal price. So if you're direct marketing, you can estimate your costs at the beginning of the season, then adjust them during harvest time for changes which have occurred.

Also, if your analysis shows a selling price that is out of line with competitors' prices, you can make adjustments in sell-ing price and/or costs in order to meet the prevailing price in the area.

For example, if the prevailing price in the area for apples is $14 per bushel, but your figures indicate you need $14.50 just to break even, it can help you see that you can meet that price and still break even if you can reduce overhead by $100, (from $300 to $200):

$P = ($200 \div 200) + $13 = $1 + $13 = 14 per bushel

or by reducing variable costs from $13 to $12.50 per bushel:

$P = ($300 \div 200) + $12.50 = $1.50 + $12.50 = 14 per bushel

or some combination of the two:

$P = ($250 \div 200) + $12.75 = $1.25 + $12.75 = 14.

In either event, by planning, the operator will be able to know beforehand what level of profits (if any) can be expected from a new venture.

NOTE: Only the simplest examples of cost-plus and break-even analysis are presented here. It is highly recommended that you confer with your extension agent or small business center before putting these theories into practice. Detailed discussions of break-even analysis are presented in many business management books.

ity-conscious customer who will pay appropriate prices. Once you've lowered prices, it's hard to raise them. It is better to move an oversupply of product by giving them out as free gifts or as samples rather than by lowering prices. You can also move excess produce by finding other ways to use it. If you have too many apples, don't drop prices for apples; make apple cider, apple pies or apple cider vinegar. Or seek other market outlets such as sales to restaurants, grocery stores or other direct marketers who don't have enough of their own produce.

Asking for a fair, honest price works. Wayne Wickerham, owner of Wickerham's Produce near Huntsville, Ohio, prices his produce above supermarket prices. Several years ago, Wayne sold California plums for 80 – 89¢ a pound. When a plentiful supply of local Ohio plums came onto the market, he sold them for 59¢ a pound, yet customers wouldn't buy them. "When we put the local plums out for 59¢ a pound, customers would say: 'Something's wrong with them!' Finally we raised the price to a level equal to the California price, and customers bought them," says Wayne.

Pricing techniques

In addition to determining *what* your prices are, you must decide *how* you want to communicate prices to the customer.

9's or 5's Pricing. With 9's pricing, all prices end with the number "9." Change making is more complicated, but many retailers use 9's pricing because this seems cheaper in the consumers' minds than pricing in even numbers. Odd-cent pricing, such as 37¢ or 39¢ a pound, however, denotes economy-grade, discount pricing, and tends to attract bargain hunters. Five-cent units, such as 40¢ or 45¢ per pound, on the other hand, denotes solid-value, high-quality pricing. For this reason, if you are trying to build a "quality" image, avoid 9's pricing.

Multiple pricing. "45¢ per pound, 3 pounds for $1.25." Offering savings by marking a price for multiple purchases as well as a price for a single item encourages multiple or higher-volume purchases.

Volume reduction. Encourage large purchases by offering volume discounts. Marketers selling large volumes of produce for home canning and freezing may, at the peak of the season, change their pricing strategy to encourage the customer to buy in larger units such as flats of berries, boxes of tree fruits, or 20- and 25-pound units of vegetables.[6]

Appropriate unit of pricing. Give some thought to the appropriate quantity or unit of sale for each item. Selling sweet corn by the dozen may not be appropriate if most of your customers are couples or single-parent families who will not be able to consume this quantity for several days or a week. Encourage smaller purchases, so the corn will still be fresh when they eat it. Then they will be more likely to come back for more.

Dual pricing. For your major commodity items, offer two price levels: a quality line and an economy line. Thus, the person who wants near-perfect slicing tomatoes will have them available at a higher price, while those who want tomatoes for canning may buy them at a lower price. Dual pricing also helps overcome the complaint that your competitor has products at a lower price. The key to using two-price scheduling is to set a narrow, rather than a broad, gap between the price levels so that the first quality is a better buy. The exception to this is if you have a lot of second-quality material that you are trying to move.

"Loss leader" advertising involves promoting items at or below actual costs, with the objective of getting customers to come into the store where they are likely to purchase additional full-priced items. In general, loss leaders do not promote an image of a high-value, quality-product store. However, loss leaders can be modified by farm marketers to promote the sale of certain produce, such as giving a free pie pumpkin away with the purchase of a painted jack-o-lantern pumpkin. The jack-o-lantern price is set high enough to cover the costs of the pie pumpkin. In general, the "loss leader" item should be a common, major commodity item, so that customers can readily compare and see that its price is lower than prices for the same item elsewhere.

Specials. When considering specials, keep in mind the expected sales volume. For instance, mid-week specials may attract extra customers during a time when business is slow. Cleanup specials may be posted near the close of a day's business, but be careful because some customers, anticipating price reductions, may put off shopping until late in the day.[7]

Farm marketing is a mixture of gimmicks including old barns, the personal, family touch, genuine affection for customers, taking orders after hours, delivering, even growing things from seed furnished by a customer for them. Kroger sure can't match that service.

—Wayne Wickerham, Wickerham's Produce, Huntsville, Ohio

Marketing outlet pricing considerations

Price your produce according to the relative amounts of time and money spent when selling through various outlets. With farmers markets, for example, the cost of transporting the product to the market must be considered as well as the time spent in selling. On the other hand, there is less investment in selling through a farmers market— no structure to build or displays to maintain.

Roadside marketers must consider the expenses in building the market, packaging and refrigerating the products, and advertising or promoting the products. Study ways to project a high-value image for your roadside market. Instead of a roadside sign, for example, that says, "Corn for sale, 85¢ a dozen," display a mouth-watering cutout of a luscious ear of corn. Pictures alone can imply quality much more effectively than naming the price.

It is important to post prices in the market, however, because some people are hesitant to ask about prices and may walk out without buying anything. But post prices *along with* information about crop variety, cooking methods, nutritional content and uses.

U-Pick. Prices may be lower for U-Pick operations, but if you add entertainment, such as clowns, live music or wagon rides, etc., figure the costs of entertainment as part of the product expense. Build the costs of the free haywagon ride into the costs of the apples, apple pies and cider, for example. Make sure that your prices cover the costs of all that you provide.

Restaurants and retail stores. Consider setting standard prices throughout the season, based on the careful records you keep of production costs, and your profit goals. Restaurants and retail stores appreciate this because they don't have to keep changing their prices.

Wholesale pricing. When selling to brokers and wholesalers, the grower has less control over prices than when selling to other outlets. The exception is with specialty crops or items that do not ship well (e.g., edible flowers and fresh herbs) in which growers may be able to set their own prices because of the product's scarcity. But if you are selling mainstream crops on the wholesale market, you will need to accept whatever the market rate is.

As with direct-market sales, know your costs and the lowest price you need to receive to break even for each crop when selling wholesale. If you can't get your lowest price, consider using excess crop as donations to soup kitchens, as demonstration samples, or as promotional giveaways to chefs or produce buyers.

Acknowledgments

David Sasseville, state horticulture specialist, Lincoln University, Jefferson City, Missouri.

Forrest Stegelin, Agricultural Economics, University of Kentucky.

Rules & Regulations

Randy Meyer only wanted to make a few improvements in his modest-sized roadside stand in El Dorado County. For this privilege, the county government wants Randy to put in a fire hydrant with a six-inch outlet. Randy smiles wryly and says that hydrant would put out enough water to blow his stand away. All this for an unanticipated cost of $5,000.
    —"On-Farm Sellers Battle To Gain Breathing Room," *Farm Link*, California Association of Family Farmers, July 1992

THIS CHAPTER is going to be about as much fun as going to the dentist—but the agony of rules and regulations is something you have to live with in marketing. Fortunately, direct marketers who sell to consumers from roadside stands, U-Pick fields or certain certified farmers markets may be exempt from sizing, standard pack and certain container and labeling requirements. However, nearly all marketing activities are affected by various federal, state, county, and city ordinances, regulations or rules.

In addition to taxes, insurance liability and incorporation issues, farmers need to review labor laws, health department requirements, land-zoning or land-use rules and the permits that go with them. Some of the other possible regulatory barriers to direct marketing are: transportation codes, business licensing regulations, product marketing orders, union contracts, weight and measure specifications, and fire and police ordinances.

When you market your product through retail channels, you will need to comply with additional state regulations. And if your product is marketed across state lines, you must comply with FDA regulations for packaging, labeling and handling.

Zoning requirements

Zoning laws govern the purposes for which a parcel of property may be used, such as commercial, residential or agricultural; types of structures permitted; and parking guidelines. Since zoning requirements vary widely from state to state and county to county, you need to check to find what zoning requirements apply to your operation. If you build a roadside market or open a U-Pick operation, for example, does this necessitate that your land be zoned commercially? Commercial zoning usually entails higher taxes than an agricultural classification, as well as additional requirements. Contact your local county or city planning commission for information on local zoning laws.

Check also with the fire and police departments to make sure that structures you plan to build conform with local ordinances. Some fire departments, for example, may require fire extinguishers or certain kinds of building materials, or have regulations relating to electricity and the availability of water.

How To Deal With Rules, Regulations and Inspectors

ALWAYS CHECK with various local, state and federal authorities before trying to market any kind of food item. Check with the officials before you start so that there are no unpleasant surprises down the road. You may be surprised at how easy it is to meet requirements, especially if you're not selling processed foods. Rules and regulations are constantly changing, so communicate regularly with local and state officers. Keep abreast of changes.

Make government inspectors your allies rather than your adversaries, and they will often give you valuable, free advice on many aspects of your operation. If you are constructing a building, for example, your consultations with inspectors will ensure that what you are building will be something they will approve. Make yourself knowledgeable about rules and regulations far enough ahead to allow sufficient time to conform with them. It is far less trouble to find out about rules and regulations ahead of time! Get a written list of requirements from each office; government officials can forget, or leave out something, so get things in writing.

Nearly all regulations add time, effort and cost to your marketing operations. Most are necessary and desirable; some may not be. If you feel that certain legal requirements are extraneous or detrimental, bring this to the attention of the proper authorities and work with them to resolve the situation. Waivers may be obtained in certain situations.

In case you are inspected. When you are inspected, accompany the inspector while she is walking around your property. Ask questions and seek her advice and assistance in meeting regulations. Ask for one of her business cards. It is important to know how to contact the inspector for follow-up purposes. You may need to obtain copies of regulations, clarify a specific situation with an inspector, or speak with someone else in the agency.

In case of violations or citations, be clear as to why you are being given a citation. Reread the regulation so that you understand it thoroughly and how it applies to your situation. If the inspector is obviously writing a justified warning, let her know you understand and will comply. If you feel you are being wrongly cited, talk to the enforcement officer.

If there is still disagreement, follow up with the appropriate agency or solicit aid from the county ag commissioner's office. The next step is to go to your board of supervisors; ask to speak with an aide and try to work the problem out. As a last resort, call or write your assemblyman. He or she may be looking for a cause, and all of them are sensitive to public opinion, especially when a bill is coming up for a vote.

Finally, be polite and be persistent. It took Joy Blumingcamp, owner of Bloomingcamp Ranch in Oakdale, California, three years to get the entire Stanislaus County, California, agricultural code amended. The incident generated a lot of unsought, yet favorable media publicity that brought lots of sympathetic folks to the farm.

"Don't make adversaries out of your county government officials," Joy advises. "Be their friend even if you have to bite your tongue and smile. They're the people you have to work with. In our situation, it wasn't easy winning this case. They really tried to work within the framework of the regulations they have to abide by. But if we had been hasty with them, it could have had a very different outcome."

Dorothy Coil

Grower of Gourmet Produce

Building permits

Building permits are required in most areas to ensure compliance with building codes. Even remodeling an existing market can be full of legal challenges. Contact the local county planning commission to obtain the proper building permits and guidelines for building code specifications.

Signs

There are numerous restrictions by federal laws, state statutes and local ordinances on the placement, size, location, and type of signs that can be used. Contact your local county planning and zoning commissions for information on sign regulations. If your property is on a state or federally funded highway, they may also be able to advise you about state and federal requirements.

The Lady Bird Johnson Highway Beautification Act prohibits signs within 660 feet of federal highways. State enforcement of this law varies widely from state to state, however, so check with your state department of transportation to find if your signs are exempt.

If your farm market is not visible from, but within 5 - 20 miles of a state highway (this distance varies from state to state), your farm market may also qualify for a Tourist Oriented Directional Sign (T.O.D.S.). Call your state department of transportation to find out. T.O.D.S. are signs along rural non-interstate highways which provide directions and distances to tourist-oriented cultural, historical, recreational and commercial establishments, similar to the logo signs providing tourist directions for gas, food, lodging and camping. If your state does not have a T.O.D.S. program, contact your state assemblyman. To find out more about the T.O.D.S. program, contact Claudia Kawczynska of David M. Dornbusch and Co., Inc., at (415) 981-3545.

Health regulations

Contact your county health department (or the county environmental health office) regarding health and sanitation regulations. There are many restrictions with which you should be familiar. Structural requirements, for example, govern such things as the availability of water and restroom facilities.

Food preparation generally is prohibited without a special permit. Operational requirements are more strict for processed foods than for fresh foods, with guidelines for food preparation, storage and the presence of hazardous substances. (A processed food is one which has been altered from its raw, natural state. Examples are homebaked goods, preserves, bottled honey, dried fruits and shelled nuts.) Some county health offices interpret food preparation regulations so as to prohibit the cutting of samples! Consult your local food inspector for information.

Organic Certification[1]

Organic food production is defined as growing food without the use of synthetic fertilizers, herbicides, or pesticides. The Federal Organic Production Act of 1990, which will go into effect in 1994, states that a harvest may not be certified organic unless the land the product grows on has had no synthetic inputs for three years. A host of other guidelines and restrictions are continually being defined. Growers wishing to sell produce as organic have to be certified by an independent agency, which will require a map of the location of crops grown, a tally of gross sales, soil samples, lists of crops, lists of everything added to the soil or crop—in short, everything that might affect the organic certification.

Contact your state department of agriculture for the state rules that will continue to be law until the federal act goes into effect.

Licenses

Business license fees will vary between activities, products handled, and location. Contact your chamber of commerce for information on obtaining a business license. You may also need a state permit to resell produce purchased from other growers.

Weights & measures

All scales used at roadside markets to weigh produce must meet the standards for commercial scales set by the National Bureau of Standards. Make sure that the scales you purchase are intended for commercial use. For certification of your scales, call the agricultural commissioner or sealer

---

of weights and measures in your county, or your state department of agriculture, or department of health. Also, if a commodity is weighed at the time of sale, the scale's indicator must be visible to the consumer.

Sales taxes

Food that is sold to be consumed on the premises, or nonfood items such as cut flowers or house plants, are usually subject to sales tax—this varies from state to state. Contact your state board of equalization (or division of taxation, department of treasury, or department of revenue) to find out information and to acquire a registration number or permit to sell taxable items. You may also ask them questions regarding which items are taxable. There may be a small fee as well as a security deposit to insure payment of the sales taxes. You must keep a record of all sales transactions, and monthly or quarterly reports must be filed with the state board of equalization.

Labeling laws

Every food product you sell to retail stores or wholesale outlets is required to be labeled. Labels make good promotional sense as well, so that people who like your product can contact you. The labeling requirements for *processed* food products are more stringent than for fresh food products; these are covered in Chapter 16, "Specialty Food Products." Packaged *fresh* food products offered for sale, including those made from the direct marketer's own produce, must meet state health department regulations. In addition, there are federal regulations which may apply to your fresh food products if you are providing voluntary point-of-purchase labeling when selling fresh produce to the public.

Processed products and fresh products sold to consumers may soon have similar labeling requirements, although fresh food items sold in bulk displays will have the option of using placards or signs rather than labels on each food item to display the nutritional content of a serving. At present, labeling of fresh produce is voluntary but the FDA may change this in the future to make it mandatory.

To find out about state laws concerning labeling, contact your state department of agriculture,

county agricultural commissioner, county extension agent, or your local food inspector.

Labor

If you sell only what you grow, you may be classified as an agricultural employer. As an agricultural employer, you may have a different set of labor regulations than those for other employers. If you sell produce or additional items obtained from others, however, you may be classified as a retailer and are covered by a different set of labor standards administered by the state. Contact your state department of labor to find out your appropriate classification and which labor regulations apply to you.

Labor laws are a big concern if you employ nonfamily members. Depending on the size and nature of your operation, you may be required to pay state disability insurance, employment and training taxes, unemployment insurance, social security, and federal and state income taxes. Depending on your gross annual sales and the ratio of processed-to-resale products that you stock, some of the taxes and deductions may apply. You should find out about workmen's compensation and minimum wage laws, as well as regulations concerning child labor, overtime limitations, overtime pay, deductions from wages, wage payment and collection, medical exams and personal appearance standards. Some states also have employee right-to-know laws.

The Federal Occupational Safety and Health Act (OSHA) requires employers to furnish a place of employment free from recognized hazards that could cause serious physical harm or health impairment. Check with your state department of

Direct Marketing Regulations Chart

		Farmers Markets	On-Farm Markets	Pick-Your-Own Operations	Processed Products	Off-Farm Restaurants*	Off-Farm Retail Outlets*	Whom To Contact (See codes below)
Tax Laws	Sales	M	M	M	M			7
	Nonprofit Exemptions	✓						7
Labeling Laws		M	M		✓		M	5, 6, 11
Miscellaneous Permits & Provisions§		✓	✓	✓	✓			1, 2, 5, 6, 12
Labor Laws		✓	✓	✓	✓	✓	✓	10, 14
Packaging Requirements		M	M	M	✓	M	M	5, 6
Insurance & Liability		✓	✓	✓	✓	✓	✓	13
Sign Regulations		✓	✓	✓				1, 12
Environmental Concerns		✓	✓	✓	✓	✓	✓	9, 16
Fire & Police Ordinances		✓	✓	M	M			3
Weights & Measure Specifications		✓	✓	✓	✓			4, 6, 15
Business License		✓	✓	✓	✓	✓	✓	4
Health & Sanitation Codes		✓	✓		✓			2, 8, 9
Building Permits		✓	✓	M	M			1
Zoning Regulations		✓	✓	✓	✓			1

* The "Off-Farm Restaurants" or "Off-Farm Retail Outlets" categories assume you are acting as a supplier for a restaurant or grocery store, etc., owned by someone else.

§ Miscellaneous permits include a driveway permit, electric service, inspection of nursery stock, Americans with Disabilities Act provisions, etc. Check with your extension agent.

Key
✓ = Yes (does apply)
M = Maybe (check with authorities)
Blank = Does not apply

Whom To Contact (Codes)

(1) municipal planning commission or zoning officer
(2) county health office
(3) fire & police department
(4) county municipal offices
(5) county ag agent or commissioner
(6) state dept. of agriculture
(7) state board of taxation
(8) state dept. of health
(9) state dept. of environmental protection
(10) federal/state dept. of labor
(11) FDA regional offices
(12) state dept. of transportation
(13) insurance company or attorney
(14) state & local government offices
(15) state dept. of law & public safety, consumer affairs division—weights & measures
(16) county or regional conservation district office

environmental protection to ensure compliance with the act.

Employees under age 16. There are limits on the number of hours children under the age of 16 can work and the type of jobs they can perform. The U.S. Department of Labor prohibits under-age workers from performing any job considered hazardous. There are many prohibited tasks.

Both federal and state laws cover labor topics such as wages and taxes, labor housing and proof of citizenship. Labor laws vary from state to state and are subject to constant change, so only limited information can be given here. Contact the U.S. Department of Labor and your state department of labor for more information.

Marketing orders

Marketing orders, or commodity boards, are set up to aid growers market a particular crop and to establish industry-wide standards for packaging, size, grade, and/or maturity. There may also be selling restrictions such as when a commodity may be harvested and sold to the public. Generally, products sold through small-scale roadside markets or pick-your-own operations are exempt from marketing order standards.

There are both federal and state marketing programs. Check with your state department of agriculture marketing branch to see if the crop you plan to grow is covered by a statewide marketing order. For federal marketing orders call: Northwest Marketing Field Office, Portland, Oregon, (503) 326-2724; California Marketing Field Office, Fresno, California, (209) 487-5901; Southwest Marketing Field Office, McAllen, Texas, (210) 682-2833; Southeast Marketing Field office, Winter Haven, Florida, (813) 299-4770; Headquarters in Marketing Order Administration Branch, Washington, DC; (202) 720-2491.

Standardization restrictions

Wholesale markets. Federal, as well as most state marketing orders, generally require that fresh fruits and vegetables for resale be packed in standardized containers. Each product has specific size and type of container requirements. Exceptions to this are products sold directly by farmers on or immediately adjacent to the site of production (roadside markets), or products sold by certified producers at either a roadside market or a certified farmers market. (These restrictions mainly apply to farmers selling to off-farm outlets such as wholesale and institutional markets.)

Not all products have standard pack requirements, especially new-to-the-market ethnic or specialty products. If the product does not have standard pack requirements, and if it can be packaged in bulk without damage, save on packaging costs by selling in bulk whenever possible.

Restaurants and retail stores. Unlike wholesale markets, little inspection is done on standard pack for retail store and restaurant sales. For most products, however, it is sensible to follow industry standards. Most of the time your restaurant or retail store clients will order quantities from you which they are accustomed to ordering for that product, i.e., "half a box of zucchini." Following standard pack simplifies procedures. For standard pack conventions of various products check *The Packer's Produce Availability and Merchandising Guide, The Red Book, The Blue Book,* or check with your local ag commissioner.

Miscellaneous permits

In addition to all of the above restraints, there may be other permits and clearances required from city, county and state offices in order for you to use your farm for direct marketing activities. Since requirements vary around the country, the best advice is to contact officials first to see what is required before going ahead with any direct marketing plans.

Acknowledgments

Ron G. Good, Division of Marketing, New Jersey Department of Agriculture.

Kevin Edberg, Marketing Division, Minnesota Department of Agriculture.

Dr. Lynn Brown, Department of Food Science, Pennsylvania State University.

Darice Bauerle, Food Processing Center, Lincoln, Nebraska.

Morris Fabian, Department of Agricultural Economics & Marketing, Cook College, New Jersey.

Jeff Patton, Lehigh County, Pennsylvania, Cooperative Extension.

Insurance

AS A FRUIT AND VEGETABLE grower, you are subject to lawsuits for injuries or claimed injuries caused by products you sell. You are also liable for accidents on your premises for almost any cause. While the risk of a lawsuit being successfully brought against you may be small if you are selling fresh fruits and vegetables through wholesale channels, direct marketing operations carry more risk. While farms in general have a high incidence of insurance claims for property loss and personal injury accidents, pick-your-own operations and rural recreation centers are especially subject to hazards and inherent risk.

Unfortunately, today's customers are decidedly "sue-oriented"—20 years ago the number of civil actions filed was not nearly as large as today. While the farm owner can take every possible precaution, it is impossible to eliminate every potential hazard. It is a good idea to post a sign, "Not Responsible For Accidents," but this does not free the owner from liability. Adequate insurance is important to reduce these risks to a tolerable level.

There are three steps you can take to minimize risk: incorporate, buy insurance, and make your farm or food processing operation as safe as possible. Incorporation is one method of protecting your family and personal possessions from business liabilities, as liability is limited only to the assets of the company in case of a lawsuit. Consult your attorney.

Liability insurance

In the event a customer trips and breaks a leg while on your property or claims he became ill from pesticide residue on the fruits or vegetables you sold him, or if an employee backs into someone's car while driving your truck, your liability insurance coverage needs to be sufficient to cover settlement.

Liability, generally, must be founded on fault of some kind, either yours or that of those who work on your behalf. You are not automatically liable because a customer is injured on your property. The operator is liable for any accidents that occur in which he has not taken "reasonable care" to prevent them. Although insurance may be expensive, you'll be gambling everything you own if you try operating without it. It is a necessary cost that should be built into your product prices.

Have your current farm insurance policy analyzed by your insurance agent and/or your lawyer to see if your current policy covers the types of marketing activities you will be doing. Many policies exclude direct marketing activities from normal farm operations. (Be aware that policies not defining farming probably *do not* cover direct marketing operations.) If your direct marketing activities are excluded from coverage under your current farm policy, you should purchase liability insurance to cover your direct marketing operations and product liability.

While there are many optional insurance coverages available, there are some basics which every farm operator should have:

- *Product liability insurance* for injuries which may arise out of products that are raised and/or sold by you.

- *Premises liability insurance* to protect you from suits based on injury or damage arising at your premises, or from operations you conduct away from your premises.

- *Workers' compensation and employer's liability insurance* to protect you from suits involving injuries to your employees.

- *Physical damage insurance* to protect against damage or loss to your property, such as buildings, equipment and merchandise.

Product liability

There has been an increase in product liability suits in recent years. If the product is dangerous, even for reasons unknown to the grower, the grower may be held liable. State laws, as well as buyers such as restaurateurs, retail store owners or brokers, may require suppliers to maintain product liability insurance for fresh produce as well as for processed products.

The main areas of concern for fresh produce are: 1) chemicals or sprays—make sure that the chemicals you use are safe and you have followed the manufacturer's application instructions in using them; and 2) shelf life—check all products regularly to be sure they are not spoiled or outdated.

Make sure that all food preparation, whether at an on-farm restaurant or food processing plant, conforms to the health standards of your local municipality and/or state. Monitor the ingredients and the quality of the products carefully, and clearly label all stored ingredients.

Premises liability

As part of taking "reasonable care," you have a duty to guarantee to the best of your ability that your premises are free of hazards. You must take every reasonable action to remove those hazards. If you cannot remove a hazard, you have a duty to warn people about it. Pay special attention to the safety of children and older people, who are more likely to be involved in accidents.

Some types of operations have built-in hazards which present high risks:

- *The entrance or parking areas.* Establish safe parking patterns and assure good visibility at entrances and exits. Post and enforce appropriate speed limits for automobiles. Make sure the parking area is not too close to a highway or road. If you are utilizing an unpaved open field or lot, maintain it regularly in order to smooth out any holes, ruts or mounds which could cause a fall. If you are transporting customers to the picking area in a U-Pick operation, make sure the transport vehicle is safe.

- *Steps, ramps and handrails.* Make sure strong, solid, splinter-free (smooth) handrails are in place.

- *"Attractive nuisances" like farm equipment, ponds or creeks, farm animals, etc.* Apply guard rails, fences, warning signs and barriers in all potentially dangerous areas that might attract people. Post ground rules regarding Do's and Don'ts for each area of your operation, including parental supervision of children. When U-Pick customers check in, instruct them as to where they should and should not go. Have field supervisors watch people to prevent them from going into restricted areas.

- Eliminate *tripping hazards* such as ruts in fields or paths, and boxes or empty crates in walkways.

- *Orchards.* Do not allow customers to use ladders or poles, or to climb into trees. Plant dwarf or semi-dwarf varieties, and have farm workers harvest what cannot be reached from the ground before customers begin to harvest.

Other potential problem areas include playground equipment, hayrides, pony rides and buggy rides.

Workers' compensation insurance and employer's liability coverage

Each state has some form of workers' compensation coverage. This coverage is required by law and provides specified benefits for the injured employees, regardless of legal liability. Agricultural employment is exempt in some states from workers' compensation. Since most state regulations are different, consult your attorney to determine your needs. Sales activities of employees working in a roadside stand and other marketing facilities which are not clearly agricultural in nature, however, may not be eligible for the agricultural exemption. Again, your attorney can offer advice in this area.

Employer's liability insurance provides coverage in case you are sued by an employee for negligence. Unlike workers' compensation, in which an injured worker is compensated regardless of any negligence, under employer's liability coverage the employer has to be found negligent for a payment to be made. Coverage will usually pay for the defense of any suit brought for injuries and pay damages awarded to the injured party. Even if you are in a state where there is an exemption for farm employees, you often will have a high degree of care required for a safe work environment and the legal liability that goes with it. Most workmen's compensation packages include employer's liability coverage—check to make sure that yours does. Also check with your attorney to make sure that the limit of liability is adequate for your needs.

Physical damage insurance (property coverage)

This provides protection for you against damage to or loss of property you own such as buildings, vehicles, equipment and inventory due to fire, windstorm, theft or vandalism. You should ask if the premium will cover loss of inventory (refrigerated products) should there be a power outage or equipment failure.

Insurance policy

When thinking about starting up any new farm operation:

• Seek out the advice of the regulatory agency involved. The local or state board of health will be able to advise you on regulations regarding equipment, storage of foodstuffs, etc. Often, farmers like to keep costs low by ignoring potential liability responsibilities, but cutting corners in the beginning can cause major liability problems later on. Find out what your responsibilities are *first*.

• Talk to an attorney who is well-versed in business law. He may be able to provide legal advice which could affect your business and insurance needs. If you are thinking of hiring a subcontractor, for example, an attorney might advise you on how you can "transfer liability" in case the subcontractor is hurt on the job.

• Talk to a qualified insurance agent regarding the total insurance program necessary for your business. Insurance premiums are not expensive compared to the cost of a large judgment against you for an injury connected with your operation.

Never assume that any new activity you are thinking of adding is covered by your existing policy. Make sure you have a written policy stating exactly what is covered.

Individual policies are available for physical loss of property, liability, workers' compensation, as well as coverage for other specific needs. The alternative most direct marketers elect is for a package policy that combines coverage in one policy. Frequently, a farmowner's policy will provide acceptable coverage for an on-farm roadside stand or pick-your-own operation if the income derived is incidental (minor) to the farm business. The dollar incidental sales limit, such as $5,000, provided for in the policy may be increased with insurance company approval. Product liability insurance may be provided by a farmowner's policy for sweet corn, apples, strawberries, etc., if the product has not been altered or processed.

If the product is processed into apple cider or strawberry jam, the farmowner's policy would not, as a general rule, provide product liability insurance. You need to obtain a rider attached to your farmowner's policy that covers value-added, processed foods.

Costs of insurance, as well as coverage offered, vary widely among insurance companies, so consult with more than one agent, and talk to other farmers regarding insurance. Make sure you are insured with a quality company that offers you the type of protection you need. Understand your insurance policy thoroughly and review it annually or more often if changes occur in your business.

Insurance costs depend on the size and nature of your business and on the risk factors, such as playground equipment, hayrides, etc. Provide all the necessary information your agent needs to properly insure you. Be open and honest about the nature of your operation, potential risks and liabilities, and seek out your agent's advice regarding appropriate coverage and limits for your situation. Consider carrying a high-deductible policy; this entails assuming some risk yourself, but it helps keep costs down.

Be sure liability limits are adequate to prevent serious financial problems in the event you are faced with a major claim. In addition to covering liability judgments, the policy should cover expenses in supplying relief at the time of an accident; costs of defending against lawsuits; the owner's expense in the investigation, defense or settlement; and costs of court bonds or interest on judgments delayed by appeals. Get insurance cost estimates before you decide to go ahead with any operation.

Setting up a safety program

Safety programs start with a serious commitment to creating a safe workplace. Preventive measures can go a long way toward reducing the chances of accidents:

• *Pesticides*. Don't apply pesticides not approved for the particular fruit or vegetable intended, and don't apply pesticides too close to harvest. Keep accurate records of spray materials used on each plot and when they were used. Make sure to wash off any fruit that has been sprayed before putting it out for sale. Keep all pesticides in locked storage, preferably in a locked building. Disposal of empty containers should follow the latest environmental regulations.

• *Employee safety training sessions*. Cultivate safety consciousness among employees. Prepare a written safety policy and work rules. The policy should outline specific rules and procedures to follow on the job. Encourage your employees to report safety hazards. Teach employees proper lifting techniques, since back injuries due to improper lifting are among the most common of all work injuries. Make sure that you and at least one employee are trained in CPR and first aid. Keep fire extinguishers and first-aid equipment handy. Make sure the local ambulance corps and fire department know how to find your farm, and keep their phone numbers beside each telephone.

Regardless of the strength of your safety program, accidents can still occur. If someone is injured on the premises, make sure the person involved receives prompt medical care. As soon as practical, notify your insurance agent of the accident. Be sure to get the injured party's name, address and phone number. In case of an employee injury, immediate attention to medical needs can greatly help limit the cost of workers' compensation claims as well as help provide care for the injured employee. Documenting an accident not only is necessary to comply with the law but also can be useful in preventing similar accidents.

Ask your insurance agent to come out to your farm to walk around with you. Point out safety measures you are taking and ask for further suggestions on how you can eliminate potential hazards. He might also help you write up any appropriate disclaimers as well as conduct a safety training session for your employees.

Be constantly on the lookout for potential safety hazards and promptly take steps to remedy them. You are in a much stronger position when an accident occurs *if* you have made an effort to make your operation as safe as possible. Your insurance policy covers you adequately *only* if you have taken positive steps to prevent accidents. Always "THINK SAFETY."

Acknowledgments

David Fleming, Pennyslvania Farmers' Association, Camp Hill, Pennsylvania.

Don Cook, United Farm Bureau Mutual Insurance, Indianapolis, Indiana.

The Sales Call

CHAPTER
27

Several years ago, Bob "Matty" Matarazzo was making the rounds of supermarkets to find buyers for his produce. He was ushered into the plushly carpeted office of a large chain store in New York and greeted by the owner and several others wearing three-piece suits. "They thought I was special," says Matarazzo. "They had never had a farmer make a personal sales call on them before. They had previously purchased only from brokers."

"THE PERSONAL SALES CALL" according to Dan Block, an agricultural consultant in Ventura, California, "is the oldest, and the most effective, form of marketing communication. People make buying decisions, and nothing beats the power of a person-to-person relationship between buyer and seller. A vegetable grower in the Bakersfield area makes regular trips to his buyers in the Los Angeles area just to say hello. He knows that a smiling face associated with his farming operation goes a long way towards differentiating his produce from his competition in the minds of his buyers."

As the farmer who grew the product you're selling, you have a big advantage. As Jeff Main of Good Hummus Farms in Capay, California, said, "Because I'm the farmer and intimately know the product, I know I can sell twice as much on any given day as a hired salesman!"

In spite of the myth that some people are "born salespersons," selling skills can be gained by common sense preparation. Go to your library or bookstore and get a good book on salesmanship! It is often the basics in selling that are the most important, such as simple courtesy. Ellen Todd, farm market manager at the Greig Farm near Red Hook, New York, recalls: "As a buyer for our retail store I went to produce terminals. In some places, I was received nicely; in some I was ignored; and in others the people were very rude. I chose the ones who were nice to me and made me feel a part of their business family."

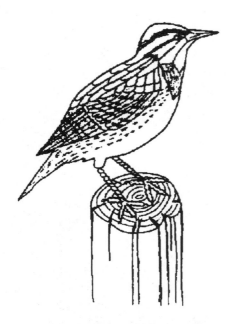

© Meadowlark Farm, 9904 Southside Blvd.,
Nampa, ID 83686 (208) 466-4806

Preparing to sell

Know yourself and your product. The most important rule in the food business is: *Never sell anything you are not completely satisfied with.* Sell only items that are healthy, top quality, and balanced with the cost.[1]

Secondly, ask yourself: What is unique about your product? Why should buyers buy from you? The biggest concerns of buyers are inconsistent quality and unreliable supply. Be prepared to tell the buyer when your supply is available, the volume you can supply, how often you can deliver, and the product size and quality. If possible, give samples and be sure that your product lives up to its samples.

Be prepared with a price list, as well as information about where and how you grow your product, nutritional information, shelf life, product uses, point-of-sales support material or educational literature you can supply, packaging samples, etc.

Know what your cost of production is for the product you are selling and your cost in getting it to market. This lets you know what terms will be acceptable and puts you in a position to negotiate. Buyers in grocery stores or restaurants usually ask what you want for your product. If your price is higher than competitors' products, be prepared to justify your higher price by mentioning your product's longer shelf life, low minimum order, or other points that make your product or service more attractive to the customer.

Never ask a prospective buyer what the best price is he can pay! That gives him the upper hand, or the idea that you do not have much respect for your product. If you've sold to other local buyers, mention them as references. If not, propose a trial period to convince the buyer you can meet his requirements.

Prospecting new accounts

Study your potential customers. Find out about the company's products and if the company is using any competitive products. If it is a retail outlet, visit them and familiarize yourself with their operation. At restaurants, look at the menu or read reviews. Obtain company literature. Studying your prospective buyer's needs allows you to pinpoint those accounts whose needs you can meet and make a profit.

Once you've identified potential customers, give them a call or write them a letter to introduce yourself. Try to make appointments to go in and see them in person. Ask them when the best times are to come by.

When you meet with the prospective customers, find out what products they use now or might be needing, packaging and delivery requirements, who has purchasing power, and the best way to work with them. Each outlet will have different requirements. Leave samples of your produce if possible, as well as printed literature stating what crops you will have available, and when.

Qualifying your customers

With limited time and resources, it is essential that you focus on people who are likely to buy your product. Develop a list of criteria that describe a good customer for your product. Then as you call on prospects, look for how well they fit your criteria. Some of the criteria might be:

- *Size of their business.* Evaluate the potential volume of business you can do with an account. It may be worthwhile to drive 15 extra miles to sell to an account that can purchase 20 extra pounds a week. Don't waste time on accounts that require greater quantities than you can offer.

The worst thing you can do is to do the same thing every year. Find out what the trends are. Talk to the people you're going to market with—consumers, grocery stores or wholesalers—and make sure there's going to be a market there before you plant.

—Ken Schmidt, Quail Mountain Herbs, San Jose, California

- *Resources and ability to pay.* Sell to places that have a budget to purchase your product consistently and pay the bill on time.

- *Geographic location.* Plan where you want to sell and how far you want to drive. Driving is expensive in time as well as in mileage costs. Evaluate the best use of your time.

- *Probability of ongoing business.* If you find an account committed to someone else's product, it may be difficult to establish a relationship. Monitor the time and resources involved against your potential returns.

Remember not to put "all your eggs in one basket"! Sell to more than one account and through more than one marketing channel.

Periodically review your accounts. Traditional marketing wisdom says that 80 percent of your business will come from 20 percent of your customers. Identify the 20 percent that give you 80 percent of your business and try to strengthen those accounts. If customers are buying apples from you and you also grow berries, would they be interested in buying berries from you as well?

Evaluate customers according to where they fit in your marketing mix. If a low-volume restaurant pays a high premium, for example, it may be worth keeping. Some growers make a practice of periodically dropping the bottom 10 percent of their customer list—a grocery store, for example, that buys in such low volume that it is not cost-effective to deliver to them. Then there is the one-in-a-hundred who isn't happy in spite of the best products and service you give him. Some people can't be satisfied! Be diplomatic—tell him you're sorry, but you're just not meeting his needs—and then move on. Your time is better spent elsewhere.

Planning the sales call

Remember that every sales call you make takes an investment of time and effort and adds to the cost associated with selling. It is important that each call be well-planned and effective.

Set your call objectives. Examples might be to gather more information about buyers' needs, provide product samples, or make a presentation about your product.

Decide on an approach. Are you going to send a letter of introduction, or call for an order or an appointment? Is it time to leave them a sample, or are you going to try to close a deal?

Set a call schedule. Take into consideration the best day and time to call on your customers. With restaurants, for example, no one will have time to talk if you show up during the lunch or dinner rush.

The sales call

The sales call consists of three phases: the introduction, the presentation or demonstration, and the close. All of these objectives may not be accomplished in one visit or phone call. The object of your first phone call or visit may be only to qualify the buyers, to find out more information about their needs, or to drop off some samples of your product.

Introduce yourself, identify your business and remind them briefly of any previous conversations. Don't forget to use their names and let the customer know you care about them and their business.

If it is an introductory call, tell them a little about yourself and your business. Try to build a human bond so they are comfortable and you establish some credibility. Don't say a lot about your product, because you don't yet know their needs.

Later on, jot down the things you need to remember, such as the name of the receptionist and assistant chef, etc.

Ask questions. Find out the buyer's current purchasing patterns and what he might need. *Remember to listen.* Contrary to the salesman's image as a talker, it's even more important to listen. The process of presentation is to talk and listen until you've learned about the customer's needs and how you can satisfy them.

The motto of the legendary salesperson Walter Hailey ("The Texas Comet") was, *"If you want to sell, then ask, don't tell."* While listening, ask yourself, "How can I best serve this customer?" This will prepare you to *demonstrate,* with the knowledge you have about your products and services, that you can meet their needs.

Make your presentation. To begin, repeat their needs, then explain how you can meet them. This is where you need to think on your feet and know your product and benefits. *"Repeat and meet"* their needs, focusing on the features and benefits that will apply. Avoid extravagant claims and exaggerations, however—this only detracts from your credibility.

Don't try to sell buyers a program you can't deliver. It's a waste of your time and the buyers' time. Commit only to what you can live up to! The quickest way to lose business and your reputation is to promise something and not be able to deliver.

Be enthusiastic! If you are excited about what you grow, this is conveyed to the customer. A sure-fire way to convey enthusiasm—the actual *experience* of your product—is sampling. Produce people buy with their senses, and this is why it's so hard to sell over the phone. Try to meet with your clients and let them see, taste, smell and feel your product! Always leave a few samples wherever you go. If you are selling in winter when no products are available, bring pictures from last season's crop.

Keep in mind that every business owner has to make money. Explain how your product will make money for them. For example: "By carrying shiitake mushrooms, you will add to your line of specialty produce items and increase your revenue base."[2]

Don't be afraid to toot your own horn. Use references of customers who like your product, especially well-known, top-of-the-line customers with whom you've established rapport.

Dealing with objections

The key to another famous selling technique—meeting and answering customer objections—is to keep a positive mental attitude. Always be positive and not defensive. Try to look at customer objections not as problems but as challenges to be solved. If someone gives you a negative response, "I don't like the appearance of your potatoes," or "Last year your shipping was inconsistent," try to look at this as information rather than a problem. Use the information to improve your operations.

In some cases, there may be misinformation or miscommunication on the customer's part; listening to the customer may help clarify this. When dealing with an objection, don't disagree with the customer—no matter how silly the objection.

As you are selling, you may begin hearing the same objections again and again. Keep a list, and note how you handled them. Neutralize objections before they are raised. If there is a common concern, use an example from another client. For example, you might say "XYZ restaurant was concerned about the price, but found that my extensive prep work actually saved them on labor costs."

Remember there are some people you will never sell to because you cannot meet their objections. For example, a customer may not be able to pay the price you have determined you need for your product. When you come across an objection you can't meet or minimize, go on to the next customer.[3]

Closing the sale

Closing the sale is an essential part of the selling process. *Ask* for the sale ("Can I make the delivery?"). The worst you're going to get is a "no," and if you don't ask, the answer is "no" anyway! The best way to close the sale is to make it easy for the customer to buy. Providing free samples, for example, permits the buyers to test an item before purchasing a large quantity. Another way to make it easy for the customer to buy is by offering a guarantee. If your customers are not fully satisfied, offer a full refund or replacement.

Other ways to close a sale include reviewing the points of the agreement ("You said you like deliveries Monday between 9 and 10 a.m., and you could use 8 pounds a week. Would it be convenient to begin delivering to you next Monday?"); or giving them alternatives to choose from ("Do you want 10 pounds delivered twice a week, or 20 pounds at a time?").[4] Or, you might offer an incentive to buy now, such as a 10-percent discount introductory offer.

If they say "No" when you ask for the order, ask "Why not?" This will bring you back to dealing with objections, and you keep moving back and forth

Features/Benefits[5]

Highlight the benefits of your product. Every product has features and benefits. A feature is a characteristic of the product. A benefit is what the feature means to the customer. For example, shiitake mushrooms have more flavor than button mushrooms (feature), so you can use fewer when you cook (benefit). *Never mention a feature without a benefit!* To say that your vegetables are homegrown, for example, means nothing to the customer. But to say that your vegetables are *fresher*, and therefore *tastier* than vegetables which have been shipped long distances, means *a lot* to the customer!

Features	*Benefits*
Locally grown	Freshness, lower shipping costs, supporting local economy
Flavorful	Complements other foods
Versatile	Adaptable to different menus and methods of preparation
Natural, healthful, nutritious	(Be careful of medical claims)
Careful packaging	Minimum bruising and spoilage

until all the objections are met or there is one you can't meet.[6]

After you've made the deal, review the order, and the amounts and conditions of the sale. A careful review of all the components of the deal will avoid misunderstandings. Be clear on whether or not the price includes delivery, for example. Suggest additional items. If you sell salad dressing along with your greens, let the customer know this. Second sales help your profits, and help the customer. If your first call on a customer doesn't make a sale, be polite and ask if you can call back. Persistence pays—Mary Kay (of Mary Kay Cosmetics) claims that many sales are closed on the seventh call!

Every sale is worth at least three sales: the initial sale when you close it; the repeat sale when you do a good job; and the referral sale when your customer tells her friends!

Follow-up and collections

Follow-up. Following up after the sale is crucial to turning one-time customers into repeat customers. Do what you said you were going to do, when you said you would do it, and for the price you agreed on.

Trustworthiness pays. Matty Matarazzo's business reputation is so extraordinary that often, when chain store produce buyers need an order immediately, they phone Matty and arrange for shipment without even asking the price. In the produce industry your word is your contract. When you give a quote over the phone, you're expected to live up to it!

Service and follow-up generate return customers. Studies show that 65 percent of business lost is because customers didn't get good service.[7] Provide your customers with merchandising support, such as information on how to prepare and use your product, or tips on handling and storage.

With new accounts, start with a small shipment to get the bugs out of the system before expanding to larger orders. After shipping an order, call the next day to ask if the order was received in satisfactory condition and in the correct amount, how they liked the product, and if there were any problems. This is also a good time to ask when they would like to place their next order.

When following up on an account, make sure that orders get processed on time, customers get replacements for bad products, and paperwork gets processed on a timely basis. Keep a customer file for each account with copies of all agreements, deliveries, bills, etc.[8] Consider a four-part invoicing procedure: 1) customer; 2) your customer file; 3) your accounts receivable file; and 4) stays in book as a daily sales history.

Everybody makes mistakes; customers expect them. Admit your mistakes immediately and do everything you can to remedy the problem. Saying that you are sorry helps too.[9] Don't give excuses and don't blame someone else.

Collections also are a part of sales. Find out who writes the checks and what the buyer's payment procedure is. The deal is not closed until the check is cleared and the money is in the bank! Be

SONOMA GRAPEVINES, INC.

© Sonoma Grapevines, Inc., 1919 Dennis Lane, Santa Rosa, CA 95403 (707) 542-5510

clear on your payment terms. As a grower you are operating on a limited cash flow, and you may need to explain to buyers that you need to be paid within 10, 14, or 30 days. Have your credit terms printed on your invoice, along with interest percentages charged for past-due balances. Be honest with yourself; maybe the slow accounts are *not* worth keeping.

If payment is not received promptly, call your buyer and verify the invoice to be sure an error was not made. In some cases a simple error on an invoice can delay payment.

Promotion

Dear CCOF:

After having been in the retail clothing business for a number of years, and an ardent fan of organically grown produce, I continually wonder why farmers don't get more money for their efforts. I think one of the biggest problems is in the area of merchandising. Why don't more farmers use the specialty "boutique" or designer approach? Why do people pay two bucks more per pair for Calvin Klein underwear over Fruit of the Loom? It's because they know something about the person who made the garment (no matter how removed) and they love the quality and cachet of buying a designer name. Building a name and an image takes thought and sometimes a little advertising or free coverage in newspapers and magazines. It could be something as simple as a distinctive twist-tie. I buy organic lettuce all the time and all the ties look the same and say simply "Organic Lettuce." Organic lettuce is more expensive than regular lettuce. Why? Who grew it? Where? Did they care? What's their story? Are they small family farms? Or are they just like the big boys? Their products look exactly the same except for the word "organic." Calvin Klein practically single-handedly brought back the widespread use of natural fibers in the mid-seventies to an upscale market. He did it by simply including a beautiful folded tag with each garment that said something like "wrinkles in this garment tell you the fabric is 100 percent linen. Unevenness in color or dying is part of the individualized look of handcrafted garments." He made it chic to have wrinkled clothes again. The same could be true of hand-grown vegetables.

Most supermarkets used to be the equivalent of K-Mart in the retail world. But now you see the sudden proliferation nationwide of upscale markets using the boutique approach. When will fruits and vegetables catch up? The Lundbergs are applying the new thinking to rice and Cascadian Farms to frozen vegetables with great success. When are the rest of all you wonderful, dedicated farmers going to "come out of the closet" and let us know who you are and why and how you grow what you do?

— Bill Lovejoy, "Profits From Designer Veggies: Advice From the Clothing Industry," California Certified Organic Farmers Newsletter

EVEN IF YOU have the best produce, service and prices available, your operation will not be successful if it doesn't attract an adequate number of customers. To attract customers, you may need to do some advertising and promotion. However, many growers and roadside marketers do not realize the importance of promotion and advertising in increasing both patronage and sales. To many marketers, advertising and promotion costs represent a high price for an invisible product, especially since there may be little immediate discernible effect.[1]

Successful direct marketers know, however, that promotion may be just as essential as production to the overall success of their business. Unfortunately, the benefits of advertising and promotion for direct marketers have yet to be consistently

Marketing vs. Selling

The MARKETING CONCEPT is a philosophy of doing business which holds that the key task of the organization is to determine the needs and wants of target markets and then adapt the organization to deliver the desired products and services more effectively and efficiently than its competitors.

	A Selling Approach	A Marketing Approach
Objective	Sell product	Meet consumer needs
Assumptions	Consumer won't buy without coercion; all consumers are alike	Consumer purchases products and services to meet needs and solve problems; seeks value; there are sub-groups of consumers who have different needs and wants
Overall Marketing Strategy	Heavy advertising; do what we've always done	Identify consumer needs and wants; adapt the organization; develop the appropriate marketing mix; communicate benefits to target market(s)
Market Research	Huh?	Heavy use of secondary research; talk to customers

The Marketing Mix

	A Selling Approach	A Marketing Approach
Product Strategies	Produce products and package them in ways we find convenient	Create product lines to meet consumer wants; add/drop products frequently; add services
Place Strategies	Do what others are doing; distribute however I can	Create channels of distribution that add utility (value) to your product; e.g., convenience. Distribute through defined, niche-market channels
Price Strategies	Follow formulas (e.g., cost plus)	Relate price to market and consumer expectations; emphasize value
Promotion Strategies	Slick brochures, clever ads	Communicates value and benefits
Results	**Solo purchases**	**Repeat business**

Courtesy of Dr. James R. Stone III, University of Minnesota

demonstrated. Promotion of farm products appears to be effective in some cases but not in others.

Effective marketing involves everything you do, from raising a top-quality crop to greeting your customers with a smile. The promotional mix involves public relations, publicity, personal selling, sales promotion and advertising. All of the elements of the promotional mix must be coordinated and integrated so that they reinforce each other and create a consistent message to achieve your promotional objectives.

Establishing your identity

To promote your business to others, you must first know what your business is, or you want it to be. A family-run business that caters to families with superior customer service? The market where customers can find one-stop shopping for dinner from your wide variety of produce? You can't be all things to all people. Adopt the image and style that fits your business and then consistently follow it in everything you do—merchandising, advertising, and service.

The best that advertising and promotion can do is cause reasonable prospects to try your product—once. If what you are promoting fails to live up to customers' expectations, all your promotional efforts will backfire. While your promotion and advertising efforts may bring customers into the store, or induce shoppers to try your products, it is the quality of your goods and services that brings them back and turns them into repeat customers.

So before you undertake a promotion or place an ad, check out your business from top to bottom. A direct marketer can measure the market's image, for example, by asking questions like:

• Are the facilities neat and clean?

• Are the displays neat, full and convenient?

• Are the products top quality, fresh, clean and graded?

• Are market employees appropriately dressed?

• Are salespeople courteous, friendly and helpful to customers?

• Are management and staff looking for ways to improve the market and benefit customers?[2]

Unless your business is ready to follow through with what your promotions promise, spend your

time and money to correct the defect, whether it be too few cash registers to handle the trade in your farm market, or less than same-day shipping service in your mail-order, gourmet food business.

Remember: promotion, at best, can bring one-time customers. Only quality products and services make *satisfied, repeat* customers. Only repeat customers make long-range *profits*.

Business name. The business name you choose is a golden opportunity to convey your unique identity. Customers relate to an individual better than to an object like a market or a product, so one way to personalize your business name is by incorporating your personal name. For example, "Bertha's Berry Farm" has a more personal ring than "The Garden Patch," conveying pride and personal interest.

Stamp your personal identity on everything you do. The lettering you use for your newspaper ad, for example, should (if possible) match the typeface and logo on the sign at your business location. The same design should be on your letterhead, on your business statements, and on your delivery trucks.

Making a promotion plan

Now you are ready to develop a promotion plan. Nothing complex, but a clear statement of what you're going to do and how you plan to do it. The plan should be prepared with 6 – 12 months' lead time, be put in writing and be specific. The basic elements of a marketing plan are:

• *Objectives.* What do you want this promotion to do for business? Increase public awareness of your farm name? Increase overall sales? Promote a new product or increase sales of a specific product?

• *Message.* What is the message you wish to convey that will bring about the desired objective?

• *Audiences.* Whom do you want to hear the message?

• *Strategies.* How will you get your message across—public relations, personal selling, news releases, or advertising? If advertising, what media will reach your audience? Select techniques or types of media to be used; determine timing, frequency and coverage.

• *Budget.* How much will this project cost?

Change Your Business From A "No-Go" To A "Go-Go" With A Logo!

© Terry's Berries, 4520 River Rd.,
Tacoma, WA (206) 922-1604

THERE IS NOTHING more synonymous with your identity than your logo. It is one of the best promotion and advertising expenditures you will make. Whether it is a picture, a name, a word or phrase, a logo is the feature that distinguishes one business from another. Your logo can do for you what Smoky the Bear did for the Forest Service! Use your logo on road signs, packaging, letterhead, containers, business cards, brochures and direct mail pieces, as well as all advertising that you do. Soon, customers will associate the logo with the experience of shopping at your market, or eating your products.

Considering that the logo is something that you will use over the entire lifespan of your business, it is a good investment, and it may be worth it to spend a little extra to get graphic design help for your logo. Although you might spend from $500 to $1500 for logo development at an advertising agency or design studio, there are less expensive ways you can get graphic design help. Look for a talented artist at a junior college or high school art program, or a newspaper staffperson. (Be careful—paste-up artists at newspapers are often not skilled in graphic design.) Ask to see samples. Try to barter: one flower grower helped pay for her logo development from an advertising agency by supplying the studio with fuchsias in exchange for half her bill.

Try to capture the essence, or "feel," of your farming operation in a simple visual statement that is unique to your farm and fits your identity. Apple baskets can be found at every market, for example, but perhaps the stream below the market or the big oak tree by the road are more symbolic of your market.

Before visiting the artist, sketch or write out some rough ideas; put together a list of the most important things you want your customers to know about your business, and show these to your artist. Take a series of snapshots of all aspects of your farm operation to show the graphic artist. Things you have lived with and never paid any attention to will "jump out" at you. Then give the designer the freedom to simplify, reorganize and structure your basic idea.

The logo may include an original cartoon character or spokesperson for your operation. Slogans or jingles can also become a sort of audio logo for radio use, providing continuity and a recognizable image in your advertising. Keep them short—five to ten words.

Keep your logo simple, clean and crisp. Logos with lots of details can distract a customer and cause her to miss the real message or theme you are trying to convey. Also, simpler logos are more likely to reproduce well in advertising. Design the logo so it looks good in one or two or more colors—this gives you some flexibility in choosing how many colors you want to print it in, depending on the cost to reproduce it.

- *Schedule.* When will it happen?
- *Evaluation.* How will you evaluate the results of your promotional campaign?

Target audience

Promotion and advertising strategies should be targeted to the type of customer to be reached. For example, if the roadside marketer is placing local newspaper ads but finds out the majority of his customers are travelers from other areas, another type of advertising should be considered. Ask yourself: Whom am I trying to reach with this ad? New customers? Old customers? Develop a customer profile. Find out who your customers are, what their interests are, where they live, what newspapers they read and which radio stations they listen to.

Talk to your customers as they come into the store, as they are leaving, or at the cash register. You can also learn a lot about your customers from a direct customer questionnaire. Ask customers what they like in the store, and what else they might like to have.

The more you find out about your customers, the more you can cater to their wishes and increase sales. If your trade largely consists of families, a "family event" promotion may be effective. If your customers have a health and fitness or "back to nature" orientation, a "good for you" message may be effective. To city dwellers with leisure time, you might promote the market's open-air, friendly atmosphere and the opportunity for a unique shopping experience. Seniors might view your U-Pick in terms of recreational value as well as an economical place to shop on a limited budget. Knowing that seniors are interested in bus tours, for example, you might contact bus tour companies and invite them to make your market a tour stop.

Budget

When you know what you want your promotion and advertising to do and whom you want to reach with your message, decide how much you should spend. Spending too much on advertising and promotion is an obvious extravagance, but spending too little (i.e., getting caught in the "low-cost trap") can be just as costly in terms of lost sales and diminished visibility. The cheapest radio spot, for example, doesn't mean the best buy. A $50 spot on WAAA, which is *not* the market you want to reach, will be more costly than a $75 spot on WBBB, which *is* the market you want to reach. Costs must be tied to results. You must evaluate your goals and assess your capabilities, and a budget will help you do this.

For each project, draw up an expenditures list. Advertising costs include media space or time, special help fees, copywriting, design, layout, photographs, illustrations, typesetting, artwork and printing. When figuring expenses for events or festivals, don't forget the time spent planning, researching, telephoning, attending meetings, as well as miscellaneous items like postage, shipping, delivery charges, office supplies and telephone expenses.

What you spend on promotion will vary depending on what your objectives are, your location, your competitions' promotional efforts, your product mix, how much free publicity or other low-cost promotional methods are available to you, and so on. Consider advertising and promotion as an investment. Promotion must increase profit margins to more than offset promotion expenditures. You'll need to spend time and effort to get free publicity, or spend money on advertising—or do both. Generally, the farther you are from customers, or the newer your product or business, or the stronger your competition, the more you need to promote. You may need to spend 10 percent or more of gross sales in the beginning; but later on, as word-of-mouth builds your business, 2 percent may be plenty!

Let's say you have a 10-acre blueberry farm right outside a major metropolitan area. You may need to spend 20 percent of your gross the first few years to make a dent in the market. Joe Huber, on the other hand, spends 2 percent of his gross on advertising and draws over 10,000 people to his farm near Louisville, Kentucky, on a weekend. Remember, it is where you place your time and effort and dollars, not how much you spend!

Utilize free promotion before spending money. Read books like *Advertising Without Money* by Salli Raspberry and *StreetSmart Marketing* by Jeff Slutsky for low-cost promotion techniques. Test everything you do so as not to lose your farm if a promotion doesn't work. Every promotion you do represents you, so allocate enough money in your budget to produce a promotion or advertisement

Brand It!

WHY WOULD ANYONE pay $2 a pint for ice cream? The consumer pays that for Haagen-Daas because she knows what she's getting. Not so with unbranded produce, whose consistency the consumer regards as varying widely. Many experts feel that brand identification is one key to getting high prices for quality food products. In a market of mass-produced, no-name products, stamping your personal identity on your product builds trust and confidence. As one successful grower commented: "A produce brand name is worth a fortune."

You don't have to be Sunkist or Chiquita to stamp your label on your product. Even the smallest farmer can utilize branding to maximize his advantage over competitors. In California, for example, "T & D Willey Farms" has become syn-onymous with the finest quality potatoes, while Warren Weber has become known in the finest restaurants for his specialty salad greens.

Ruth Waltenstiel, owner of Timbercrest Farms near Healdsburg, California, points out that her farm dried over 600 truckloads of tomatoes this year for the line of processed tomato products that they market. She gives much of the credit to their farm brand name, "Sonoma." "Even if you're only selling to one restaurant, use a brand name," she advises. "If your name is Dokes, call it 'Doke's Okie Dokie Produce' and go from there." One advantage of having a brand name, Ruth points out, is the feedback that customers give you: "If your product is good, customers will tell you; if it's bad, they'll tell you. But with-out your name on the product, how can they tell you?"

Remember, however, that "the quality goes in before the name goes on." Don't just stick a label on your product and expect it to sell. Consistent quality is crucial to branding your products. Bad products will ruin your brand name. Frieda Caplan, explaining why her company subjects each new product to arduous taste-test procedures, says: "If a consumer picks up something with a Frieda label and they don't have satisfaction, there're 250 other items they're not going to buy. There are certain things that you just can't brand," she adds: "They don't have the potential or the shelf life. It's not that simple. You have to have a program to market your brand, and you have to have consumer confidence."

that communicates quality. A poor-quality promotion or advertisement is not neutral; it will create a negative image about you.

When defining your target audience, do not overlook your existing customers. Remember the 80/20 rule: 80 percent of your business comes from 20 percent of your customers. Always promote to your best audience on a regular and thorough basis before spending money on your second-best audience. Your existing customer base is your most important and easily targeted group. It may be wise, for example, to spend the bulk of your advertising and promotional dollars in areas where existing customers live rather spending promotional money in an effort to draw customers from new areas.

Allocating the budget

Set up a promotion calendar, both to help you plan your promotional campaigns, and as a guideline in appropriating funds for the year. Keeping a calendar also helps you run a consistent, ongoing promotional program so that you know when the slow periods are and when you need to do promotions.

The percentage-of-sales method is useful to determine how much money to allocate for each time period. The standard practice is to match sales with advertising dollars. Thus, if the month of February accounts for 5 percent of sales, you might designate 5 percent of the total advertising budget for that month. Other growers believe that when business is slow, that's the time to spend the money. When people hear about you, they think you're busy and will be attracted to visit your store.

Your first budget will be the most difficult to develop, but it will be worth the effort. The budget will help you analyze the results of your advertising. After the first year you will have a more factual basis for budgeting.

Evaluating your promotional campaigns

Ways of tracking promotion results range from talking to customers ("How did you hear about us?"), to asking customers to fill out a short questionnaire at the point-of-sale, or sending them a return-mail postcard. Try to have a way to track inquiries with every promotion you do. Count returned coupons, and code all your advertisements. Keep track of sales by product type, by day of the week, by season, and by zip code.

At the end of the year and shortly after each promotion, evaluate your promotional campaigns. Keep a promotion book in a three-ring binder. For each event describe the promotion, budget, consumer feedback, and include copies of any paid advertising or free publicity. Did you reach your target audience? Did you achieve your goals? Could you have prepared better for unforeseen circumstances? Did you stay within the budget? How can you improve future promotional campaigns on the basis of this experience?

Keep and compare sales results and promotional expenses on a monthly and yearly basis—mapping seasonal as well as yearly trends helps you figure effects of your promotional programs. Note facts such as last year's sales, this year's sales, months of the year and days of the week when traffic is heaviest, current prices and available items, weather or traffic conditions that affected the week's volume, etc. Look at both your products and your promotions and figure which products or types of promotion are the most cost-effective for you.

While you obviously need to change what's not working for you, don't change for the sake of change. Consistency and repetition are often cited as two key elements in advertising. Through a combination of promotion and advertising, keep your name in front of the public at all times. A lot of retailers put their names on the radio, for example, for a month or six weeks and then go off the air completely. When they return to the air, they've got to spend money to bring their names back up again. The goal of promotion is the cumulative effect. Even if you drop individual promotional or advertising methods, your overall promotional efforts must be unceasing. Experts say that consumers need to hear your message seven to nine times within an 18-month period before they will act on it!

Public relations

Everyone's time is limited. But public relations is not only good for your business—it is good for your soul! Do give as much of yourself as you reasonably can to contribute to the pleasure or satisfaction of another. It will come back to you a thousandfold.
—Linda Morgan, author of *The Success MAP* for Your Herb Business (*Marketing, Advertising and Publicity)*

Customers *do* talk about you, whether for ill or for good, and public relations is the all-important "word-of-mouth" factor about your business. Public relations includes your relation with the media; the way your delivery van looks; the time you take to speak to someone, teach them something or show them something; your reputation for honesty and quality; the way you answer the phone, and more!

Nothing goes unnoticed in public relations. While the country image cultivated by many farm operations might suggest overalls and checkered shirts, for example, the homespun identity does *not* excuse dirty clothes or sloppy printed material.

Word-of-mouth. The best and most economical way to attract and hold customers is through personal recommendation, or "word-of-mouth." According to a recent study, over half of the consumers learned about the roadside markets they patronize through word-of-mouth. And according to the book, *Talk Is Cheap: Promoting Your Business Through Word of Mouth Advertising,* one study estimates that homemakers rank word-of-mouth as the "single most important influence on a decision to try a new food product." (See "New World Bookshelf," p. 301 for information on ordering this book.)

Although word-of-mouth advertising is not purchased, it's not free. It is *earned* each time you provide your customers with outstanding service and a quality product. A customer who is "sold" on your high-quality goods and services is more likely to use your business repeatedly and recommend your business to others than is someone responding to an ad offering a low price.

Studies also show that every *satisfied* customer tells 5 friends; every *dissatisfied* customer tells 10 friends! So instead of plowing money into excessive advertising, spend it on improving products, services and customer satisfaction. Make what you offer a happy experience, and word-of-mouth promotion will follow.

There are a few additional things you can do to help fuel word-of-mouth about your business. Ask satisfied customers to recommend your services or products to their friends: "I'd sure appreciate it if you would tell your friends!" Set up a referral program to encourage customers to tell others about your farm or market, and reward customers who bring in new customers with a basket of strawberries, a jar of honey, a recipe book, etc.

Another way to remind customers of your products and services is to have your farm logo, along with a map, printed on your paper bags, cartons and other containers. Brochures are also an excellent way to help spur word-of-mouth about your business. A committed customer will be happy to take three or four brochures to pass out to friends.

When someone compliments you—"Wow! We had a *great* time at your farm!"—ask: "Would you mind putting that in writing?" Customer quotes in the window, or in your newsletter, are another excellent way to help spread the good word about your operation. Buy an instant camera and interview your clientele. Collect customer testimonials (along with their photos) to quote in your advertising and promotional copy.

Develop a reputation for being a "giver" business. Give customers their money's worth and *then some* by giving something away free. Make it something that doesn't cost a lot, yet is attractive to the customer—food samples, a pumpkin or a small basket of strawberries, hayrides, etc. One market owner gave away free Polaroid pictures of the kids with Santa. It cost $800 per thousand pictures, but sales quadrupled that weekend.

Community involvement. Contributing to your community earns you the kind of reputation that money can't buy. Community involvement means joining the chamber of commerce or the Farm Bureau, donating fresh vegetables for the Big Brother/Big Sister fund-raising dinner, hosting free demonstrations or workshops, or holding a benefit sale. On Mother's Day, for example, you might hold classes on garden planting or on growing perennial plants and herbs.

Be a joiner! Let's say you've joined a local restaurant association, and each month they have a dinner meeting hosted by one of their member restaurants. This gives you the opportunity to get your specialty product on their menu, and on the plates of restaurant and country club owners, their management staff and their chefs.

Community service activities help keep your name in front of the public. Chambers of commerce and civic groups often are willing to work with growers to plan and promote events that benefit the entire community. Set up a "Friends of the Farm" for your farm market or pick-your-own operation, offering free educational seminars or early season PYO specials. Invite the local bicycle club to stop by for apple cider as a rest stop on their outings. Help organize benefit auctions for the various organizations you join. Contribute bags or boxes of your product, and include a sales brochure—recipients will show up later at your farm.

Sponsor a local high school club that is community-minded. Club projects might include cleaning up a public eyesore, reading and running errands for residents of a nursing home, and rounding up gifts or food and delivering them to the underprivileged during holiday seasons.[3]

Set up displays in malls with family members present to make personal contact with the public. Exchange business cards with business owners you meet and offer to let them place posters at your farm store in return for letting you place your posters at their places of business.

Goodwill. Consider giving food contributions to charitable organizations, or providing small scholarships for special programs to local school-children. Dennis Simonian, owner of Simonian Farms near Fresno, California, is active in the community and regularly contributes food to the Salvation Army, a local hospital, a rescue mission, schools, and various church food programs. "Sometimes the churches mention us as program sponsors," he says, "but mostly we just feel it's part of our goodwill with the community."

Farm festivals are also a golden opportunity to serve your community. At Silver Bend Farm near Clarksburg, California, owner Bob Kirtlan hosts several events each year in which part of the proceeds go to local nonprofit charitable groups. Kirtlan calls it "an investment in the community. It comes back to you tenfold," he says. At the Silver Bend Farm's Fall Harvest Festival, for example, gate proceeds go to a different children's charity each year, and food concession proceeds go to the local volunteer fire department and youth groups.

In organizing a nonprofit event, work with a radio or TV station or newspaper to co-sponsor and help promote the event. Instead of an "here's-the-check" approach, request the beneficiary group to take an active part in the festival, such as having an information booth to answer questions. In staging nonprofit events, look for goodwill, future sales and long-term promotion rather than immediate profit. Don't give away the farm, just budget according to your capacity. Most of all, look for the "extra something" that comes with giving.

Publicity

An industry rule-of-thumb is that editorial coverage is seven times as valuable as paid coverage. Readers may not believe you when you say in a paid advertisement that your strawberries are the best, but they *will* believe it when a reporter writes an article in the local newspaper stating that your strawberries are great! A good piece of publicity can be worth hundreds or even thousands of advertising dollars. So before spending money on advertising, *first* utilize all the free publicity and promotion available.

Since very few people react to just one ad or news story, effective marketers often will use both publicity and advertising to increase the odds that consumers will see or hear their message. That's why a campaign that repeatedly places your message before your audience gets results.

While publicity can be useful to introduce a new company to the public, launch new products or services, build a reputation, or promote an event, advertising is often effective for promoting specific products. If your pick-your-own strawberries are ready to be harvested in a few weeks, for example, a classified ad is more reliable to move your product than a news release, which may or may not be printed. A newspaper article on your farm festival, on the other hand, can be used to promote your farm to the public and increase sales throughout the season for all your crops.

News releases

Good publicity is the by-product of a good story for the media. If you approach publicity thinking only about what you will get out of it, you'll probably fail. Think about what the public would be interested in, present it to the media in a professional way, and you'll reap the benefits.
—Pattie Belmonte, Belmonte Media Services, Olympia, Washington

One of the most effective low-cost promotional methods is the publicity available through local newspapers, radio and TV stations. Lots of farmers are hesitant to call busy newspaper editors, but remember that you are doing them a favor, since they are always looking for interesting stories to fill their newspapers or air time. In fact, 75 percent of what appears in print has been "planted" by PR people!

You don't have to run an advertising agency or work for a conglomerate to send out news releases. Media people get so many slick press releases from large firms that they often favor "homemade" newsy items from small businesses, especially if they are local. Besides, food editors *love* getting free food samples sent to them, and if they like it, they will likely do an article on your product!

Subject matter for news releases. The key to getting press releases accepted is to send information about something that is *unique* or *new*, and is

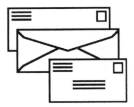

Profile: Media Whiz
Matty Matarazzo

CONSISTENT WITH his marketing philosophy: "Spend as little money as possible and get the most out of it," Matty Matarazzo, media-whiz owner of Matarazzo Farms near Belvidere, New Jersey, is a master at using the media to gain free publicity. "Don't be the biggest secret around," he advises. Matty has a whole album full of press clippings about his farm, largely as the result of sending out at least one news release a week. "Press releases are the cheapest and most effective advertising you can get," he says.

Matty holds up a front-page spread in a newspaper about an upcoming Matarazzo Farm festival: "You can't buy that kind of advertising," he enthuses. "If you don't have the money, you spend the energy."

Milking publicity for further publicity, Matty makes reprints of published articles to send to other newspapers along with suggestions for other stories. This often results in another article in another newspaper. "Sending press clippings along with your press packets gives you added credibility," Matty explains.

Matty is constantly looking at his operations from different angles to find interesting, newsworthy stories. "The year Alar wiped out the apple industry was a big year for us," he points out. "Because of articles that had been written about our transition to organic growing methods, customers knew we were organic, and they would go into grocery stores to ask for our apples."

Blowups of newspaper articles about the farm, along with thank-you notes from schoolchildren, are posted along the walls of the retail store. "When visitors come in and see all the stories written about you," says Matty, "it makes them think they've come to a famous place."

---

of real *interest* or *usefulness* to the readers, rather than blatantly self-promotional pieces. Editors want news, not advertising. The name of your farm or business and its location, worked in with the rest of the story, is sufficient to enable readers to come out to your farm or get in touch with you.

Find a "hook." Sharon Schafer of Kerman, California, markets natural raisins, as well as a variety of yogurt- and candy-coated raisins and nuts, under her own "Grapes-N-More" label. An article in *The Fresno Bee* put her retail store on the map. "Other small business owners had told us you can't get into *The Bee*," she says, "but we didn't make it just another store-opening story; we made it an agricultural story. There was a lot of news about failing vineyards at that time, so we used the opening of our retail store as an example of what to do when normal things aren't working in agriculture."

Get in the habit of thinking "possible PR story." Write your ideas down and file them. As you develop media contacts, this allows you to offer them several suggestions for stories about your farm. You may be surprised at what reporters consider newsworthy. Maybe your prize ewe just gave birth, or you're holding a "Best Scarecrow Contest"—these make wonderful stories. Or invite a group of kids out to the farm to pick vegetables, then give them the opportunity to sell the produce they've picked at your farmers market stall. Free events, or community service events such as a food-tasting, or a demonstration or lecture by an expert, are especially suitable for the community bulletin board slots offered by media.

Uniqueness. Ask yourself: What is *unique* about your market or your products? Do you grow an unusual food item not normally obtainable in grocery stores?

Recipes. A newsworthy item for people selling food products is to offer recipes and cooking tips to local food editors for the types of produce that are coming into season. Or create a tip-sheet: ten tips on how to raise mushrooms or sprouts, ten tips for easy-to-prepare food gifts for the holidays, etc.

Turn adversity into triumph. Joy Blumingcamp relates that when she started her farm market near

---

Matty Matarrazo, of Matarrazo Farms near Belvidere, New Jersey

Business news. Look for possible business angles about your operation that might make a newsworthy story such as new products or services you offer, business expansion or relocation, awards or promotions, exhibits, success stories, conferences, speaking engagements, interesting backgrounds of you or an employee, hobbies, or noteworthy accomplishments.

Community activities also make interesting news stories: offer a lecture series; host a special event or festival; take part in a fund-raising event; sponsor a scholarship; or put on a community exhibit or demonstration.

Contests. A bake-off and recipe contest is a three-way winner: contestants each submit a recipe along with their entries. Not only do you generate customer interest and response, but you can collect the recipes to print in your weekly newsletter as well as to send to newspapers!

Where to send news releases. To find media contacts, look in the yellow pages under "Newspapers," "Radio" and "Television Stations." Go to the library and study the available publications. What is their format? How can you make your story acceptable to them? What are the papers' deadlines? Do they accept photos? Do they publish information about free classes, etc.?

Compile a media list of reporters and editors who might be interested in your story. Note the names of those reporters who write for sections of the paper like Food, Leisure, Lifestyle, Agriculture, Business, etc. Learn to tailor your stories for their specific needs, i.e., one angle for the business section of the paper, another for the features editor, etc. For TV and radio, get the names of the news directors and the names of producers for talk programs.

Next, contact people on your media list. First ask if it's a convenient time to talk. Then tell them that you have such-and-such a farm and that you feel there is a newsworthy story about your business and you would like to send them information. Better yet, take the release in person to the person you are sending it to—this is a good way to initiate an ongoing media relationship. Ask what types of articles they consider helpful, how you can tailor your news to fit their needs, and when their deadlines are.

Don't neglect the smaller newspapers, the weeklies, as well as small special-interest newspapers such as senior citizen, church and PTA bulle-

Oaksdale, California, she had a squabble with the state's transportation agency about placing a farm sign out on the road. *The Modesto Bee* picked up the story, and sympathetic customers responded. "I didn't do this to pick up business, but that's what happened," Joy says.

Send the world-weary media a *positive story.* A U-Pick farm, for example, might send the news: "90-year-old grandmother won't miss a strawberry season"; or "60-year-old farm still in the family and things are 'berry good.' "

Current events. Use current happenings to promote your business. Consumer concern about pesticides is big news; send the newspaper a story of the trials and triumphs of going organic. Write a letter to the editor. Tie in with a holiday by checking for special weeks listed in *Chase's Annual Events,* available at many libraries.

How To Write A News Release

WRITE FOR THE readership. Always include a local angle, and make sure your release says something of value to the audience you are addressing. Ask yourself: Is this news? Sending too many releases without news value will cause editors to quit reading any further material you send them.

If possible, write the article yourself since no one knows your business as well as you do. If your grammar is shaky, write the first, rough draft yourself and have a friend edit and polish the final draft. Write from the heart. Tell not only *what* you do but *why* you do it. Be informal but accurate. Editors want interesting and accurate information, not advertising hype.

If you need help drafting an interesting news release, look for a moonlighting reporter at the local newspaper or the local college newspaper. The basic input should come from you, however; it needs your personal stamp on it.

Content should focus on one thought—the announcement of a single item or event. At the top of your news release include your business name, address and phone number. At the top left, date your news release. Underneath that, type: FOR IMMEDIATE RELEASE, or FOR RELEASE [SPECIFIC DATE]. At the top right of your press release type FOR MORE INFORMATION, CONTACT: then list the names and phone numbers of the persons who can give that information. Reporters often work evenings, so include an evening number.

To help get attention, start off with a headline, often a short summary statement. Then tell your story. Make your press release a good story, not simply a listing of facts, figures, and superlatives. In addition to the basic "five W's"—Who, What, When, Where and Why—add another: "Who Cares?" Why is this important? Why would anyone be interested in it?

Paragraph 1: Get to the main point immediately. Start with a grabber, something that will make the reader think, "Tell me more." Answer the "Who Cares?" question. Then answer the "five W's."

Paragraph 2: Amplify the main story, provide some quotations, identify the folks most likely to be interested in this story ("Who Cares?"), and add a few significant facts or features. People enjoy reading about other people, so provide some strong human interest material.

Paragraphs 3 and 4: Finish up with all the facts and pertinent details. Add quotes from secondary sources or supporting experts. Include the important details but don't get too wordy.

Last paragraph: Short wrap-up, where people can call or write for information. CAUTION: If the editors have a policy against including direct sales information in an article, they may omit this last paragraph, so be sure to weave in enough information (name and place of business) in the preceding paragraphs so that a reader or listener can contact you.

Except in the case of major events, try to keep your release to one page—these are accepted more readily than longer pieces. Double-space (so the editor can edit between the lines), and always title and number the pages if your release extends beyond the preferred one-page format. Make sure your release is neatly typed and professional looking. Avoid large words or promotional hype such as *tremendous, fantastic,* etc. At the end of your story (copy) finish off with a symbol such as ### to mark the end of your copy.

Send along three or four 5-by-7 black-and-white, glossy photos with your release, showing persons involved in what the story is about. Use action rather than "grin shots."

If your story is good it may be assigned to a reporter to develop into a larger story, either before or during the event. If the newspaper does not send a reporter to cover the event, however, take pictures to send along with a follow-up story.

tins. With small budgets, they're often receptive to contributed articles. Find out also whom to send free calendar listings to—the one-paragraph, "Who, What, Where, When" notices.

Don't wear out your welcome by inundating the same paper or reporter with news releases. When you are written about in one newspaper, send your story to other media outlets, written from a different angle.

Timing. For most events, send your release to allow about three weeks' lead time. Follow up with a telephone call the day before the event: "I just want to remind you we're having our herb demonstration and we hope you can cover it!"

For major events, send a short release four months ahead of the event to notify the media about the date of the event and anything that might be new this year. Then ask them: Whom should we contact about this?

Several months in advance of the major event send a major, detailed news release (three or four pages). Follow it up a few weeks later with a two-page update confirming the event schedule, who will appear, etc. Then 10 or 12 days prior to the event send a one-page update with any schedule changes, and to confirm any arrangements with reporters.

Follow-up. Follow-up calls are a must. Reporters get tons of mail, and your news release could easily have gotten lost. Four or five days after you've sent a press release, follow up with a call to the person you've sent the release to. Initiate the conversation with a "thank you"—perhaps for some previous coverage—and then ask if they received the press release you sent. If not, send them another. If they have looked at your release, ask *when* (not *if*) they will run the story. Then ask, "Do you need anything else? Further information? More photos?"

If the story is *not* going to run, politely ask why, so your next release will be more appropriate. You might add a soft sales pitch: "People are calling to ask when our strawberry festival is, and we'd really appreciate you printing something about it in your paper." Or, try to gain some after-the-fact coverage; plus, there's always next year if it's an annual event.

If you feel a media outlet is unfairly ignoring you, tell the editor: "Your reporter didn't cover this, and I feel it's important to your public." *Next* time they may cover your story. Don't give up. There are frequent staff changes in the media, and the person who rejected your story a year ago may have been replaced with a new editor—perhaps the very reporter you have made friends with!

TV & radio news releases

Make sure your news release copy can be read easily. TV and radio are "now" media; use the present tense whenever possible. Keep it short. TV and radio announcements, or "spots," are 20-, 30- or 60-seconds long. Read it aloud, time it, and tailor it to one of those times.

Type the release using double spacing. At the upper left hand corner, label it NEWS RELEASE. State the subject of the release, the name of the business sending it, a contact person, his or her phone number, and the date. Indicate on the upper right corner the reading time, e.g., 30 SECONDS.

Newscasters have a lot of air time to fill and may be willing to come out to cover your event or interview you. You might suggest, for example, that they do a story on where produce comes from and what goes into bringing it to market. Invite the media out to your farm and have them get some shots of you getting ready, loading it up and bringing it to the market. For extra impact, send a video tape to a TV station, or an audio tape of an interview with you to a radio reporter. Don't overlook cable TV stations; a certain amount of their time is mandated for community service programs and they are often responsive to suggestions for programs.

ROBERT J. MATARAZZO
RD#1, BOX 258 RT. 519
BELVIDERE, NEW JERSEY 07823
(908) 475-3872

April 18, 1992
FOR IMMEDIATE RELEASE

FOR MORE INFORMATION CONTACT:
Robert (Matty) Matarazzo (908) 475-3872

GARDENING EXPO AT MATARAZZO FARMS IS PERFECT MOTHER'S DAY OUTING

A Gardening Expo certain to make mom's special day is planned for Mother's Day weekend, May 11th and 12th, at Matarazzo Farms in Belvidere, New Jersey. Featuring a myriad of "how-to" education tours through the sample garden plots for the novice and green thumb alike, the Expo runs from 10 a.m. to 5 p.m. each day.

The Gardening Expo will provide participants with expert advice and helpful tips on topics such as starting a garden, growing vegetables and shrubs, and cultivating plants or flowers. Staff members will be leading guided tours throughout the weekend, lending their experiences and insights to each informative tour.

In honor of Mother's Day, each mom attending the Gardening Expo will receive a special gift, compliments of Matarazzo Farms. Family members can select their perfect gift for mom from the farm market's wide variety of spring flowers, plants and shrubs, not to mention gourmet food items and gift baskets.

"There couldn't be a better way to celebrate the beauty of Spring than with our new event on gardening," said Robert (Matty) Matarazzo, owner of Matarazzo Farms. The tours offered during the Gardening Expo are free of charge and begin at 11 a.m. each day. Reservations for the programs must be made in advance by calling Matarazzo Farms at (908) 475-3872 (ask for Suzanne or Valerie).

Matarazzo Farms is located on Route 519 in Belvidere, N.J. (Warren County), just 3 miles north of Route 46 and 6 miles south of I-80, Exit 12.

–###–

Media relations

"Free" publicity is not really free; it is a regular, ongoing effort. Cultivate relationships with the press; trust is built over time. Keep in touch with reporters on a regular basis. At Tehrune Orchards, located near Princeton, New Jersey, there is nothing that can't be found at many other farms, but owners Pam and Gary Mount point out that they've gotten terrific coverage because they've worked hard at developing a rapport with the media. "The media is royalty around our place," says Gary. "Pam spent all morning one day with a writer taking pictures for an article."

Similarly, Richardson's Seaside Bananas, located near Santa Barbara, California, is a small banana plantation, the only one in the U.S. It received so much local press that the *Los Angeles Times* and, later, *Newsweek* magazine picked up its story. The farm became a national event all because owner Doug Richardson had something new and different to talk about, assiduously courted the media, and was available for interviews.

In order to help reporters get to know you, prepare a press kit to send along with your releases. This should contain a fact sheet about you and your farm, what you grow, as well as copies of articles that have been written about your farm. Be assertive but not aggressive or demanding. A simple courtesy like a "please" or a "thank you" goes a long way! Sending a thank-you note after your release has been printed is important. Be sure to let reporters and editors know that the article has generated response.

Always be polite, but persistent. When Ann Burckhardt, a bed-and-breakfast owner in St. Peter, Minnesota, wanted to get her business story published in *Country Inns Bed & Breakfast* magazine, she requested twelve of her most loyal customers to write laudatory letters to the magazine. A year later, the magazine ran a nice, glossy feature on her business.

Establish yourself as a reliable media source so that any time reporters are looking for a local tie-in for a story with a wider scope—on farm prices, food safety, or the drought, for example—you are the person they think of to call. Let them know you are available for comment on issues that affect your business. Let your farm advisor know about your areas of expertise; often he or she is the first person the newspapers call when they want to do an agricultural story.

Court the media. If you're sponsoring a farm tour or festival, for example, send reporters free press passes, and an offer to send them pictures in case they can't attend the event. Invite them out for a special day, serve them refreshments, and give them special tours of your farm. (If you're serving blueberry pie, invite me!) Or take baskets of fruit to newspaper editors or TV announcers, and put them on their desks with a note saying: "This is compliments of (Your) Farm."

When the media comes. When a reporter comes to interview you, be prepared to answer questions—controversial as well as sympathetic—in a positive, factual manner. Never react with anger; customers *do* have concerns, and you need to address them. The issue of pesticides is an example: the public is eating your food, and they have a right to know your growing practices.

Control the interview. Rehearse anticipated questions. Be aware that you are never off the record. "Don't quote me" means nothing—what you say will be printed. If you suspect an interviewer's intentions, tape the interview, or ask for a list of questions beforehand. Or you can refuse the interview.

When speaking, say your most important points first, then fill in with a few supporting statements. Don't ramble; try to answer questions within 30 – 50 seconds. Use a conversational style rather than a prepared speech. Personalize the points you are trying to make. How does this affect you? How does it affect the customer?

Making speeches and teaching classes

Giving speeches, or teaching or sponsoring classes or seminars not only generates a tremendous amount of local media publicity, but helps establish you as an authority on your subject. Volunteer your services to community organizations such as the local civic, business or service clubs, garden clubs, senior citizens' groups and local schools. Make your speeches interesting to your audience rather than blatantly self-promotional.

Check with the organization's publicity chairperson to see if they are sending out news releases about the event; if not, do so yourself. Bring along flyers, business cards, coupons or giveaways so that audience members take something home. See that everyone attending leaves with the information they need to find you. Save everything—your notes, visual aids, and a copy of your speech to form the basis for future writing or material for your newsletter or catalog. Bring along a gift certificate or products from your store which the sponsoring organization can use for a door prize or raffle.

Look for opportunities to share your expertise through the media. Send a proposal to your local newspaper offering to write a weekly or monthly gardening or cooking column, or a regular column about your specialty products or about farm issues. Or you might tape a cooking show for your local public broadcasting station, showing off the latest recipes for the products you grow.

Conduct workshops and classes at your farm or invite local extension people to do so. Jo Ann Arvanigian, owner of the Sierra Nut House in Fresno, California, conducts classes for groups on uses of nuts such as making candy, and holds open houses in which areas of the store are turned into "events" for syrup tastings, candy-making, or putting together gift packs. You might also teach a course related to your field in conjunction with a local college. If the class is free, there are plenty of TV or radio community bulletin boards that will announce your event.

Radio and TV talk shows.[4] Many TV and radio stations and cable companies have local talk show hosts who invite the audience to phone in questions for their guests to answer. With many of the talk shows, in fact, you may not even have to leave your home—they interview you over the phone. Talk show producers are always on the lookout for new and different subjects to attract a varied audience. Simply call or write those in your area about your specialty.

The trick in getting on talk shows is to present yourself to the media so they will know that you have interesting things to say. Think of ten questions your customers ask you most often. Write them down clearly and concisely, and volunteer yourself to the media to provide the answers. Once you are on the talk show, however, is not the time for one-line answers—they want a story!

Do not push your business in a blatant, self-promotional manner. Discreetly and briefly mention your product or farm market a time or two, and request that the host give out information about how customers may reach you at the end of the interview. Insist on this—in fact, bring a "prep card" with you and hand it to the host at the time of the interview. You can also make an offer to local newspapers and radio or TV stations to write a column or to tape brief programs about your field with tips to readers, viewers and listeners.

Acknowledgments

Linda Stanley, JAMarketing, Elmhurst, Illinois.

Advertising

My accountant did a lot of research into advertising. He said it was all elusive, that no one really had the answers. . . Sometimes they ask you to spend a lot of money and there's no guarantee!
　　—Sharon Schafer, Grapes–N–More, Kerman, California

"FIFTY PERCENT of advertising works, and 50 percent doesn't," goes an old Madison Avenue advertising adage. "The problem lies in figuring out which 50 percent doesn't!" For a large farm with corporate-size advertising budgets, it may be OK to waste 50 percent of its advertising dollars, but for the small grower, advertising should work or it's not worth doing. Your advertising dollars should work as hard as your tractor! For many farmers, as with many retailers, the story of advertising has often been a case of spending too much—"pouring money down the advertising hole"—or too little, not realizing the benefits of an ongoing promotion and advertising campaign. Try to exhaust your resources for free publicity and promotion before spending a lot of money on advertising. Evaluate ad results constantly, so that you don't keep spending money on ads or promotional campaigns that aren't working.

William Wicher, in his book *You Can Spend Less and Sell More*, summarizes the most important principles of advertising:

• *Keep it simple.* Who are you? Who is your customer? What is the most cost-efficient way to reach that customer with a selling message?

• *Be consistent.* Project the same image in everything you do. Make sure that all of your advertising efforts reflect the identity or style you wish to convey. (Keep in mind that "homespun" does not excuse tackiness; your ad is competing with professionally produced ads that the customers see and hear every day.)

• *Sell!* The purpose of advertising is to sell! Don't be so clever and creative with your advertising that you forget to sell your product! If your advertising doesn't make the cash register ring, something's wrong and you should find out what . . . fast!

Making your advertising pay

Tailor your advertising and promotions to your current and prospective customers. Patty Belmonte, a marketing consultant from Olympia, Washington, tells the story of a client with a blueberry farm in Bellevue, an affluent suburb of Seattle, who wanted to promote U-Pick. Belmonte advised studying the farm's current customers. As they watched customers step out of their BMW or Mercedes cars in suits, high-heels and dresses, they quickly realized they were *not* U-Pickers!

"We found that the grower's primary customers were specialty food buyers who came in for a pint of blueberries that they could use for dessert at their evening meal," says Belmonte. "My client decided to emphasize convenience and freshness, such as washed berries, freezer packs and small quantities, conveying to customers that even in the

---

Advertising　　　　　　　　　　　　　　　　　　　　　　　　　219

heart of a metropolitan area they could get fresh, local blueberries." The ad—a picture of a stop sign with a caption: "Fresh Blueberries in Bellevue!"—brought in a rush of business.

Find the most comprehensive, cost-effective medium to deliver your message to your desired audience. When you approach the media, ask for an audience profile. Find a media outlet with a similar target audience as yours. Another way is to quiz your customers about their reading or listening habits (what media do they use?), and then choose your media accordingly.

Tailor your message to the chosen media. An upcoming special event needs the immediacy of television and radio coverage, for example. Yet a detailed tour description of your farm trail operation is best presented in a colorful brochure.

The amount of money you place in each advertising medium, such as direct mail, newspapers, radio, etc., should be determined by past experience, industry practice and ideas from media specialists. Normally, it's wise to use the same sort of media your competition uses.

Don't do an ad unless you can afford to repeat your presentation at least three times. Only a small fraction of any audience is paying attention to a promotion at any given time, and only a percentage of that fraction will take action on the first contact. Study what other people are doing. See how many times they run their ad and where. If they place an ad in a certain paper over a period of time, it probably means the ad is working for them.

Do only what you can afford to do, and do it well, rather than doing a lot of things in a mediocre fashion. If you are aiming for a high-end, gourmet market, competing with companies who put out slick direct-mail ads, it may be penny-wise and pound-foolish to try to save on your ad make-up. If you can't afford a sharp-looking direct-mail ad or display ad, consider starting with classifieds and build from there. Start slowly when allocating advertising dollars to a new medium. If you're new to the TV scene, try it out with 20 to 30 percent of your total ad budget; then adjust this figure upwards if you see some positive results.

Your basic message in advertising is to show customers how they can benefit from purchasing your product, or shopping at your store. What makes you unique? What products or services do you offer that are different and/or better than your competitors'? You can also advertise specials on

selected items. Advertising a different item each week is very effective in promoting both the item and the market. Pick a high-demand, excellent-value item on which to run a special. Once customers are in the store, use your layout, displays and point-of-purchase materials to sell them other products. Be sure to stock a reasonable amount of the special you are advertising, and place signs, or a copy of the ad, next to the product so that people can find it in the store. "Loss leaders" are specials advertised at near or below cost in the expectation that once customers are in your store, they will make additional purchases.

Evaluating your advertising

Keep tabs on how much you are spending for your advertising and what works and doesn't work. Experiment, monitor and adjust. Instead of running a big newspaper ad four weeks in a row for opening day, for example, run a full-page ad in the local paper a few days before the event; then 1/2 size the second week of your season and 1/8 size the third week. Once the word-of-mouth is out, classified ads or occasional small display ads may be sufficient to draw the customers you need.

Pre-testing introduces advertisements or promotional programs to a small sample of consumers or "focus groups" for their comments and opinions before directing the program to your entire target audience. One way to do this is simply to ask people what they think of your ad before you run it.

Post-testing involves tracking each ad, such as counting coupons brought into the checkstand or returned to you in the mail, or by checking the sales of advertised items. If the same ad is in several media, code your ad. A radio commercial might offer a gift or discount when listeners tell you they heard your ad on that station. Talk to people coming into the store: "Where did you see my ad?" Tabulate sales at the end of each week for four weeks, and try to make a judgment as to how many of the sales resulted from the advertisement. If the ad doesn't work, don't repeat it! On a long-run ad, try cutting the ad for a week or two and see if it makes any difference in sales. Look at long-term results also. Try to monitor whether your sales are

Personalize Your Product!

THE STORY OF George MacLeod, a retired grower from Kenwood, California, is a lesson in the importance of personalizing your product. A former general manager, as well as marketing director in electronics with Monsanto Chemical Company, George retired in 1979 and planted five acres of dwarf Gravenstein, Jonathan, and Red and Gōlden Delicious apples on his ranch. For awhile, George successfully sold all his apples direct from the farm, but as the trees began to produce more and more, things got out of hand. "When apples get ripe and everybody's selling them, you have to have a niche," says George. "From my marketing days, I knew I had to personalize my product."

George's daughter, Susan, drew a caricature of him, and he began selling his apples up and down the Sonoma Valley with in-store, point-of-sales signs saying "George's Kenwood Apples." The signs also carried a brief description of the apple variety, its flavor, aroma, texture and application, such as eating as is, or in pies and applesauce, or packing in school lunches.

"The stores were extremely happy," George recalls. "Even now, three years after I've stopped selling them, customers go into stores asking: 'Do you still have George's Kenwood apples?'"

up two months later as a result of your ad. An important function of advertising is to build store traffic and thus generate purchases of unadvertised items. Remember, your goal is the repeat customer.

To see if your advertising is paying for itself, figure the cost of the advertisement, plus the money for production of the ad. If an ad pulls ten times its cost, it's producing a good result—this represents a 10-percent advertising cost on your sales. Long-term advertising costs, however, usually represent only about 2- or 3-percent (net) cost of sales. Customers brought in by advertising, however, will also be attracted to something not advertised. This may bring down the high 10-percent figure to the profitable 2 to 3 percent. You can do this if your store is well-stocked, efficiently staffed, and has attractive displays.

Getting the most bang for your advertising bucks

Spread out your advertising costs by using design elements in several advertising media. An expensive artwork piece you've used for a large newspaper display ad, for example, can be used also on signs, brochures or posters. Utilize the reduction and enlargement modes of the copier at your local copy shop. Perhaps your flyer, with a little revision or juggling, can become an effective display ad for a newspaper.

Look for barter arrangements instead of hiring professionals or an ad agency. Trade produce or gift certificates with an artist-customer to help you develop a logo. For help with ad copy and layout, perhaps a community college journalism teacher can put you in touch with college marketing students who are looking for "real" projects for class assignments. You might also trade gift certificates for radio air time or newspaper ad space. Trade only with those media you would spend real money on; otherwise, your time and resources are wasted.

Too often, farm stories about going to an ad agency are disaster stories. First, there is the sheer cost of using an advertising agency. Second, you have to teach them your business. No one knows or can sell your product like yourself. Use professionals on an "as needed" basis for the tasks which you or a staff member can't do. Hire a consultant on a one-time basis, for example, rather than signing an ongoing contract with an ad agency. Ask to look at samples of their work and ask for references so that you can see if efforts with previous clients have been successful. Set specific objectives and ask for a cost estimate of what it will take to achieve this. "This is what I've got to spend. What can you come up with for that amount of money?"

If you choose to work with an agency or professional, make sure they are honest, competent, and *have worked with other food marketers*. They should also be marketing-oriented and have some experience in local store marketing. They should be able to help you define whom you're trying to reach and advise you on what it takes to reach them. Don't let them sell their style to you if it is not appropriate for your product. Professional advertising people are sometimes creative solely for the sake of being creative. Your goal is to sell products.

Road signs

The road sign identifies your business and directs customers to your farm. A good sign is relatively inexpensive, yet works for you on a daily basis. In a survey of customers at an Ohio road-side stand, 75 percent indicated they had learned about the market through highway signs. A professionally made sign, 4-by-8 feet, costing about $500 and lasting five years, costs only 27.4 cents a day!

Place an advance road sign 2 – 10 miles from your market (one in each direction) to alert motorists when to start looking for your market. Place another sign one-half mile from your farm, with perhaps another sign one-quarter mile from the market, and your best sign at the market location. (Be sure to include the words "Next Exit" where appropriate!) Too many signs, too closely spaced,

only confuse the driver and cheapen the image of your market.

Road signs can also be used to show the dates and hours you are open; a customer who has driven several miles only to find your market closed is likely to be perturbed! Consider constructing your road signs with individual panels hanging from the bottom of the main sign, listing the types of produce in season. When strawberries are in season, for example, you can suspend a panel saying "strawberries."[1]

Road signs are usually the first impressions customers have of your market, so make sure your signs are professional-looking, neat and clean. If signs are appealing, customers are much more likely to stop. Plywood cut-outs of fruits or vegetables, or wood with scenic carvings and delicately shaded colors, help depict a farm-fresh image. To create a professional-looking sign at low cost, use a slide projector to blowup your logo and some typeset script onto a wooden signboard. Then paint in the colors.

The use of signs is restricted by federal laws, state statutes and local ordinances. Contact your local county planning and zoning commissions for information on zoning restrictions and other regulations.

Size of signs. If your customers are primarily transient, you might want to make your signs large to attract their attention. But if most of your customers are local and are aware of your market, smaller signs that merely remind them you are open, and give news about new or in-season products, may be sufficient. Also, if a small sign would be overshadowed by others near it, it is probably advisable to use a larger sign if you can afford it.[2]

Signs must be easy to read, so keep the message short. Six words is about all people can comprehend while whizzing by on the highway. Focus on what appeals most to your customers, such as a seasonal product you are featuring. Use selling words like "fresh," "homegrown," "organic," etc. Periodically change some of the copy or design element on your signs to create continued interest. On top of a fruit stand near Watsonville, California, there is a 15-foot, hand-lettered banner with a different message each week: "Lettuce pray for peachy weather," or "We got the beet!," or "An apple a day keeps us in business," etc.

Pictorial symbols such as your farm logo or a fruit or vegetable caricature convey ideas better

than words. Do not mention prices. Signs at or near the checkin station are better for showing prices. If your prices are higher than the supermarkets', customers may not stop, but if they *see* how fresh and tasty and delightful your corn looks, then notice the higher price, they won't be as reluctant to buy from you.

Make sure the letters are large enough that drivers can read your signs. Allow a minimum of 1-inch of letter size for each 10 miles per hour of the speed of traffic passing your site. If traffic goes 40 m.p.h., in other words, use 4-inch letters or larger. Test your sign's legibility by driving past your business and seeing if you can read it from a distance.

Colors. Choose colors which contrast well with each other. Consider also the image you are trying to convey: reds, yellows and oranges project warmth, action and excitement, while blues and greens are "cool" colors.

Newspapers

Advantages:

- reaches a large number of people;
- relatively inexpensive for the number of people reached;
- can use coupons to track response;
- easily and quickly changed;

- can be placed in a particular section of the paper to reach and appeal to a selected audience; and
- can be clipped and saved if people are interested.

Disadvantages:

- nonselective, largely wasted circulation among nonclientele readers;
- consumers don't read all of paper;
- frequency and color are expensive; and
- no reader involvement.

If you advertise in a daily paper, you can choose where and when your ad will appear. Many growers like Friday editions to help bring people out on weekends. Some growers prefer to place ads in the food section or another section with a high percentage of women readers, or in recreation supplements that list places to go and what to do. If you are advertising in a large paper and only need to reach a specific geographic area, you can save on costs by checking to see if zone editions are available. You might also check the cost of using newspaper inserts, which can be an effective way to advertise.

Besides comparing circulation figures, note how completely a prospective newspaper reports local news—this is often an indication that readership is high. Besides daily and weekly newspapers, consider "shoppers." These are picked up by people who are specifically searching for bargains or are shopping for particular items. A survey of retailers showed that coupon ads in shoppers realize a much higher return than in daily newspapers.[3]

Newspapers will often help design your ad at no extra cost, but be careful. Study samples of previous ads in the newspaper and check their quality. Then watchdog your ad and ask for a proof before it goes to press. Newspaper employees are usually busy, and their layouts and designs probably will look like every other ad in the newspaper, meaning a waste of your advertising dollars. A freelance designer or artist more likely will be able to give your ads a distinctive look.

Display ads

Display or "space" ads are more costly than classified advertisements, but are larger and can be placed in designated parts of the paper. Display ads placed in the food or entertainment section, for example, are effective in attracting new customers.

A knockout, peak-season, large display ad (1 or 2 columns by 4 or 5 inches) with a coupon, placed in one or two key papers, is more attention-getting than a run of smaller display ads. Use the display ads to sell a new product, to announce a special, or to promote an event. Especially on a short season crop such as strawberries, you need to advertise "open soon" and "get the pick of the crop."

Don't spend money on a display ad without making it effective. Your display ad should always carry your logo, indicate your location and hours, feature one to three items, and have a coupon or other response element. Featuring only one or several items is more effective than trying to list all your products.

Classified ads

Classified ads are probably the most common form of newspaper advertising used by direct marketers. They are inexpensive and are read by a surprisingly high percentage of consumers. Classified ads are good for promoting items to people specifically looking for the products you have to offer, e.g., committed U-Pick customers. Another advantage of classifieds lies in the accommodation of last-minute price changes, something food producers often need for dropping prices of oversupply items. To make your classifieds stand out, request the newspaper to place a box around them. If your newspaper doesn't already have it, request them to create a classified section for "Fresh Produce."

Classifieds should be interesting and demand a reader's attention with the first two or three words. The lead words should be powerful and specific to the topic—e.g., "Luscious Strawberries." After the headline or lead-in, tell your prospects everything necessary to get them to act now. "Phone for free brochure. . ." or "Call today" will increase response. Then, condense and polish your copy. Use proven motivational words such as "you," "new," "free," "save" and "discover."

Radio

Advantages:

- usually local;
- frequency of message;
- can be tied to a specific program or time of airing to reach a selective audience;
- can be purchased or canceled on relatively short notice;
- emotional power with use of music and sound; and
- alive, friendly, conducive to warm, conversational messages.

Disadvantages:

- relatively expensive;
- need for brevity and repetition;
- difficult to measure response;
- often fails to get listeners' full attention; and
- must be repeated frequently because of the short exposure time.

Because of its "act now" nature, radio is good for bringing people out to events such as fairs, festivals, grand openings or family-fun days. And since it has the advantage of getting your message to the consumer quickly, radio is particularly helpful when you have an over-supply situation due to weather or other factors. Groups such as farm trails or growers' associations might find it easy to get free community service spots telling what products are coming on, or what's to be found at the farmers market. Investigate the idea of sponsoring a radio program. If your station has a program that's geared toward homemakers, this could be an effective media buy. Another radio tip is to take your local deejay a tantalizing sample of your product and ask him or her to eat it on the air—this is usually an offer they can't refuse!

Since ads cannot contain much detailed information and people often do not pay close attention, radio is usually a supplementary medium. A radio ad usually runs from 10 to 60 seconds. For radio and TV messages to be effective, they must be heard at least three times. For customers to hear the ad three times, the ad generally must be run a minimum of 12 spots.

Radio rate cards are negotiable, so bargain for lower prices. Radio stations also are often receptive

Linda Stanley, of JAMarketing, shows some of her advertising materials at a farm conference trade show

to tradeouts, i.e., trading air time for products you offer which they can use as listener prizes in radio promotions. For example, a rural attraction farm might trade "Pumpkin Fantasy Land" tickets in exchange for radio spots.

One way to save money with radio or TV ads is by making "donuts"—an identical opening and close with a hole in the middle for your message. You can change the message whenever you want—update the spot, sell a different item, and so on.[4]

To write good copy for radio:

- Speak informally, as if you are talking to another friend. One way to do this is to give the radio interviewer two or three questions he might ask you, then answer them.

- Talk benefits. Say at the beginning what you offer.

- Say your name at least two or three times. Often listeners are not tuned in at the start of a commercial; then a word or phrase will catch their attention.

- Organize your topic. Be very familiar and confident with the product(s) you are advertising.

- To make your ad stand out, find someone other than the on-duty deejay to do the speaking. If you are a good spokesperson for your business, do it yourself! Practice at home with a tape recorder until your tone of voice is natural and your delivery is confident. Time yourself and tape it. Listen for anything that sounds unbelievable or stilted.

Make music a part of your message. Call the music department at your local college to find a talented music student eager to compose and produce a musical jingle for your business. Or go through the music library at your local radio station and look for music cleared for commercial use. Select music that fits your company's identity and appeals to your target audience.

Link your radio ads to your print media ads for maximum effectiveness. Gear your copy to the listening format of each radio station: down-home copy for a country music station, and a more sophisticated approach for a classical music station. One way to find ideas for radio ads is to listen to out-of-town stations and borrow some ideas from them!

For more information on radio advertising write: Radio Advertising Bureau, Inc., 485 Lexington Ave., New York, NY 10017.

Television

Advantages:

- combination of sight, motion and sound is the closest to personal selling; and

- potentially large audience.

Disadvantages:

- expensive air time and costs;

- nonselective audience; and

- long preparation time.

Most big city TV stations cover a large area and are prohibitively costly. For less expensive local or cable TV stations, however, television may be a cost-effective advertising medium. According to Jay Levinson, author of *Guerrilla Marketing*, prime time satellite TV spots can be purchased for less than $20 for a 30-second ad, and produced for less than $1,000. It is often possible to buy local advertising inserts on nationwide cable TV channels. ESPN's travel channel, for example, offers the

LADYBUG™
PRODUCE

© Organically Grown Co-Op, 2545-I Prairie Rd.,
Eugene, OR 97402 (503) 689-5320

opportunity to target advertising to a travel audience.

Locally produced programs or cable TV are good places to look for free promotion for new food products. Local stations often are searching for new program ideas or may provide community service programs concerning nutrition and food. They often need material for "shorts" at the end of newscasts. Ask if one of their reporters is interested in doing a news story on some interesting and newsworthy aspect of your market or product.

Contact local stations regarding production services. Compare their facilities, prices and quality. Ask stations to recommend advertising agencies with good reputations for lower-cost, high-quality commercial production. Here are some tips on producing your own TV spot:

- Speak in an informal, conversational manner.

- The voice, or audio, describes the details. The video is the background for your message. Music determines the mood. You can save money by shooting silent footage and adding the sound later.

- Focus on one subject. Gear your presentation toward one specialty area. Make a storyboard to help you keep to the point and to guide those working with you. Take a large sheet of paper and sketch rough pictures for the visuals you plan to use. Under each portrayal write the words you plan to use with that scene.

- Ensure good production. Watch the station you are planning to use. Note the quality of their commercials. If the station cannot produce the quality of commercial you require, check in the yellow pages for independent production companies. Or consider using quality color slides. Beautiful photography, with appropriate music and a friendly voice-over, makes an attractive, economical alternative to video.

- Ask questions. *TVBooks* (from the Television Bureau of Advertising) contains excellent guidelines for beginners. TV salesmen should have these, along with sample scripts.

Brochures

Advantages:

- can be delivered to a selective audience;

- allows longer copy length; and

- permanence of print—customers can keep them.

Disadvantages:

- expensive if trying to reach a large audience.

Brochures help fuel word-of-mouth. Unlike flyers, an attractive brochure is something customers often want to save and pass along to friends. With words and striking pictures, your brochure portrays what you want people to know about your farm. Make sure your brochure is eye-catching, accurate, and includes your farm logo, store or farm hours open to the public, and a map of how to get to your farm.

In addition to handing out brochures at fairs or trade shows, or to customers who come to your store, also place brochures wherever there is a collection of people who would be interested in hearing about you. Such places include businesses, gift shops, malls, historical attractions, restaurants, museums, service stations, bed-and-breakfast inns, hotels and motels, travel agencies and fairs. Contact your chamber of commerce for community cooperative ads that may be available, as well as your state division of tourism. Before producing your brochure, check with various visitors' centers to find out their guidelines for brochures. Brochures can also be used as a direct mail piece to elicit new business. Include a cover letter and business reply card.

Choose the right printer for the job. Get several estimates and ask to see examples of their work. Study especially how they print photographs—not all printers do justice to a good photograph. It is usually not too expensive to add an additional color or two to your brochure. Four-color, or full-color, is more complicated, expensive, and time-consuming. A color photograph, however, is often more beautiful in print than the original. Another consideration is that color may be helpful in bringing out the qualities of your food product.

JAMarketing in Elmhurst, Illinois, offers four-color printed "blanks" with farm themes and images (see "Chapter Resources"). These can be imprinted with your farm name, logo and copy to make a quick and colorful brochure.

Flyers

Advantages:

• inexpensive;

• selective; and

• quick to get out—good for announcements.

Disadvantages:

• limited message.

Flyers are an inexpensive yet effective way to advertise. Businesses are more likely to display flyers in their windows than large posters, and they also can be used as mailers. Flyers can be 8-1/2-by-11 inches, legal size (8-1/2-by-14 inches) or 11-by-17 inches folded for self-mailers. You don't need to put a lot of money into flyers, yet neither should they look tacky. They may announce a special sale, a new expanded service or a new product, or they may invite the reader to a special event. Be sure to include a coupon in the flyer and offer specials or discounts.

Look for places to pass out your flyers such as food fairs, home shows, or pre-season festivals. Flyers also can be used as point-of-purchase sales pieces or as handouts to those who pass your store or trade show booth. Don't litter your neighbors' parking lots or yards by sticking your flyers under windshield wipers. Include this message at the bottom: "We sincerely hope you'll redeem this valuable coupon at (name of your market). However, if you can't, please dispose of it in a proper receptacle. Thank you for not littering!"

Direct mail

Advantages:

• personalized approach;

• can reach a specific audience;

• lengthy copy can be presented;

• often costs less per customer;

• rapid feedback;

• can be saved if recipient is interested; and

• offers a large variety of formats, such as letters, flyers, coupons, or recipe cards.

Disadvantages:

• worthless if list is not carefully selected (must use an accurate, up-to-date mailing list); and

• may be treated as junk mail.

Direct mail can be used to announce new products, or services; to welcome new customers or help regain lost customers; to thank all customers for their business at least once a year; to notify or remind customers and prospects of special events and so on. A mailing piece to a group of seniors, for example, might be designed in large, easy-to-read type, and promote the "real farm experience." Direct mail is a costly advertising medium; yet because of the high percentage of returns, it can be one of the cheapest in terms of results (cost per inquiry or sale).[5]

The quality of the customer list you mail to is the most important factor in direct-mail response. The best list is your current and previous customers' names obtained from receipts or checks, surveys and coupons, or a customer sign-up sheet. Offer customers free announcements of product availability or discounts on purchases as an inducement to sign your mailing list. Make it a *service* to your customers–e.g., "I see you bought some strawberries. If you would fill out this section, we'd be glad to notify you next season when strawberries are coming on." Personalize your form letters or messages by including friendly and folksy personalized comments.

Group the names on your mailing list according to current customers, inactive customers, and prospects. You may, for instance, want to make a mailing to inactive customers with a special inducement to become buyers again. When customers bring the coupons in, have the checkout clerk note the dollar amount purchased on the back.

This way you can make a computer listing of addresses of "large purchasers." Drop names you have not heard from in two or more years. Instead of keeping the lists physically separate, code the names in a single list to help prevent duplications. This can be done easily with a computer.

Printing and postage are expensive, so send mailings only to genuine prospective customers. Postal rates make checking the mailing list for outdated and inaccurate addresses imperative (see "Mail Order," Chapter 12). If you do more than one direct mailing a year, consider getting a bulk-rate permit.

Postcards

Postcards can be used to send prospective customers information about your store or products, as birthday cards for your regular customers, or to let them know about new goods or "preferred customer" sales, etc. Postcards are the least expensive way to mail first class. Like all first-class mail, they will be returned if undeliverable, so you can delete old names from your list. Many mail order marketers "clean up" their list at least every other year by mailing first class, using a simple postcard. Post cards cost about $200 for 500 cards, including design, printing and postage.

Newsletters

A personalized newsletter offers a soft-sell approach that allows you to keep in touch with your customers. Newsletters help you build a close relationship with existing patrons who are also your best prospects. They make customers feel like part of the farm "family."

Here are some other advantages of a newsletter:

• Saves postage and printing costs by compiling all your announcements, news, sales bulletins, classes offered, etc., into one mailing rather than several small mailings or numerous advertisements.

• Expands visibility—your newsletter is a reminder to customers that you're in business and have something valuable to offer them.

• Helps establish you as an authority in your field—by sharing your expertise with customers, you increase interest and sales.

• Addresses the most commonly asked questions—a newsletter allows you to answer the questions only once rather than over and over again.

In addition to promoting sales, new products, or announcing contests or events, etc., newsletters can be used also for educational and recognition purposes. The more you educate people about food, agriculture and farming, the more they will understand and support you. Include tips regarding food storage, recipes, craft projects, gift suggestions, etc. Your extension home economist can supply you with educational articles about food and nutrition.

Don't be put off by thinking you are not a great literary talent. Just imagine you are talking to friends—your customers. Do a monthly profile on one of your farm employees, highlighting what they do and why. Thank people or organizations who have helped you, or write about a related service or product your customers might want to know about. Invite your customers to participate in your newsletter through contributed articles such as recipes or new ways to use your products.

Include enough entertaining features and valuable information that your newsletter is of interest to your readers, something they look forward to. Don't forget, however, that your newsletter's main function is to increase sales. Most of your articles should have a marketing slant. Thus, if you do an article on one of your staff, highlight how that employee's expertise can serve the customer; use your recipe space for food items which are on promotion at your market, and so on.

In addition to mailing your newsletter to regular customers, place a complimentary copy in each

"Come & Pick 'Em–Farm-Fresh Blueberries" blueberry newspaper ad insert from the JAMarketing Catalog

customer's bag as they leave the store. Don't keep sending it to people who aren't bringing you business. Ask readers from time to time if they want to continue receiving the newsletter. When the newsletter gets popular enough, consider selling advertising space to neighboring businesses.

Outdoor advertising

Advantages:

- high exposure over a long period of time; and
- geographically selective—can reach customers near your business.

Disadvantages:

- limited amount of information can be presented;
- difficult to purchase, change or cancel on short notice;
- billboards are governed by local ordinances;
- large investment to cover entire market area; and
- audience may resent intrusion on landscape if poorly done.

Outdoor advertising such as posters, banners and billboards is usually designed to create aware-ness, or if placed near a store, as a last minute reminder. Try to place signs on at least one major thoroughfare coming from each direction toward your business. You might also consider placing signs on nearby freeways or major traffic routes, or even other streets close to your market. Outdoor advertising specialists are listed in the yellow pages under "Advertising–Outdoor." Don't forget to place a sign on the side of your delivery truck in order to make it a "traveling salesman"!

Outdoor advertising calls for clear, bold and quick communication. Short and simple copy is best—no more than five lines. Think of your billboard copy as a print headline with no wasted words. Attention-getting phrases are more effective than complete sentences.

Balloons. Bobbi Machado, of Machado Orchards Farm Market near Bowman, California, calls the 15-by-5-1/2-foot advertising blimp they purchased for $450 "the best advertising investment we've made." Machado says the apple-shaped blimp has increased sales 30 to 40 percent. The balloon comes with velcro attach-on letters, so that the sign can change with the seasons, from cherries to peaches to apples, etc.

Miscellaneous media

Keep your eyes and ears open to the many possibilities available for publicizing your products and services.

Printed bags serve as a reminder to come again, and are an effective advertising tool for year-round markets.

Trade publications. These ads generally are geared to wholesaling products, and your success will depend on what you are offering and how valuable it is to the industry.

Business cards. Be sure to have the map to your farm printed on the back of your business cards.

Fairs, exhibits, display booths. You can gain a tremendous amount of community goodwill through these means. You can also hand out samples and brochures, and collect names and addresses for your mailing list.

Buyers' and consumers' guides. Many states publish directories of U-Pick operations, rural recreational farms and roadside markets. Check with your state department of agriculture or local extension agent to find out how to be included.

Writing Advertising Copy

SIT DOWN AND put in writing 15 ways that your products or services benefit your customers. Vine-ripened taste? Unusual or gourmet produce? Friendly atmosphere and fantastic customer service? Answer the questions: "Why should I buy this?"; "Why should I come to your farm?'"; or "What's in it for me?" A special attention-getter is a statement indicating chemical-free fruits and vegetables (if such is the case).

You can't compete with the big companies on price, so promote freshness, nutritiousness and local ownership. Beware of advertising "quality," however. Everyone says, "I have the best." You have to *show* yours is the best. Perhaps you've won awards at the county fair, or can gather glowing testimonials from satisfied customers.

Keep it simple. Focus on one benefit at a time, and repeat it. People remember one key message, not ten reasons why they should patronize a market or roadside stand. Use a "benefit" headline—an informative statement rather than a "label"; then amplify this message in your copy and subheads. The illustration should express the idea the headline conveys. Long copy is OK, if what you have to say is important in selling your product.

Tell a story. As a small entrepreneur, don't try to be General Foods. We live in a society in which everything is wrapped in plastic, and people want to hear your personal story. Put lots of personality into your copy; tell how your farm got started, your early struggles, or your ethnic background.

Remember the AIDA formula. Get *Attention*, stimulate *Interest*, create a *Desire* or need for the product, and finally, give a call for *Action*, the part of the ad that tells readers what to do.

A few more rules are:

- Express your ideas clearly. Promise what you can deliver in an engaging, upbeat style.
- Feature a special, an announcement or an event.
- Sell specifics, i.e., "14 varieties to choose from" is better than "wide choice of offerings."
- Never disparage your competition.
- Repeat the name of your product or market several times.
- Clearly state what you are selling, as well as store location, hours open, and telephone number.
- Include customers' testimonials to assure your readers that what you say is true. Any time someone compliments you on your product, ask, "May I quote you in my ads?" Then jot down their name and actual words.
- Sell! Ask for the order. Give the reader a reason to act now with the use of a coupon or by specifying a designated time period for the promotion or event.

Local business directories or newcomer guides often are published by the chamber of commerce. Or you might consider putting together a buyers' guide, directory or map with the cooperation of a local farm trail or growers' association. (See "Group Promotion," Chapter 30.)

Yellow pages are worth using only if prospects would ordinarily look there for your type of business. See if other similar companies are listed under what you offer, e.g., "Farm Markets," "Gifts," "Flowers," "Fruits and Vegetables," etc. If you try the yellow pages, experiment first with a small-size ad to see if it works.

Unlike newspaper display ads, in which you list only one or two items, inform readers of the full range of services you offer, such as farm-fresh fruits and vegetables, pick-your-own strawberries, etc. Give a map and clear directions on how to find you. State clearly the hours and days you are open.

Coupons

Coupons can be included in newspaper display ads, in flyers or direct mailings, etc. By offering the customer a "bonus" or "extra" for bringing the coupon into your store, coupons act as an incentive to act on the ads or leaflets advertising your

Design and Production

UNLESS YOU ARE a talented designer, seek help with graphic design. A designer can help you avoid costly mistakes and produce a superior ad or brochure that may be used for years with only minor revisions. A shoddy-looking advertisement sends an implied message that your business is cheap, no matter what you say in the ad copy.

Perhaps you have a talented customer, friend, or student at a nearby college who is open to barter arrangements. Your printer may employ a good designer or be able to suggest someone. Ask to see their portfolio and be sure their work appeals to you. Or find a locally produced brochure or ad that you like and find out who designed and produced it.

If you decide to produce your own ads, do some homework. Go to the library and learn all you can about design. Study other ads and brochures, and compare those you like with those you don't like. What appeals to you? Design? Colors? Copy?

Some guidelines to follow with visual media are:

• Make your ads easy to recognize. In newspaper advertising, for example, the logo, the borders, the headline placement and the general layout should be the same from ad to ad. If you change the look of the ad each time, you constantly have to re-educate readers as to who you are and what you are selling.

• Use a simple, visually appealing layout with a dominant element such as a large picture, illustration or headline. Too many styles of type and dazzling illustrations or borders distract the reader. Strive for a layout that is pleasing to the eye, with at least 40 percent white space.

Ads with artwork generally perform better than ads without artwork. When you choose illustrations, make your advertising "farm-specific," instead of supermarket ad look-alikes. Stress the fresh air and sunshine aspects of the farm experience. If you have a U-Pick strawberry farm, for example, don't use a picture of a single berry in your ads—that's the image carried by all the supermarkets. Depict a smiling customer sampling a berry or customers carrying their fruit to the checkout stand.

In addition to becoming a "clip-art" collector, you might hire a photographer to shoot some of your popular products or your farm scenes. Ask for black-and-white copies of each shot if you're not printing four-color. Or you might hire an artist to do illustrations of some of your popular products, displays or farm scenes. An artistic illustration is often more appealing than a photograph, especially in newspapers.

Save money on typesetting costs by using laser printer "desktop publishing" output, available in many print shops. This is adequate for all but the highest-quality magazine advertisements. For an example of what "desktop publishing" looks like, you're looking at it! This book was produced on a Macintosh LC, with WriteNow and PageMaker software, and output to an Apple Laserwriter LS printer.

market or product. Coupons might be for a specific amount or a percentage discount off the cost of an item, a free cup of cider, a free recipe booklet, or a free coloring book for the children, etc. Coupons act as a loss leader: as customers bring in coupons for the free or discounted item, they usually purchase other items as well.

Coupons also serve as an effective, low-cost way to test advertisements or promotions. Code each coupon so you will know where it came from–

this allows you to test the effectiveness of that medium. As each coupon is returned, have the checkout clerk write on the back of the coupon: the customer's zip code (or town name), dollar amount purchased, and whether they are a new or old customer. With this data, you can see if your ads are working and alter your newspaper ad placements based on these tabulations. If the coupon offers a specific item at a reduced rate, the offer will bring in only those customers who have a need for that item. A better way to monitor your ad's effectiveness is to include a coupon for 10 percent off on the customer's next purchase.

Make sure each coupon includes your business name, location and hours, and gives an expiration date, as well as a clear explanation of the amount and terms of the coupon offer.

Promotions & gift certificates

Promotions do more than simply create immediate business. They can be used to build mailing lists, introduce new products or services, and create goodwill. Let's say you have an event in which you offer discount certificates as a promotion. To be eligible for a prize, a person is asked to come to the store to fill out a registration form. The promotion should bring in enough prospective customers and sales to pay for the cost of the certificates, plus provide a profit. In addition, you can use the names and addresses of the registrants as a nucleus for your mailing list in future direct-mail advertisements and promotions.

Some other promotional ideas include:

• Take a tip from the health food stores by punching a card with each purchase. When the card has been completely punched in for $100 in purchases, the customer gets $10 off the next purchase.

• A bakery ran an ad in the local paper six nights each week. The ad was always the same size and in the same location. Each night the owner selected one name from the phone directory and, in one corner of the ad, invited that person to call for a free pie. It was one of the most highly read ads in the paper.[6]

Gift certificates. The only extra costs involved with gift certificates are printing them and placing a few signs inside your store to announce that you have them available. When the recipient of the gift certificate comes into your store, you may have gained another steady customer. Include a small notice of the availability of gift certificates in every customer's bag; hand them out to shoppers as they enter; display signs announcing them in your store; and mail out notices of their availability with your newsletter or direct-mail pieces.

Acknowledgments

Linda Stanley, JAMarketing, Elmhurst, Illinois.

Group Promotion

We do not compete on price; we compete on quality and service to our consumers. I think the future is bright for those of us who are willing to improve ourselves and our marketing skills.

—Joe Huber, one of the founders of the Starlight Fruit and Vegetable Growers Association in Starlight, Indiana

I N UNION THERE is strength; it pays to promote with your fellow growers. Many growers feel they are competing with their neighboring farmers. This is not necessarily true! The more attractions in an area, the better to attract the crowds—more brings more.

Group promotion can start on a simple basis like going in with a few neighboring farmers to sell each others' produce at farmers markets. Or you might go in with a local bakery, restaurant or ice cream shop to place ads in the newspaper: "Fresh strawberry season is here!" While you hand out flyers for the bakery at your farm, the bakery places your farm brochures in customers' take-home bags, or allows you to place a small display on its counter or in the store window. Local retail stores are often happy to cooperate. They like the image of supporting local farmers.

Or you might create a "Strawberry Festival" promotional printed piece with recipes and coupons, to be distributed by all the partners in the promotion. The flyer offers coupons for a free box of pectin with a $10 purchase at the grocery; a free piece of strawberry pie with dinner at the local restaurant; a free tart with a dozen Danish rolls at the bakery; a free gourmet cooking class, "Cooking with Berries," at the gourmet food store; free jar toppers with a case of jelly jars at the hardware store; and $1 off on the next $10 purchase of U-Pick berries at your farm. Everyone benefits by having the promotion offered to other businesses' customers.

Some other co-promotion ideas include: high school home economics students demonstrate jam making on Saturday afternoon at your farm and sell the jam to raise money. You advertise it and put photos in the newspaper. Or invite local church groups to come out to your place and make pies for a bake-sale fund raiser.

Bartering is another way to benefit by pooling talents and resources. If you are offering farm recreational experiences on your farm, provide space also for a local baker. The baker provides high-quality baked goods and you share the profits. For a third of the take or more, hire school teachers to give weekend farm tours to children.

Growers can join together to create festivals on a scale that would be impossible for an individual grower. The Starlight Strawberry Festival in Starlight, Indiana, for example, attracts 16,000 people for its two-day event, and requires more than 160 people to run the show! Look for churches, organizations or civic groups in town to co-sponsor a festival along with your farmers' group. Donate festival proceeds to a worthy charity. Farmers will benefit from selling produce and will gain additional exposure for their farm attractions.

On a broader scale, growers can cooperate with other local businesses and governmental agencies to attract tourists and travelers to a growing area. Two-thirds of all Americans take at least one weekend trip a year, with 22 percent taking six or more weekend trips per year. Travelers are seeking increased diversity in their vacations, and country offerings are a welcome respite to city-weary travelers.

Cooperative advertising

Cooperative advertising is an economical way to achieve a broad advertising effect. Any number of noncompetitive businesses can buy advertising together. In newspaper co-op advertising, for example, growers buy a full page and subdivide it among several advertisers. Each pays a fraction of the cost of a full-page ad, while being part of a well-designed, interesting presentation.

Start a co-op ad campaign gradually. You can always buy more space or time as the season progresses. But if you commit yourself to a season's worth of ads and then decide that co-op advertising isn't working, you've wasted valuable time and money.

Direct marketing associations

The purpose of local *direct marketing associations* (sometimes called *farm trails*) is to bring city folks out to the farms. Each local farm trail publishes a map to help travelers locate the member farms. Farm trail maps not only can show city people where to buy farm-fresh produce, but also where to find local specialty items such as crafts or confections, or where to ski, swim, or eat at a good restaurant on their way back to the city. By offering a wide variety of farm attractions and products in a regional area, farm trails can draw customers from long distances and allow growers to specialize without losing sales. By pooling their promotional dollars, growers can reach more consumers and

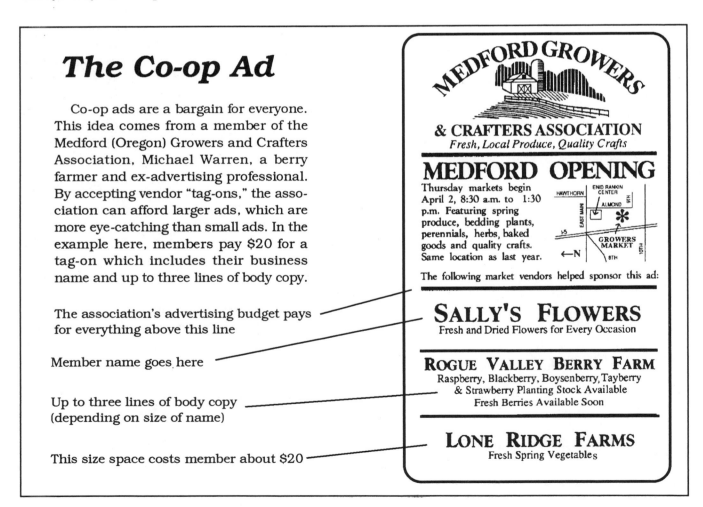

The Co-op Ad

Co-op ads are a bargain for everyone. This idea comes from a member of the Medford (Oregon) Growers and Crafters Association, Michael Warren, a berry farmer and ex-advertising professional. By accepting vendor "tag-ons," the association can afford larger ads, which are more eye-catching than small ads. In the example here, members pay $20 for a tag-on which includes their business name and up to three lines of body copy.

The association's advertising budget pays for everything above this line

Member name goes here

Up to three lines of body copy (depending on size of name)

This size space costs member about $20

MEDFORD GROWERS & CRAFTERS ASSOCIATION
Fresh, Local Produce, Quality Crafts

MEDFORD OPENING
Thursday markets begin April 2, 8:30 a.m. to 1:30 p.m. Featuring spring produce, bedding plants, perennials, herbs, baked goods and quality crafts. Same location as last year.

The following market vendors helped sponsor this ad:

SALLY'S FLOWERS
Fresh and Dried Flowers for Every Occasion

ROGUE VALLEY BERRY FARM
Raspberry, Blackberry, Boysenberry, Tayberry & Strawberry Planting Stock Available
Fresh Berries Available Soon

LONE RIDGE FARMS
Fresh Spring Vegetables

take advantage of advertising media which they might not otherwise be able to afford.

Another benefit of farm trails is informal networking. Let's say you grow strawberries, and your neighbor grows kiwis; you tell customers about her farm, and she sends customers over to you. Ellen and Bill Adamson, owners of the Happy Haven Ranch near Glen Ellen, California, claim that their $120 membership in Sonoma County Farm Trails brings them all the customers they need. "Farm trails are the best advertising tool for the money," they say.

Organization. Direct marketing associations are often organized by producer associations, state departments of agriculture, and/or cooperative county extension services. It doesn't work just to have a group of farmers put their names on a farm trail map and expect the public to come out to their farms, however. The farmers have to be willing to work and keep the association going.

Startup. Have at least one general meeting to draw up plans for a farm trail. Begin the meeting by explaining the concept of a farm trail and reviewing the reasons such an organization would benefit those present. Have someone from another farm trail relate his/her experiences, or show slides, videos and press clippings of other successful farm trails.

Work with existing businesses and organizations to get started. When the Yosemite Apple Trails organization started, the Oakhurst Chamber of Commerce provided insurance coverage for the fledgling organization in return for receipts from some booths and from the pancake breakfast at a festival sponsored by the organization.

Funding. Most farm trail maps are funded through membership fees, while others receive cooperative extension assistance. Some associations allow business card ads on their farm trail maps; others have fund-raising events.

Location. Because of the greater diversity of products offered, it should be possible to draw customers from farther away than a single independent stand could. Nevertheless, the farm trail should be within a reasonable distance of a sizeable metropolitan population, or on a roadway leading to a popular tourist recreational area.

Membership. Establish guidelines for member eligibility and responsibility. What percentage of products sold by each member should be homegrown? Most farm trails require that all members

Massachusetts grown... and fresher!

be bona fide producers, although some allow them to supplement their displays with a specified proportion of purchased items. Include producers of a variety of products in your farm trail in order to widen appeal and stretch out the season. A diversity of operations helps attract customers and encourages them to spend a longer time in the area.

Institute special memberships for nonfarming local businesses and interested supporters. Businesses selected for inclusion in the farm trail map should be in harmony with the tourism or "country feel" of the map. Examples are motels and tourist attractions, bed-and-breakfasts, antique shops, old-time general stores, and "country-theme" restaurants and bakeries. Your map also might list area attractions such as parks and beaches, craft shows and music festivals, square dancing, nature trails, and recreational vehicle parks.

Fees. Establish a sliding scale for producer members (per gross income) ranging from $50 to $150, with a lower fee for nonfood operations and a still lower fee for citizen supporters.

Legal status. Filing for nonprofit status has several advantages: the group may be eligible for certain government assistance and grant monies; and the group can use free public service announcements (PSA's) made available by radio and TV stations.

Geographic limits. Limit the geographic boundaries. Too small or too big an area reduces effectiveness.

Tasting Events

A TASTING EVENT is a high-end farmers market, with growers displaying their produce at booths. The idea is not to sell goods on the spot, but to make contacts with food professionals such as restaurateurs, specialty brokers, food caterers, independent growers, and specialty wholesalers or distributors. Food buyers connect with farmers, and farmers connect with buyers who are looking for produce they can't get through conventional suppliers. The Tasting puts many potential high-end buyers together at one place in a fun, festive way. Nearly every farmer who comes to a well-organized Tasting makes some solid business contacts.

Funding. You'll need to look for seed capital, since some expenses need to be paid before the ticket proceeds come in. Look for corporate donors, such as supermarkets and commodity food groups, as well as city government sponsors. Civic groups often are receptive to a Tasting, since they like the idea of their city being a center for gourmet foods. Tickets might be sold for $10 to $20. In addition to selling them individually to food professionals attending the show, try to sell them in blocks to wholesalers or corporations as goodwill gifts to clients. Grow-

ers' booth fees can range from $50 and up.

Planning. The key to forming a strong, ongoing Tasting event is to gather a broad base of support. Include a variety of members on the planning committee, such as farmers, state personnel, retailers, wholesalers and chefs. Do not lose the farm focus of the Tasting, however. One booth requirement might be that the farmers themselves must grow the produce displayed, and at least 50 percent has to be fresh produce.

Appoint an overall coordinator, as well as committees: grower, comparative tasting, food coordination, marketing, volunteer, site and equipment, and finance.

Calendar. Allow at least six to nine months to gather donor support, generate farmer involvement and enthusiasm, and to roll out the publicity. The glossier the publicity and programs, the longer the lead time.

Comparative tastings. Comparative tasting booths are an essential ingredient of the Tasting. Farmers donate produce that is cut up into bite-size samples to allow people to compare different varieties of the same commodity. The purpose is education; the public and even food professionals are often surprised at the many varieties of a product.

Food events. Part of what makes the Tasting more than a glorified farmers market is the food event. Tastings are not just a trade show; they are also a celebration—a fun, classy affair. This is important, because you're trying to attract the high-end buyers.

The Tasting food event allows restaurants to put on food and beverage demonstrations with produce donated by the farmers, both to show the use of the farmers' products and to allow restaurants to display their culinary talents. Give the restaurateurs a separate cooking area, and let them hand out samples of their creations.

Education. Another important function of the Tasting is education, both for the buyers and public, about specialty produce and growing methods. The influence of Oakland's "Tasting of the Summer Produce" on direct marketing of high-quality specialty products in the Bay Area, for example, was enormous.

Enjoyment. While consumers exclaim, "Those were the best I ever ate!," growers and buyers report that the Tastings give them a chance to get together with people they work with but don't see on a daily basis.

Quality control. Establish guidelines for product quality, sign construction and display, etc. The success and reputation of the farm trail will depend upon the quality of the products offered. Establish some enforcement mechanics such as expulsion or a fine.

Committees. Establish membership, fund-raising and map committees.

Precautions. Some factors which can hamper farm trail organizations are:

- inadequate inspection to ensure that standards are maintained—make sure that operators comply with regulations;

- unrealistically high requirements of the percentage of produce which must be homegrown;

- excessive dependence on public agencies which are often instrumental in establishing the organization; and

- limited or thinly spread membership which fails to draw the public or maintain farmer interest.

Farm trail maps

Consumer guides, or farm trail maps, are pamphlets or booklets that inform consumers about farmers who sell products directly to consumers within a specific area, such as a county, region or state. The guides list products including fruits, vegetables and herbs, etc., offered for sale by direct marketers.

Contents. List each producer's farm name along with their farm trail member number; their location and telephone number; the season and hours of operation; a listing of products offered by the producer; and the methods of sale. List available products alphabetically followed by code numbers which identify the growers who produce these items. Include also a pictorial map on which the various farm operations are located, a calendar showing harvest dates for the crops in the region, and tips for buying or harvesting.

I ♥ N.Y.
VEGETABLES!

© New York State Vegetable Growers Association, Inc.
P.O. Box 356, Ithaca, N.Y. 14851-0356; (607) 539-7648

Keep in contact with the growers to maintain their interest in the farm trail. Find out if there have been changes in the crops they're growing since the previous map was published, and if they have an adequate supply of produce for the coming season.

Distribution. Supply farms and business members with all the maps they need to give out to their customers, visitors, family and friends. Work with other agricultural events such as festivals and farm equipment shows. Invite the public, through TV and radio public service announcements, to obtain a map by sending a self-addressed, stamped envelope. Distribute the maps through local businesses, state tourism bureaus, state departments of agriculture, county extension offices, parents' magazines, AAA's *Motorland* magazine, and various insurance, company and travel magazines. Tourist companies should get a good supply, as well as bus companies, convention and business bureaus, realty companies, hotels, motels, gas stations, chambers of commerce, visitors' centers, newcomer clubs or welcoming committees, and the like.

One of the best ways you can promote your farm trail map is to ask your area newspaper to print it as an insert, together with a series of articles. Find helpful food or features editors who might interview farmer members. Suggest that reporters include a map to farm locations and a seasonal availability chart. Give them ideas for complementary articles on preparing fresh produce, and additional features highlighting pick-your-own fields, organic growers and harvest festivals.

Signs and logos. Farm trail membership entitles farmers to display the farm trail sign and logo on their farm; have them put their number on the signs corresponding to their listing in the map.

Regional commodity marketing associations

The purpose of a regional commodity marketing program is to promote a wide range of regional farm products. Sonoma County, California, farm advisor Paul Vossen, who was instrumental in organizing the Sonoma County Agricultural Marketing Program (SCAMP), told Sonoma County growers: "Local individual competitors are a drop in the bucket. Our *real* competitors are not other Sonoma County apple growers, but the big New York and Washington state apple growers."

SCAMP aims to promote local products under the "Sonoma County Select" label. Most mainstream consumers in Sonoma County didn't buy homegrown food before the SCAMP program was instituted; nor did they know what crops were produced in the county. Without a strong local marketing group, apples imported from Washington were selling for $1.19 a pound in supermarkets, while local apples were selling for six pounds for a dollar. SCAMP's aims are twofold: to convince consumers that they should buy local produce; and to help local growers and processors market their products in the nearby Bay Area, and eventually throughout California.

SCAMP's marketing efforts include continuing promotions and publicity; grocer and supermarket demos; development of the Sonoma Select logo and point-of-purchase materials; market research; cooperative advertising in newspapers, radio and television; a "Tasting of Sonoma County" trade show for regional food professionals; a co-op catalog sent out to food professionals; and marketing seminars. SCAMP also has hired a part-time merchandising salesperson to act as a liaison between SCAMP members and local markets.

Many states also have successfully organized collaborative agricultural marketing programs. The sale of New Jersey agricultural products increased by 50 percent within the first year of the New Jersey Fresh campaign.

Cooperative promotion

Network with convention bureaus or chambers of commerce who can help get the word out about nearby agricultural products and events. Make contact also with business and industry groups, service clubs, farm bureaus, travel agencies, church groups, and women's organizations. Many are willing to hear a speaker from your association, or view a slide show or video about your group. Contact convention bureaus and offer farm tours as meeting breaks or off-hours recreation.

Encourage other groups and associations to include your farm attractions in their calendar of events, and include those with a country theme in yours. Encourage restaurants to promote "A Taste of (Your) County" recipes, either as specialties or regular menu items. Promote a farm-map placemat to local restaurants. Provide local motels with apples and farm trail maps to place in rooms. Farm employees, in turn, can refer travelers to restaurants, lodgings, and other attractions in the area.

Contact the "gatekeepers": motel clerks, restaurant employees, campground hosts, state park employees, gas station attendants, etc., who deal with tourists and travelers—the very people you're trying to let know about your farm attractions! Tell them about your farms. Then they will have a ready

© California Certified Organic Farmers, 303 Potrero St., Ste. 51, Santa Cruz, CA 95061 (408) 423-CCOF

Group Festivals: A Checklist

☐ *Goals and objectives.* If your community's commerce centers around agriculture or even a specific commodity, it may be a natural to turn your function into a community-wide event. Invite participation from local clubs, church groups, county extension personnel, and the local chamber of commerce. The more you can involve the whole community in planning and participating in the event, the easier it will be to secure funds, equipment and other donations. Farming should be the focus, however; make sure that agriculture is not lost in the hoopla of crafts, carnivals and entertainment events.

☐ *Event planning.* Festival planning takes a lot of time, energy and ideas. Begin working early—at least six months to a year before the event. Select a date early in order to avoid conflicts with county fairs or other major local events. Form a committee for each group in charge of a specific function. An overall events chairperson should coordinate planning and operations. Other committees you will need include publicity, program, finance, facilities, cleanup, and special activities. Additional committees might include refreshments, parking and safety, decorations and props, or other special functions. For each committee, a master checklist should be compiled, with a list of all the assigned tasks and deadlines, to assure that jobs are completed on time.

☐ *Fund-raising.* You will need some finances to get started. Equipment and facilities may have to be rented beforehand. In addition, promotional efforts, contract agreements with entertainment groups, acquisition of supplies and prizes all require some funding prior to the event. If direct appeals for donations and volunteer efforts do not produce enough funds and facilities to stage your event, you might ask your local chamber of commerce for financial support. Solicit private donations, such as having a business underwrite the children's program, with their name(s) on the program. Provide for additional fund raisers, such as raffles, auctions, a pancake breakfast, garage sales, T-shirts, game booths, advertisements in the event's printed program, fund-raising dinners, booth fees, etc.

☐ *Volunteers.* Volunteers are the lifeblood of a festival. "Do you want to work at the apple fair—it's a lot of fun?" Treat volunteers like royalty, with a banquet at festival's end. Offer booth space to nonprofit groups in exchange for volunteer help. Remember, however, that these activities must relate as much as possible to the overall theme of the event. Make sure that all staff and volunteers are fully informed about their duties, and have back-ups in case any problems crop up or some workers do not show up.

☐ *Site selection.* A spot with its own natural beauty is best. If an outdoor site is selected, however, you may need to cancel or postpone the event in case of bad weather. Can the site handle your anticipated attendance? Is there adequate parking? Are there adequate sanitation facilities—both restroom and trash cans? Are there separate rest areas available? Can the site accommodate your anticipated food service requirements? Have you checked it for safety hazards? Utility servicing may need to be done by a licensed electrician.

☐ *Rules & regulations.* Make sure your event meets all local requirements for food booths, toilet facilities and other crowd-related regulations such as parking and traffic control. Contact city and county agencies early in the planning stage to obtain needed permits and licenses. Meet with state or local departments of health to discuss plans for the health and safety of event attendees, and to help booth participants obtain any needed permits. Contact local police, highway patrol and county agencies to make sure you meet requirements for parking and traffic control.

☐ *Insurance.* Make sure your event is covered by insurance. Provide a detailed list of activities and crowds expected to your insurance company. Some insurance companies will offer one-time coverage for special events.

Group Festivals: A Checklist *continued...*

☐ *Crowd control.* Make sure you have adequate staff and plans for the control, safety and comfort of those who attend the event. To prevent problems in this area, make a high estimate of the anticipated attendance, take a pessimistic outlook toward the weather, and consider any unfortunate results which could occur because of the nature or location of event activities. Get in touch early in the planning stage with local law enforcement agencies to find what security precautions you need to take. Police and firemen, ambulance and hospital personnel, Boy and Girl Scouts and other "service" people should be identified and recruited.

☐ *Entertainment, exhibits and educational events.* Encourage local talent as well as celebrities. Have ongoing demonstrations and workshops such as weaving, horseshoeing, etc. Devote a special area for children with story tellers, puppet shows, jugglers and musicians. No purely carnival-type concessions (such as bumper cars)— keep it clean, family *country* fun. Create lots of opportunities for children; they have a *major* influence in choice of family outing activities.

☐ *Food.* Providing food and refreshments for crowds can be a challenge: ask your local extension home economist for help in planning quantity food serving.

☐ *Special considerations.* Plan for:
• special requirements associated with the handicapped, small children and senior citizens;
• a lost-and-found booth;
• a spotlight and operator for the entertainers;
• electrical requirements for vendors;
• hospitality for VIP's;
• a planning session to advise staff on what to do in case of emergencies;
• a central communications point for staff to facilitate communications; and
• an "emergency kit" of miscellaneous items such as safety pins, tape, wire cutters, marking pens, etc.

☐ *Money matters.* Accountability and security are important. See that a system is set up to account for all monies, and arrange for someone to pick up money from concessionaires.

☐ *Promotion.* Make contacts with the media as early as possible. Public relations, in fact, should be a year-round effort. Send out initial news releases to create an early awareness of the event, then follow up with more detailed information that highlights specific activities to be offered.

☐ *Before the event.* Your pre-event "to-do" list might include: news releases, posters, slide shows to local community groups, billboards, signs, talks to local groups, mayor's proclamation, event name or slogan contests, reduced-price ticket sales, invitations, street banners and marquees, radio and TV coverage, bumber stickers, fund drives, newspaper supplements, etc.

☐ *During the event.* Invite a celebrity such as a local deejay or a food columnist to cook on-stage or judge a pie contest. Other promotional ideas include newspaper, TV and radio coverage, searchlights, prize drawings, balloon ascensions, guessing contests, etc.

☐ *After the event.* Post-event promotional ideas include news releases, speeches to civic groups, letters of thanks, volunteer recognition banquets, announcement of contest winners, etc.

☐ *Cleanup crew.* Volunteers are often not reliable in cleaning up and staff will be exhausted, so it may be wise to put aside money to pay a crew to do this. Close supervision of cleanup crews is necessary; see that only trash and garbage are thrown away and that those things which do not belong to you or which you wish to save are set aside. Everything borrowed or rented must be returned immediately.

☐ *Evaluation.* After the event, the planning committee should make an evaluation in the interest of improving it for next year. Evaluation methods can include crowd estimates and financial accounting, personal observation or comments from committee members and participants, questionnaires, personal interviews, etc.

answer when guests ask what there is to do in the area. Take free produce or snacks to them and give them free passes to your farms.

Go in with nonfarm businesses to offer package deals to tourist companies. This might include reduced prices for a ski resort's lift rides, a bed-and-breakfast stay, and a theater presentation. Special group tours might visit farms and farm festivals, packaging and processing facilities, and nurseries and restaurants. The Southwest Michigan Tourist Council offers a Lake and Country Tour, an Apple Country Tour, and an Orchard Tour, among many other tours. Make arrangements for reduced-rate overnight accommodations for groups; this encourages people to stay for more than a day.

Many tourists hesitate to purchase local agricultural products, thinking they will spoil before they get home. Educate them on how to transport fruits and vegetables. Just a simple suggestion such as keeping the produce out of the sun may be sufficient. Use protective, recyclable containers; customers won't mind the extra cost. For storage tips, write to the commodity group of whatever crop you grow; they are likely to have pamphlets available on storage and different ways to use the product. Ask if it's OK to use this pamphlet with your name and logo printed on it, with due acknowledgment to the commodity group.

Tourists often think that they have to purchase farm products in large quantities; they are concerned about spoilage while traveling and prefer small quantities. Let them know that small quantities are available, with special packaging if needed for traveling.

Tourists sometimes think that on-farm products are more expensive than grocery store products. If your products are *not* expensive, let your customers know this. If your products *are* more expensive, emphasize the "extras"—the fun, educational experience of visiting farm trail farms, and the homegrown authenticity of the products.

Media promotion

Your media promotion campaign might include press releases to newspapers and other publications, public service announcements for radio and TV stations, flyers and posters, and possibly paid advertising. Publish a cookbook, such as the *Appletizing and Appeeling Cookbook*, published by

© Tennessee Department of Agriculture

Yosemite Apple Trails in Oakhurst, California. Consider publishing a newsletter to keep both producers and consumers informed. Send it to food professionals as well as to the public and include a wholesale sheet listing farmers who are willing to deliver products to restaurants or stores.

The key to a successful publicity campaign is to make your group events newsworthy and timely. Emphasize "human interest" and "community service" aspects. All radio and TV stations are required by the Federal Communication Commission to offer free public service announcements on behalf of nonprofit organizations. Public service announcements are generally 20-, 30-, or 60-second spots. If your group is registered as a nonprofit organization, participate in as many of these as possible.

Try to get farm trail members booked as guests on local TV or radio talk shows; hopefully, these will develop into ongoing programs. Similarly, supply food editors with material for regular features on crops which are in season and recipes for their use. When anything noteworthy affects your farm trail, marketing association or farmers market, send out a press release. The media want stories about people, not organizations, so feature individual farmers. If somebody wins a prize for the biggest pumpkin, publicize it! Encourage members to mention their affiliation with the organization whenever they are contacted by the media. When publicizing events, spotlight several farmers, not just one.

Court media people, restaurant and motel personnel, or others who deal with tourists, by inviting them on bus tours of your farm trail, or by giving them gift certificates to be used at the farms. Sponsor a media dinner, or a press picnic, with food supplied by member-producers. Make it a meal to remember, so that the press will go back to

their desks and write mouth-watering stories! If you are serving blueberry pie and ice cream, send me an invitation!

If the importance of the story merits it, call a press conference. Send a press release announcing the press conference three or four weeks ahead to news and assignments editors. Morning conferences before 10 a.m. are best, and they should not last more than 30 minutes. Prepare releases, fact sheets and background information for distribution at the conference.

Develop a "farmer's media guide," to train member-producers of your organization in dealing with the press. For an excellent example of a farmer's media guide, send a self-addressed, stamped envelope to Southland Farmers' Market Association, 1010 S. Flower St., Suite 402, Los Angeles, CA 90015.

Making a good impression with the media does not require special skills; it is a matter of being lively, informative and friendly. When approached by a reporter, be prepared to talk about your crops (as well as those of other farm members), and talk about the benefits you receive from being a member of the organization. Stress the uniqueness of the food, pointing out that many of the items they can purchase from you or from fellow member-producers are not in grocery stores.

Acknowledgments

Harriet Moyer, Tourism Research and Resource Center, University of Wisconsin.

Dennis Propst, Department of Park & Recreational Resources, Michigan State University.

Sharing The Bounty

*Feeding the Hungry, Saving Farmland,
and Fighting for Farmers' Rights*

CHAPTER
31

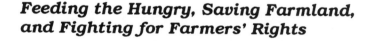

Kind hearts are the gardens.
Kind thoughts are the roots.
Kind words are the blossoms.
Kind deeds are the fruits.
    —Kirpal Singh

Feeding The Hungry

THE PROCESS OF sharing is something that comes naturally to farmers, who are used to working every day in the bounty of nature's harvest. The sunlight, soil, water and air given freely to us are constant reminders that we are caretakers, not creators, of the crops we grow. We are therefore beholden to share our harvest with our brothers and sisters.

How can there be hunger in this land of abundance?

Bonnie MacGregor, program coordinator for the California Food Network, which distributes food to the needy through churches, soup kitchens, day-care centers, senior meal programs, shelters, and hospices, lists a number of reasons, including diminishing governmental funds to help the needy.

"But mostly it's because with the high cost of living and the low minimum wage, there's little money left for food, especially for people with fixed incomes. Housing costs especially are a big problem—affordable housing is just not a reality anymore. The most tragic thing for me is the seniors and children who can't work themselves out of it.

"I think we've had the mistaken view," concludes MacGregor, "that the people who are hun-

---

Sharing The Bounty

That All May Be Fed:
The Rescue Mission

THEY WALK IN, ride bicycles or pull up in decrepit cars—alone, couples or entire families, an average of 288 of them a day, Monday through Friday. There is one common thread among them—they're hungry. At Sister Ursula's Kitchen in Visalia, free, hot lunches are provided to all who enter. Said Sister Kenneth Quinn of the St. Vincent de Paul Society, who runs the kitchen: "We never have enough food, but we do what we can."

Three-year-old Matthew's face lights up as Sister Kenneth hands him a teddy bear from the thrift shop next door. As Mat-thew, his two-year-old brother, and his mother and father prepare to leave, Sister Kenneth explains that for Matthew, as for many others who come to the kitchen, it may be his one meal of the day.

Matthew's father, a farm worker, is unemployed now that the harvest season is over. Others needing assistance, Sister Kenneth says, may be single-parent families; single men from Mexico seeking employment; migrant families from the South; families whose income is not enough to cover food, clothing, and housing; or the disabled.

Tulare County has an estimated 45,000 people living below the poverty level, most of them elderly, handicapped, or children. "Almost all of these people are people who are in bad circumstances but who want to work," explains Sandy Beals, executive director of Tulare County Food Resources, Inc. Pointing to boxes of fresh kiwifruit in the warehouse, she says, "Some children will be better fed because of this donation."

—"Rescue Mission," by Eric Gibson, *California Farmer*, December 1987

gry don't want to help themselves. But we find that there are many people who are working and still go hungry."

What you can do

The best way to share your harvest is to contact a food bank, community center, service group or church in your county which has a food distribution system to see if they will accept your surplus vegetables and fruit.

You can donate other things besides food. Many of the food distribution centers double as warehouse and transportation operations, so donations such as freezers, food drying equipment or office furniture are appreciated. As one food program coordinator said: "Just giving something to a charitable thrift shop helps enormously. Your good wishes, prayers and just plain caring are also important—they help keep our spirits up."

Look into ways that any farmers' group you belong to can help. Donations from farm festivals, for example—either unsold food or booth pro-ceeds—might be donated to needy programs. Each week at the Marin County Farmers Market, farmers donate 500 to 1,000 pounds of unsold food to the Marin Community Food Bank. The market also has plans to serve the community by providing easier access to the market for seniors and low-income citizens, and by working with schools to help students learn how to grow and market vegetables.

Many farmers markets participate in the federally funded Women, Infants and Children (WIC) farmers market food coupon program. Under the WIC program, $10 to $20 worth of food coupons are issued once each summer to low-income, nutritionally at-risk households. The coupons are redeemable for locally grown fresh fruits and vegetables sold at participating farmers markets. Everyone benefits: low-income women and needy children gain the nutritional benefits of fresh produce, while growers report as much as a 30-percent increase in sales as a result of the program, both from sales made through the coupons, and through additional cash purchases made by the same customers who often return to the market as regular shoppers. For information about WIC, contact the National Association of Farmers Market Nutrition Programs at (512) 445–5748 or (203) 296-9325.

Another thing you might do to help surmount world hunger is to become a vegetarian and utilize farm animals for purposes other than human consumption. According to many social scientists, the meat industry is the foremost cause of world hunger. In the book *Diet for a Small Planet* author Frances Moore Lappe documents the great waste of the world's protein and food (caloric) energy supply that results from feeding human-edible crops to "food" animals. It takes about two acres of grain to produce one beef cow, whereas one hundred human beings can be fed using the same amount of grain. To find out more about the health, social, ethical and spiritual reasons for becoming a vegetarian, send for the pamphlet *You Are What You Eat*, available free from New World Publishing (see Order Form, last page).

Gleaning programs

When you reap the harvest of your land, you shall not be so thorough that you reap the field to its very edge, nor shall you glean the stray ears of grain. Likewise, you shall not pick your vineyard bare, nor gather up the grapes that have fallen. These things you shall leave for the poor. . .
—Holy Bible, Lev. 19: 9 - 10

One of the best ways to support food distribution programs is through gleaning programs in which farmers invite volunteers to harvest the food that is either too big, too small, cosmetically blemished (but otherwise perfect in food value), or overripe for marketing.

In Contra Costa County, California, Project Glean harvested 288,000 pounds of surplus produce last year. According to former Project Glean coordinator Jill Kohler, about a third of the food goes to seniors living on supplemental Social Security incomes of $500 a month or less, and another third goes to children.

Everyone benefits from gleaning: food that would rot on the ground goes to people who need it, and insect pests that might be attracted to the

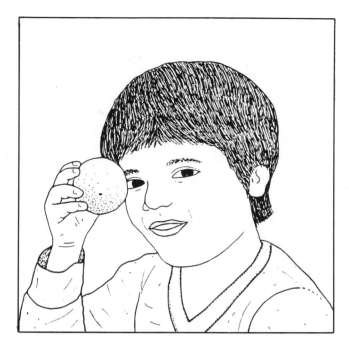

Delicious! This happy scene is made possible by the kind hearts of Project Glean volunteers.

rotting fruit are foiled. Mostly, though, farmers simply participate in the joy of giving to those in need.

Some farmers express the following concerns about gleaning:

• *Volunteers might damage the crop or might pick in nondesignated areas.* Make sure that the volunteers have been well-instructed, and that a field supervisor will be present to monitor their harvesting.

• *Giving away food will hurt the market for the crop.* A reputable food distribution group will give only to those in need. The people going to a soup kitchen cannot afford the food otherwise.

• *Liability.* Volunteers working for a hunger program are generally not a sue-happy group. Some states have "Good Samaritan" laws that absolve farmers from liability. The gleaning volunteers can sign a waiver of liability. Some gleaning groups take out liability insurance.

• *Farmers don't want to give to people they think could be working to support themselves.* Most of the people served by food distribution programs are children or seniors, single parents, or the disabled, who are living on low incomes.

For the gleaning volunteers, the benefits of gleaning include a sense of purpose and a feeling of self-worth; the opportunity for physical exercise and social interaction; and a way to fulfill the need to be needed.

Emile and Margaret Lacrampe, Project Glean volunteers, put on work clothes and sun hats a couple of times a week and join other volunteers harvesting surplus fruits and vegetables. "The work is hard, and sometimes it would be easier to stay home and let someone else worry about feeding the hungry," the Lacrampes exclaim. "But there's a huge amount of enthusiasm, and it's very rewarding, knowing that what you're doing is helping others."

To find out more about starting a gleaning program, send for the pamphlet *Gleaning: Pointers On How To Begin,* which is available free from New World Publishing (see Order Form, last page).

Saving Farmland

Every hour in this country we are bulldozing 220 acres of American farmland for housing tracts and shopping centers. I know whereof I speak, for I have read every general plan for every city in the county of Fresno, as well as the county's general plan, and in point of fact, agricultural land is considered an "interim use." It is good for agriculture until the city needs room for housing or commercial development.

—"How We Treat Our Precious Dirt," Elizabeth Scott-Graham, *Fresno Bee,* November 22, 1992

Metropolitan farmers—those farming near a city—have a golden nest egg. The average value of land and buildings on metro farms is more than twice as high as on nonmetro farms ($1,429 vs. $661 per acre). Proximity to urban consumers provides direct access to ready-made markets for high-value produce; metro farmers account for 60 percent of U.S. direct-marketing sales. Yet metro farmers, like their country cousins, are in trouble. Farming near an urban area brings skyrocketing prices for land, labor and water. Development also brings neighbors who complain about the smell of cows or the noise of the tractor, and bring political pressure to zone agriculture out of the area. Many farmers would rather take the money offered by developers than fight to save their farmland. Sonoma County farm advisor Paul Vossen gives the example of a Sonoma County farmer who recently was offered $800,000 for fewer than 20 acres. "That's pretty hard to turn down," Vossen comments.

Metropolitan growth may be killing the goose that laid the golden egg—the ability of farmers to farm. Over one million acres of farmland a year nationwide are being converted to nonagricultural uses. Orchards and fields are torn up; family farms are put up for sale, and farmers move out. In the bulldozer's wake, all the benefits of nearby farmland disappear: fresh, local produce, ag-related jobs, tourism, and the open spaces in which to breathe and to live.

What to do

Renew your commitment to farming. Many farmers are ambivalent about the issue of farmland protection. They want to protect ag land, but they are reluctant to install regulations for fear of foreclosing the possibility of selling their own land for a high profit.

Push for agricultural elements in general plans, and right-to-farm ordinances at county, statewide, and federal levels. In Sonoma County, farmer Ray Peterson spearheaded a group of farmers to stave off a proposed county zoning ordinance that effectively would have taken away his farming operation. "The county board of supervisors is constantly pressured by developers," Peterson explains. They believe that if a city is not growing, it's dying. Those of us in agriculture spend our time farming. Our lack of presence in the political area is a disadvantage. We must convince more farmers to get involved. Without participating, we get what others want."

Work for stricter agricultural zoning with permanent urban boundaries. Help elect officials with spine enough to enforce the regulations. The local farm bureau is a good way to work locally; they have good credibility and are well-staffed.

Work with local planning agencies to adopt such policies as land trusts and Purchase-of-Development Rights (PDR) programs, with the idea of creating agricultural "open space" districts. Under PDR programs, government or nonprofit land trusts purchase a farmers' development rights,

The Organic Grain Company

paying him the difference between the land's value for development and the land's agricultural value. The idea is to protect agricultural land against development. The farmer gives up the right to subdivide the land, so that it can't be subjected to development speculation.

Many feel that the issue of farmland preservation has become a do or die matter; once the furrows are paved over, there's no turning back. As Petaluma, California, dairyman Dan Silacci suggests, "Maybe the people will realize the value of agriculture when they have to tear up streets to plant crops so they can eat."

Fighting For Farmers' Rights

A lot of small farmers together can do things that only a big farm can do.
—Matty Matarazzo, Matarazzo Farms, Belvidere, New Jersey

Finally, "sharing the bounty" implies joining hands with your fellow farmers to better your mutual livelihood and help preserve a way of life that enriches us all. As Mark Mulcahy, produce manager at the Good Nature Grocery store in Walnut Creek, California, said: "Farmers used to be looked upon as some of the most important members of society, and that should happen again."

The farmers' road back to respectability, however, is a long one. As California Association of Family Farmers president Al Courchesne said: "On issues like farm-labor housing, farm-labor relations, chemical controls, fuel-on-the-farm, quality control standards, taxation or marketing orders—the whole system is geared to deal with the large operations. The whole attitude of government seems to be that if you're small, you're not important."

One of the first things farmers can do is write or call their congressmen and push for a national right-to-farm act. As quoted in *Missouri Farmer* (now *Small Farm Today*), (July/Aug. 1989), Jeff McFadden of Richmond, Missouri, said to the Senate Agriculture Committee: "The next farm bill should include a national right-to-farm act. Nationwide, many farms are being put out of business by spreading cities, restrictive zoning, nuisance lawsuits, and taxation of farmland at higher than commercial or residential values. Some states have addressed this problem with a right-to-farm bill, which guarantees that no operating farm can be zoned, reclassified for tax purposes, or nuisance-sued out of business for normal farm operations."

Another major challenge to modern agriculture—skyrocketing land costs—needs to be addressed with broad political action. In many areas of the country, land costs have become so extravagant that it is difficult for the farmer who owns land to remain in farming, and impossible for the average person to buy land and get into farming. Many observers feel that only cooperative action up to the level of broad public-policy governmental directives involving land trusts, long-term leases with options to buy, or low-interest loans to the farmer, can help stem the tide of skyrocketing land costs.

What to do

What can one farmer do to "shout from the tractor" and let her views be known?

Get involved! Clayton Mize, a peach and mixed vegetable farmer near Sacramento, California, made national news for taking on Cal Trans with his claim that they killed several of his trees when their crews sprayed along the road that borders his peach orchard. Cal Trans tried to deny the claim, but through media coverage and expert testimony, Mize brought the bureaucrats to their knees and they paid him for the damage. This case led to the passage of a state law to limit herbicide use by Cal Trans.

Similarly, Matty Matarazzo, of Matarazzo Farms in New Jersey, is a member of his local county zoning board. With his farm surrounded by $400,000 homes, he's concerned that farming rights will be swallowed up. "Are we going to let politicians determine our rights or let the state tell

"Those Damn Farmers!"

RECENTLY, A COFFEE and doughnut shop in Woodland, California had raised the price of its pastry products. A sign on the wall explained the price increase as a result of the high price of wheat. A townsman was overheard as he read the sign to remark bitterly, "Those damn farmers!"

Those three little words, indeed spoken by a townsman in a community which owes its existence to the surrounding farms, reflect the utter ignorance of urban Americans about the food supply system which nourishes their daily lives. According to a study produced by the USDA for Congress, the farmer, while being the most essential part of the system, got only 24 cents out of every dollar spent by consumers for food in 1990. In the case of wheat, the study showed that the farmer got only 5 cents of the dollar spent on bread.

—Robert Drynan, in *California Wheat* newsletter, Summer 1992

us how we can market?" Matty asks. Too many government regulations, Matarazzo asserts, prevent the farmer from being a good marketer. When a local health board shut down a U-Pick farm because a customer slipped and broke his arm, Matty participated in a cooperative effort to change the state law. "In New Jersey, the law now ensures that a farmer can't be successfully sued just because someone falls off a reasonably safe wagon," Matty says.

Call and write a letter to, or go see, your local newspaper editor. Tell him: "Hey, I watch your TV news program every day, and I never see any stories about farming!" As Matty Matarazzo says: "Papers *owe* it to their constituents to cover the positive aspects of farming. Publicity is not something farmers should have to pay for, and it's more important for newspapers to cover a few farm stories than every traffic accident that occurs."

Join a farmers' organization. Writing in *Rural Enterprise* magazine, editor/publisher Karl Ohm

III comments: "Eventually, we must reach the point where direct marketing's contribution to the agricultural economy is more fully recognized. Direct marketing associations are needed to make sure that tax-supported institutions will respond to certain needs. For example, funds still seem to flow more easily into agricultural production research instead of marketing."

Farmer associations *are effective!* For example, a few of the accomplishments of the California Association of Family Farmers are: 1) helping win passage of federal farm credit legislation that provides greater protection for family farm borrowers; 2) protecting prime farmland by successfully opposing "Super Collider" siting in California; 3) successfully lobbying for legislation creating the state sustainable agriculture research program; and 4) co-sponsoring the state's annual Farm Conference.

Stage an event. During Earth Day, April 22, 1991, Cable News Network did a special feature on the ecological benefits of farmers markets by following Lynn Bagley, director of the Marin County Farmers Market, as she shopped at the market. During the interview, Bagley suggested farmers market shoppers "vote with their fork" by supporting family farmers and the agricultural foodbelt/greenbelt surrounding cities through their purchases of fresh, local produce.

Influence your legislators. Pay them a personal visit in their office, call them, or write a letter. Be brief, clear, and to the point. Mention the bill and your reasons for being either for or against it. Don't use a form letter; use your own paper and words. Illustrate local support for your opinion. Never underestimate the power of a letter. Keep in mind that legislators must decide on *many* bills and issues, most of which they admit to being only partially informed about, and they often rely on the "mail count" to make quick decisions.

Once you have developed communication with your legislator's district office, invite their aides out to your farm to see firsthand the challenges that you are facing.

Educate the public about agriculture. Look upon your pick-your-own farm or your roadside market as an important agricultural education tool. Don't just talk to customers about food; talk about farms and farmers as well!

Encourage and support local grade school and high school agricultural programs. Support state-

Our salvation can come only through the farmer.

—Mahatma Gandhi

wide programs like *Ag In The Classroom*. With less than one percent of the population involved in farming, it is important to educate people about agriculture and how important it is to everyone. People will not support something they don't understand!

As Bob Kirtlan of Silver Bend Farm expresses it, "The future of agriculture in this country is not in the hands of farmers; it's in the hands of city folk, because they out-number us. So it's important to get them out to the farm and show them the problems and challenges we face here."

Farm tours. In an era when agriculture is coming under increasing public scrutiny, public (farm) tours that show the life and work down on the farm are not only sensible, they're becoming necessary. And in times of increasing competition, strengthening consumer loyalty by inviting customers and potential customers for farm visits is a winning marketing strategy.

Since 1988, Ron Mansfield, owner of Goldbud Farm in Placerville, California, has hosted a two-day "Cherries Jubilee" festival on Father's Day weekend. "The Highway 50 corridor (between Sacramento and Lake Tahoe) is fast becoming a suburban area and I need to look ahead," says Mansfield. He regards his high-profile farm operation as the kind of approach necessary to keep agriculture viable in the area while at the same time taking advantage of the increasing potential customer base.[1]

Similarly, at the Good Nature Grocery store in Walnut Creek, California, produce manager Mark Mulcahy organizes "Meet The Grower" Tasting Faires, inviting growers who supply the store to hand out samples of their products and bring pictures of their farms to show the customers. He also organizes farm tours, arranging carpools to take customers out to the growers' farms, letting the farmers explain their farming methods, the seasonality of their products, and so on.

Start a "buy local" campaign. Educate urban residents about agriculture, and encourage them to "vote with dollars" by purchasing locally produced food. Let the public know that if they wish to enjoy the scenic vistas provided by farms, they have an obligation to buy locally produced food to keep the farms financially viable.

According to Andy Lee, author of *Backyard Market Gardening*, Vermont—like many other states—imports nearly 90 percent of the food that it eats. "Our challenge," he says, "is to convince and encourage our friends and neighbors to buy from us instead of from the supermarkets. While our neighbors are spending their money at the supermarkets, local farmers are going out of business."

Acknowledgments

Tom Haller, director, California Association of Family Farmers.

Enjoy!

Festivals,
Farm Humor and more. . .

Three-time California fiddle champion
Jay Belt lights into "Rag-Time Annie"

Festivals

There will always be sufferings and problems, but we have to take time in the year to recognize other processes in ourselves and in nature and rejoice. And that, to me, is what festivals are all about.

—Leslie Weedman, "The Farmer and the Festivals," 1991 Eco-Farm Conference

WITH THE HAY IN the barn, the pumpkins on the fence, and the checks deposited in the bank, it's time to enjoy! One of the best ways to enjoy and celebrate farming is to have a festival or fair. The Sonoma County Harvest Fair, for example, features a blacksmithing contest, a scarecrow contest, "the longest apple peel" contest, a box social, and a draft horse barn. The Sonoma County Retail Store, selling local farm products from mustards to jams, did over $100,000 dollars worth of business in three days. According to its coordinator Saralee Kunde, "People see the quality of our local produce, so they feel they don't have to go to Hickory Farms for Christmas."

At the Marin County Farmers Market, director Lynn Bagley views the annual Harvest Faire as an extension of the twice-weekly market. "People come to the Faire who ordinarily wouldn't come to the market," she says. "They make ongoing contacts with the farmers, who often double their take on Faire day. The Faire really helps build the market."

Lynn Bagley feels that, although harvest fairs are helping revive the appeal of farming life, farmers too often are lost in the glitter. "A harvest fair should emphasize the harvest and the farmer," she states. "Farmers don't like to go to fairs where they feel there is too much emphasis on entertainment. The people should come expecting to buy produce."

For all its upscale reputation, the Marin County Farmers Market Harvest Faire is a throwback to traditional harvest fairs, with a country breakfast, crafts fair, live animal farm, live music, food and farm demonstrations, and a hayride. "We get calls all year from people asking: 'When is the fair this year?' " notes Bagley. "A true old-fashioned country fair is hard to find. People tell us this is what the county fairs used to be like. We feel it's important to get the farmers and the community together to celebrate."

For the real down-home feel, nothing beats the annual "Hoes Down" Festival in Guinda, California. As coordinator Dru Rivers explains, "It's time to put your 'hoes down' and have some fun!" The event is sponsored by the Committee for Sustainable Agriculture and is held on the Full Belly Farm owned by Rivers and her husband Paul Muller.

"Having the event somewhere else might be easier or more convenient," comments Rivers, "but we thought that having the festival on the farm is the best way to introduce people to farming life." Demonstrations include horseshoeing, compost making ("a lot of people who come are home gardeners"), seed saving, sheep shearing, almond shelling, and an herb garden tour.

During the milking demonstration, some city folks actually do discover that milk comes from cows. "I'm not ridiculing anyone," comments Rivers, "but people really have lost connection. It's important that people realize where their food comes from!"

Everything is hands-on at the Hoes Down Festival: "Urban people really don't get to do things with their hands too much," Rivers explains, "and just to feel the wool from the sheep in the spinning demonstration is fun for them."

Similarly, the idea of the contests, such as the sack races, corn husking, apple bobbing, and the straw bale toss, is to get people involved, instead of just sitting down and being entertained. Then there is the Manure Pitch-Off: participants race with their wheelbarrows to a manure pile, fill their barrows, race back to the starting line and pitch the manure 20 feet into a bucket. Whoever gets their bucket fullest within the five-minute limit wins!

One year, instead of the scheduled one-time farm tour, Paul Muller found himself taking folks out on the wagon five times to see the farm. "A lot of people come here who had seen us at the farmers markets," he said. "They wanted to get a picture in their mind of where their food comes from."

Some very special events each year at the Hoes Down Festival are the kids' activities, with apple bobbing, water balloon tosses, and story telling in

© Frog Hollow Farm, P.O. Box 872, Brentwood, CA 94513
(510) 634-2845

the Enchanted Tepee. "I'm always amazed at how kids respond to the farm," comments Rivers. "They're fascinated with horses. It's important to give them the freedom to let loose and have some fun."

The most fun part of the festival, as Rivers sees it, is not the event itself so much as people getting together. The Hoes Down Festival starts with "three of us meeting as a committee for eight months, organizing the details, everything from the music to the food. Then the day before, about 25 to 30 people help set up. The day of the event, we have 40 to 50 volunteers, and then 25 to 30 the day after to help clean up."

Harvest fairs may not singlehandedly bring back the family farm, but at least, as Dru Rivers sees it, it's a start at getting people committed to the rural way of life. "It's just farmers and friends working toward a common goal," she says. "Lots of times we're so involved in our own lives, we don't have a chance to get involved with other people."

According to noted biodynamic farmer/philosopher Trauger Groh, festivals traditionally have served the deeper, spiritual purpose of helping give meaning to the annual rhythms of sun, moon, the planets and earthly seasons. "Festivals help give structure to the year," he says. "In addition, the festive mood brings out of people something of their true being. We see sides of people we've never seen before."

Trauger Groh points out that festivals can be a solitary event as well as a social one. In winter, for example, our spirits, like nature, tend to be more contractive and inward rather than expansive and outward as in summer months, and winter is the natural time to take a solitary walk around the farm and "meditate," or visualize what you'd like the farm to become in the coming months. "Walk every field and go to every corner," Groh says.

"Create images of what will be there in the summer."

Festivals, Groh agrees, are made for children. He tells how on his own CSA (community supported agriculture) farm, third graders are invited to the farm to plant rye seed. They are invited back to see it sprouting up, and then again a year later at harvest time when, as fourth graders, they help thresh the rye with bottles to separate the seed out and ceremoniously hand over the yield to the next class of third graders to plant. "In the U.S. we can establish something entirely new because we are not burdened by tradition," Groh explains. "But we must do something to reconnect us with the seasons of the year."

For Leslie Weedman, a farmer from Los Molinos, California, festivals are also a time to get together with people other than just the farmers in your community. For their annual festival, she points out, they invited everyone in the community from gas station attendants to sales clerks. "If you're a farmer, all you ever see is what's *not* done. But when people come to a festival, they see what *is* done!"

While it helps to plan festivals by studying past traditions and adapting them to your community and farm, Leslie points out that they are "a living, evolving thing. Each year they become deeper and more special because of people's participation. You can judge a community, like a family, by its traditions. In our culture we've lost that, but we're trying to rebuild it."

Echoing Trauger Groh's thoughts about the spiritual nature of festivals, Leslie recalls a late spring day, the day of their annual festival, that turned out to be cold, gray and rainy. "The sun hadn't come out all that morning, and we finally started the maypole dance," she recalls. "And as we were doing it, about halfway through, the sun came out on the maypole for about 30 seconds. Then it poured and hailed and stormed. But that was the *only* time in the whole day that the sun came out. To me, it was symbolic that in festivals there *is* something more than we see happening."

Farm Humor

This woman decided that what she really wanted to do was to be a farmer. So she went into the country and she cut down some timber and she stored it in piles and she got a portable mill and she made planks and she made fence posts, and she built her fences and she built her house.

So after she'd done that, she got a horse, and she got a plow, and she plowed her field, and she planted her hay. She planted her wheat, and it grew! She harvested it, and she got her chicks, she fed them the wheat, she got a cow, she put it out to the pasture, and she used her excess wood in a fossil fuel stove.

She got milk from her cow, she took it in her house and she lovingly churned the butter. She had the most wonderful milk. She was so happy! But you know, after she'd taken all those ingredients into her kitchen and baked her cake, she swore that the work was too hard. She'd never bake a cake from scratch again!

—Sue Moore, contestant, Ecological Farm Conference Laff-Offs

One way to enliven your fair or festival is to have a joke-telling contest! In the annual Laff-Offs Contest at the Committee for Sustainable Agriculture's Eco-Farm Conference, farmers play to standing-room-only crowds, tell jokes, laugh their heads off, and compete for the first place prize—a trip to Hawaii!

Humor is one of the best ways to celebrate farming—and life—year-round. As Laff-Offs coordinator Amigo Cantisano comments: "It takes a real extrovert to get up in front of an audience and crack jokes. But really, the best humor is the everyday occurrences on the farm—things that happen that farmers just make light of."

James Myers, author of *A Treasury Of Farm And Ranch Humor*, points out: "It is a fact that since colonial days, farm and ranch jokes have been a major source of laughter for Americans in all walks of life. We are a laughing people, and when life is hard, when weather or prices or bugs are against us, we laugh the hardest because that is when we need those healing stories and jokes that bring us laughter."

According to Dr. Marilyn Spiegel, associate professor with the Ohio State University Cooperative Extension Service, who conducts stress-management workshops for families in Ohio, humor is a miracle drug with no bad side effects. "Humor relieves stress and anger, helps us learn better, work better, and solve problems more creatively," she says. "We sometimes ignore its value and forget how powerful a tool it is."

Although it is difficult to analyze humor in a laboratory, Spiegel says, there are indications that the benefits of humor have a scientific basis. Laughter not only lessens the pulse rate and releases muscular tension in the body; it stimulates the cardiovascular system through the deep respiration that accompanies it, and increases production of chemical endorphins, the body's natural pain-killers. "Laughter really is the best medicine," Spiegel asserts.

Humor is natural to farm life—there are often kids and animals on the farm, and they help us to see the humor in everyday situations. But farms have become more sophisticated, more specialized, notes Spiegel. "Today's farmers are subject to the same stresses as other businessmen, and it's important to remember to relax once in awhile!"

So if things have gotten just too businesslike on the farm and it's hard to see much of anything funny, try *working* at it—in a fun way, of course. "Just try to see the funny side along with the serious side," Spiegel says. Look for humor in everyday experiences. Learn to reframe stressful situations as humorous ones. Post cartoons behind the cash register, and offer a one dollar reward for the joke of the week.

Incorporate humor and fun in meetings, parties and conversations. If you're the boss, set the tone by letting employees know it's OK to laugh and enjoy themselves once in awhile. Humor helps develop trust, opens up communication, and promotes closer relationships. Everyone's a winner.

No one has to tell Doug Carrigan, of Carrigan Farm in Mooresville, North Carolina, about farm humor. For April Fools' Day one year, he stuck $20 worth of marshmallows on peach tree buds. Then, assuming the role of a farm advisor, he had a friend play the role of the farmer, and they called in the media for a press conference about their marshmallow crop! On the day the TV crews came out, however, it was raining, so naturally it turned into a story about how things looked disastrous for the marshmallow crop, and how the state's marshmallow industry would probably experience a $40 million loss because of the rains!

So keep smiling—it'll make people wonder what you've been up to. As Amigo Cantisano says: "We need a little break once in awhile, to be able to poke fun at ourselves." And as Zia Sonnabend said at the Ecological Farm Conference Laff-Offs: "It's important for farmers to cultivate a sense of humor. . . hoe! hoe! hoe!"

What the world needs now is a sense of humus.

*Time to relax! This shanty on Highway 41 near Lemoore,
California, is the handiwork of Robert Gonzales. "I like old
things," he explains, "and it seemed like a fun thing to do."*

Section X: Resources

General Resources

Craig was the first person to really listen to us and our concerns and to come up with answers. He hunts through books we can't afford and through sources that we can't get to—and gets back to us.

—Leo and Holly Dumont, San Martin, California, on Santa Clara County farm advisor Craig Kolodge, *Small Farm News*, March/April 1992

TO MAKE SOUND DECISIONS about growing and marketing, you need up-to-date, accurate and reliable information. Reading books and journals on farming, maintaining a good filing system, keeping a personal daily journal, making friends with other growers with whom you can exchange information, and attending meetings, workshops and seminars should all be scheduled into your routine.

Your first step in seeking resources and information should be your local cooperative extension office. Extension agents have access to a wide array of resources, and they can advise you concerning the resources you need for your particular enterprise. Contact also state, county and federal offices for help with your marketing questions.

Also seek the help of local small businesses, economic development groups or community colleges. Many of the resources listed in this section are available through libraries: check your county extension library, as well as local county, university or college libraries. Many state and local chambers of commerce are also establishing small business councils and information referral centers. They can help you comply with local laws, licenses, and restrictions.

In addition to reading some of the agricultural trade books and journals listed in this section, take an occasional peek at journals of related industries such as *Craft Reporter, Gifts and Decorative Accessories, Giftware News, Professional Merchandising, Natural Foods Merchandiser, Fancy Food, Grocer, Packaging Digest, Food and Drug Packaging, Cooks, Restaurateur,* and so on.

Trade associations such as vegetable and fruit growers' associations are an excellent way to obtain specialized knowledge for growing and marketing your products. These groups provide newsletters, workshops and conferences from which you can gain a wealth of ideas, and make personal contact with other growers. Trade associations also serve as support groups, and often provide co-op advertising, group purchasing and sometimes group insurance packages.

Using the Resources Section: While "General Resources" lists resources which cover a broad range of topics, "Chapter Resources" lists information specific to each chapter topic—e.g., farmers markets, advertising, etc. In addition to sending away for some of the resources listed here, you should also contact your state cooperative extension printing service, since they may have information more specific for your state. These are listed in "General Resources."

Remember that additional information is always available from each resource. Before spending money to purchase a book or subscribe to a magazine, etc., you may want more information than is available here. Call or write the organizations listed to request a descriptive brochure or catalog of the resources they offer.

The prices listed in this resources section are subject to change. In order to assure a return delivery of whatever you send for, you may want to include a note mentioning this book as your source of information, the date (1993), and a note saying "Please bill me for any additional charges due to subsequent price changes."

To my knowledge, all the listings here are correct as of the date of publication of this book. Any resource directory begins to go out of date almost as soon as it is printed, since businesses are always moving, books go out of print, or periodicals cease publication or change names,

A dedicated county extension agent, or farm advisor, is your single most valuable resource. Shown here: Sonoma County, California, farm advisor Paul Vossen.

etc. If you find that any of these listings are no longer valid, you may have to do some research on your own—for example, calling or writing some of the other resources listed in this section—for help in finding more up-to-date information.

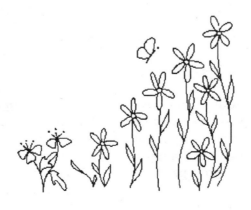

General Resources Contents

1. Cooperative Extension Services 257
2. Books & Publications Suppliers 259
3. Books 259
4. Pamphlets & Booklets 260
5. Directories & Resource Books 261
6. Periodicals & Newsletters 261
7. Associations 262
8. Conferences 263
9. Audio & Video Tapes 264
10. Databanks 264
11. State Programs 265
12. U.S. Government Resources 265
13. Consultants 265

14. Direct Marketing Supplies 266
    Barrels, baskets, crates, buckets ..266
    Cider & juice making equipment ..266
    Roadside banners 266
    Miscellaneous direct marketing ....
      supplies 266
    Scales 266
15. Miscellaneous Resources 266
16. Packaging Supplies 266
17. Wholesale Marketing Resources ...267
18. Cooperative Resources 268
19. Organic Resources.......................268
20. Postharvest Handling 269
    Cooling units 269

1. Cooperative Extension Services

Write to the Cooperative Extension Publications Department *for your own state* to request a catalog of agricultural and small business publications.

Alabama. Cooperative Extension Service, Auburn Univ., Auburn, AL 36849.

Publications Dept., Tuskegee Univ. Cooperative Extension, Tuskegee Institute, Tuskegee, AL 36088.

Cooperative Extension Program, Alabama A&M Univ., Normal, AL 35762.

Alaska. Information Office, Cooperative Extension Service, Univ. of Alaska, Fairbanks, AK 99775-5200.

Arkansas. Cooperative Extension Service, 1201 McAlmont, Univ. of Arkansas, Box 391, Little Rock, AR 72203.

California. (See ANR Publications, "Books & Publications Suppliers.")

Colorado. Bulletin Room, Colorado State Univ., Fort Collins, CO 80523.

Connecticut. Agricultural Publications, U-35, 1376 Storrs Rd., Univ. of Connecticut, Storrs, CT 0269-4035.

Delaware. Extension Service, The Univ. of Delaware, Newark, DE 19717-1303; (302) 451-2506.

Florida. Editorial Dept., G022 McCarty Hall, Institute of Food and Agricultural Science, Univ. of Florida, Gainesville, FL 32611.

Georgia. Extension Publication Office, Hoke Smith Bldg., The Univ. of Georgia, Athens, GA 30602. Make checks payable to Cooperative Extension Service, The Univ. of Georgia.

Hawaii. CTAHR Publications Order Desk, 2500 Dole St., Krauss Hall 121, Univ. of Hawaii, Honolulu, HI 96822.

Idaho. Agricultural Communications Center, Ag Publications Bldg., Bldg. J40, Idaho St., Univ. of Idaho, Moscow, ID 83843-4199.

Illinois. Office of Agricultural Communications & Education, 69-C2 Mumford Hall, 1301 Gregory Dr., Urbana, IL 61801; (217) 333-2007. Make checks payable to Univ. of Illinois.

Indiana. Agricultural Communication Service, Media Distribution Center, 301 S. 2nd St., Lafayette, IN 47901-1232; (317) 494-6794. Make checks payable to Purdue University.

Iowa. Publications Distribution Center, Printing and Publications Bldg., Iowa State Univ., Ames, IA 50011; (515) 294-5247.

Kansas. Distribution Center, Cooperative Extension Service, Umberger Hall, Kansas State Univ., Manhattan, KS 66506.

Kentucky. Dept. of Ag Communications, 131 Scovell Hall, Univ. of Kentucky, Lexington, KY 40545-0064.

Louisiana. Publications Office, Rm. 128, Knapp Hall, Louisiana State Univ., Baton Rouge, LA 70803.

Maine. Information and Publications Editor, Cooperative Extension Service, Univ. of Maine at Orono, Orono, ME 04469.

Maryland. Publications Office, Cooperative Extension Service, Univ. of Maryland, College Park, MD 20742.

Massachusetts. Dept. of Agricultural and Resource Economics, 201 Draper Hall, Univ. of Massachusetts, Amherst, MA 01003.

Michigan. Michigan State Univ. Bulletin Office, 10-B Agriculture Hall, E. Lansing, MI 48824-1039; (517) 355-0240; Bulk: (517) 353-6740.

Minnesota. Marketing Division, Minnesota Dept. of Agriculture, 90 W. Plato Blvd., St. Paul, MN 55107; (612) 297-4648.

Mississippi. Extension Information, Mississippi Cooperative Extension Service, Mississippi State Univ., MS 39762.

Montana. Extension Service, Montana State Univ., Bozeman, MT 59715; (406) 994-3273.

Nebraska. Cooperative Extension, Institute of Agriculture and Natural Resources, Univ. of Nebraska-Lincoln, Lincoln, NE 68583.

Nevada. Agricultural Information Office, College of Agriculture, Univ. of Nevada-Reno, Reno, NV 89557-0103.

New Hampshire. Cooperative Extension Service, Univ. of New Hampshire, Durham, NH 03824.

New Jersey. Publications Distribution Center, Cook College, P.O. Box 231, Rutgers Univ., New Brunswick, NJ 08903. Make checks payable to Rutgers, The State University of New Jersey.

New Mexico. Bulletin Office, Dept. of Agricultural Information, Box 3AL, New Mexico State Univ., Las Cruces, NM 88003-0031.

New York. Farming Alternatives Project, 443 Warren Hall, Cornell Univ., Ithaca, NY 14853-7801.

North Carolina. Publications Office, Box 7603, North Carolina State Univ., Raleigh, NC 27695-7603.

North Dakota. Distribution Center, NDSU Extension Service, Morrill Hall, P.O. Box 5655, North Dakota State Univ., Fargo, ND 58105-5655; (701) 237-7883.

Ohio. Publications Office, Cooperative Extension Service, 2120 Fyffe Rd., Columbus, OH 43210-1099.

Oklahoma. Central Mailing Services, Oklahoma State Univ., Stillwater, OK 74078-0550.

Oregon. Bulletin Mailing Office, Industrial Bldg., Oregon State Univ., Corvallis, OR 97331-4202.

Pennsylvania. Publications Distribution Center, College of Agricultural Sciences, 112 Agricultural Admin. Bldg., Pennsylvania State Univ., University Park, PA 16802; (814) 865-6713.

Purdue University. Lonni Davenport, Purdue Univ., Horticulture Dept., 1165 HORT Bldg., West Lafayette, IN 47907-1165; (317) 494-1314.

Rhode Island. CE Education Center, Greenhouse Conservatory, Univ. of Rhode Island, Kingston, RI 02881-0804.

South Carolina. Bulletin Room, P & AS Bldg., Clemson Univ., Clemson, SC 29634-5609.

South Dakota. Ag Communication Bulletin Room, Box 2212A, South Dakota State Univ., Brookings, SD 57007.

Tennessee. Mail and Supply Office, P.O. Box 1071, Univ. of Tennessee, Knoxville, TN 37901-1071; (615) 974-7300.

Texas. Dept. of Agricultural Communications, Texas A & M Univ., College Station, TX 77843-2112.

Utah. Bulletin Room, Utah State Univ., Logan, UT 84322-5015.

Vermont. Vermont Extension Service, Univ. of Vermont, College of Agriculture, 178 S. Prospect St., Burlington, VT 05401; (802) 656-3036.

Virginia. Virginia Cooperative Extension Service, Virginia Tech, 101 Hutcheson Hall, Blacksburg, VA 24061-0401; (703) 231-4528.

Washington. Bulletin Office, Cooperative Extension, Cooper Publications Bldg., Washington State Univ., Pullman, WA 99164-5912.

West Virginia. Extension Specialist - L.A., Rm. 2092, Ag Sciences Bldg., P.O. Box 6108, West Virginia State Univ., Morgantown, WV 26506-6108.

Wisconsin. Agricultural Bulletin, Rm. 245, 30 N. Murray St., Univ. of Wisconsin, Madison, WI 53715.

Wyoming. Bulletin Room, P.O. Box 3313, Univ. of Wyoming, Laramie, WY 82071-3354.

2. Books & Publications Suppliers

agAccess, P.O. Box 2008, Davis, CA 95617; (916) 756-7177; FAX (916) 756-7188. For orders, UPS rate is $3 for 1 book, $2.50 each for 2 – 4 books.

ANR Publications (University of California), 6701 San Pablo Ave., Oakland, CA 94608-1239; (510) 642-2431. Make checks payable to UC Regents.

Distribution Center, 3 Coffey Hall, 1420 Eckles Ave., St. Paul, MN 55108; (612) 625-8173. Educational materials on community tourism development, marketing, promotion and advertising. Send for list of publications, "Educational Materials Order Form." Make checks payable to Univ. of Minnesota.

KSU-Small Business Development Center, 2323 Anderson Ave., Ste. 100, Manhattan, KS 66502-2912; (913) 532-5529. Make checks payable to KSU Foundation.

Northeast Regional Agricultural Engineering Service (NRAES), 152 Riley-Robb Hall, Cooperative Extension, Ithaca, NY 14853-5701; (607) 255-7654.

Products and Services Catalog. Listing of publications published by the United Fresh Fruit and Vegetable Growers Association (see listing in "Associations"). Books are available for nonmembers as well as members including *Encyclopedia of Produce; Supply Guide; Training Resources for the Produce Industry Guide Book; The Produce Industry Fact Book; Facts and Pointers On Fruits and Vegetables; Specialty Produce Chart* and more.

The Small Business Directory: Publications and Videotapes for Starting and Managing a Successful Small Business. U.S. Small Business Administration publication listing numerous low-fee publications and videos useful for small businesses on small business management, pricing, marketing, personnel management and financing.

For an order form and complete listing write to the SBA and request 115-A (Small Business Directory). SBA Publications, P.O. Box 30, Denver, CO 80201-0030.

Superintendent of Documents, U.S. Government Printing Office, Washington, DC 20401. Make checks payable to Superintendent of Documents.

3. Books

Note: For additional books, please see "New World Bookshelf," p. 301.

1988 Marketing: Agriculture Yearbook. From the USDA "Yearbook of Agriculture" series, issue devoted to broad range of marketing topics. $9.50. Superintendent of Documents, Government Printing Office, Washington, DC 20402. SN #001-000-04517-2.

1990 Direct Marketing Resource Notebook. Starting a Business, Marketing Research, Types of Markets, Location of Markets, Financial Topics, Personnel Management, Insurance, Computer Programs, Cost of Production and Pricing, Postharvest Care, Weights and Measures, Tourism, State Regulations, Resources, Market Terminology. $15 plus $4 p/h. Ramsey County Extension Service, 2020 White Bear Ave., St. Paul, MN 55109; (612) 625-9292.

50 Small Farm Ideas. Briefly describes 50 successful small farms of 3 – 10 acres. Unique products and special niche markets. $3.75. Island Meadow Farm, 295 Sharpe Rd., Anacortes-Fidalgo Island, WA 98221.

Gardening For Profit, by Peter Henderson. This is the classic book on market gardening, written over 100 years ago! Its ideas are still valid: raise only high-value crops, capture lucrative early and late markets, farm the best land you can, concentrate on freshness and quality, farm as close to your market as possible, be a price setter,

not a price taker. Weatherproof your farm as much as possible. Topics include high-value vegetable crops, crop rotation, monthly garden calendar, planting tips, pest control and more. $24.95 postpaid. American Botanist, P.O. Box 532, Chillicothe, IL 61523; (309) 274-5254.

Grow Fruits & Vegetables the Way They Used to Taste, by John F. Adams, Wynood Press, 1988. New York, NY. 207-page paperback for creating an heirloom garden, including grafting, propagation techniques, seed sources, step-by-step illustrations.

How To Grow More Vegetables ($17.50 postpaid) and *The Backyard Homestead Mini-Farm* ($11.50 postpaid), by John Jeavons. Ecology Action/Common Ground, 5798 Ridgewood Rd., Willits, CA 95490.

How To Make $100,000 Farming 25 Acres by Booker T. Whatley. How to set up a subscription farming operation, and more. $19.95 postpaid. The New Farm magazine, 222 Main St., Emmaus, PA 18049.

How To Make Money Growing Plants, Trees and Flowers: A Guide to Profitable Earth-Friendly Ventures, by Francis X. Jozwik. 180 pp. $19.95 plus $2.95 p/h. Also from the same author and publisher: *Perennials for Profit or Pleasure: How To Grow and Sell in Your Own Backyard*. 80 pp. $9.95 plus $2 p/h. Also: *The Greenhouse and Nursery Handbook: A Complete Guide to Growing and Selling Ornamental Container Crops*. 514 pp. $49.95 plus $6 p/h. Andmar Press, P.O. Box 217, Mills, WY 82644.

Knott's Handbook for Vegetable Growers, by Oscar A. Lorenz and Donald M. Maynard. A complete resource book for growers of any vegetable crop. Cultural practices, nutrient requirements for vegetable crops, common planting practices, useful soil science, irrigation, harvesting and storage, and packing. 390 pp. $45.95. SN #WIL037 From agAccess. See "Books & Publications Suppliers."

Managing for Success: A Manual for Roadside Markets, by James Beierlein and Cathleen Connell. Information on enterprise feasibility, pricing, budgeting, laws and regulations, legal structures, insurance, farm market layout, product handling and storage, product display, computers, advertising and promotion, business and record keeping, personnel management and salesmanship. $13. Penn State Univ., Dept. of Agricultural Economics and Rural Sociology, Armsby Bldg., University Park, PA 16802-5502; (814) 865-0469.

Market Gardening, by Ric Staines. Growing techniques, crop requirements and nutrition, machinery and equipment, pest and weed control, plus a chapter on marketing which contains an overview of selling through farmers markets, roadside stands, subscription services, pick-your-own, farm stores, restaurants, caterers, grocery stores and specialty shops. 192 pp. $14.95 plus $2 p/h. Fulcrum Publishing, 350 Indiana St., Ste. 350, Golden, CO 80401; (800) 992-2908 or (303) 277-1623.

Pay Dirt: How To Raise Herbs and Produce for Serious Ca$h. This book is written mainly for the beginning farmer or market gardener, or the layperson thinking of taking the leap into making a living from the land; yet even established growers can profit from the creative marketing ideas presented here. 214 pp. $12.95. Prima Publishing, P.O. Box 1260BK, Rocklin, CA 95677; (916) 786-0426.

Quality Control In Direct Produce Marketing, by W. Hurst, 1988. From the Univ. of Georgia. See "Cooperative Extension Services."

Secrets To A Successful Greenhouse Business, by T.M. Taylor. Nationwide plant buyers list, which plants sell best, when and how to grow them, selling to national chains and local markets, plans to build a solar greenhouse, nursery supply directory. See "New World Bookshelf," p. 300.

The Shiitake Mushroom Marketing Guide for Growers. Although written for growers selling shiitake mushrooms, many portions of this excellent guide are applicable to growers of other gourmet specialty produce items. Contains sections on market assessment, distribution, packaging, pricing, promotion, personal selling, a worksheet section to develop your own marketing program, and more. $30 plus $3.50 p/h. The Forest Resource Center, Rte. 2, Box 156A, Lanesboro, MN 55949; (507) 467-2437.

Specialty and Minor Crops Handbook is a loose-leaf binder handbook with information sheets on some three dozen specialty crops, most of which are suitable for a California climate. Covers seed sources, production methods, cultivation, postharvest care, specific weed and pest problems, and marketing options. Publication #3346, $30. From Small Farm Center. See "Associations."

Vegetable Production Handbook. Written especially for fresh market growers. Covers most popular vegetables. $4 postpaid. Publication #1241 from Univ. of Illinois. See "Cooperative Extension Services."

4. Pamphlets & Booklets

Considerations in Enterprise Selection and *How to Determine Your Cost of Production.* SN #ANRP-011. $2. From Small Farm Center. See "Associations."

Direct Farm To Consumer Marketing: A Profitable Alternative for Family Farm Operators, by G. H. Sullivan, V. Kulp, R. Treadway, P. Kirschling. Roadside farm markets, pick-your-own operations, and community farm markets. Trends, market planning, market layout, produce display, and management. 115 pp. #HO-160. $3. Purdue Univ. See "Cooperative Extension Services."

Farmer To Consumer Marketing. A 6-part series. Part 1: An Overview, #PNW0201; Part 2: Production and Marketing Costs, #PNW-0202; Part 3: Merchandising, Pricing, Promotion, #PNW0203; Part 4: Place of Business and Product Quality, #PNW0204; Part 5: Personnel Management, #PNW-0205; Part 6: Financial Management, #PNW-0206. Each part costs 25¢. Washington State Univ. See "Cooperative Extension Services."

A Guide To Successful Direct Marketing, by Charles R. Hall and Jeff L. Johnson. Includes overview of direct marketing alternatives; business plans for direct marketers; market research; farmers market, pick-your-own and roadside stand basics; merchandising, advertising and promotion tactics; pricing strategies and more. 32 pp. $12. Checks payable to Texas Agricultural Extension Service Account 20696. Texas Agricultural Extension Service, Dept. of Agricultural Economics, College Station, TX 77843-2124. Attn: Dr. Charles R. Hall.

Marketing. Direct Marketing and Quality Control, Marketing Cooperatives and Setting Up a Roadside Stand. #ANRP010. $3. Small Farm Center. See "Associations."

Marketing Fruits and Vegetables, by Schmidt and Acock. 11 pp. A Mississippi State Publication, #570. See "Cooperative Extension Services."

Marketing, Promoting and Advertising Nursery Products. Free. Contact: Lydia Wiggins-Azimi, Cooperative Agricultural Research Program (CARP), Tennessee State Univ., Box 522, John Meritt Blvd., Nashville, TN 37209-1561.

Opening Your Doors: A Guide to Opening and Operating a Bed and Breakfast, by Steven Brown. 28 pp. $3. From KSU Foundation. See "Books & Publications Suppliers."

Running An Herb Business or Any Other Business, by Louise Downey-Butler. Louise Downey-

Butler, 3 River St., Bethel, VT 05032; (802) 234-9928.

The Small Business Directory: Publications and Videotapes for Starting and Managing a Successful Small Business. A free pamphlet which lists a variety of low-cost publications on financial management, management and planning, personnel management. For orders add $1 p/h. Make checks payable to U.S. Small Business Publications. SBA Publications, P.O. Box 30, Denver, CO 80201-0030.

Understanding Produce Marketing, by W. O. Mizelle. B-859. 15 pp. Univ. of Georgia. See "Cooperative Extension Services."

5. Directories & Resource Books

Common Harvest: An Alternative Food and Agriculture Resource Directory. Provides personal models to encourage gardening, food preservation, dietary changes, community supported agriculture, community gardening, and better municipal food policies. 150 pp. $9 plus $1.50 p/h. Food Action Network, Inc., 5324 Park Ave., Minneapolis, MN 55417-1720; (612) 822-7607.

The Directory of American Agriculture. Reference source for agricultural organizations and leaders including state and national organizations, departments of agriculture, USDA state offices, state extension offices, colleges of agriculture, state youth organizations, major agricultural broadcasters and publications, state fairs, and more. Over 5,500 listings. $49.95 (includes p/h) from Directory of American Agriculture, ARC, Inc., P.O. Box 67212, Topeka, KS 66667-0212; (913) 456-9705.

Directory for Small-Scale Agriculture. Lists nearly 500 key state and federal government experts who can answer questions about small-scale, diversified agriculture. SN #001-000-04539-3. $5.50. Superintendent of Documents. See "Books & Publications Suppliers."

Gardener's Source Guide. 13-page directory of 510 nursery and seed mail order companies who send free catalogs. $5 from Gardener's Source Guide, P.O. Box 206-NW, Gowanda, NY 14070.

Gardening By Mail, by Barbara Barton. Mail order source for gardeners including seed companies and nurseries, garden supply and service companies, plant and horticultural societies, trade associations, gardening and horticultural libraries, books, magazines and newsletters. See "New World Bookshelf," p. 300.

Herbal Resource Guide. A networking resource with more than 3,000 listings. 176 pp. Maureen Rogers, HGMN P.O. Box 245, Silver Spring, PA 17575-0245; (717) 898-3017.

Marketing Services Guide. A resource book with over 1,300 listings of agricultural companies, consultants, agencies, associations, radio shows and publications, and more. $30 postpaid from Century Communications, 6201 Howard St., Niles IL 60714; (708) 647-1200.

Sustainable Agriculture for California: A Guide to Information, by D. Bainbridge and S. Mitchell. Listings and information on agricultural libraries, organizations, books, journals, electronic databases throughout the U.S. on a wide variety of subjects. 198 pp. $12. ANR Publications. SN #3349. See "Books & Publications Suppliers."

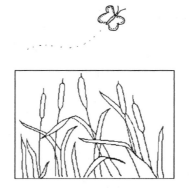

6. Periodicals & Newsletters

American Fruit Grower and *American Vegetable Grower.* Production, marketing, research and all aspects of commercial fruit (or vegetable) growing. $14/year. Meister Publishing Co., Fruit Grower Magazine Circulation, 37733 Euclid Ave., Willoughby, OH 44094; (216) 942-2000.

American Small Farm covers small farm topics. 10 issues/year. $15/year. Features, columns, calendar listings and more. American Small Farm Magazine, P.O. Box 5075, Chatsworth, CA 91313-5075.

The Business of Herbs. Features interviews, marketing hints, industry news, new products, plant profiles, business tips, sources and resources for herb growers. "Books From Northwind Farm" is their book list about herbs—crafting, medicinals, growing, marketing and more. Send self-addressed, stamped envelope for information and book list. $20/year/USA, $23/Canada. Sample issue $3. Northwind Farm Publications, Rte. 2, Box 246, Shevlin, MN 56676; (218) 657-2478.

The Farming Alternatives Newsletter. Quarterly publication of the Farming Alternatives Program at Cornell Univ. The newsletter covers events, programs, research and resources related to farm diversification, sustainable agriculture and marketing. The newsletter is free; donations are welcome. Make checks payable to Cornell University. The Farming Alternatives Program, Warren Hall, Cornell Univ., Ithaca, NY 14853; (607) 255-9832.

The Flora-Line. Quarterly newsletter on growing, drying and marketing flowering herbs. $16.95/year. Berry Hill Press, 7336-B Berry Hill, Palos Verdes, CA 90274.

Greenhouse Grower Magazine, 37733 Euclid Ave., Willoughby, OH 44094; (216) 942-2000.

Growing for Market. 12-page monthly newsletter. Broad coverage of production and marketing topics for the market gardener and small niche-market farmer. $24/year. Single copies $2. Fairplain Publications, P.O. Box 365, Auburn, KS 66402.

The High Value Crop Newsletter. Discusses climate requirements, cultural care, and marketing issues for a variety of crops. Sample copy $6. $60/year. Claude Sweet, Sweet Enterprises, 7488 Comet View Ct., San Diego, CA 92120-2004; (619) 286-9255.

HortIdeas. Reports on research, methods, tools, plants, books, etc., for vegetable, fruit and flower gardeners. $17.50 per year. Contact Greg and Pat Williams, 460 Black Lick Rd., Gravel Switch, KY 40328.

Marketing for Success is Robert "Matty" Matarazzo's monthly marketing newsletter. This publication serves as a reminder of ongoing marketing and promotional activities, and offers innovative, cost-efficient, and profitable ideas to generate new business for the present month. Topics include developing free media coverage, utilizing the slow season for planning purposes, entertainment agriculture, and more. $30/year. Sample copy $5. RJM Marketing, RR03, Box 258, Rte. 519, Belvidere, NJ 07823; (908) 475-3872; FAX (908) 475-3555.

New World Update, from New World Publishing, acts as an update for the book you are now reading, with news about small-farm marketing and small business. See p. 299.

On The Cutting Edge. Bimonthly newsletter with articles and recipes, from Frieda's, Inc., the nation's premier marketer and distributor of exotic fruits and vegetables. Focuses on the latest food and produce industry trends. $11.95/year. Frieda's, Inc., P.O. Box 58488, Los Angeles, CA 90058.

Rural Enterprise. A magazine devoted exclusively to the subject of farm direct marketing. Direct marketing ideas, resource contacts, news and information, marketers' network and advertising, business tips, feature stories and more. This magazine was recently discontinued but back issues are still available at $3/copy. Send a self-addressed, stamped envelope with a request for a back issue order form to Rural Enterprise, P.O. Box 878, Menomonee Falls, WI 53052-0878; (414) 255-0100.

Rural Heritage. Quarterly how-to magazine dedicated to preserving the traditional rural lifestyle and its use of draft-horse power. $14/year. Sample copy $5. Contact: Gail Damerow, Rural Heritage, 281-C Dean Ridge Ln., Gainesboro, TN 38562-9685; (615) 268-0655.

Rural New England Magazine. How-to and lifestyle magazine for rural New Englanders. Monthly. $12/year. Rural New England Magazine, P.O. Box 504, Sherman, CT 06784; (203) 350-0555.

Small Farmer's Journal, featuring practical horse farming, "the champion of the small family farm." Superb artwork plus lively fiction. Quarterly. $19/year. Sample issue $6. SFJ, P.O. Box 2805, Eugene, OR 97402.

Specialty Crop Digest. Biannual publication from the publisher of *Backyard Cash Crops.* Money-making ideas for market growers on high value crops, containing production and marketing tips. 2-year subscription $10. Sample copy $1. *Special Reports* are designed along specific topics. $9 each or three for $21. Sample titles: *Making Money With Oyster Mushrooms, Ornamental Grass Nursery, Profitable Culinary Herbs, Profits in Antique Roses, Bamboo Bounty,* etc. Write for complete list. Homestead Design, Inc., P.O. Box 1058, Bellingham, WA 98227; (206) 676-5647.

University of Wisconsin Cooperative Extension Direct Marketing Newsletter. 4-page bimonthly newsletter on a wide variety of direct marketing topics. The January 1992 issue contains a directory of topics covered from Sept. 1987 to Nov. 1991. Contact: John Cottingham, Agricultural Marketing Specialist, Cooperative Extension Programs, Univ. of Wisconsin-Platteville, 1 University Plaza, Platteville, WI 53818-3099; (608) 342-1392.

7. Associations

American Horticultural Society, 7931 E. Boulevard Dr., Alexandria, VA 22308-1300; (703) 768-5700. Nonprofit organization of gardeners. $45/year membership. Monthly magazine, seed exchange, toll-free gardeners' information service, and book discounts.

Association of Specialty Cut Flower Growers (ASCFG), 155 Elm St., Oberlin, OH 44074. Information center for the fresh and dried flower industries. Newsletter, conferences, membership directory.

ATTRA (Appropriate Technology Transfer for Rural Areas), P.O. Box 3657, Fayetteville, AR 72702; (800) 346-9140 or (501) 442-9824. U.S. Fish and Wildlife Service program which gives free information on low-input agricultural practices to agriculture professionals. Call ATTRA for answers on a wide variety of sustainable ag production, conservation, and marketing topics.

California Association of Family Farmers (CAFF), P.O. Box 363, Davis, CA 95617; (916) 756-7420. Small farm advocacy, education, member networking, insurance, bimonthly newsletter.

California Rare Fruit Growers, Inc., The Fullerton Arboretum, California State Univ., Fullerton, CA 92634. Excellent source for information on production of rare or leading-edge fruit varieties. Publishes *The Fruit Gardener,* a bimonthly magazine.

The Herb Growing & Marketing Network, P.O. Box 245, Silver Spring, PA 17575-0245; (717) 898-3017. Publishes a 36-page trade journal, *The Herbal Connection,* as well as an annual resource guide, *The Herbal Resource Guide*.

International Herb Growers and Marketers Association (IHGMA), 1202 Allanson Rd., Mundelein, IL 60060; (708) 566-4566. Quarterly newsletter containing trade news, marketing and growing hints, technical information and more. Special seminars, annual conference and trade show. Excellent information source for products, suppliers, etc.

Missouri Alternatives Center, (800) 433-3704. Places potential producers in touch with advice sources on a wide range of agricultural marketing and production topics.

National Farmers Direct Marketing Association (NFDMA), c/o Ed Stritzkes, 14850 Countryside Dr., Aurora, OR 97002; (503) 678-2455. National organization of direct marketers. Publishes newsletter, acts as resource for farm direct marketing ideas and resources, and hosts the annual National Farmers Direct Marketing Conference.

National Retail Federation, Inc., 100 W. 31st St., New York, NY 10001-3401; (212) 244-8780. Offers many services for the retailer. Contact the Publications Order Department for their *Catalogue of Books and Films*, which offers books and videos on finance and accounting, merchandising, personnel, and advertising and sales promotion topics.

North American Strawberry Growers Association, c/o Dr. J.W. Courter, P.O. Box 160, W. Paducah, KY 42086-0160; (502) 488-2116. Newsletter, conferences, marketing program aids and materials. Contact for current membership dues.

Office for Small-Scale Agriculture, H.W. Kerr, Jr., USDA/CSRS, OSSA, Ste. 328-A, Aerospace Center, Washington, DC 20250-2200; (202) 401-1805; FAX (202) 401-1804. Provides information to small-scale and specialty agricultural producers. Services include an excellent free newsletter and the

Directory For Small-Scale Agriculture (see "Directories & Resource Books") which lists numerous sources and resources for the grower and marketer.

Professional Plant Growers Association (PPGA), P.O. Box 27517, Lansing, MI 48909-0517; (517) 694-7700; FAX (517) 694-8560. Newsletter, conferences, seminars, books and marketing aids. Mostly for greenhouse crops but general interest as well.

Seed Savers Exchange, c/o Kent Whealy, 203 Rural Ave., Decorah, IA 52101. Gardeners dedicated to finding and spreading heirloom vegetable varieties before they are lost.

Small Farm Center, Univ. of California, Davis, CA 95616; (916) 757-8910. Offers a wide variety of services for the small farmer including workshops and conferences and a free bimonthly newsletter, *Small Farm News*. The Center maintains a library with an extensive selection of books, magazines, reports and videos on production, specialty crops and direct marketing for small farmers. When ordering pamphlets or books, make checks payable to UC Regents.

Teleflora, 12233 W. Olympic Blvd., Los Angeles, CA 90064. Membership directory of florists, monthly magazine *Flowers And*.

United Fresh Fruit and Vegetable Association, 727 N. Washington St., Alexandria, VA 22314; (703) 836-3410 or (800) 336-3065; FAX (703) 836-7745. Services include generic promotion of fresh fruits and vegetables, trade shows and conventions, market development, and The United Information Center, a source of information for the produce industry. Call or write for information.

Wholesale Nursery Growers of America, 1250 "I" St. NW, Ste. 500, Washington, DC 20005; (202) 789-2900. Grower division of the American Association of Nurserymen, a national trade organization whose mission is to educate, promote and

foster a favorable business climate for the nursery industry. Call or write for membership information and publications catalog.

8. Conferences

Next to visiting similar operations in person, the next-best way to research a new enterprise is to go to a conference. Not only do you learn a lot from the workshops, you will meet dozens of other growers involved in alternative enterprises. It is frequently expressed at marketing conferences that if you go home with one new idea it will pay for the cost of the conference.

Conferences are like an enormous smorgasbord of production and marketing ideas for alternative enterprises. Farm Conference '91 in San Diego, for example, offered 52 workshops such as: "Opportunities In Gourmet Produce," "Profitability and Demand for Culinary Herbs," "Merchandising for Higher Sales," "Selling to Restaurants," "Successful Roadside Stands," "Effective Expansion of Your Markets Through Direct Mail," "Marketing and Certification of Organic Produce," "The Use of Beneficial Insects for Pest Management," "Sources of Seeds," and so on.

You don't learn much by keeping secrets; you'll learn a lot more by sharing your own trade secrets and getting feedback. When you go to a conference, get the names and numbers of presenters, speakers and people you meet. That way, you can call them back later for more in-depth details of things you discussed with them or heard them present.

The "biggie" is the annual National Direct Marketing Conference sponsored by the National Farmers Direct Marketing Association. But there are many others, including the Ohio Roadside Marketing Conference, the Mid-Atlantic Direct Marketing Conference, Herbs '93 (and Herbs '94, etc.), the Ecological Farming Conference, the Illinois Fruit and Vegetable Growers Convention, and so on. The locations for these conferences change each year, so keep posted about upcoming conferences by reading the "Calendar" or "Meetings" sections of farm trade magazines such as *American Vegetable Grower* and *American Fruit Grower*.

If you can't attend a conference in person, remember that many conference proceedings are available in the form of books or audio cassette tapes. Call or write the conference organizers to ask about availability; inquire also about proceedings or tapes available from past conferences.

9. Audio & Video Tapes

Audio Productions, 8806 S. Lake Stevens Rd., Everett, WA 98205; (800) 488-5455; FAX (206) 334-7866. Ecological Farming Conference, 1993 National Farmers Direct Marketing Conference.

Follick Recording Service, 1402 S. Madison, Normal, IL 61761; (309) 452-9073. 1992 National Farmers Direct Marketing Conference; North American Strawberry Growers Association annual conferences.

High Value Marketing. Farmers demonstrate ways in which they have increased the value of what they sell. Strategies include direct and cooperative marketing, processing and organic certification. Part of a Farmer-to-Farmer video series. Produced by Rooy Media and Rodale Institute. Rooy Media, 7407 Hilltop Dr., Frederick, MD 21702; (301) 473-8695.

10. Databanks, computer networks and information services

Electronic databases allow you to do searches for articles or books in minutes that would take days by hand. They are most useful for recent journal articles. Many uni-versity libraries and private libraries subscribe to services that provide on-line access via telephone to these databases. They may be able to provide search assistance by appointment for a modest fee. If you can't afford an on-line search, and your database of choice isn't available in CD-ROM format (see below), it will often be available in printed form which you can search manually.

These databases can also be accessed on-line by most home computers with a telephone modem through vendors. Off-peak rates are often much cheaper than daytime charges.The vendors also provide training materials and special services. Note that many of the important agricultural and databases which you may want to search are now being produced in compact disk format (CD-ROM). This allows libraries to operate the databases on microcomputers within the library (as opposed to accessing them "on-line" via telephone). Usually you can search these for free.

agAccess Information Service. This agricultural bookstore in Davis, California, also offers a computer information service which utilizes their worldwide network of information sources. They offer research help in market research, new crop production techniques, specific technical queries, project development and more. agAccess, P.O. Box 2008, Davis, CA 95617; (916) 756-7177.

Agricultural OnLine Access (AGRICOLA). Database for the USDA's National Agricultural Library, is tied to a worldwide network of agriculture data collections. Electronic bibliographic index to more than 2 million books and articles relating to all aspects of agriculture. Emphasis on federal and state material as well as journal articles. Accessible through two nationwide information retrieval systems, DIALOG and BRS; (301) 504-5479.

AGRICOLearn, a stand-alone, computer-based video training course, is available for individual instruction on searching the AGRICOLA database. AGRICOLA Training, Reference and User Services Branch, National Agricultural Library, Rm. 111, 10301 Baltimore Blvd., Beltsville, MD 20705; (301) 504-5204.

Agricultural Library Forum. National Agricultural Library's forum for the exchange of agricultural information via computer bulletin board. The system provides a convenient tool for electronically accessing information about NAL products and services, and for exchanging agricultural information and resources; (301) 504-6510, 504-5111, 504-5496, 504-5497. Systems Operator, (301) 504-5113. For a free copy of the Guide to Using ALF write: NAL, Public Services Division, Rm. 111, 10301 Baltimore Blvd., Beltsville, MD 20705-2351.

FARM Net USA is a computer on-line information service for agriculture. 937 Via Ondulando, Ventura, CA 93003; (805) 644-5460.

Prodigy Information Service. This computer network has a Commercial Vegetable Farm topic on its Homelife Bulletin Board in which growers nationwide share ideas. Requires Prodigy on-line service and dedicated software. $14.95/month subscription fee. Contact Prodigy Information Service, 445 Hamilton Ave., White Plains NY 10601; (800) 776-3449.

World Sustainable Agriculture Network. A computer network of interest to growers and supporters of small-scale agriculture. It is run by EcoNet, a network of people and organizations interested in environmental preservation. $15 one-time sign-up charge, plus $10/month fee. Contact EcoNet, 18 DeBoom St., San Francisco, CA 94107; (415) 442-0220.

11. State Programs

Contact your state department of agriculture to find out what state resources are available to you for help with production and marketing. Aggressive state programs have sprung up nationwide to promote locally grown and processed products through direct marketing, diversify farm income into high-value specialty crops, and develop locally owned food-processing industries.

12. U.S. Government Resources

Agricultural Information Center, USDA Office of Public Affairs, 14th and Independence Avenues, SW, Rm. 102A, Washington, DC 20250; (202) 720-2791. Provides information and referrals on USDA programs, and sells currently available USDA publications.

Agricultural Trade and Marketing Information Center, National Agricultural Library, 10301 Baltimore Blvd., Beltsville, MD 20705-2351; (301) 504-5509.

Federal-State Market News Service. USDA and Cooperating State Agencies. Federal-State Market News is a compilation of market prices, supply, demand, quality, etc., on fruits, vegetables, ornamentals and specialty crops collected from major terminals and other handlers. Subscriptions are available for daily, weekly and monthly issues. Telephone recordings with 24-hour market news information are also available from many shipping point and terminal market news offices. For information or to subscribe, contact: USDA, AMS, Fruit and Vegetable Market News, P.O. Box 96456, Rm. 2503-South Bldg., Washington, DC 20090-6456; (202) 720-2745. Call your county extension office for local state listings.

Food and Nutrition Information Center, USDA, National Agricultural Library, Rm. 304, 10301 Baltimore Blvd., Beltsville, MD 20705; (301) 504-5719. Provides information and educational materials in the area of food and human nutrition. Books, journal articles and audio visual materials pertaining to human nutrition, food service management, and food science.

How to Get Information From the United States Department of Agriculture. Free publication from USDA-OPA/OPVC, Rm. 507-A, Washington, DC 20250-1300.

List of Available Publications of the United States Department of Agriculture. Available free from USDA-OPA/OPVC, Rm. 507-A, Washington, DC 20250-1300.

National Agricultural Library, USDA, Reference Section, Rm. 111, 10301 Baltimore Blvd., Beltsville, Maryland 20705-2351; (301) 504-5755. A telephone research service is also available: call the reference desk (301) 504-5479. This institution houses the world's largest collection of information on farming and gardening; everything from farm financing, appropriate technology, systems of marketing and more. Assistance in accessing NAL's extensive collections, referrals to related organizations or experts, and access to bibliographies on agricultural topics.

Guide To Services from the National Agricultural Library. Free publication from NAL, Rm. 204, 10301 Baltimore Blvd., Beltsville, MD 20705-2351.

The NAL provides *Quick Bibliographies* on a variety of agricultural topics. They can be obtained by sending a self-addressed mailing label for each QB requested. Some useful titles include: *Farmer To Consumer Marketing* (QB 86-71) and *Marketing of Horticultural Products* (QB 92-01).

USDA Agricultural Marketing Service, Office of the Administrator, P.O. Box 96456, Rm. 3071 South Bldg., Washington, DC 20090-6456; (202) 720-5115. Compiles weekly and annual lists of what price commodities sold for at various nationwide terminal markets.

The lists include conventional commodities, as well as herbs, oriental vegetables and many other kinds of specialty produce, with up-to-date reports on prices and shipment sizes.

USDA Information Center, Rm. 103A Administration Bldg., 14th and Independence Avenues, SW, Washington, DC 20250; (202) 720-2745. Provides information on the USDA and its programs and gives telephone numbers of department offices and personnel. Current USDA publications are available on a walk-in basis only.

13. Consultants

Agriland Concepts, Inc., P.O. Box 935, 6 Wilcox St., Simsbury, CT 06070; (203) 676-2686. Agricultural business planning and management.

Patty Belmonte, 504 75th Way, NE, Olympia, WA 98506; (206) 943-1998. Marketing, advertising and promotion.

Ransom Blakeley, P.O. Box 449, Dryden, NY 13053; (607) 844-4714. Direct marketing, including on-farm markets, pick-your-own operations and farmers markets. Consults on topics including determination of sales potential, site selection, market layout, personnel training, advertising planning, and evaluation of market operations.

Vance Corum, 441 Merritt Ave., Oakland, CA 94610; (510) 465-8714. Farmers markets, public markets, farm direct marketing, special events, conference planning and market research.

Carol Klesow, 115 W. 8th St., Santa Rosa, CA 95401; (707) 528-3203. Direct marketing, special gardens, foods and events.

Robert (Matty) Matarazzo, RR03 Box 258, Belvidere, NJ 07823; Phone (908) 475-3872; FAX (908) 475-3555. Farmers markets, direct marketing, special events (entertainment agriculture), marketing plan development and promotion, advertising programs.

Curt Stutzman, 4943 Cosgrove Rd., SW, Kalona, IA 52247; (319) 683-2495. Farm diversification and planning.

14. Direct Marketing Supplies

Barrels, baskets, crates, buckets

The Bradbury Barrel Co., P.O. Box A, 100 Main St., Bridgewater, ME 04735; (207) 429-8141 or (800) 332-6021.

Texas Basket Co., 100 Myrtle Dr., P.O. Box 1110, Jacksonville, TX 75766; (903) 586-8014 or (800) 657-2200; FAX (903) 586-0988.

Cider & juice making equipment

Day Equipment Corp., 1402 E. Monroe, Goshen, IN 46526; (219) 534-3491.

Frontier Technology, Inc., 609 N. Eastern Ave., Allegan, MI 49010; (616) 673-9464.

GoodNature Products, Inc., P.O. Box 866, Buffalo, NY 14240; (716) 855-3325. Non-citrus fruit and vegetable juicer.

Happy Valley Ranch, 16577 W. 327 St., Paola, KS 66071; (913) 849-3103.

Orchard Equipment & Supply Co., P.O. Box 540, Conway, MA 01341; (800) 634-5557.

Roadside banners

Bannerscapes, 726 Raddick Ave., Santa Barbara, CA 93103; (800) 676-1283.

Litho Screen, P.O. Box 715, Sheboygan, WI 53082; (800) 262-1677.

Miscellaneous direct marketing supplies

Design Decorators, Inc., 3076 Jasper St., Philadelphia, PA 19134; (215) 634-8300 or (800) 331-5644. Farm market theme balloons such as Big Apple, Sally Strawberry, Jack O'Lantern Pumpkin, etc.

High Sign Inc., 1486 CTH DB, Mosinee, WI 54455; (715) 693-6201. Farm market balloons.

JAMarketing, 942 Virginia Ln., Elmhurst, IL 60126; (708) 279-5806. Fruit and vegetable marketing materials. Road signs, color postcards, letterheads, buttons, flyers, signs, banners, giant balloons, tee shirts, clip art, and more.

Pumpkin Ltd., P.O. Box 61456, Denver, CO 80206; (303) 722-4442. Pumpkin carving kit.

Scales

Orchard Equipment & Supply Co., P.O. Box 540, Conway, MA 01341; (800) 634-5557.

15. Miscellaneous Resources

Florapersonnel specializes in jobs in the growing industry—greenhouses, nurseries, arboretums, parks and other horticulture-related areas. For more information: Florapersonnel, 1450 S. Woodland Blvd., #201, DeLand, FL 32721-1732.

16. Packaging Supplies

A-Roo Co., 963 Schriewer Rd., Seguin, TX 78155; (800) 446-2766. Floral packaging including sleeves and bags.

Action Bag Co., 501 N. Edgewood Ave., Wood Dale, IL 60191; (800) 824-BAGS. Polybags, cotton drawstring bags, ziplock shipping supplies.

Adelman-Fisher Packaging, 207 Walnut St., Kansas City, MO 64106; (816) 842-4961. Produce boxes, plastic bags, bushel baskets, display baskets, etc.

Agri-Pack/ Division of Liberty Carton Co., 870 Louisiana Ave., South, Minneapolis, MN 55426; (800) 328-1784. Berry and farm market suppliers, fruit and vegetable containers, fruit and jam gift containers.

Essentials 'N Such, 3999 N. Chestnut Ave., Ste. 368, Fresno, CA 93726. Bottles, jars, vials, caps, tea bags, etc.

Fresh-PAK, P.O. Box 256, Stevensville, MI 49127; (616) 429-3295. Produce packaging.

Independence Box Co., 935 N. Main St., Independence, OR 97351; (503) 838-3763.

Inland Container, Park Fletcher Station, Box 41264, Indianapolis, IN 46241; (317) 248-8086. Produce boxes.

Ivex Floral & Nursery Products, 221 E. Greenwood, Grant Park, IL 60940; (815) 465-2092. Cut flower sleeves, flower boxes.

The Nu-Era Group, Inc., 727 N. 11th St., St. Louis, MO 63101; (800) 325-7033 or (314) 231-3662. Padded shipping bags, floral, gift and jewelry boxes.

Package Containers, Inc., 777 NE 4th Ave., Canby, OR 97013; (503) 266-2721. Contact person: Greg Leo. Tote bags, herb ties and twist ties.

Packaging Corp. of America, 1603 Orrington, Evanston, IL 60204; (708) 492-5713.

Pacific Isles Trading Ltd., 450 7th Ave., Rm. 3105, New York, NY 10123; (212) 465-8027. EarthSaver ecological alternatives to throwaway bags.

Pacific States Box and Basket Co., 1295 S. Los Angeles St., Glendale, CA 91209; (818) 244-8688. Berry baskets.

Polybags Plus, P.O. Box 3043, Port Charlotte, FL 3949. Ziplock, muslin, cellophane.

Rockford Package Supply, 10421 Northland Dr., Rockford, MI 49341; (800) 444-7225.

Sunburst Bottle Co., 7001 Sunburst, Citrus Heights, CA 95621. Vinegar bottles, glass vials, canning jars, lip balm jars, corks, push-on capsules, potpourri boxes, etc.

17. Wholesale Marketing Resources

The Blue Book. Credit rating information of growers/shippers, brokers, and receivers of produce including wholesalers, chain stores and cooperatives. Transportation section with truckers, trucker brokers and other produce haulers and Supply/Commodity Index. Service includes spring and fall *Blue Book*, weekly credit updates, confidential reports, problem assistance and access to collection assistance. $400/year. Produce Reporter Co., 315 W. Wesley St., Wheaton, IL 60187; (708) 668-3500.

Consumers' Guide To Farm Marketing Contracts. Audio tape from Marketplace '92; (#47). $6 postpaid. Studio A, 105 Broadway Ave., Bismarck, ND 58501; (701) 223-8980.

Developing A Marketing Plan For Fresh Produce, by C. Moulton and L. Burt. SN #PNW241. From Washington State Univ. Cooperative Extension. See "Cooperative Extension Services."

Floral Marketing Directory and Buyers' Guide. Listings of produce managers, addresses and phone numbers. $35. Floral Marketing Division, Produce Marketing Association, 700 Barksdale Plaza, Newark, DE 19711; (302) 738-7100.

Handling, Transportation, and Storage of Fruits and Vegetables. AVI Publications, Westport, CT.

Marketing Fresh Fruits and Vegetables, by R. Brian How. Comprehensive overview of the fresh fruit and vegetable wholesale marketing system, including market information sources and communication networks, market prices and price analysis, trade practices and credit ratings, cooperative marketing, marketing orders, pesticide use and food safety, nutritional marketing, international trade and shipping point operations, transportation, wholesaling at destination and terminal market facilities, food retailers and retailing, the food service industry, and direct marketing. $46.95 postpaid (add state sales tax). Make checks to "Van Nostrand Reinhold." Send to Van Nostrand Reinhold, Attn: Order Processing, 7625 Empire Dr., Florence, KY 41042-0668; (800) 926-2665.

National Florists Directory. Lists over 40,000 retail florists. $90. Contact National Florists Directory, P.O. Box 258, Paragould, AR 72450; (800) 643-0100.

National Directory of Organic Wholesalers. State-by-state listings of organic growers, wholesalers, distributors, support businesses and suppliers, and organizations dealing with organic and sustainable agriculture. $34.95 plus $5 p/h. California Action Network, P.O. Box 464, Davis, CA 95617; (800) 852-3832 or (916) 756-8518.

The Packer. Weekly newspaper of the fruit and vegetable industry. It lists current prices of produce, buying trends expected, and has related articles and advertisements. $49/year/USA, $80/Foreign. Subscription includes *Produce Packaging Digest*—packaging equipment and techniques for fresh produce; *Fresh Trends: A Profile of Fresh Produce Consumers*; and *The Produce Availability & Merchandising Guide*, which shows buyers by commodity. It contains listings of distributors and wholesalers, suppliers, merchandising sources, shipping container information, ripening, temperature and display charts, commodity information on availability, varieties, care, merchandising and

nutrition, and more. (It is available for $20 if ordered separate from subscription.) Contact Vance Publishing, 7950 College Blvd., P.O. Box 2939, Shawnee Mission, KS 66201; (913) 451-2200 or (800) 255-5113.

Produce Marketing Association, P.O. Box 6036, Newark, DE 19714-6036; (302) 738-7100. Training, marketing, information and networking resources for retailers, wholesalers, restaurant/institutional operators, food service distributors and their suppliers. Assortment of books, guides, posters and charts on identifying, transporting, storing and handling bulk produce. Regional conferences and an annual convention, annual International Trade Seminar & Floral Marketing Seminar. Can provide fruit & vegetable market bibliographies to nonmembers.

Protecting Perishable Foods During Transport by Motortruck. SN #001-000-04535-1. $3. Superintendent of Documents. See "Books & Publications Suppliers."

The Red Book. Contains descriptive information, trading performance and credit ratings on firms such as chain stores, wholesalers, brokers and trucking companies in the fresh produce industry. The semiannual book includes a weekly update bulletin. Used by growers and shippers selling to accounts throughout the U.S. and Canada. $400/year. The Red Book, P.O. Box 2939, Shawnee Mission, KS 66201; (800) 252-1925.

Regulations Governing Contracts Between Growers and Handlers of Agricultural Produce: A Primer for Small-Scale Producers. 8 pp. SN #21425. $1.50. From ANR Publications. See "Books & Publications Suppliers."

Should I Grow Fruits and Vegetables? Non-Direct Marketing for Fruits and Vegetables. R. M. Lloyd, J. R. Nelson and S. Westphalen. F-182. 5 pp. Oklahoma State Univ. See "Cooperative Extension Services."

18. Cooperative Resources

U.C. Center for Cooperatives, Univ. of California, Davis, CA 95616; (916) 752-2408.

USDA Agricultural Cooperative Service (ACS). Provides research, management and educational assistance to growers interested in starting a cooperative. Sample by-laws, incorporation, membership forms, etc.; possible in-person follow-up visits to help in organizational development. Requests for assistance should be directed to Dr. Randall Torgerson, Office of the Administrator, USDA-ACS, P.O. Box 96576, Washington, DC 20090-6576. ACS publishes many publications on nearly all phases of cooperative topics including starting, managing and running a cooperative. They are listed in *Farmer Cooperative Publications,* CIR 4, 56 pp. Free.

State councils for agricultural cooperatives operate in 33 states. Activities include providing publications, information, and legislative and technical assistance to cooperatives. Contact your state department of agriculture.

Also visit other cooperatives in your state to learn from their experience.

19. Organic Resources

Acres. Send for subscription rates and book catalog. Ecological agriculture monthly newspaper. Emphasis is on production of quality food without the use of toxic chemicals. Acres, P.O. Box 9547, Kansas City, MO 64133; (816) 737-0064.

Alive and Well. 35-minute video. $40. Five key steps to sustainable soil fertility. Available from Visual Media, Univ. of California, Davis, CA 95616; (916) 757-8980.

Alternative Farming Systems Information Center, USDA, National Agricultural Library, AFSIC, Rm. 304, 10301 Baltimore Blvd., Beltsville, MD 20705-2531; (301) 504-6559. Information and data on alternative farming practices, including organic, low-input and sustainable agriculture. Send for free brochure listing services available.

ATTRA (Appropriate Technology Transfer for Rural Areas). P.O. Box 3657, Fayetteville, AR 72702; (800) 346-9140. Their packets on both IPM and organic certification are excellent.

Consumer's Organic Mail-Order Directory. Lists farmers and distributors who sell organically grown produce direct to the public via mail order. $9.95 plus $2.50 p/h. California Action Network, P.O. Box 464, Davis, CA 95617; (916) 756-8518 or (800) 852-3832.

A Grocer's Guide To Selling Organic Produce, $20. Greenleaf Produce, 1980 Jerrold Ave., San Francisco, CA 94124; (415) 647-2991.

Healthy Harvest: A Directory of Sustainable Agriculture & Horticulture Organizations, edited by Sanzone and Pearson. This book contains 1,400-plus entries of groups working in all sectors of sustainable agriculture: organic growers' groups, schools, publishers, distributors, communities, seed exchanges, political groups, reforestation projects, and more. Includes a geographic index, a subject index and full descriptions, as well as contact persons and phone numbers. 110 pp. $19.95. Available from agAccess. See "Books & Publications Suppliers."

Healthy Harvest News. A bimonthly newsletter published by the Healthy Harvest Society. Newsletter on organic agriculture and healthy food. 16 pp. Write to: The Healthy Harvest Society, 1424 16th St., NW, Ste. 105, Washington, DC 20036.

Increasing Organic Agriculture at the Local Level: A Manual for Consumers, Grocers, Farmers, & Policy Makers, by Hansen, Maren, et al. A group of citizens determined to increase the amount and selection of organic produce available in their area created this manual to show how they accomplished their goal. They discuss obstacles and the steps they took to overcome them. The emphasis is on consumer education and marketing. 98 pp. $16. Available from agAccess. See "Books & Publications Suppliers."

Natural Food & Farming. Bimonthly magazine, $20/year (includes membership in NFA). Natural Food Associates (NFA), Box 210, Atlanta, TX 75551; (903) 796-3612.

The New Farm. Farmer-based publication "dedicated to putting people, profit and biological permanence back into farming." $15/year. The New Farm, 222 Main St., Emmaus, PA 18098.

Organic Farmer: The Digest of Sustainable Agriculture is a quarterly journal on organic and sustainable farm and food practices and policies. $15/year. Organic Farmer, 15 Barre St., Montpelier, VT 05602.

Organic Farming Directory. 24-page directory of organic organizations, farm suppliers, consultants, periodicals, classes and apprenticeships. #21479. $3.50. From Small Farm Center. See "Associations."

Organic Food Production Association of North America (OFPANA), P.O. Box 31, Belchertown, MA 01007. The trade organization for the organic industry in North America.

Organic Market News and Information Service (OMNIS). A detailed listing of prices for organically grown fruits, vegetables and herbs. $45 for 25 issues. Sample issue for $2. Send payment (checks only) to OMNIS, P.O. Box 1300, Colfax, CA 95713.

Successful Small-Scale Farming: An Organic Approach, by Karl Schwenke. How-to guide for organic farming. See "New World Bookshelf," p. 301.

Sustainable Agriculture. 30-minute video. Strategies of sustainable agriculture, with sections on soil fertility, pest management, and biological diversity. Available from San Luis Video Publishing, P.O. Box 4604, San Luis Obispo, CA 93403; (805) 545-5426.

Sustainable Agriculture Resources. Lists books, videos, periodicals, internships, and apprenticeships. Available free from the Wisconsin Dept. of Agriculture, Trade and Consumer Protection, Sustainable Agriculture Program, P.O. Box 8911, Madison, WI 53708-8911; (608) 273-6408.

Teaching Children About Organics. Video to help schools use a fun and exciting method for teaching science and get the sustainable agriculture message across. Life Lab Science Program, 1156 High St., Santa Cruz, CA 95064.

20. Postharvest Handling

American Fruit Grower & American Vegetable Grower magazines (see "Periodicals") have annual issues listing companies that supply products for postharvest handling. *The Packer* newspaper (see "Wholesale Resources") also has listings for suppliers and packaging companies.

The Commercial Storage of Fruits, Vegetables, and Florist and Nursery Stocks (Ag Handbook #66), by R.E. Hardenburg, A.E. Watada & C.Y. Wang. 130 pp. SN #001-000-04478-8. $7. From Superintendent of Documents. See "Books & Publications Suppliers."

Cooling Requirements of Fruits and Vegetables, by Michael Boyette. Notebook binder containing specific cooling requirements for different types of produce. Free from Michael Boyette, 210 Biological and Agricultural Engineering Bldg., North Carolina State Univ., Raleigh, NC 27695-7625.

Postharvest Technology of Horticultural Crops. 192 pp. $17.50 ANR061. From agAccess. See "Books & Publications Suppliers."

Produce Handling for Direct Marketing. Bulletin which describes produce-handling techniques, general guidelines on field handling and market displays, with sections on iced and refrigerated displays. Discusses the principles of refrigerated storage and options for cold storage rooms and refrigeration equipment. Also lists recommendations for handling more than 40 types of vegetables and fruits. 26 pp. SN #NRAES-51. $5.50 postpaid from NRAES. See "Books & Publications Suppliers."

Product Handling & Storage. $3.20. Available from Innovative Rural Enterprises, Dept. of Agricultural Economics and Rural Sociology, Ohio State Univ., 2120 Fyffe Rd., Columbus, OH 43210. Indicate the title, the number of pages (16), and the item topic (Farmers Markets - R). Make checks payable to OSU/IRE.

Refrigeration and Controlled Atmosphere Storage for Horticultural Crops. $5.75 from NRAES. See "Books & Publications Suppliers."

Cooling units

Barr Equipment Co., 7701 County Rd. FF, Pickett, WI 54964; (414) 589-2721. Coolers, freezers and chillers.

Cool-and-Ship. A mobile home air conditioning unit in a box that will take berries or tomatoes from a field temperature of 80° F. down to 50°. Cost is less than $2,000. For more information contact: North Carolina State Univ. Cooperative Extension, Dept. of Ag Communications, Box 7603, Raleigh, NC 27695; (919) 515-3173.

An Evaporative Cooler For Vegetable Crops, by J. F. Thompson and R.R. Kasmire, California Agriculture, March/April 1981. Describes how to build a simple, low-cost energy-efficient evaporative cooling system. For a reprint of this article, send a self-addressed, stamped envelope to Richard Van Rankin, Rutgers Cooperative Extension, Atlantic Co., 1200 W. Harding Hwy., Mays Landing, NJ 08330.

Mini-Reefers. CMF Corp. manufactures several models of self-contained slip-in fiberglass coolers for mini-trucks and conventional 8-foot pickups. The cooling unit is charged overnight with a standard 110v plug-in; thus, the unit can be used as a free-standing cooler when not installed on the pickup. Prices start at $5,250. CMF Corp., 1524 W. 15th St., Long Beach, CA 90813; (310) 437-2166.

Selecting Coolers for Fresh Fruit, Vegetables, and Flowers by R. F. Kasmire and J. F. Thompson. Summary of various methods used for cooling products prior to shipping, and how to select a cooler for the crop you grow. For a free copy, write to Joe Ahrens, Mann Laboratory, U.C. Davis, Davis, CA 95616; (916) 752-1412.

ThermaCover is a shiny, thin-filmed radiant space-blanket material that, according to its manufacturer, ThermaGard, Inc., blocks out 97 percent of all radiant energy. The protective blanket has a variety of uses, from protecting your produce at the farmers market to draping over pallets or pickup loads of produce. The company also makes boxes that provide an alternative to Styrofoam. ThermaGard, Inc., 6312 Shortcut Rd., Moss Point, MS 39563; (601) 474-2314.

Chapter Resources

Note: For a list of related books on these subjects, see the "New World Bookshelf," p. 301.

Chapter 2. Choosing Your Enterprises

Break-Even Analysis for Comparing Alternative Crops, by James H. Hilker, J. Roy Black and Oran B. Hesterman. 12 pp. 75¢. From Michigan State University, Bulletin #E2021. See "General Resources—Cooperative Extension Services."

Evaluating Farm Based Alternatives—A Guide for Selecting Rural Income Options, by Allen Bjergo. 31 pp. Free. #EB94. Montana State University. See "General Resources—Cooperative Extension Services."

Farming Alternatives: A Guide to Evaluating the Feasibility of New Farm-Based Enterprises. Helps you assess personal, family, and business goals; inventory your resources; research local and regional markets; analyze production feasibility, profitability, and cash flow; and make final go/no-go decisions. 88 pp. $6 from NRAES. See "General Resources—Books & Publications Suppliers."

Farm Management. Considerations in Enterprise Selection, Farm Leases and Rents, How to Determine Your Costs of Production and How to Finance a Small Farm. #ANRP011. $2. From Small Farm Center. See "General Resources—Associations."

Steps In the Management Process of Evaluating Farming Alternatives. A "mini-workbook" for decision making. 10 pp. $2. Make checks payable to Cornell University. The Farming Alternatives Program, Warren Hall, Cornell Univ., Ithaca, NY 14853; (607) 255-9832.

Chapter 3. Deciding What To Grow

Backyard Cash Crops: The Source Book for Growing and Marketing Specialty Plants, by Craig Wallin. See "New World Bookshelf," p. 301.

Health resources

American Cancer Society (see local information for your state).

The American Dietetic Association, 216 W. Jackson Blvd., Ste. 800, Chicago, IL 60606.

American Heart Association, 7320 Greenville Ave., Dallas, TX 75231.

Consumer Information Center-F, P.O. Box 100, Pueblo, CO 81002.

Contact also your local county extension office for nutritional pamphlets or brochures published by state groups.

Chapter 4. Market Research

"Consumer Surveys—Critical To Direct Marketers," by John Cottingham. *University of Wisconsin Cooperative Extension Direct Marketing Newsletter*, July 1989. See "General Resources—Periodicals & Newsletters."

Do It Yourself Marketing Research, Breen and Blankenship, McGraw-Hill. Available through bookstores.

Researching Your Market. $1. #MT8. From SBA Publications. See "General Resources—Books & Publications Suppliers."

Chapter 5. Making A Marketing Plan

"Beginning Business Planning for Direct Marketers," by Timothy M. Baye, *University of Wisconsin Cooperative Extension Direct Marketing Newsletter*, November 1988 and March 1989. See "General Resources—Periodicals & Newsletters."

Business Plan for Retailers. $1. #MP9. From SBA Publications. See "General Resources—Books & Publications Suppliers."

Business Plan Guidelines, by Fred Rice. 3 pp. Free. From KSU Foundation. See "General Resources—Books & Publications Suppliers."

The Business Planning Guide, by David Bangs. Available in libraries and bookstores, or from Upstart Publishing, (800) 235-8866.

"Marketing Plans for Direct Marketers," by Kenneth Huddleston. *University of Wisconsin Cooperative Extension Direct Marketing Newsletter,* January 1990. See "General Resources—Periodicals & Newsletters."

Sources of Financing in the '90s. Audio tape from 1992 National Farmers Direct Marketing Conference. Contact Follick Recording Service. See "General Resources—Audio & Video Tapes."

Twelve Tips to Get Micro Business Financing. Audio tape from Marketplace '92. $6 postpaid. #28. Studio A, 105 Broadway Ave., Bismarck, ND 58501; (701) 223-8980.

Chapter 6. Is Direct Marketing For You?

"Direct Marketing Alternatives," by John Cottingham. *University of Wisconsin Cooperative Extension Direct Marketing Newsletter,* January 1988. See "General Resources—Periodicals & Newsletters."

Family-Based Business: Why Have a Home-Based Business? Advantages and Disadvantages. 25¢. #HE-FS-3096. From University of Minnesota Tourism Center. See Chapter 30 (Group Promotion) resources.

How to Make Money at Produce Auctions. 20¢. Available from Innovative Rural Enterprises, Dept. of Agricultural Economics and Rural Sociology, Ohio State Univ., 2120 Fyffe Rd., Columbus, OH 43210. Indicate the title, the number of pages (1), and the item topic (Direct Marketing - R). Make checks payable to OSU/IRE.

Marketing. Direct Marketing and Quality Control, Marketing Cooperatives and Setting Up a Roadside Stand. $3. #ANRP010. From Small Farm Center. See "General Resources—Associations."

Chapter 7. Farmers Markets

Establishing a Municipal Retail Farmers Market. 270 pp. $30. #NB06. MSU Distribution Center, 10 "B" Agriculture Hall, East Lansing, MI 48824-1039; (517) 353-6740.

Establishing and Operating a Community Farmers Market, by Forrest Stegelin. University of Kentucky. #AEC-77. See "General Resources—Cooperative Extension Services."

Establishing and Operating a Farmers Market, by R. P. Jenkins. #PB847. From University of Tennessee Cooperative Extension. See "General Resources—Cooperative Extension Services."

Farmers Markets '96, by Eric Gibson. Latest trends in farmers markets. See "New World Bookshelf," p. 303.

Food Stamps and Farmers Market Promotion Manual. A guide to promotion and certification. $5.

Contact The Hartford Food System, 509 Wethersfield Ave., Hartford, CT 06114; (860) 296-9325.

How to Organize and Run a Successful Farmers Market. $3. Massachusetts Federation of Farmers Markets. Dept. of Food and Agriculture, Division of Markets, 100 Cambridge St., Boston, MA 02202.

Tips: Retail Farm Market Sales Persons. #MP10. New Jersey Publications Distribution Center. See "General Resources—Cooperative Extension Services."

Chapter 8. Roadside Markets

Construction and Management of an Iced Produce Display, $1; *Walk-In Cooler Construction,* $1. Available from Monika Crispin, Cornell Cooperative Extension, 615 Willow Ave., Ithaca, NY 14850.

Designing Your Market. 40¢. Available from Innovative Rural Enterprises, Dept. of Agricultural Economics and Rural Sociology, Ohio State Univ., 2120 Fyffe Rd., Columbus, OH 43210. Indicate the title, the number of pages (2), and the item topic (Direct Marketing - G). Make checks payable to OSU/IRE.

Facilities for Roadside Markets. Booklet on planning a farm market. Covers planning for display area, checkout area, back room and preparation area, refrigerated storage, office area, parking area, and other facilities. Also discusses zoning ordinances, site drainage and parking lot construction, market lighting, signs, security, and fire-resistant construction. 32 pp. $5.50 from NRAES. See "General Resources—Books & Publications Suppliers."

Management of Roadside Markets, by F. Stegelin. 1986. #AEC-41. From University of Kentucky. See "General Resources—Cooperative Extension Services."

Managing for Success: A Manual for Roadside Markets, by James Beierlein and Cathleen Connell. See "General Resources—Books."

Principles of Layout for Retail Produce Operations. Research Report #590, USDA Agricultural Marketing Service. Superintendent of Documents. See "General Resources—Books & Publications Suppliers."

Produce Handling for Direct Marketing. Booklet discusses handling through harvest, transport, storage and display. Includes recommendations for fruits and vegetables and reviews the basics of refrigerated storage, assisting in selection of equipment that will maximize produce shelf life. 29 pp. $5.50 from NRAES. See "General Resources—Books & Publications Suppliers."

Roadside Marketing Manual, 128 pp. $10. #NB03. From Michigan State University. See "General Resources—Cooperative Extension Services."

Roadside Market Stand Plan. Blueprints for an 8-by-16 foot roadside stand. $1. University of Delaware, Extension Agricultural Engineer—Plan Service, 058 Townsend Hall, Newark, DE 19717-1303. Make checks payable to University of Delaware and specify Plan #5983, Roadside Stand.

Chapter 9. Pick-Your-Own

Is Your Farm Suited To Pick-Your-Own?, by J.W. Courter. Available free from Ohio State University. See "General Resources—Cooperative Extension Services."

Management of Pick-Your-Own Marketing Operations. 66 pp. $1. From Delaware Cooperative Extension. See "General Resources—Cooperative Extension Services."

Pick Your Own. $1.40. Available from Innovative Rural Enterprises, Dept. of Agricultural Economics and Rural Sociology, Ohio State Univ., 2120 Fyffe Rd., Columbus, OH 43210. Indicate the title, the number of pages (7), and the item topic (Pick Your Own-D). Make checks payable to OSU/IRE.

Pick-Your-Own Farming, by R.J. Wampler and J.E. Motes. Covers all aspects of pick-your-own farming, including parking, insurance, containers, labor and advertising. 194 pp. $21.95. #UOK001. From agAccess. See "General Resources—Books & Publications Suppliers."

Pick-Your-Own-Marketing, #HM1; *Estimating the Trade Area for PYO Farmers*, #HM6; *Liability and Insurance*, #HM2. Fact sheets from Dept. of Horticulture, Univ. of Illinois, Plant Science Lab, 1201 S. Dorner Dr., Urbana, IL 61801.

PYO, by G. H. Sullivan, V.H. Kulp and R.W. Treadway. Free pamphlet from Purdue University Cooperative Extension. See "General Resources—Cooperative Extension Services."

Chapter 11. Subscription Farming

Basic Formula To Create A Community Supported Agriculture, by Robyn Van En. Handbook on how to start and operate a CSA, including prospectus, budgets, job descriptions, outreach tactics, bibliography, and CSA directory. 60 pp. $10. Robyn Van En, Indian Line Farm, RR3, Box 85, Great Barrington, MA 01230.

Community Related Agriculture: An Introduction. 10 pp. Biodynamic Association, P.O. Box 550, Kimberton, PA 19442. In addition to the brochure, the Biodynamic Association will also send a list of CSA projects in the U.S. Send $1 and a self-addressed, stamped envelope for a copy.

Community Supported Agriculture of North America (CSANA), 20001 "L" St., NW, Ste. 801, Washington, DC 20036; (401) 785-5135; FAX (202) 785-5214. CSANA assists and encourages CSA's to grow and improve their operations through publications, seminars, as well as technical assistance and research in CSA-related areas. CSANA also promotes and disseminates CSA information to the public. CSANA is compiling a directory of existing CSA's throughout North America and publishes a quarterly newsletter.

CSA Information Packet. $3. Homestead Design, Inc., Box 1058, Bellingham, WA 98227.

Farms Of Tomorrow by Trauger Groh and Steve McFadden. See New World Publishing Bookshelf (p. 301).

It's Not Just About Vegetables. A video that describes the beginnings of Indian Line Farm and introduces CSA concepts. 18 min. VHS. Interviews with core group and running dialogue of CSA logistics. $35 postpaid. Available from Bio-Dynamic Association, P.O. Box 550, Kimberton, PA 19442, or from Robyn Van En (address above). Canada and foreign orders allow for U.S. funds & check processing.

Chapter 12. Mail Order

Direct Marketing Association, 6 E. 43rd St., New York, NY 10017; (212) 689-4977.

Mail Order Connection. How-to newsletter. Request sample copy. Stilson & Stilson, P.O. Box 1075, Tarpon Springs, FL 34286.

Mail Order Made Easier, by John Kremer. Forms, sample letters, worksheets, records, formulas, flow charts, etc. Ad-Lib Publications, 51 N. 5th St., P.O. Box 1102, Fairfield, IA 52556-1102.

Mail Order Moonlighting. Ten Speed Press. Provides a detailed list of 900 books, tapes, newsletters, seminars and articles on selling by mail. Available in bookstores and libraries.

National Mail Order Association, 5818 Venice Blvd., Los Angeles, CA 90019-5097; (213) 934-7986.

Selling By Mail Order. $1. #MT9. From SBA Publications. See "General Resources—Books & Publications Suppliers."

Uncle Dutchie's Gourmet Co-op is the brainchild of Jeff Lawrence, who began pooling with other gourmet food entrepreneurs in order to market his own Cajun spice. In addition to taking out group space ads in high-profile magazines, the co-op publishes a newsletter, which consists of paid "advertorials," and is sent to food connoisseurs and professionals nationwide. Uncle Dutchie's Gourmet Co-op, 2298 S. Elliott Rd., SW, Stockport, OH 43787; (614) 557-3245.

Chapter 14. Selling To Restaurants

The Chef's Source Book. Contains listings for specialty producers, regional distributors, and gourmet manufacturers. Read by chefs and other food service professionals who buy for restaurants and hotels. Cuisine Publications, 25 Kearny St., Ste. 500, San Francisco, CA 94108; (415) 982-0701.

Food Arts (magazine), 387 Park Ave. South, New York, NY 10016.

The *Fresh Connection Newsletter* (State of Massachusetts) acts as a link between restaurants wanting to buy from growers, and growers who sell to restaurants. Write to Massachusetts Dept. of Food and Agriculture, Bureau of Markets, 100 Cambridge St., Boston, MA 02202; (617) 727-3018.

Getting on the Menu, by Deborah S. Weschsler. Article reprint available from Rodale's *Organic*

Gardening magazine, Sept. 1986. Rodale Press, Inc., 33 E. Minor St., Emmaus, PA 18049.

Chapter 15. Selling To Retail Outlets

Progressive Grocer's Marketing Guidebook. Profiles of supermarket chains, distributors, wholesalers and brokers; names, addresses and phone numbers of buyers and management personnel; demographic and distribution profiles of market areas; retail supermarket share data by market; listings for food brokers, candy, media, nonfood distributors, and more. $270 (National Edition), $120 (Regional Edition). Contact Progressive Grocer's Trade Dimensions, Attn: Directory Sales, P.O. Box 10246, Stamford, CT 06913-0184; (203) 977-2900.

Chapter 16. Specialty Food Products

Encyclopedia of Associations, Gale Research Co. Available in libraries.

Food and Fiber Center, c/o Mississippi Cooperative Extension Service, P.O. Box 5446, Mississippi State, MS 39762. Publishes *New Product Introduction: A Practical Guide for Evaluating Product Potential.*

Food Processing Center, University of Nebraska-Lincoln, 60 H.C. Filley Hall, East Campus, P.O. Box 830928, Lincoln, NE 68583-0928; (402) 472-5791. Offers technical and marketing assistance as well as seminars on all phases of food processing.

From Kitchen To Market: Sell Your Gourmet Food Specialt Stephen F. Hall. See "Ne Bookshelf," p. 301.

Small Home Processing, S 75¢. From sity. S op

Tradeshows & Exhibits Schedule. Directory with information on more than 11,000 trade shows in the U.S. and Canada. $170. Successful Meetings, Tradeshows and Exhibits Schedule, 633 3rd. Ave., New York, NY 10164-0635; (800) 253-6708.

Labeling laws

Food Labeling: A User's Manual is a comprehensive guide to food labeling published by the National Food Processors Association. The cost for members is $350; for non-members, $500. Available from the National Food Processors Association (Attn: Publications), 1401 New York Ave., NW, Washington, DC 20005; (202) 639-5900.

The Food Processing Center at the University of Nebraska-Lincoln has compiled a summary of the new labeling regulations. Send $10 to the Food Processing Center, Univ. of Nebraska - Lincoln, 143 Food Industry Building, Lincoln, NE 68583-0919; (402) 472-5791.

Chapter 17. Merchandising

Barry Ballister's Fruit and Vegetable Stand: A Complete Guide to the Selection, Preparation and Nut tion of Fresh Produce, by Barr lister. See "New World Bo p. 301.

Eat More Fr bles—5-A-Dai Four-color fresh fr a pl k

tion. See "General Resources—Associations."

Marketing Checklist for Small Retailers. $1. #MT4. From SBA Publications. See "General Resources—Books & Publications Suppliers."

Merchandising Agricultural Products. A fact-sheet style reference on ordering and receiving merchandise, budgets, policies, vendors and middlemen, suppliers, purchase orders, invoicing, determining selling prices, labeling, product life cycle, and retail price legislation. 29 pp. $2.15 plus $2.50 p/h. #E-108. Cornell Instructional Materials Service, 109 Kennedy Hall, Cornell Univ., Ithaca, NY 14853; (607) 255-9252. Make checks payable to Instructional Materials Service.

Organic Produce Merchandising Manual. Send $5 to Albert's Organics, P.O. Box 786, Kennett Square, PA 19348. (Parts of Chapter 17 are reprinted, with permission, fro... this booklet.)

Produ...
Yo...

The Quaker Oats Company, P.O. Box 049001, Chicago, IL 60604-9001. Attn: Coordinator Trade Educational Programs.

Chapter 18. Customer Service

Courtesy Is Contagious. Suggests ways to improve marketing skills of people in the tourism industry. $2. #CD-FO-3271. From Distribution Center. See "General Resources—Books & Publications Suppliers."

Good Customer Relations With Improved Personal Selling. #EC814. Free. From North Dakota State University. See "General Resources—Cooperative Extension Services."

Retaining Customers b... Handling Complaints ... ...ree. From Nort... ...rsi... ...op-

Chapter 23. Business Smarts

General

1989 Yearbook of Agriculture: Farm Management, How to Achieve Your Business Goals. 336 pp. $9.50. OPA #001-000-04537-7. From Superintendent of Documents. See "General Resources—Books & Publications Suppliers."

Barter News. Listings of barter opportunities. Call (714) 495-6529.

"Crop Budgets for Direct Marketers." *University of Wisconsin Cooperative Extension Direct Marketing Newsletter,* May 1988. See "General Resources—Periodicals & Newsletters."

Guide to Starting a Small Home Business. Michigan State University Cooperative Extension Service. $25 payable to Michigan State University. Send to Irene Hathaway, Extension Specialist, Family Resource Management, 203 Human Ecology, Michigan State Univ., East Lansing, MI 48824.

Home-Based Business. . . Is It For Me?, by the North Dakota State University's Cooperative Extension Service. Publication on financing, legal forms of ownership, marketing, pricing, recordkeeping, tax considerations, license permits and ...ning, insurance, time manage...ent, employee relations, etc. 26 ... Free. #EB-44. North Dakota ...te University. See "General Re...ces—Cooperative Extension ...ces."

...me Business Digest. Quar...ewsletter published by the ...ooperative Extension Ser.../year. See "General Re...—Cooperative Extension

...ade Money: Your Home...ess Success Guide for ...Barbara Brabec. See ...ookshelf," p. 301.

...ome Business Re...ewsletter for home...s. $24/year. Sam...Brabec Produc-

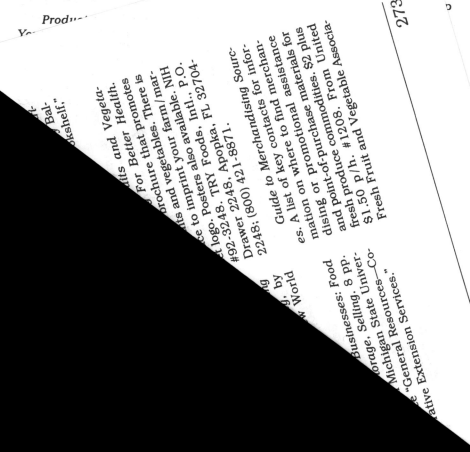

273

tions, P.O. Box 2137, Naperville, IL 60567.

Starting A Home-Based Business, by Fred Rice. 99 pp. $6. From KSU Foundation. See "General Resources—Books & Publications Suppliers."

Computers

Computers on the Farm. 25¢. #F2277. From Washington State University. See "General Resources—Cooperative Extension Services."

Enterprise Budget Worksheet. Software program from University of Idaho. $20. #MCUG-14. See "General Resources—Cooperative Extension Services."

Market Model. A computer program developed at Ohio State University that allows growers to work "what if" scenarios by plugging in production or price figures from individual operations. Allows the grower to make profit comparisons between different crops. Contact Professor Franklin Hall, Dept. of Entomology, Ohio State Univ., OARDC, 1680 Madison Ave., Wooster, OH 44691; (216) 263-3726.

Microcomputers On The Farm, by D.E. Erickson, et al. 1990. Essentials of acquiring and using a small computer in agricultural operations. Includes a source list for on-line information services. 108 pp. $9.95. #IOW060. From agAccess. See "General Resources—Books & Publications Suppliers."

Updated Inventory of Agricultural Computer Programs. Lists about 1,500 computer programs for agriculture, forestry, home and family. 186 pp. $3.90 plus $2.50 p/h. #G-201. Cornell Instructional Materials Service, 109 Kennedy Hall, Cornell Univ., Ithaca, NY 14853; (607) 255-9252. Make checks payable to Instructional Materials Service.

Recordkeeping

Cornell Farm Account Book. 60 pp. $4 plus $2.50 p/h. #E-111. Cornell Instructional Materials Service, 109 Kennedy Hall, Cornell Univ., Ithaca, NY 14853; (607) 255-9252. Make checks payable to Instructional Materials Service.

Farm Business Records. $13. Make checks payable to Cornell University. Contact: Penny Evans, Cornell University Resource Center, 7 Cornell Business and Technology Park, Ithaca, NY 14850; (607) 255-7660.

Recordkeeping In A Small Business (#FM10, $1); *Checklist For Developing A Training Program* (#PM1, 50¢) and *Employees: How To Find and Pay Them* (#PM2, $1). From SBA Publications. See "General Resources—Books & Publications Suppliers."

Small Farm Bookkeeping System, by the editors of *Small Farmer's Journal.* 144 pp. $8.95 postpaid. Send to Farmer's Book Service, Small Farmer's Journal, P.O. Box 2805, Eugene, OR 97402.

Personnel management

Farm Personnel Management, by Kenneth H. Thomas and Bernard L. Erven. Provides principles and guidelines for hiring and keeping good farm employees. 23 pp. #NCR329. From University of Illinois. See "General Resources—Cooperative Extension Services."

"Training Helps Farm Market Employees Succeed," by Bernard L. Erven, *Rural Enterprise,* Fall 1991.

Organizations

Small Business Administration (SBA): In addition to the low-cost publications listed in *The Small Business Directory,* the SBA has an "answer desk" for questions regarding government regulations, training and counseling services available. (800) 8-ASK SBA. See "General Resources—Books & Publications Suppliers."

Small Business Development Centers. Resources, individual counseling and training available at no cost to small business owners. Contact: Small Business Development Center, SBA, 409 Third St., SW, Washington, DC 20416.

Small Business Institute, Office of Business Development, SBA, 409 3rd St., SW, 6th Floor, Washington, DC 20416. Extensive business consulting offered free of charge through universities and colleges, for small business owners.

Chapter 24. Pricing For Profits

A Pricing Checklist for Small Retailers (#FM12, $1); *Pricing Your Products and Services Profitably* (#FM13, $1); *Simple Break-Even Analysis for Small Stores* (#FM11, $1). From SBA Publications. See "General Resources—Books & Publications Suppliers."

Putting A Price On Your Products. 80¢. Available from Innovative Rural Enterprises, Dept. of Agricultural Economics and Rural Sociology, Ohio State Univ., 2120 Fyffe Rd., Columbus, OH 43210. Indicate the title, the number of pages (4), and the item topic (Direct Marketing - E). Make checks payable to OSU/IRE.

Chapter 25. Rules & Regulations

"Hiring Rules for Roadside Markets and Pick-Your-Own Businesses," by Mike McCoy. *University of Wisconsin Cooperative Extension Direct Marketing Newsletter,* May 1990. See "General Resources—Periodicals & Newsletters."

"Roadside Marketing Requires Reviewing Laws and Regulations," by Stan Ernst, *Rural Enterprise,* Winter 1987.

The Nutrition Edge: A Labeling Education and Marketing Guide for Retailers. This program includes a poster, video, instruction booklet and workbook; posters are also sold separately. Available from Director of Nutrition, Produce Marketing Association (PMA), P.O. Box 6036, Newark, DE 19714-6036.

Chapter 26. Insurance

How to Avoid Lawsuits for Negligence—A Primer for Direct Marketing Farmers, by L. Leon Geyer. #448-008. Free from Virginia Cooperative Extension Service. See "General Resources—Cooperative Extension Services."

"Insurance," Chapter 6 in *Managing for Success: A Manual for Roadside Markets*. See "General Resources—Books."

Liability & Insurance for U-Pick Operations, by Donald L. Uchtmann. #HM-2-79. From University of Illinois. See "General Resources—Cooperative Extension Services."

Risk Liability & Insurance for Direct Marketers. 80¢. Available from Innovative Rural Enterprises, Dept. of Agricultural Economics and Rural Sociology, Ohio State Univ., 2120 Fyffe Rd., Columbus, OH 43210. Indicate the title, the number of pages (4), and the item topic (Direct Marketing - E). Make checks payable to OSU/IRE.

Chapter 27. The Sales Call

Creative Selling: The Competitive Edge. 50¢. #MT1. SBA Publications. See "General Resources—Books & Publications Suppliers."

Fundamentals of Successful Selling. #FS023. Cooperative Extension Service, Cook College, Rutgers—The State University of New Jersey. See "General Resources—Cooperative Extension Services."

"Salesmanship," Chapter 14 in *Managing for Success*. See "General Resources—Books."

Chapter 28. Promotion

Direct Farm Marketing: A Guidebook for Promotion and Publicity. $6. Publication from Minnesota Dept. of Agriculture. See "General Resources—Cooperative Extension Services."

How To Advertise and Promote Your Retail Store, by Dana Cassell. See "New World Bookshelf," p. 301.

Promotion & Advertising. University of Kentucky. See "General Resources—Cooperative Extension Services."

The Publicity Manual, by Kate Kelly. How to increase the visibility of your business through free publicity in newspapers, magazines, newsletters, trade journals, radio and television. 234 pp. $19.95. Available from Para Publishing, P.O. Box 4232-190, Santa Barbara, CA 93140-4232; (800) 727-2782.

Chapter 29. Advertising

Advertising. MT11. $1 from SBA Publications. See "General Resources—Books & Publications Suppliers."

Advertising: An Investment In Your Business' Future. Advertising tips and techniques. Media chart comparing coverage, audience and costs, plus sample budget and planning worksheets. For owners of small businesses. $1.50. #CD-BU-3539. From Minnesota Dept. of Agriculture. See "General Resources—Cooperative Extension Services."

Advertising Resource Book. $14.95 postpaid. Advertising Resources, Inc., P.O. Box 6136, East Lansing, MI 48826.

Direct Farm Marketing: A Guidebook for Promotion & Publicity. $6. From Minnesota Dept. of Agriculture. See "General Resources—Cooperative Extension Services."

Evaluating Tourism Advertising with Cost-Comparison Methods. $2. #CD-FO-3372. Describes how to translate advertising rates into

"customers obtained." From Minnesota Dept. of Agriculture. See "General Resources—Cooperative Extension Services."

Guerrilla Marketing, by Jay Conrad Levinson. $8.95. Available in bookstores.

Handbook of Advertising Phrases. Descriptive words, phrases and sentences on quality and appearance for 90 fruits and vegetables. Helps in writing copy for ads and for making signs. $2.50 plus $1.50 p/h. Order code #HM8026. United Fresh Fruit and Vegetable Association. See "General Resources—Associations."

How To Advertise and Promote Your Retail Store, by Dana Cassell. See "New World Bookshelf," p. 301.

The Success MAP* for Your Herb Business (*Marketing, Advertising and Publicity), by Linda Morgan. $5 postpaid. Antique Orchid Herbary, Rte. 6, Box 734, Abingdon, VA 24210.

Clip art resources

Dover Publications, 31 E. 2nd St., Mineola, NY 11501; (516) 294-7000. (Many Dover books also are available in bookstores.)

Fruit and Vegetable Clip Art for Direct Marketers. $5 postpaid. Make checks payable to the University of Illinois and send to Jeff Kindhart, Univ. of Illinois, Dixon Springs Agricultural Center, Simpson, IL 62985.

Wheeler Arts, 66 Lake Park, Champaign, IL 61821-7101; (217) 359-6816 (2 – 5 p.m.).

Chapter 30. Group Promotion

Community Travel and Tourism Marketing (#CD-FO-3272, $3); *Tourism Advertising: Some Basics* (#CD-FO-3311, $3); *Tourism Brochures to Boost Business* (#CD-FO-3273, $2). From Distribution Center. See "General Resources—Books & Publications Suppliers."

Events and Festivals—Information and Resource Book. $20. A compilation of information on how to manage and operate a successful event or festival. From Tourism Center (address below).

How To Conduct A "Tasting" Event, by the Board of Directors, Tasting of Summer Produce. Information packet to assist organizations interested in producing "Tasting" events. Available from Small Farm Center. See "General Resources—Associations."

Marketing Crafts and Other Products to Tourists. Offers a profile of tourists, examines successful marketing strategies and suggests ways to make crafts part of community tourism. 12 pp. Available from Publications Office, Cooperative Extension, Univ. of Nebraska, IANR Communications and Computing Services, Lincoln, NE 68583.

Rural Tourism Development Training Package. Workbook and video explaining how rural communities can develop and expand their tourism and travel industry. $55 (guidebook only, $30). From Tourism Center (address below).

Starting a County-Wide Ag Marketing Program. Available free from Paul Vossen, Farm Advisor, Univ. of California Cooperative Extension, Co. Administration Center, 2604 Ventura Ave., Rm. 100, Santa Rosa, CA 95403.

Tourism & Your Community. 12 pp. 30¢. #E0729. From Michigan State University. See "General Resources—Cooperative Extension Services."

Tourism Center. Offers educational programs and materials for the visitor industry on small business management and community tourism development. Ask for their catalog, *Educational Materials Order Form,* which contains an extensive list of available publications, including *Tourism Brochures To Boost Business* (#CD-FO-3273, $2); and many others. Tourism Center, 101-C Green Hall, Univ. of Minnesota,1530 N. Cleveland Ave., St. Paul, MN 55108; (612) 624-4947.

Tourism USA: Guidelines for Tourism Development. A University of Missouri-Columbia, University Extension publication. $3 payable to Tourism USA. Send orders prepaid to United States Travel and Tourism Administration, Attn: Tourism USA, Dept. of Commerce, Rm. 1860, Washington, DC 20230; (202) 377-0140.

"Tips On Developing Publicity for Farm Markets," by Jeffrey Patton, *Rural Enterprise,* Winter 1992.

Farm marketing organizations

Farm Markets Of Ohio, Two Nationwide Plaza, P.O. Box 479, Columbus, OH 43216; (614) 249-2430.

Massachusetts Federation of Farmers Markets (MFFM), c/o Charlie Touchette, Executive Director, 1499 Memorial Ave., West Springfield, MA 01089.

Sonoma County Agricultural Marketing Program (SCAMP), c/o Betsy Timm, Coordinator, SCAMP, 1055 W. College Avenue, Ste. 194, Santa Rosa, CA 95401; (707) 829-5528.

Chapter 31. Sharing The Bounty

Feeding the hungry

To donate to the food service agency nearest you, call the home economist at your cooperative extension office. Also contact:

Farmers Market Nutrition Program (FMNP). Brochures, newsletters, info sheets. Contact National Association of Farmers Market Nutrition Programs (FMNP), 509 Wethersfield Ave., Hartford CT 06114; (203) 296-9325.

Food First. 145 9th St., San Francisco, CA 94103. A research and education center dedicated to searching out the underlying causes of world hunger.

Gleaning: Pointers On How To Begin. Free pamphlet on how to organize a gleaning project. Send a self-addressed, stamped envelope to New World Publishing. See Order Form, last page.

Growing Food for the Hungry Garden Project. Model program for gardeners helping the hungry. Contact Organic Garden and Nutrition Club, P.O. Box 3626, Santa Rosa, CA 95402; (707) 539-6598 or (707) 527-2621.

Save Three Lives: A Plan for Famine Prevention, by R. Rodale and M. McGrath. Sierra Club Books, California, 1991.

Second Harvest. Call their national headquarters at (312) 263-2303; they will put you in touch with the regional office nearest you.

Seeds. Monthly publication exploring the issue of hunger from a Christian perspective. $16/year. Contact Seeds, 222 E. Lake Dr., Decatur, GA 30030.

"A Win-Win Situation: Both Growers and Low-Income Families Benefit from the Farmers Market Nutrition Program," by August Schumacher, Jr. and Hugh Joseph. *American Vegetable Grower,* June 1992.

You Are What You Eat: Some of the Health, Social, Ethical and Spiritual Reasons For Becoming a Vegetarian. Free pamphlet. Send a self-addressed, stamped envelope to New World Publishing. See Order Form, last page.

Saving farmland

The *American Farmland Trust (AFT)*, 1920 "N" Street, NW, Ste. 400, Washington, DC 20036; (202) 659-5170. AFT is a private, non-profit organization dedicated to protecting our nation's farmland. AFT works to stop the loss of productive farmland and to promote farming practices that lead to a healthy environment. Its programs include public education, technical assistance in policy development and direct farmland protection projects.

The *Farmland Preservation Directory* is a sourcebook of organizations, models, and printed materials oriented toward helping preserve farms and farmland. Write to: National Resources Defense Council, 122 E. 42nd St., New York, NY 10168; (212) 949-0049.

LandOwner. Practical tips on farmland ownership for high-return and safe investment. 3-month trial subscription, $10. LandOwner, 219 Parkade, P.O. Box 6, Cedar Falls, IA 50613.

Saving America's Countryside, by S. Stokes, et al. 1989. A comprehensive, step-by-step guide to protecting a rural community's resources. How to organize a conservation effort, inventory available resources, pass effective new laws, set up land trusts, take advantage of federal programs, and change public attitudes. 306 pp. $16.95. #JOH025. From agAccess. See "General Resources—Books."

Saving the Farm: A Handbook for Conserving Agricultural Land, from the American Farmland Trust. This volume is an invaluable tool for locating resource information and organizations. It defines procedures for implementing conservation programs by networking with local government agencies. Private options for land conservation are included. $20 postpaid. Contact American Farmland Trust, Western Regional Office, 1949 5th St., Ste. 101, Davis, CA 95616-4026; (916) 753-1073; FAX 753-1120.

Sustaining Agriculture Near Cities, published by the Soil and Water Conservation Society. 296 pp. $12. Contact SWCS, 7515 NE Ankeny Rd., Ankeny, IA 50021-9764.

Fighting for farmers' rights

Business and Economic Development Strategies for Small Communities, by Fred Rice. 24 pp. $3. From KSU-Small Business Development Center. See "General Resources—Books & Publications Suppliers."

The *Center for Rural Affairs (CRA)*, P.O. Box 406, Walthill, NE 68067; (402) 846-5428. CRA is dedicated to provoking public thought about social, economic and environmental issues affecting rural America such as emerging technologies, sustainable agriculture, rural economic policy, and rural community development.

Ecology Action/Common Ground, 2225 El Camino Real, Palo Alto, CA 94306; (415) 328-6752.

Grants For Your Small Town (#31), *How to Organize Successful Fundraising Drives in Your Community* (#30), *How Your Community Can Put Together a Winning Economic Development Proposal* (#29), *100 Do's and Don'ts For Successful Community-Building* (#37). Audio tapes from Marketplace '92. $6 each postpaid. Studio A, 105 Broadway Ave., Bismarck, ND 58501; (701) 223-8980.

"Politics," *Southland Farmers Market Association Newsletter*, Volume 3, Number 1 gives some excellent tips on media and legislative influence. Send $1 to SFMA, 1010 S. Flower St., Rm. 402, Los Angeles, CA 90015.

Rural Information Center (RIC), c/o National Agricultural Library, Rm. 304, Beltsville, MD 20705; (301) 504-5372 or (800) 633-7701. Provides information on rural economic revitalizations, local government planning projects, rural health services, funding for rural development projects, research studies, and other topics related to maintaining the vitality of America's rural centers.

Miscellaneous

If you're opposed to genetically engineered food and want to make a statement about it, here's a free camera-ready symbol you can reprint on your produce packages that reads "We DO NOT grow genetically engineered food." Request it from the Pure Food Campaign at 1130 17th St., NW, #630, Washington, DC 20077-6095.

Chapter 32. Enjoy!

A Treasury Of Farm And Ranch Humor. $10.95 plus $2 p/h. Lincoln Herndon Press, 818 S. Dirksen Parkway, Springfield, IL 62703.

Section XI: Appendices

Produce Handling & Storage

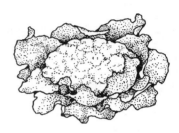

Adapted from Vegetable Crops Fact Sheet VC-33, prepared by Dr. Mark Sherman, University of Florida.

FRESH PRODUCE is alive, and after harvest it depends upon its own food reserves for the energy needed to remain alive. The strategy for the produce manager must be to manage the postharvest environment so that product deterioration is minimized.

The postharvest environment is determined by three critical factors: temperature, humidity, and atmosphere. Most produce handlers lack facilities to store each crop at the optimum conditions. Products in the same display and storage area should have similar requirements with respect to temperature, humidity and atmosphere (see Table I).

Temperature

Temperature is the single most important factor that managers can control. High temperatures accelerate depletion of a product's food reserves, increase water loss, and encourage decay. Prompt cooling of a product to its optimum storage temperature will result in the best shelf life and maintenance of quality.

Roadside markets that do not have refrigeration equipment should harvest highly perishable produce more frequently to maintain a supply of quality produce. Care should be taken to prevent storing and displaying products in the sun at the market.

Managers who have refrigeration equipment should use it wisely. Keep products sensitive to chilling injury away from ice, cold and refrigeration. Chilling injury can result in decay, discoloration, pitting, and loss of flavor and ripening ability (see Table III).

Humidity

The humidity of the surrounding air greatly influences loss of water in fruits or vegetables. Postharvest water loss should be minimized because it is a major cause of quality deterioration and reduced consumer appeal, due to shriveling, wilting, softening, and loss of crispness. Water loss also reduces salable weight.

Minimize water loss by the following practices:

- Maintain a high relative humidity in the air around the product. Sprinkle or mist, in conjunction with proper temperature management.
- Reduce excessive air movement around products.
- Trim the tops from root crops and shanks from sweet corn.
- Use protective packaging on very perishable items. Plastic wraps can maintain a high relative humidity immediately surrounding the products and restrict wilting and shriveling. Package ventilation must be provided. A few small holes will permit adequate gas exchange and still maintain high relative humidity due to limited movement of water vapor.

Atmosphere

Fresh produce, being alive, undergoes a process known as respiration. Respiration is the conversion of food reserves to usable energy. This process involves the intake of gaseous oxygen and release of gaseous carbon dioxide.

When a product is packaged to reduce water loss, its storage atmosphere is also modified. A rapidly respiring product may deplete the oxygen within the package. Storage of products under these conditions can lead to off-flavors and rapid deterioration.

All plants produce ethylene gas to varying degrees. It is a natural product of plant metabolism and is considered to be a natural aging and ripening hormone. Ethylene, however, can have some undesirable effects: 1) accelerated ripening and softening of fruits when not desired; 2) accelerated loss of green color in some immature fruits (cucumbers, squash, snap beans)

and leafy vegetables; 3) russet spotting on lettuce; 4) bitterness in carrots; 5) loss of leaves from cabbage, cauliflower, and foliage ornamentals; and 6) shortened storage life and reduced quality of cut flowers.

Keep ethylene-sensitive crops separate from ethylene producers. You should ensure that products negatively affected by ethylene are not stored with crops producing more than trace amounts of ethylene. Follow the guidelines for display and storage in the tables below. Some crops that produce significant amounts of ethylene are apples, avocados, bananas, litchees, mangos, papayas, peaches, pears, plums, cantaloupes, honeydew melons and tomatoes.

Market sanitation

Good sanitation practices are essential to maintaining a market with a comfortable, pleasant, shopping atmosphere. Here are some guidelines:

- Promptly remove decaying products from displays and the market.
- Disinfect contact surfaces of display cases by washing with water containing one teaspoon of household bleach with one gallon of water. Do this on a regular basis.
- Provide for routine removal of trash to a site remote from the market.

TABLE I: Suggested Storage Groups For Selected Vegetables		
(Crops within a group are compatible with respect to temperature, humidity, and ethylene sensitivity or production.)		
Group 1	Temperature = 32 – 40°F Relative Humidity = 90 – 95% Ethylene Sensitive or Low Ethylene Producing	Beets, Broccoli, Brussels Sprouts, Cabbage, Chinese Cabbage, Carrots, Cauliflower, Celery, Swiss Chard, Collards, Sweet Corn, Endive & Escarole, Horseradish, Kohlrabi, Lettuce (All Types), Mustard & Turnip Greens, Green Onions, Parsley, Parsnips, Peas (All Types), Potatoes (Irish), Radishes, Rutabagas, Spinach (All Types), Strawberries, Turnips
Group 2	Temperature = 40 – 45°F Relative Humidity = 50 – 60% Low Ethylene Producing	Dry Onions, Garlic
Group 3	Temperature = 50°F Relative Humidity = 90 – 95% Chilling And Ethylene Sensitive Crops	Beans (All Types), Cucumbers, Eggplants, Okra, Peppers, Yellow Squash, Zucchini Squash
Group 4	Temperature = 45 – 55°F Relative Humidity = 90 – 95% Chilling Sensitive Crops That Produce Ethylene	Honeydew Melons, Muskmelons, Ripe Tomatoes, Sweet Potatoes, Watermelons
Group 5	Temperature = 60 – 65°F Relative Humidity = 60 – 70% Crops Tolerant To Higher Temperatures	Pumpkins, Acorn & Butternut Squash, Mature Green Tomatoes

SELL WHAT YOU SOW!

Table II: Fruit and Vegetable Products Which are Incompatible in Long-term Storage			
Products			**Effects**
Apples or Pears	with	Celery, Cabbage, Carrots, Potatoes, Onions	Ethylene from apples and pears damages or causes off-flavors in vegetables. Potatoes cause "earthy" flavor in fruit. Potatoes are injured by cold temperatures. High humidity causes root growth in onions and potatoes.
Celery	with	Onions or Carrots	Onion flavor is transmitted. Ethylene from celery causes bitterness in carrots.
Dairy	with	Apples and Citrus	Fruit flavors are taken up by dairy products.
Leafy Greens & Flowers	with	Apples, Pears, Peaches, Tomatoes and Cantaloupe	Ethylene produced by the fruit crops damages greens and flowers.
Cucumbers, Peppers and Green Squash	with	Tomatoes, Apples, Pears	Ethylene from tomatoes, apples, and pears causes loss of green color. This is aggravated by storage temperatures of 45 - 50°F which are too warm for apples and pears.

Source: Produce Handling for Direct Marketing, NRAES-51. Ithaca, NY: Northeast Regional Agricultural Engineering Service. February 1992.

Table III: Display Considerations for Vegetables			
Should be displayed on ice		**Should not be displayed on ice**	
Asparagus, Beets (bunched), Broccoli, Brussels Sprouts, Carrots, Cauliflower, Celery, Endive, Leeks, Lettuce, Onions (green), Parsley, Radishes, Spinach, Watercress		Beans (snap), Cucumbers, Cantaloupe, Eggplant, Peppers, Squash (all kinds), Tomatoes, Watermelon	
Non-Chilling-Sensitive Commodities		**Chilling-Sensitive Commodities**	
Fruits	**Vegetables**	**Fruits**	**Vegetables**
Apple,* Apricot, Berries, Cherry, Fig, Grape, Kiwifruit, Nectarine, Peach, Pear, Persimmon,* Plum, Prune, Strawberry, Pea, Radish, Spinach, Turnip	Artichoke, Asparagus, Bean (lima), Beet, Broccoli, Brussels sprouts, Cabbage, Carrot, Cauliflower, Celery, Sweet Corn, Garlic, Lettuce, Onion, Sapote	Avocado, Banana, Cherimoya, Citrus, Feijoa, Guava, Jujube, Mango, Olive, Papaya, Passion fruit, Pineapple, Plantain, Pomegranate	Snap Bean, Cucumber, Eggplant, Muskmelon, Okra, Pepper, Potato, Pumpkin, Squash, Sweet potato, Tomato, Watermelon

* Some varieties are chilling sensitive

Source: Produce Handling for Direct Marketing, NRAES-51. Ithaca, NY: Northeast Regional Agricultural Engineering Service. February 1992.

Produce Display

Showing Off With Product Display

Courtesy Forrest Stegelin and Brad Porter, Dept. of Agricultural Economics, University of Kentucky.

SNAP BEANS and lima beans in pods can be displayed in bulk or in a variety of containers for ease and speed in serving customers. Shelled limas retain quality better if they are exhibited in closed plastic bags or boxes covered with film wrap.

Sweet corn usually is put out for sale on bulk display. This item benefits greatly from refrigeration or use of ice. Even though the display is restocked frequently with a fresh supply, corn quality will deteriorate rapidly on hot days if the corn is not cooled.

Peppers are most attractive when the reds, greens, yellows and purples are shown together, either in containers or on dump displays. Root vegetables including carrots, beets, radishes, green onions, leeks, and kohlrabi may be offered in bunches with the tops on and laid horizontally and parallel to the front of the display with tips all in the same direction. If bunches are held together snugly with rubber bands or plastic twists, customers may pick them up and inspect the tops and roots for freshness.

Locally grown cantaloupes are excellent traffic builders. Bulk dis-plays are best, but should be kept at a convenient height for shoppers.

Potatoes and dry onions may be ready-bagged and pre-weighed in several sizes of containers, as well as bulk, to meet various shoppers' needs. Protect potatoes from bright interior lighting and sunlight to prevent discoloration.

Fresh fruits are enjoyable to work with because their naturally lively colors catch the eye of shoppers. Apricots, nectarines, peaches, pears and plums that are ready to eat bruise easily, so handle them gently and not often. Small containers please customers who want fresh fruit to eat out of hand. Point-of-sale information to aid shoppers in selecting the best variety for special uses may be as important as the display and price cards.

Grapes are an impulse item. Bulk displays of table grapes show off nicely when placed in bunches on a white background to emphasize the color and quality. This also makes it easier for shoppers to pick what they want. Berries and cherries are most presentable in small containers. Pint and quart sizes accommodate the special handling requirements of those perishable fruits. Refrigeration is essential to minimize loss of quality.

Broccoli and cauliflower may be laid upright or on their sides, preferably not more than two lay-ers deep. Pick them up by the stem and stack them carefully because the flowers damage easily. Brussels sprouts are usually cut off the stalk and placed in clean boxes.

Cabbage is best offered in bulk, but don't stack too high or handle carelessly to injure the leaves. Cabbage may be stacked with the stem end up or down. It is more attractive with the stem end down even though shoppers will tear off more leaves while handling the heads.

Head lettuce may be stagger-stacked if the heads are not wrapped. Stagger-stacking reduces damage from handling and allows proper air circulation if they are not more than two layers deep. Wrapped lettuce heads are more attractive if they are shown with the stems down.

Spinach and other greens should be displayed so as to gain the greatest impact from leaf colors. Don't pack them because this will injure leaves and cause discoloration. It is better to replenish frequently than to overload the display initially. All of these vegetables should be kept cool at 35 – 40 degrees F.

What about potted plants?

Annual bedding plants, vegetable plants and hanging baskets fit nicely into many direct market operations. These plants add variety to the product line, especially during the early part of the season when homegrown produce is scarce. The foliage and blooms add versatility to displays and add color to the market's appearance.

Plants are perishable, too, and they need special care and handling. If you purchase plants to sell, check them when they arrive and water immediately if the soil is dry. Make a daily inspection to check water needs and remove discolored leaves, dried blossoms, and any plants you would not buy for your home. Place plants in a protected area, shielded from wind, rain and extreme temperatures. Attract attention to the plants by showing them at a convenient height. Never place them on asphalt or concrete, as they will dry out quickly and shoppers may trip over them.

Fertilize plants that have been on display more than a week. Use a commercial water soluble fertilizer according to directions. Label the plants so shoppers may identify them, and include the prices. Provide customers with information about care, handling, and planting so their experiences will be satisfying. Keep only fresh, top-quality stock, rotating and consolidating often so the plants do not have a picked-over appearance.

Methods of Displaying Fresh Produce

Courtesy Monika Roth Crispin, Cornell Cooperative Extension.

Vegetables

Asparagus
- Protect tender tips. Display either upright or on side. If on side, do not "shingle-stack."
- Lay bunches horizontally and parallel to front of case with tips pointing in same direction to form neat rows.
- Do not stack too high.
- Trim excessive "white" butt ends. Bunch in 1, 1-1/2, or 2-lbs.; wrap narrow band of parchment paper around each bunch before applying twist-em tape or rubber bands.
- Alternatively display standing upright in shallow pan partially filled with water in order to keep butt ends moist.

Beans (green, wax, pole)
- Beans bruise easily and should be handled carefully.
- Cull out rusty or decayed beans.
- Display bulk on produce rack, or in containers.

Beans (lima)
- Tend to mold and decay—cull out poor quality.
- Display in bulk or shell and sell in pint and quart baskets.

Beets, Carrots, Radishes, Turnips (bunched with tops)
- Lay bunches horizontally and parallel to front of rack with roots to the flow of traffic.
- Bunch carrots with rubber band around the roots.
- Display packed carrots in rows to give ribbon effect on rack.
- Keep moist, sprinkle lightly with water.

Broccoli
- Remove yellow heads.
- Display with heads up or on side one layer high. Stack carefully — flowers damage easily.
- Sprinkle only if refrigerated.
- Keep out of sun.

Brussels Sprouts
- Sell with outer leaves trimmed and before they turn yellow.
- Display bulk on stems.
- Sprouts cut from stems should be sold in baskets or poly bags.

Cabbage
- Do not strip too much. Remove off-condition leaves.
- Display with stem up or down; fewer leaves are torn off if stem is up, but this is less eye-appealing.

Cauliflower
- Avoid handling flower heads.
- Leave protective leaves; trim to one inch over flower.
- Display on stem end, heads-up, not over two high to avoid bruising.
- If head becomes discolored, trim and break into segments, place in poly bag for quick sale.
- Sprinkle only if refrigerated.

Celery
- Trim off discolored or broken stalks; trim butts for fresh look.
- Display in even rows butt end to traffic flow.
- Rubber bands around stalk lessen damage.
- Bunch loose stalks together and sell for chop suey.

Corn
- Keep it FRESH! Strip a few ears to show quality.
- Do not overload display; frequent replenishment indicates rapid turn-over and freshness.
- Keep surplus under refrigeration; quality deteriorates rapidly when temperature is over 35 degrees.
- Prebag in dozen units or use bulk display.

Cucumbers
- Keep dry and cool, temperatures below 40° F cause damage.
- Sort out undersized, shriveled, deformed fruit.
- Place in rows on rack, or when in volume display in bulk or original container (bushels, cartons).

Eggplant
- Sort out brown-spotted fruit.
- Avoid high stacking—stems may puncture fruit.
- Sell by unit or pound.
- Temperatures below 40° F cause damage.

Endive and Escarole
- Trim off brown and broken leaves.
- Sell by head or pound (depends on uniformity of heads).
- Break leaves back so bleached heart shows.
- Ribbon effect is best display method.

Green Onions, Leeks, Scallions, Shallots

- Trim broken leaves; sometimes leaves are cut to make all bunches equal length.
- Display flat horizontal to the front of the case with the roots first in shopping view.
- Sprinkle if refrigerated.

Lettuce

- Trim off broken and rusty leaves. Trim butts.
- Display with stem up to reduce customer damage. (To pick up head, the customer must take hold where the leaves are anchored.) Losses through loose leaves are reduced.
- "Bulk" look of displaying lettuce with rubber bands on each head protects leaves during selection.
- Display in rows (2 – 3 high) or in bulk display.
- Sprinkle if refrigerated.

Mushrooms

- Bulk display or prepackaged.
- Keep dry, and sell before they turn dark.

Onions, Dry (white, red and yellow)

- Watch for decayed or smutty onions; rotate; watch for sprouting.
- Display in bulk; many customers like to select a few for their needs or in packages: 2-lbs. for white, 3-lbs. for yellow seem to be best-selling units, with red in bulk.
- Keep dry.

Onions, Spanish

- Watch for decay, check necks of onions.
- Spanish sell best single.
- Imported Red Italian onions come in a braided string and make a fine impression hung from a structure and sold by the sack or pound; also can be bagged in 2-lb. poly.
- Keep dry.
- Do not display with apples or pears.

Parsley

- Display in small bunches.
- Keep cool and damp. Watch for mold.
- Keep in jars of water in a cooler.

Peas

- Display and handle like lima beans.

Peppers (all types)

- Sort out broken or decayed fruit.
- Sprinkle if refrigerated.
- Don't pile so high they will fall on the floor. A damaged pepper generally is a total loss.
- Temperatures below 40° F and above 50° cause damage.

Potatoes

- Discard bruised, scabby or decayed potatoes.
- Potatoes bruise easily. Handle carefully; do not toss bags onto the display.
- Moisture loss will occur; shriveled potatoes are hard to sell. Late in the season rotation controls sprouting.
- Sold bulk in 5-, 10-, 20- and 50-lb. bags. Experience soon tells what sells best. New potatoes generally sell best in bulk.
- Keep out of sun.

Potatoes (Sweet) and Yams

- Watch for decayed ends — trim and sell quickly.
- Keep away from drafts.
- Don't drop crate—damage will speed up decay.
- Ideal temperature is 55 to 65 degrees F.
- Display in bulk or 2-, 3-, or 4-lb. bags.

Squash (Yellow and Zucchini)

- Handle minimally.
- Squash should be clean and not too mature.
- Display in original container.
- Sell by unit or weight in bulk displays—arrange in neat rows.

Squash (other types)

- Must be clean.
- Sell by pound or unit.
- Large squash can be cut, poly

wrapped and priced by the pound (Hubbard, Delicious, etc.).

Spinach and other greens

- Remove severely damaged and discolored leaves.
- Display to show leaves. Do not compact leaves; let them be fluffy—helps to lessen leaf damage.
- Do not pile too high; replenish often.
- Sprinkle if refrigerated or display on ice.

Tomatoes

- Sort and display by size and color.
- Do not display more than 2 layers high; pressure bruises, stems puncture.
- Sell in bulk (lb.), quart and 2-quart baskets.
- Inspect for decay or bruising.
- Do not place under refrigeration or display in refrigerated case.
- Store at 55 – 65 degrees for best quality.

Fruits

Apples

- Do not expose to excessive heat or sunlight which causes skins to shrivel.
- Inspect for decay or bruising.
- Display in bulk, cartons, baskets or poly bags.
- Be sure grade is on each display or package.
- Keep refrigerated for maximum quality.
- Keep dry and away from sun.

Apricots

- Sort out decayed or bruised fruit.
- Sell by pound or in quart baskets.

Avocados

- Display in container or bulk.
- Sort out soft, overripe fruit.
- Generally sold by unit or twos.

Berries

- Sort out soft, overripe or moldy fruit.
- Display one tier only, quarts or

pints.
- Display on flat surface (tie-in shortcakes).
- Store backroom stock in cooler.
- Cello caps prevent customers selecting berries from different containers.

Cantaloupes
- Sort out bruised, overripe and cracked melons.
- Do not pile over four high, to avoid bruising.
- Cut melons and cello wrap to increase sales.

Cherries
- Sort out decayed cherries.
- Display bulk in original container, or pack into quart containers.
- Keep under refrigeration.

Cranberries
- Watch for decayed berries.
- Pack in poly bags or sell in pint/ quart containers.
- Rotate stock.

Grapes
- Remove decayed and discolored berries from bunches.
- Avoid excessive handling, causing berries to drop from bunches.
- Temperature changes cause sweating and decay.

Honeydews
- Check for ripeness; reduce price of bruised, spotted or overripe fruit.
- Sell customers only ripe fruit.
- Sell by single unit, multiples, or as cut melons covered with cello.

Peaches, Nectarines
- Handle with care; sort out bruised, spotted fruit.
- Sell only ripe fruit.
- Display in stair-stepped displays, quarts, pound, peck, 1/2 bushel and bushel.
- Mark varieties; advise which variety is good for canning, freezing, etc.

- Large premium fruit can be sold by unit.

Pears
- Bruise easily. Never dump; pile by hand on soft base.
- Never pile more than three deep.
- Sell in bulk, prepackaged in quart containers and cardboard trays. Some full bushels and half bushels sell for canning.

Plums
- Handle carefully. Don't bruise. Sort out bruised and soft fruit.
- Bulk displays sell well; keep varieties separated; sell by quart or larger units.
- Mix-em-or-match-em varieties increase sales.

Watermelons
- Wipe melons clean if soiled.
- Keep good display of cut melons.
- Melons in cooler may sell for premium.

THE THOMAS JEFFERSON AWARD

With each edition of Sell What You Sow!, we'd like to present an award to the farmer or farmers who we feel exemplify the book's ideals of a master marketer and who, in addition, are good neighbors, community pillars and overall friends to farmers everywhere. And the winners of the first edition Sell What You Sow! Thomas Jefferson Award are. . . Tom and Denesse Willey, of T & D Willey Farms!

IT SEEMS FITTING that one of the co-recipients of the first edition *Sell What You Sow! Thomas Jefferson Award* is also the originator of the award's title. With regard to large-scale, "overexpanded and overcapitalized" farming, Tom Willey said at a recent farm conference: "The Jeffersonian ideal of the yeoman farmer making a modest but very self-sufficient livelihood and being the backbone of true democratic society has all but disappeared."

For Tom and Denesse Willey, the issue of small farm survival is an urgent one, as their 40-leased acres near Clovis, California, have been marked by city officials as a possible site for a new elementary school. The couple expect to have to move next year. Tom Willey would like to own land near Clovis, but most farmland slated for development is too expensive. The land he farms is valued at $6,000 an acre as farmland, but near $60,000 an acre as developed land. "Unless you have deep pockets, it won't pencil out," he says.[1]

Tom has been attending meetings of the Clovis City Council and the Fresno County Board of Supervisors, pitching the idea of a trust to protect small farms around Valley cities. "We belong to this community and we don't fell like being run out. We think we can still contribute here."[2]

For the past ten years the Willeys have raised and marketed a variety of organic, premium-qual-ity peas, beans, potatoes and a variety of specialized vegetables. These range from English peas and sugar snap peas in the early spring to baby savoy spinach, arugula and Red Irish and white rose potatoes in the winter. In specialty grocery stores in the Bay Area where they ship much of their produce, the Willey's brand name has become synonomous with quality. In addition, the Willeys recently made an agreement with a local specialty food store-delicatessen-cafe, The Valley Gourmet, to supply the store with certified organic vegetables. The local outlet particularly pleases Tom. "Up till now, Fresno has acted like farmers," he says: "Send away the best and have the second-best for themselves."[3]

"I can outline on a thumbnail those attributes of our farm operation responsible for our survival and relative prosperity," Tom notes: "Innovation, avoidance of debt, direct marketing, transition to organic methods, operating and managing with a husband and wife team, specialty crops, selective low-volume/high-margin wholesaling, closeness and responsiveness to customers, use of low-cost technology, maximizing the value of our own labor, and minimizing the use of hired labor."[4]

As we talk, Denesse Willey is sifting meticulously through green beans being boxed for shipment. Each T & D Willey shipping crate bears a label saying "Naturally Good, Good Naturally" and

carries both Tom and Denesse's signatures. "Everyone who farmed used to pack and ship under their own label," Denesse says. "The beautiful old fruit labels provided an identity. Reputations were developed based on quality. Behind each label stood a family farm, and with the label there was the farmer's signature. Each single box that leaves our farm either has been packed or inspected by myself or Tom. Our name is on the box and we know what goes in it."

In addition to selling through specialty brokers and wholesalers, the Willeys also market their produce through farmers markets and specialized retailers. The face-to-face contact they experience with their farmers market customers is a facet of direct marketing the Willeys try to carry over into their wholesale and retail marketing. They seek out retailers, for example, who are willing to display their name and product information along with their produce. They also send cartoons or personal notes along with their produce for display on the stores' bulletin boards. The Willey's "Public Information Documents" (P.I.D.'s) are simple photocopied messages inserted in each box of produce, containing storage tips, recipes and serving suggestions, or educational statements about the Willey's growing practices, and broader agricultural issues. One delightful P.I.D. reads: "There's a lot of ugliness in this world that a potato's eyes were never meant to see. So keep these innocent things in the dark, and you'll both rest easier."

The Willey's organic produce commands about a 30-percent premium over conventional produce.

"Our policy is to compete on quality and service rather than cheap prices," Tom says. "Our methods are working presently, but we—and other small operators—must make widespread efforts to convince the general public to pay more for higher quality, for more flavorful, healthful products." Tom points out that in 1930, people in the U.S. were paying about 25 percent of their disposable dollars for food; by 1986, this figure had fallen to 14.8 percent, approximately half of what people in other countries pay for their food. As the demand for organic and specialty crops grows, and production from larger growers increases, Tom views customer loyalty and product identification as essential for the smaller grower.

Besides making a right livelihood for themselves and three children, community participation is an important part of Tom and Denesse's farming life. They are often-called-upon speakers at various seminars and conferences.

One of the major challenges facing Fresno County agriculture is that of agricultural land preservation. "The whole (Central) Valley is getting to be a bedroom community for L.A. and the Bay Area," Tom says. For the Willeys, the fight against the onslaught of urban spread means trying to educate the public about the need to support agriculture with their food dollar. "When farmers can make a decent living in agriculture, they will stand up to the developers."

Through their organic growing practices and active participation in the California Certified Organic Farmers (CCOF) organization, the Willeys have tried to serve as an example of how farms can coexist harmoniously with an urban environment. "Within my farming lifespan organic farming has moved from being a small group of fringe farmers into mainstream agriculture," Tom notes.

For her part, Denesse is fully aware that in the face of diminishing farmland, skyrocketing land prices and an increasingly competitive marketplace, it will take some effort to maintain the Willey's marketing strategy of high quality, fair price and personal attention. Denesse, who spends as much as 60 percent of her day talking to buyers, acknowledges this challenge with characteristic spirit. "Personalized marketing of farm produce can be a lot of work," she admits. "To me it is a lot of fun. Why spend all that effort, money and time raising a crop if you're not going to sell it right?"

And The Winners Are. . .

SOME FEW THERE ARE AMONG YOU who received a letter last year from an intrepid journalist who was writing a book about agricultural marketing and asked for your logos to enhance the book. Who would have thought that these farmers, who have bugs, bad weather and politicians to do battle with, would have responded to this mailpiece with anything but a ceremonial toss to the can? Yet respond they did, with creativity and vision, submitting logos penned in the characteristic high spirit of their profession. These logos are "homemade" in the best sense of the word. To the three entrants we've selected as Grand Prize Winners, we are sending complimentary copies of *Sell What You Sow!*; to all whose logos were printed in the book, a 30-percent discount coupon; and to all who submitted a logo, a 10-percent discount coupon. To all, our heartfelt thanks! And the winners are. . .

To see this logo in a larger size, please see p. 18

SOMERSET GOURMET/Noah's Ark is owned by David O. Harde and his wife Toby Y. Landis. (Somerset Gourmet is the farm name; Noah's Ark is the brand name for their farm products.) Somerset Gourmet grows a wide variety of certified organic fresh vegetables which are marketed direct to restaurants and retail stores in El Dorado and Sacramento counties, California. David and Toby opened a retail store this year at 535 Placerville Drive, in Placerville, where they sell their fine produce and also have a sandwich and salad bar.

When it comes to marketing, David favors a no-holds-barred approach. "The key to marketing success is with samples," he says. "Take the best examples of your farm produce and get your product out to as many places as you can. Whether it's going to the farmers market or taking your product direct to people's homes, the number of places you can direct-market your products to is limited only by your imagination—the sky's the limit!"

Like businessmen of all types, David puts out a seeming paradox: have a product so good that customers will come to you, and then take it to them anyway. "A high-quality product sells itself," David chuckles, "but at the same time, you need to be assertive. Once you've called on a customer, you need to call again and check back, because most customers will not call you. Don't just sit by your phone—call them." David makes weekly reminder calls even to his regular restaurant and retail customers. They get this kind of service from their wholesale suppliers, so why shouldn't they expect it from an independent marketer?

Our one regret with the Noah's Ark logo, which was designed by David and rendered by Placerville artist Sue Nerwinski, is that we weren't able to print it in full color. Its rainbow colors are stunning. "Color is everything," David says. "People say: 'Why put so much into a beautiful logo if it just goes on your boxes?' But we use the logo on everything—aprons, market bags, T-shirts, sweat shirts—even the sign out in front of our market."

To see this logo in a larger size, please see p. 17

To see this logo in a larger size, please see p. 55

FARMER BROWN ENTERPRISES, INC., located near Meridian, Idaho, markets corn, pumpkins, potatoes and Belgian draft horses, yet their most important "crop" is farm recreation. The farm started out as a horse-drawn, haywagon-ride operation; now its produce crops are sold mainly through a farmers market. Citing the frequently heard phrase, "I saw this on grandpa's farm when I was growing up," operations manager James Teeter explains, "We try to give urbanites a sense of what farming was like."

For Teeter and the rest of the members involved in the family-owned farm, Farmer Brown's incorporates a deeper purpose, inherent in the Amish-based value system that sustains the operation. "We raise Belgian draft horses," Teeter explains, "as a way to help keep draft-horse farming alive. We are trying to preserve not only a heritage but the values that went along with them." Traditional Amish values, he says, are "a simplicity in life, a sort of 'back to the basics' lifestyle. We believe in being stewards of the land. We look at modern life and mass marketing in stores, and we also believe it's important to keep in touch with traditional values.

"Modern society has lost a lot of family values," Teeter asserts. "When I was a child growing up on a farm we needed our neighbors' help to do things. Now with modern machinery people can do more things by themselves but they lose touch with other folks. We believe neighbors should be neighbors!" One example of the cooperative Amish spirit is the farmers market through which the operation sells much of its products—it is held on the farm with neighboring farmers invited as participants on a cooperative basis. "There are a lot of traditional values tied up in rural life," Teeter muses.

The Farmer Brown logo was penned by James' wife Susan, who is a professional artist, typographer and graphic designer. "Farmer Brown" is Farmer Brown Enterprises, Inc. owner Rich Brown.

FOR MIGUEL URIBE, owner of Living Earth Organic Agriculture, farming is a living, symbiotic relationship with Mother Earth for which his Native American background provides a rich example. "Working with the earth demands sensitivity, intelligence and respect on both sides," Miguel says. "According to my heritage the earth is a personage, a spirit, rather than just some material object or food factory from which we're trying to pump profits. Working with nature is a participatory kind of thing, a loving relationship governed by natural and cosmic laws. If you observe these laws there is triumph on both sides, not just a 'taking' kind of thing—it should be a win-win situation."

Modern civilization finally is beginning to take the ancient ecological wisdom seriously. "The ecological approach is the only way to work with natural resources," Miguel concurs. "We want to go for the long-term gain rather than short-term profits. Why should one generation rape the earth's resources at the expense of our lineage?"

Putting his theories into practice as a grower/ packer/shipper and organic agricultural consultant on 350 acres in the Imperial Valley, San Diego and Mexico, Miguel is the head of a family-owned business centered in Valley Center, California. Living Earth Agriculture grows some 16 different organic fruits and vegetables on its sparse desert soil. "Our goal is to exemplify the scientific and economic viability of organic agriculture," Miguel states. "We want to show other growers it can be done." Slowly the company is breaking ground, bringing organic produce to the marketplace at comparable prices to conventional agricultural products.

The Living Earth Organic Agriculture logo, an original idea of Miguel's, is visionary, with each detail joyously symbolic: the personification of Mother Earth, the planting stick, and the full moon signifying planting time. The logo was drawn by noted artist Gary Knack who later featured it in an artbook collection of his work.

Footnotes

Introduction
1. "Niche Marketing Targets Consumers," *Rural Enterprise*, Spring 1992.
2. "Consumers Rediscover Farmers Markets," by Tracy Walmer and Kevin Johnson, *USA Today*, Sept. 21, 1990.

1. Planning For Profits
1. "Planning Sessions," by Daniel W. Block, *California Farmer*, Nov. 21, 1987.
2. *A Guide To Successful Direct Marketing*, by Charles R. Hall and Jeff L. Johnson. Texas Agricultural Extension Service.
3. *Choosing An Enterprise*, by Curt Stutzman, Adapt 3 Conference.
4. *Windows of Opportunity: The Market for Specialties and Organics*, by Nancy Lee Bentley.

2. Choosing Your Enterprises
1. "Plan for Success Before You Invest," by Craig Cramer, *The New Farm*, Jan. 1990.
2. "Do Your Own Market Research," by Judy Green and Nancy Grudens Schuck, *USDA Yearbook of Agriculture*, 1988.
3. *Choosing An Enterprise*, by Curt Stutzman, Adapt 3 Conference.
4. "Plan for Success Before You Invest."
5. *Farming Alternatives: A Guide to Evaluating the Feasibility of New Farm-Based Enterprises*. Northeast Regional Agricultural Engineering Service (NRAES), Cooperative Extension, Ithaca, NY.
6. "Plan for Success Before You Invest."

7. *Farming Alternatives: A Guide to Evaluating the Feasibility of New Farm-Based Enterprises.*
8. *The Shiitake Mushroom Marketing Guide for Growers.* The Forest Resource Center, Lanesboro, MN.
9. *Farming Alternatives: A Guide to Evaluating the Feasibility of New Farm-Based Enterprises.*
10. Ibid.
11. Ibid.
12. Ibid.
13. "Plan for Success Before You Invest."

3. Deciding What To Grow
1. "Viability of Small Farms Near Urban Areas," by Ron Voss. *Small Farm News* (University of California's Small Farm Center), May/June 1992.

4. Market Research
1. "Do Your Own Marketing Research," by Judy Green and Nancy Grudens Schuck, *1988 USDA Yearbook of Agriculture.*
2. Ibid.
3. "Measuring Your Chances for Success," by Cathleen M. Connell. Chapter 1 in *Managing for Success: A Manual for Roadside Markets*, by James Beierlein and Cathleen Connell, Penn State University.
4. "Do Your Own Marketing Research."

5. Making A Marketing Plan
1. "Planning Sessions," by Daniel W. Block, *California Farmer*, Nov. 21, 1987.

6. Is Direct Marketing For You?
1. "In '90s Cuisine, The Farmer Is The Star," by Trish Hall, *New York Times*, July 8, 1992.

7. Farmers Markets
1. *USDA Office for Small-Scale Agriculture Newsletter*, Fall 1992.
2. *A Guide To Successful Direct Marketing*, by Charles R. Hall and Jeff L. Johnson.
3. Ibid.
4. Ibid.
5. *Backyard Market Gardening*, by Andy Lee. Good Earth Publications, Burlington, VT, 1992.
6. Ibid.
7. *A Guide To Successful Direct Marketing*, by Charles R. Hall and Jeff L. Johnson.
8. "Make Your Market Stand A Standout," *Growing For Market*, Feb. 1992.
9. Ibid.
10. *USDA Office for Small-Scale Agriculture Newsletter*, Fall 1992.
11. "Recipe for a Successful Farmers Market: Price Guidelines and Creative Promotions," by Joyce Schillen, *Growing For Market*, Oct. 1992.
12. Ibid.
13. "Stretching the Farmers Market Concept," *Farm Link* (California Association of Family Farmers newsletter), Nov./Dec. 1992.
14. *Backyard Market Gardening*, by Andy Lee.

8. Roadside Markets

1. *Marketing Fresh Fruits and Vegetables,* by R. Brian How. Van Nostrand Reinhold Publishing Co. See "General Resources—Wholesale Marketing Resources."
2. *A Guide To Successful Direct Marketing,* by Charles R. Hall and Jeff L. Johnson.
3. *Facilities for Roadside Markets.* Reprinted with permission from the Northeast Regional Agricultural Engineering Service (NRAES).
4. *A Guide To Successful Direct Marketing,* by Charles R. Hall and Jeff L. Johnson.
5. Ibid.
6. Ibid.
7. *Facilities for Roadside Markets.* Northeast Regional Agricultural Engineering Service (NRAES).
8. "Fundamentals of Farm Market Layout," by Ransom Blakeley, Chapter 7 in *Managing for Success: A Manual for Roadside Markets,* by James Beierlein and Cathleen Connell.
9. "Managing a U-Pick Operation for Success," by Bev Klauer in *Rural Enterprise,* Summer 1992.
10. *Facilities for Roadside Markets.* Northeast Regional Agricultural Engineering Service (NRAES).
11. *A Guide To Successful Direct Marketing,* by Charles R. Hall and Jeff L. Johnson.
12. *Facilities for Roadside Markets.* Northeast Regional Agricultural Engineering Service (NRAES).
13. Ibid.
14. Ibid.
15. Ibid.
16. Ibid.
17. Ibid.
18. *Backyard Market Gardening,* by Andy Lee.
19. "Mobile Marketing," *The New Farm,* Sept./Oct. 1991.
20. *Facilities for Roadside Markets.* Northeast Regional Agricultural Engineering Service (NRAES).

9. Pick-Your-Own

1. "Managing a U-Pick Operation for Success," by Bev Kauer, *Rural Enterprise,* Summer 1992.
2. *A Guide To Successful Direct Marketing,* by Charles R. Hall and Jeff L. Johnson.
3. Ibid.
4. *Marketing Fresh Fruits and Vegetables,* by R. Brian How. Van Nostrand Reinhold.
5. *A Guide To Successful Direct Marketing,* by Charles R. Hall and Jeff L. Johnson.
6. *Marketing Fresh Fruits and Vegetables* by R. Brian How. Van Nostrand Reinhold.
7. *A Guide To Successful Direct Marketing,* by Charles R. Hall and Jeff L. Johnson.

11. Subscription Farming/ Community Supported Agriculture

1. *Backyard Market Gardening,* by Andy Lee.
2. Ibid.
3. Ibid.
4. Ibid.
5. Ibid.
6. *The New Farm,* Jan.1991.
7. *Backyard Market Gardening,* by Andy Lee.
8. Ibid.
9. Ibid.
10. Ibid.
11. Ibid.

13. Marketing To Retail Outlets: Introduction

1. *The Shiitake Mushroom Marketing Guide for Growers.*

14. Selling To Restaurants

1. "Tapping the Restaurant Market," *Growing for Market,* July 1992.
2. "Ways-to-Grow Project Offers Small-Scale Farmers Alternatives," *Rural Enterprise.*

16. Specialty Food Products

1. "One-Stop Shopping Boosts Sales," *The New Farm,* Feb. 1987.
2. *From Kitchen To Market: Selling Your Gourmet Food Specialty,* by Stephen F. Hall. Upstart Publishing Co., Dover, NH, 1991.

3. "Souped-Up Selling," *In Business,* Jan./Feb. 1990.
4. *Starting A Food Processing Business,* University of Nebraska Food Processing Center.

17. Merchandising

1. *Produce Handling for Roadside Markets,* by Dr. Mark Sherman, Vegetable Crops Fact Sheet VC-33, University of Florida.
2. *Backyard Market Gardening,* by Andy Lee.
3. *Tips for Retail Farm Market Salespersons,* Cooperative Extension Service, Cook College-Rutgers, New Jersey.
4. *Showing Off With Product Displays,* by Forrest Stegelin and Brad Porter.
5. Ibid.

18. Customer Service

1. "Free Recipes," by Linda Stanley, *Rural Enterprise.*
2. "Food Safety and the Direct Marketer," by Mary E. Mennes, *University of Wisconsin Cooperative Extension Direct Marketing Newsletter,* Nov. 1989.

19. The Wholesale Picture

1. *Backyard Market Gardening,* by Andy Lee.
2. Ibid.
3. Ibid.
4. "Marketing Through Wholesalers and Shippers," by Louie Valenzuela and Stephen Brown. *Small Farm News,* Sept./Oct. 1992.
5. Ibid.
6. Ibid.
7. Ibid.
8. Ibid.
9. Ibid.
10. Ibid.
11. Ibid.
12. Ibid.

20. Wholesale Marketing: Getting Your Product To Market

1. "Marketing Through Wholesalers and Shippers," by Louie Valenzuela and Stephen Brown. *Small Farm News,* Sept./Oct. 1992.
2. Ibid.

---

3. "Pack It Right," by Parry Klassen. *American Vegetable Grower*, June 1992.
4. *Developing a Marketing Plan for Fresh Produce*, by C. Moulton and L. Burt, PNW 241, Pacific Northwest Extension Publication.
5. Ibid.
6. *The Shiitake Mushroom Marketing Guide for Growers*. The Forest Resource Center.
7. Ibid.
8. *From Kitchen To Market*, by Stephen Hall.
9. "Deliver Quality," by Jean Aylsworth, *American Vegetable Grower*, June 1992.

21. Wholesale Marketing: Making It Pay

1. *Marketing Tennessee Fruits and Vegetables*, by R. Jenkins, Agriculture Extension Service, University of Tennessee.
2. *Growing For Market*, Jan. 1992.
3. *Marketing Tennessee Fruits and Vegetables*, by R. Jenkins.
4. Ibid.
5. "Marketing Through Wholesalers and Shippers," by Louie Valenzuela and Stephen Brown. *Small Farm News*, Sept./Oct. 1992.
6. *Developing a Marketing Plan for Fresh Produce*, by C. Moulton and L. Burt, PNW 241, Pacific Northwest Extension Publication.
7. *Marketing Fresh Fruits and Vegetables*, by R. Brian How.
8. *Regulations Governing Contracts Between Growers and Handlers of Agricultural Produce: A Primer for Small-Scale Producers*, by Desmond Jolly and Karen Lopiato. University of California Cooperative Extension, Division of Agriculture and Natural Resources. Leaflet #21425.
9. *Developing a Marketing Plan for Fresh Produce*, by C. Moulton and L. Burt, PNW 241, Pacific Northwest Extension Publication.
10. Ibid.

22. Wholesale Marketing: Cooperatives

1. "Cooperatives Let Small Growers Enter Big Markets," by Buffy White and Lynn Byczynski. *Growing For Market*, Sept. 1992.
2. Ibid.
3. *Opportunities for North Carolina Farmer Supply and Marketing Cooperatives*, by Edmund A. Estes, professor and extension economist, North Carolina State University.
4. Ibid.
5. "Cooperatives Let Small Growers Enter Big Markets," by Buffy White and Lynn Byczynski.
6. *Opportunities for North Carolina Farmer Supply and Marketing Cooperatives*, by Edmund A. Estes.

23. Business Smarts

1. *Farm Personnel Management*, by Kenneth H. Thomas and Bernard L. Erven.
2. Ibid.
3. Ibid.
4. Ibid.
5. Ibid.
6. "Incentive Plans Encourage Farm Employees," *Rural Enterprise*, Summer 1992.
7. "Cuddling Your Customers," *International Herb Growers and Marketers Association (IHGMA) Newsletter*, 1988.
8. *Managing Employees and Customers In Your Market*, by Kelso Wessel, Proceedings, 1991 Illinois Specialty Growers Convention.
9. Ibid.

24. Pricing For Profits

1. "Putting a Price On Your Products," Gerald R. Campbell, *University of Wisconsin Cooperative Extension Direct Marketing Newsletter*, July 1988. Also, "Pricing Relative To Costs," Jan. 1989.
2. *Marketing Tennessee Fruits and Vegetables*, by R. Jenkins, Agriculture Extension Service, University of Tennessee.
3. Ibid.
4. *A Guide To Successful Direct Marketing*, by Charles R. Hall and Jeff L. Johnson.

5. Ibid.
6. Ibid.
7. Ibid.

25. Rules & Regulations

1. *Pay Dirt*, by Mimi Luebbermann, Prima Publishing.

27. The Sales Call

1. "Personal Selling," Chapter 7, in *The Shiitake Mushroom Marketing Guide for Growers*. The Forest Resource Center.
2. Ibid.
3. Ibid.
4. Ibid.
5. Ibid.
6. Ibid.
7. Ibid.
8. Ibid.
9. Ibid.

28. Promotion

1. *A Guide To Successful Direct Marketing*, by Charles R. Hall and Jeff L. Johnson.
2. Ibid.
3. *How To Advertise and Promote Your Retail Store*, by Dana Cassell, Cassell Communications.
4. Ibid.

29. Advertising

1. *A Guide To Successful Direct Marketing*, by Charles R. Hall and Jeff L. Johnson.
2. Ibid.
3. *How To Advertise and Promote Your Retail Store*, by Dana Cassell, Cassell Communications.
4. Ibid.
5. Ibid.
6. Ibid.

31. Sharing The Bounty

1. "In The Public Eye," by Sibella Kraus, *California Farmer*, June 1, 1991.

The Thomas Jefferson Award

1. "Farmers Feel City Pressure," *The Fresno Bee*, May 10, 1993.
2. Ibid.
3. "New Shop Will Keep Valley's Best At Home," *The Fresno Bee*, May 22, 1993.
4. Sibella Kraus, *Organic Food Matters*, 1991.

Index

Symbols

30-mile marketing principle 52

A

Advertising 219–232. *See also*
   Cooperative advertising
  ad agency 222
  brochures 226
  business cards 229
  consumers' guides 229
  cost-effectiveness 221–222
  coupons 230
  design and production 231
  direct mail 227
  evaluation of 220–221
  fairs and exhibits 229
  flyers 227
  making it pay 219–220
  miscellaneous media 229
  newsletters 228
  newspapers 223–224
    classified ads 224
    display ads 223
  outdoor 229
  personalizing product 221
  postcards 228
  printed bags 229
  promotions and gift certificates
    232
  radio 224–225
  road signs 222–223
  television 225
  testing 220
  trade publications 229
  writing copy 230
  yellow pages 230
Advertising Without Money 207
Ag In The Classroom 249
American Fruit Grower 80

B

Backyard Cash Crops 24
Backyard Market Gardening
    14, 144, 249
Bagley, Lynn 18, 63, 248, 250
Bags, printed 229
Balance sheet 20, 172
Ballister, Barry 127
Barry Ballister's Fruit and Vegetable
    Stand 18, 127, 140
Bartering 233
Belmonte, Patty 219
Block, Dan 19, 136, 197
Blonz, Kay 15
Blue Book, The 145, 149, 156, 162
Blum, Jan 15
Bon Appetit 24, 100
Brand names 208
Break-even analysis 179, 183–184
Brochures 226–227
Brokers 124–126, 145, 146–147
Building permits 189
Business 171–177
  computers 174
  financial planning 171–172
  personnel management 174–177
  recordkeeping 172–173
Business name 205
Business plan
  making a 20–21
Buss, Anne 34
Bussell, Al 83

C

C.O.D. 103, 161
California Association of Family
    Farmers 187, 247
Cantisano, Amigo 252
Caplan, Frieda 113, 137
Capper Volstead antitrust protec-
    tion 168

Cash flow statement 20, 172
Cash registers 72, 130–131
Chez Panisse restaurant 17
Chun, Ina 15
Classes, teaching 217
Classified ads 224
Code of Federal Regulations 121
Commercial Vegetable Production
    Recommendations 34
Commission merchants 145, 146
Community involvement 210
Community supported
    agriculture. *See CSA*
Competition
  studying the 29
Computers 174
Consumers' guides 229
Containers, shipping 153–155
Contests 85
Coody, Lynn 90
Cook, Roberta 138, 145
Cookbooks 64
Cooking From The Garden 15, 24,
    33, 141
Cooks 24, 255
Cooper, Frank 138
Cooperative advertising 234
Cooperative Extension 255
Cooperative promotion. *See Group*
    promotion
Cooperatives 167–170
  advantages/disadvantages 167–
    169
  informal cooperatives 170
  management challenges 169
  marketing agreements 169–170
  tips on running 170
Corum, Vance 136
Coupons 230–232
Courchesne, Al 12, 247
Courter, J.W. "Bill" 75
Craft Reporter 255
Creasey, Rosalind 15, 32, 141

Crispin, Monika 283
Crops
  selecting 32
CSA 91–96
  advantages 92
  community involvement 95
  distribution and delivery 94–95
  how to start a 94–95
  member recruitment 94
  plan 93
  special challenges 92
  suitable crops 93
Customer service 136–142. *See also Customers, educating*
  customer relations 140
  customer suggestions 137–138
  handling customer complaints 141
  nutritional information 139
Customer surveys 41–44
  designing 41–42
  example of 43
  gathering data 42–44
  interpreting results 44
  written 41–44
Customers
  educating 62, 139, 141, 248

D

Dealers 146
Demos (In-store demonstrations) 115
Dickens, Charles 11
Diet for a Small Planet 245
Direct mail 227–228
Direct marketing 49–55
  advantages 50–51
  characteristics of (chart) 53
  choosing marketing outlets 54
  disadvantages 51–54
  30-mile marketing principle 52
Direct Marketing Newsletter, Univ. of Wisconsin 141
Display ads 223
Display, produce 131–133, 281–285
  color and texture 132
  fixtures 131
  stocking 131–133
  tips 60
  working display items 134
Distributors 124–126
  specialty 147
Diversity
  in marketing 31
  in production 31

E

Edible flowers 33
Educating customers. *See Customers, educating*
Enterprises checklist 27–28

Enterprises, choosing your 23–31
  evaluation 29
  identification of 24
  marketing requirements 26
Erven, Dr. Bernard 176

F

F.O.B. 156, 159
Facilities for Roadside Markets 70
Fairs and exhibits 229
Fancy Food 255
Farm
  family 11, 15
Farm tours 109, 165, 249
Farm trails 234–237
Farmer
  small 12, 16
  specialty 12, 13
Farmers market food coupon program 63, 244
Farmers markets 56–65
  advantages 57
  checking out 58
  disadvantages 57
  evaluating profitability 65
  growth in 56
  pricing tips 61
  promotion tips 64
  selling tips 60, 62–65
  special considerations 57
  startup tips 63
  what to bring 59
Farmers' rights, fighting for 247
Farming
  and society 8
  conventional 12
  income 17
  lifestyle 18
  love of 17
Farming Alternatives 23
Farming Alternatives Program 23
Farmland preservation 246–247
FDA 190
Feenstra, Gail 15
Festivals 85–86, 250–252
  checklist 239
  group 239
Financial assistance 21–22
Financial planning 20, 171–173
Financial projections 29–30
Florist Review 102
Flyers 227
Focus groups 41
Food
  quality 13
  taste 13
  trends 14, 32–33
  variety 13
Food and Drug Packaging 255
Food banks 244
Food buyers' clubs 91
Food Guide Pyramid, The 140
Food safety 141–142

Food system
  centralized vs. decentralized 15. *See also Middleman marketing*
Frieda's, Inc. 33
From Kitchen To Market 118

G

Gale's Directory of Associations 105
Gift certificates 232
Gifts and Decorative Accessories 255
Giftware News 255
Gleaning programs 245–246
Gleaning: Pointers On How To Begin 246
Goals, setting 23
Gourmet 24, 100
Grading 35, 150, 163
Green, Judy 23
Grocer 255
Groh, Trauger 251
Group promotion 233–242
  commodity marketing associations 238
  cooperative advertising 234
  cooperative promotion 238–241
  farm trail maps 237
  farm trails 234–237
  festivals 239
  marketing associations 234–237
  media promotion 241–242
  tasting events 236
Grower. *See Farmer*
Grower, The 33
Growing for Market 102
Guide To Successful Direct Marketing, A 28

H

Hall, Charles R. 28
Hall, Stephen 118
Health claims 33
Health regulations 189
Healthy Harvest 149
Home Business Booklist 171
Home delivery 96
Homemade Money 171
How To Grow More Vegetables 36
How To Make $100,000 A Year Farming 25 Acres 90
Huber, Joe 179, 233
Huber's Family Farm, Orchard and Restaurant 85
Humor, farm 252–253
Hunger programs 63
Hungry, feeding the 243–244

I

In Business 16
In Search of Excellence 176

Income statement 20
Institute of Food Technologies 119
Insurance 193–196
    for wholesale markets 163
    liability 78, 193
    physical damage 194
    policy 195–196
    premises liability 194
    prevention measures 196
    product liability 105, 121, 194
    property coverage 195
    workers' compensation 195
Intensive production 36
International Cherry Pit Spitting
        Competition 85
Inventory. See Resources, inventory

J

Jeavons, John 36
Jefferson, Thomas 8, 16
Johnson, Jeff L. 28

K

Kerr, Howard "Bud" 7, 16
Knott's Handbook 34, 153
Knox County Regional Farmers
        Market 64
Kona Kai Farms 17
Kraus, Sibella 8

L

Labels 129–130
    labeling laws 122, 190
    nutritional labeling 33, 190
    specialty food products 122
    wholesale marketing 155
Labor
    rules and regulations 190
Lappe, Frances Moore 245
Laurel's Kitchen 140
Lee, Andy 14, 144, 249
Liability insurance 78, 193
Licenses 189
Logos 206
Logsdon, Gene 16
Lotus vs. Supercalc 16. See also
        Middleman marketing

M

MacGregor, Bonnie 243
Mail order 97–99
    advantages/challenges 97
    customer base 99
    mailing list 98
    packaging/shipping 98
    promotion and advertising 99
    sales package 98
    spin-offs/catalogs 98
    suitable products 97–98
Management
    contingency plans 20

staffing 20
Margins and markups 180–181
Market research 26, 30, 39–44
    assistance with 40
    finding customers 101
    goals of 39
    planning 39
    primary research 40–41
    secondary research 40
    in wholesale marketing 148–150
Market windows 26, 149
Marketing
    direct. See Direct marketing
    diversity 36
    marketing vs. selling (chart) 204
    multi-level 54
    retail stores. See Retail stores
    specialty. See Specialty marketing
Marketing associations 234–237
Marketing orders 192
Marketing plan 19–22, 45–48
    benefits 19–20
    elements of 20
    making a 45–48
Marketing vs. selling 204
Matarazzo, Matty
        108, 111, 114, 197, 247
    (profile) 212
Medford Growers and Crafters
        Association 64, 234
Media promotion 241–242
Media relations 217
Mennes, Mary E. 141
Merchandising 127–135. See also
        Display, produce
    bulk displays 130
    cash register savvy 130
    labels 129–130
    packaging 127–129
    point-of-purchase (P.O.P.) 133
    prepackaging 130
    produce display 131–133
    produce handling 133–135
    samples 134
    unit pricing 130
    weight 130
Middleman marketing 12
Mission statement 20
Mobile markets 73
Morgan, Linda 209
Myers, James 252

N

Natural Foods Merchandiser
        33, 255
New Farm, The 17, 23
New World Publishing 245, 246,
        298
New York Times 64, 104
News releases 211–215
    how to write a 214
    sample 216
Newsletters 228–229

Newspapers 223
North American Strawberry Growers
        Association (NASGA) 136, 141
Norton, Michael 17
Nutrition Handbook 140
Nutritional Almanac 140
Nutritional information
    on labels 33
Nutritional Labeling and Education
        Act (NLEA) 122

O

Ohm III, Karl 8, 248
Operating statement 172
Organic certification 189
Organic produce
    marketing tips 36
    profitability 35–36
Organic Wholesalers Directory 149

P

Packing facilities, private 147
Packaging 127–129
    environmental considerations
        155–156
    for direct markets 129
    prepackaging 130
    specialty food products 120–121
    suppliers 128
Packaging Digest 255
Packer, The 149, 160
Perishable Agricultural Commodi-
        ties Act (PACA) 162, 164
Permits. See Rules and regulations
Personal interviews 40
Personal touch, The
    in retail marketing 113
    in wholesale marketing 165
Personnel management 174–177
    employee motivation 176, 177
        incentive programs 177
    finding personnel 174
    training 175–177
Pick Your Own Farming 75
Pick-your-own 75
    advantages 76
    checkin/checkout 79–80
    customer service 82
    disadvantages 76
    labor 78
    location 76
    management 78
    parking 78–79
    pricing policies 80–81, 186
    primary trade area 76
    promotion 81
    special considerations 76
    suitable products 77
    supervision 82
Point-of-purchase materials (P.O.P.)
        116, 133
Porter, Brad 282

Postharvest handling 37–38. *See also Food safety; Produce handling and storage*
Postcards 228
Potted plants 282
Precooling 37
Premises liability 194
Price signs 132
Pricing 178–186
  break-even analysis 179, 183–184
  by the unit 130
  by weight 130
  estimating 26
  evaluation of 182
  for different marketing outlets 186
  for high-value products 180
  for wholesale markets 159
  low price policies 182
  margins and markups 180–181
  market considerations 181
  pricing strategies 178–181
  specialty food products 123
  techniques 185
  tips 61
Processed products. *See Value-added products. See also Specialty food products*
Processors 147-148
Produce and Availability Merchandising Guide 26, 153
Produce handling and storage 74, 133–135, 279
  atmosphere 279
  humidity 279
  market sanitation 280
  temperature 279–280
Produce Handling for Direct Marketing 71
Produce Marketing Association 149
Produce News, The 149, 155
Product differentiation 46
Product liability 105, 121, 194
Production
  deciding what to grow 32–38
  diversity in 16, 31
  estimating costs 25
  plan 20
  tips on 36
Professional Merchandising 255
Profitability
  evaluating 29
Progressive Grocer's Marketing Guidebook 149
Promotion 89, 203–218. *See also Media promotion. See also Group promotion*
  budget 207–208
  establishing identity 205
  evaluation 209
  free promotion 207
  marketing vs. selling (chart) 204
  promotion plan 205–207

  target audience 207
Property coverage 195
Protecting Perishable Foods During Transport By Truck 158
Public relations 209–211
Publicity 211–218

Q

Quality
  food 13
  how to grow for 35
  in wholesale marketing 150

R

Radio 224–225
Recipes 141
Recordkeeping 172–173
Recreational farming. *See Rural attractions*
Red Book, The 145, 149, 156, 162
Rent-A-Garden 88
Rent-A-Tree 88
Resources
  inventory of 24
  finding 255
Restaurant purveyors 147
Restaurants, selling to 104–109
  advantages 105
  delivery 107
  disadvantages 105
  establishing a working relationship 107
  getting the accounts 101–102, 106
  grower-chef relationship 109
  increasing order size 108
  market research 105–106
  payment and pricing 106
  pricing policies 186
  promotion 108
  servicing the account 108
  suitable products 100
  working with other growers 103
Restaurateur 255
Retail stores, selling to 110–116
  advantages 110–111
  communication with buyer 114
  delivery 114
  finding market outlets 112–113
  getting the accounts 101
  personal touch in 113
  point-of-purchase materials (P.O.P.) 116
  pricing policies 186
  products 111–112
  retailers' concerns 111
  sales call 113
  service 116
  special considerations 110–111
  terms 113
Riggs, Dale 170
Road signs 222

Roadside markets 66–74
  advantages 67
  checkout 73
  disadvantages 67
  equipment 72
  facilities and buildings 69–70
  lighting 72
  location 68
    on-site vs. off-site 69
  market decor 72
  market layout 71–72
  parking 70
  pricing policies 186
  rules and regulations 67
  safety and security 74
  special considerations 67
  storage and handling 73
  suitable products 68
Rodale Press 90
Rules and regulations 187–192
  building permits 189
  direct marketing (chart) 191
  health regulations 189
  inspectors, how to deal with 188
  labeling laws 190
  labor 190
  licenses 189
  marketing orders 192
  sales taxes 190
  signs 189
  specialty food products 121–122
  standardization restrictions 192
  weights and measures 189
  zoning requirements 187
Rural attractions 83–89
  business of 87–89
  contests 85
  educational tours 86–87
  festivals. *See Festivals*
  promotion 89
  themes and activities 84–85
Rural Enterprise 8, 12, 248

S

Sales
  by the unit 130
  by volume 80
  by weight 80, 130
Sales call, The 197–202
  closing the sale 200–201
  dealing with objections 200
  features/benefits 201
  follow-up and collections 201–202
  preparation for 198, 199
  prospecting new accounts 198
  qualifying customers 198–199
  steps involved in 199–200
Sales taxes 190
Samples 64, 103, 134, 149. *See also Demos (In-store demonstrations)*
Scales 72

School tours 86–87
Schools and institutions, selling to 148
Secondary outlets 35
Seed catalogs 24
"Self-serve" selling 74
Selling tips 62–65
Shepherd, Renee 15
Sherman, Dr. Mark 279
Sherrill, Donna 112, 116
Shippers 145, 147
Shipping. *See also Wholesale marketing*
 long distance 14
Signs
 colors 223
 rules and regulations 189
Singh, Kirpal 243
Small Farm Today 247
Small Time Operator 171
Sonoma County Agricultural Marketing Program (SCAMP) 170, 238
SOS(BAM) marketing plan 45–48
 action plan 48
 budget 47–48
 measurement 48
 objectives 45
 situation 45
 strategies 46–47
  people 47
  place (distribution) 47
  position 47
  price 47
  product 46
  promotion 47
Specialty and Minor Crops Handbook 34
Specialty crops 16, 17, 33
Specialty distributors 147
Specialty food products 117–126
 advantages 118
 brokers and distributors 124–126
 developing a new product 119
 distributors 124
 facilities and equipment 120
 getting started in marketing 123
 labels 122
 packaging 120
 pricing 123
 rules and regulations 121–122
 sales representatives 124
 suitable products 118
 trade shows 125
Specialty marketing 34
Speeches, giving 217
Spiegel, Dr. Marilyn 253

Staffing 20
Standard Rate and Data Service 149
Standardization restrictions 192
Stanley, Linda 66, 136, 141
Startup capital 21–22
Startup tips 22
Stegelin, Forrest 282
Storage of crops. *See Postharvest handling*
StreetSmart Marketing 207
Stutzman, Curt 22, 52
Subscription farming 90–91
 food buyers' clubs 91
 home delivery 91
 membership club 90

T

Taste, in food 13, 14
Tasting events 236
Tasting of the Summer Produce 8
Tehrune Orchards 83
Television 225
Temperature control 74. *See also Postharvest handling*
Terminal markets 146
Test-marketing 44, 119–120
Thomas Jefferson Award, The 286
Thomas Register of Manufacturers 128
Toynbee, Arnold 8
Trade shows 125
Treasury Of Farm And Ranch Humor, A 252
Trends. *See Food, trends*
 market 26
Trucking 156

U

U.P.S. 98
U.S. Postal Service 98
Uniform Pricing Code (U.P.C.) 129
United Fresh Fruit and Vegetable Association 149
USDA 150
 Federal Crop Reports 160
 Market News Service 159

V

Value-added products 31, 35. *See also Specialty food products*
Van En, Robyn 92
Vandertuin, Jan 91
Variety, in food 13

Variety trials 25
Vegetarianism 245
Vitamin Bible 140
Vossen, Paul 170, 238, 246

W

Wallin, Craig 24
Waters, Alice 8
Weights and measures
 rules and regulations 189
Wessel, Kelso 13
Whatley, Booker T. 90
Wholesale marketing 143–170
 commission merchants 146
 characteristics of (chart) 151
 dealers 146
 getting accounts 149–150
 grading 150
 grower protection 162–164
 insurance 163
 market reports 150
 market research 148–150
 meeting market requirements 150–152
 miscellaneous outlets 147
 packing 153
 payment 162
 payment practices 160–161
 personal touch, the 165
 pricing 159–160
 private packing facilities 147
 processors 147
 relations with buyers 164–166
 restaurant purveyors 147
 schools and institutions 148
 shippers 147
 shipping 156–158. *See also Shipping*
  containers 153
 specialty distributors 147
 terminal markets 146
(WIC) Farmers Market Nutrition Program 63, 244–245
Willey, Tom and Denesse 111, 286–287
Word-of-mouth 209
Workers' compensation 195

Y

Yellow pages 230
You Are What You Eat 245

Z

Zoning requirements 187

About New World Publishing...

New World Publishing consists of the husband and wife team of Eric and Andrea Gibson. Eric is an agricultural journalist whose articles have appeared in *Rural Enterprise, California Farmer, Farm Journal, Furrow, American Small Farm,* and dozens of other farm trade magazines. Previously, he worked as the publisher and editor of *New World,* a community resources publication for California; as a sports reporter and paste-up person on newspapers; as a typesetter and cameraman in print shops; and as an oilfield laborer. Andrea is an illustrator, publisher's assistant, and former schoolteacher. When they're not at the computer or drawing board, or interviewing farmers, they enjoy gardening and going for walks!

Now it's your turn. . .This book is a first for us, and we'd like to keep revising it and publish future editions, as well as publish additional books on farm marketing, small business and right livelihood. We'd appreciate your ideas and suggestions for these books as well as for our annual newsletter, *New World Update,* which will serve as an ongoing update for this book. As a purchaser of *Sell What You Sow!* you are automatically entitled to a sample issue of *New World Update.* (If you purchased this book through someone other than *New World Publishing,* please take a moment to send us the postcard inserted in this book so we can put you on our mailing list for a free newsletter.) This book has been written based upon interviews with successful small farmers, and your contributions will help make future editions even more helpful to those who follow.

With love and best wishes,
Eric & Andrea Gibson

BUSINESS & MARKETING

MARKETING YOUR PRODUCE: Ideas For Small-Scale Farmers, by Lynn Byczynski. The best marketing articles from Growing For Market newsletter, 1992-1995. Topics include getting started, specialty produce, selling to restaurants, farmers markets, community supported agriculture, selling to supermarkets, expanding your market, & resources for market gardeners. 112 pp. $20.

THE NEW FARMERS MARKET: Farm-Fresh Ideas To Make Market Sales Sizzle!, by Eric Gibson. Growers and market managers around the country were surveyed and interviewed to find the best new ideas in fresh products, value-added products, display ideas, merchandising tips, selling styles, market promotions, key issues & challenges, best markets & more . Available Sept. 2000 $19.95

SECRETS TO A SUCCESSFUL GREENHOUSE BUSINESS, by Ted Taylor. Cash in on one of the high-profit business opportunities of the '90s by growing foliage plants, herbs, holiday flowers, trees or vegetables. How to sell to national chains & local markets, which plants sell best, plans for building a solar greenhouse, a nationwide plant buyers list, a wholesale plant price guide, a directory of the best grower supplies, & more.
152 pp. $19.95.

SELL WHAT YOU SOW! The Grower's Guide To Successful Produce Marketing, by Eric Gibson. The definitive book on marketing farm products, topics include: deciding what to grow, selling through farmers markets, roadside markets, pick-your-own, subscription (CSA) farming, mail order, grocery stores & restaurants, wholesale channels & cooperatives, developing specialty (value-added) food products, merchandising & customer service, advertising & promotion, pricing, & more. "This is the best book to date about the alternative marketing options available to farmers."—David Visher, U.C. Davis Small Farm Center. 304 pp. $22.50.

SHARING THE HARVEST, by Rose Henderson. Comprehensive book on CSA's (Community Supported Agriculture). $24.95.

THE SMALL COMMERCIAL GARDEN: How To Make $10,000 A Year In Your Backyard, by Dan Haakenson. A successful commercial gardener shows you how to turn your backyard garden into a profitable business. Includes information on marketing, garden design, planning, growing & harvesting, recommended crops & the business of gardening. 208 pp. $17.95.

GROWING

AMERICAN GINSENG, Green Gold, by W. Scott Persons. Detailed coverage on cultivation, harvesting, production & growing methods, as well as the economics of growing ginseng, marketing opportunities, history & use, medicinal properties & government regulations. The resources chapter includes root buyers, equipment, seed & seedling suppliers. 216 pp. $17.95.

APPLE GROWER, THE: A Guide for the Organic Orchardist, by Michael Phillips. This book combines the half-forgotten wisdom of a century ago with the latest scientific knowledge about pests that can plague apples and other tree fruits. Practical growing and marketing advice, as well as physical and biological controls that you can test yourself. 300 pp. $35.00.

BUGS, SLUGS & OTHER SLUGS: Controlling Garden Pests Organically, by R. M. Hart. Hundreds of ways to stop pests without risk to the user or the environment—from folk remedies to the latest scientific discoveries. 224 pp. $12.95.

CARROTS LOVE TOMATOES: Secrets of Companion Planting for Successful Gardening, by Louise Riotte. This classic gardening book is now available in a completely revised edition to inspire and instruct a new generation of gardeners. Lists hundreds of plants and their ideal (and so ideal) companions. 240 pp. $14.95.

GARDENER'S BUG BOOK, by Barbara Pleasant. This completely revised and updated garden guide shows how to identify and control more than 70 common garden insects using the best homemade and commercial control strategies. 160 pp. $14.95.

GARDENER'S GUIDE TO PLANT DISEASES: Earth-safe Remedies, by Barbara Pleasant. The antidote for the 50 most common plant diseases: what they look like, where they are found, what to do about them, and what they will do to the plant. The only organic plant disease reference guidebook available. 192 pp. $14.95.

GARDENER'S WEED BOOK, by Barbara Pleasant. This easy-to-use reference covers the pros & cons of the presence of weeds, recommends proven organic methods for controlling unwanted weeds, & presents an illustrated encyclopedia of dozens of the most common weeds. 201 pp. $14.95

MUSHROOM BOOK (THE): How to Identify, Gather & Cook Wild Mushrooms & Other Fungi. From DK Publishing, this book is a mushroom forager's delight. $29.95

THE NEW ORGANIC GROWER: Tools & Techniques For The Home & Market Gardener, by Eliot Coleman. Loaded with practical advice, including topics such as rotations, use of soil blocks for transplanting, specialized garden tools, row covers & season extenders. 304 pp. $24.95.

ORGANIC GARDENER'S HOME REFERENCE: A Plant-by-Plant Guide to Growing Fresh, Healthy Food, by Tanya Denckla. 288 pp. $21.95.

PRUNING MADE EASY, by Lewis Hill. Practical guide to pruning shade trees, fruit trees, nut trees, forest trees, evergreens, hedges, vines, garden plants, flowers, fruit & flowering bushes, ground covers, house plants, bonsai, espalier & topiary. 208 pp. $19.95

SAVING SEEDS, by Marc Rogers. Saving seeds is a time-honored gardening tradition. This book has practical, easy-to-use plant-by-plant advice on how to raise, harvest, and store seeds. 176 pp. $12.95.

SECRETS OF PLANT PROPAGATION, by Lewis Hill. Primer on starting flowers, vegetables, fruits, berries, shrubs, trees & house plants. Also covers topics such as seeds, division, layering, cuttings, grafting, bud grafting & tissue culture. 168 pp. $18.95

SECRETS TO GREAT SOIL, By Elizabeth P. Stell. How to create fertile, productive soil anywhere with step-by-step instructions for making compost and using soil boosters like organic mulches, soil amendments, and green manures. Gardeners will learn how to fix problem sites; overcome drainage, texture, and pH problems; eliminate soilborne diseases; and customize soil for different purposes. Includes more than 300 illustrations, problem-solving call-out boxes, quick-reference charts, and a calendar for year-round soil building. $19.95.

SEED SOWING & SAVING, By Carole B. Turner. Sowing seeds from more than 100 common vegetables, annuals, perennials, herbs, and wildflowers, plus complete directions for harvesting and storing seeds, starting seeds indoors and out, creating the ideal soil conditions, thinning and transplanting seedlings, extending the gardening season, and more. $19.95.

SUCCESSFUL SMALL-SCALE FARMING: An Organic Approach, by Karl Schwenke. How-to guide for organic agriculture with a broad range of proven techniques & practical advice on improving soils, buying & using machinery & other farm skills, along with guidelines for raising & marketing specialty crops. 131 pp. $14.95.

KEEPING THE HARVEST

KEEPING THE HARVEST: Preserving Your Fruits, Vegetables & Herbs, by Nancy Chioffi & Gretchen Mead. Help keep your fruits & vegetables fresh all year using preserving techniques such as freezing, canning, pressure canning, drying, pickling, & making jams & jellies. This reference for gardeners & cooks includes the latest techniques, equipment, & USDA guidelines for home preserving. 208 pp. $14.95.

MAKING & USING DRIED FOODS, by Phyllis Hobson. Different methods of drying—sun, oven, homemade dryer or dehydrator—& the pros & cons of pretreating. Includes step-by-step instructions to help you dry & store more than 100 types of fruits, vegetables, grains & herbs, with dozens of recipes. 192 pp. $14.95.

ROOT CELLARING: Natural Cold Storage Of Fruits & Vegetables, by Mike & Nancy Bubel. Root cellaring is a simple, energy-saving way to keep food fresh all year. This book explains building & using different types of root cellars & which vegetables & fruits store best. Includes specific storage requirements for nearly 100 garden crops. 320 pp. $14.95.

HERBS & FLOWERS

ENCYCLOPEDIA OF MEDICINAL PLANTS. From DK Publishing, this book contains hundreds of color photos of medicinal plants. $39.95.

ENCYCLOPEDIA OF HERBS. From DK Publishing, this book contains hundreds of color photos of herbs. $39.95

FLOWER FARMER, THE: An Organic Grower's Guide to Raising and Selling Cut Flowers, by Lynn Byczynski. Detailed, manageable plans for flower growing on a scale from a backyard border to a half-acre commercial garden. Includes information on the best varieties of cut flowers, how to cut, store, dry, and preserve flowers, flower-arranging basics, and extending the season with woody shrubs and trees. Also includes profiles of successful flower farmers from Vermont to California. 288 pp. $24.95.

FLOWERS FOR SALE: Everything You Need To Know To Start A Cut-Flower Business, by Lee Sturdivant. Tips on variety selection, harvesting, conditioning, selling, pricing, display, business & taxes, & how many successful growers operate.

Also a comprehensive list of varieties of annuals, perennials, bulbs, trees, shrubs, vines, herbs & wild plants with commercial value. 200 pp. $14.95.

GROWING FLOWERS FOR MARKET: A Practical manual for Small-Scale Field Production and Marketing of Fresh Flowers, by Mike Madison. This comprehensive book covers finding the small grower's niche; planning your flower operation; the grower's tools; relationship to the land; managing the soil; producing a crop; wind, weeds, pests and disease; harvest and post-harvest; business matters and health hazards in floriculture. 260 pp. $19.95

HERBS FOR SALE: Growing & Marketing Herbs, Herbal Products & Herbal Know-How, by Lee Sturdivant. Information on growing & selling culinary herbs, manufacturing & selling herbal extracts & potpourri, blending & selling medicinal herbal teas, opening an herbal restaurant or shop, teaching herb classes, & more. 256 pp. $14.95.

FROM SEED TO BLOOM: How To Grow Over 500 Annuals, Perennials & Herbs, by Eileen Powell. How to germinate & grow more than 500 flowers & herbs from seed. Includes growing zones, directions for sowing seeds indoors & out, spacing, germination & propagation requirements, & general plant care. Includes a list of seed sources. 320 pp. $19.95.

WILD HERBS IN YOUR BACK-YARD, by Brigitte Miner. A pocket-sized field guide for identifying & using commonly found plants of exceptional medicinal & nutritional value. Identify plants on your next outing, improve your diet & health, harvest a bountiful natural resource, & learn how wild plants help humanity. Recipes, charts & more! 80 pp. $6.95.

MISCELLANEOUS

MARKET FARM FORMS: Spreadsheet Templates for Planning and Tracking Information on Diversified Market Farms. Market Farm Farms work with your Excel spreadsheet software. Enter your own farm data and the embedded formulas do the calculations for you. Specify your configuration: Mac or PC; Excel 97 (PC only), or Excel 3.0, 4.0 or 5.0. $45.

GROWING FOR MARKET (newsletter): News & Ideas For Market Gardeners, Lynn Byczynski, editor/publisher. A must-read for market gardeners, small-scale farmers, flower & herb growers, & greenhouse/nursery operators, this 16-page monthly newsletter packs a lot into each issue: growing & marketing ideas, pricing information, management tips, networking updates, & how-to stories & profiles. $30 postpaid per year. ($33 Canada)

COMING SOON!

GROWER'S GUIDE TO THE INTERNET: Online Research & Promotion For Farmers & Market Gardeners, by Eric Gibson. The internet is an exciting new marketing and research tool for small-scale farmers and market gardeners alike. Includes designing websites to sell your fruits, vegetables, flowers & herbs; finding horticultural information on the internet; directory of small-farm and market-garden related web sites, and more. (Check order form for availability and ordering information.)